John G. C. Brown.

Purchased August 2013.

Haslemere, GU27 2HE

Bon Record

Bon Record

A HISTORY OF ABERDEEN GRAMMAR SCHOOL

Brian R. W. Lockhart and Arthur L. McCombie

[illegible] Arthur L. McCombie

Jan 2013

First published in Great Britain in 2012 by
John Donald, an imprint of Birlinn Ltd

West Newington House
10 Newington Road
Edinburgh
EH9 1QS

www.birlinn.co.uk

ISBN: 978 1 906566 46 3

British Library Cataloguing-in-Publication Data
A catalogue record for this book is available on request from the British Library

Typeset by Mark Blackadder

Printed and bound by CPI Group (UK) Ltd, Croydon, CR0 4YY

For Vaila, and for Isaac and Dorian

CONTENTS

LIST OF ILLUSTRATIONS

Plate section 1

16. James Dun, Rector, 1744–98, served sixty-six years on the School staff.
17. James Melvin, Rector, 1826–53, was the greatest Latinist of his day and a famous teacher.
18. Rector Melvin's Snuff-Box, which was presented by the FPs in 1853 acknowledging their debt to him.

Plate section 2

19. William Barrack, Rector, 1860–8, was the last Rector at Schoolhill and the first at Skene Street.
20. Alexander Martin, Rector, 1869–81, was promoted to Rector from the staff.
21. James Moir, Rector, 1881–93, and Co-Rector 1893, was a popular, distinguished scholar whose career ended in disappointment.
22. Henry F. Morland Simpson, Rector, 1893–1920, laid the basis of the modern Grammar School.
23. J. Mackay Thomson, Rector, 1920–1, left for a successful career as an HMI and became Secretary of the Scottish Education Department.
24. Douglas G. Miller, Rector, 1921–24, witnessed the War Memorial, Byron Statue and Rubislaw Pavilion.
25. David M. Andrew, Rector, 1924–42, led the School carefully through the inter-war problems and the early stages of WWII.
26. Sir James J. Robertson, Rector, 1942–59, was knighted for his services to education at home and abroad.
27. John Vass Skinner, Rector, 1959–72, faced the introduction of comprehensive education.
28. Robert D. Gill, Rector, 1972–87, saw the introduction of co-education and the devastation of the 1986 fire.
30. The old pavilion at the rear of the School in the 1880s.
31. The Melvin Window in King's College commemorates Scotland's great Latinists – Buchanan, Johnston, Ruddiman and Melvin.
32. Chalmers School was established by the Chalmers family of Westfield.
33. Plaque on Chalmers School for 'the Poor Girls of Gilcomstoun'.
34. Westfield School, 1900, was the site of the first gymnasium and technical departments.
35. The original Hall was the centre of School life but underwent many modifications.
36. Samuel Pope conducted Art and Writing Classes in the School from 1867 till 1912.

Plate section 3

ACKNOWLEDGEMENTS

As long ago as 1906 when Morland Simpson, the then Rector of the Grammar School of Aberdeen, was presenting his collection of records and reminiscences in *Bon Record* he expressed his surprise that no one had produced a History of the School, though there had been a number who could have done so successfully. More than a century later the situation remained the same despite high but vain hopes that the late Dr Douglas Simpson, the former Rector's son, might undertake the task. To rectify this, Arthur McCombie and Brian Lockhart have taken up the challenge and collaborated to produce the much overdue History of Aberdeen Grammar School.

Arthur L. McCombie is a former Deputy Rector of the Grammar and erstwhile Principal Teacher of History at the School. He has long been an interested and informed commentator on all things connected with Aberdeen and is keen to fill a glaring gap by writing a history of one of the oldest institutions of the Town. Brian Lockhart, the former Headmaster of Gordon's College and himself a former Principal Teacher of History, brings expertise in the researching and writing of school histories having produced books on Heriot's, Gordon's and The High School of Glasgow.

Nowadays schools usually go to some lengths to publicise their Former Pupils and they naturally like to take some credit for the success stories. The authors determined at an early stage to include in the book short biographical sketches of the School's most famous notables. They had not appreciated just how many contenders there would be for inclusion.

As 'objective' criteria, Grammar pupils who gained an entry in the *Oxford Dictionary of National Biography* (*ODNB*); *Who's Who* (*WW*); *Who's Who in Scotland* (*WWS*); *Who Was Who* (*WWW*); or Debrett's *People of Today* (Debr.) were included in this volume. Others given short profiles were included to show the diversity of occupations and careers of Former Pupils and priority was also given to those in the modern period who had been loyal supporters of the FP Association. Theodore Watt's remarkable *Roll of Pupils 1795–1919* and the *School Magazines* were a mine of information but in truth did not make selection for inclusion any easier to decide, precisely because of the enormous number of talented individuals who have attended the School. There are only a very few schools anywhere which have seen their like.

Unfortunately, a considerable number of individuals who attended the School have not published details of their schooling. Others who perhaps merit inclusion may have been inadvertently missed. The authors apologise for any such omissions.

All works of this nature are much dependent on previous research and the authors acknowledge their debt to Morland Simpson, Theodore Watt, and David K. Yule, the last for his compilation of *1256 and All That.* Both authors also benefited from the scholarship and friendship of the late Don Withrington.

With regard to archival material, we are grateful for the assistance and courtesy shown to us by the staff of the University of Aberdeen's Special Libraries, especially Michelle Gait and June Ellner; the regional archivists in Old Aberdeen, especially Ruaridhi Wishart; the Town House Archival staff and the staff of the Public Library in Aberdeen. Thanks also go to Andrew Murray, archivist at Fettes College.

We have been very grateful for the help provided by Former Pupils. When the project was first mooted we received enthusiastic support from Jock Hendry, the Secretary of the FPs, who secured the Club Executive's approval of the venture. He provided help, advice and facilities for our research. Similarly, Brian Crookshanks was approached to help. With his vast knowledge of the School and its pupils through his long connection with the Club and the Magazine, he very willingly cooperated in supplying information about the careers of many Former Pupils. Theodore Watt's son, the late Alan Watt, himself a former Secretary and Magazine Editor, contributed a collection of documents relevant to the School's history.

To secure illustrations we were able to call on the University of Aberdeen, where Neil Curtis and Shona Elliot provided assistance. We also had the help of Julian McCormick. In the School we had access to the pictures and photographs it holds and we are grateful for the assistance of Craig Gibson, the Head Janitor, in opening areas for our inspection.

We were fortunate when Mrs Joyce Fogg alerted us to her friend, Miss Anne Simpson, the granddaughter of Morland Simpson. Miss Simpson provided us with much information about the early life and career of her grandfather and the difficulties which he encountered during the First World War. Morland Craig also provided a useful personal perspective while Fiona Bennett and Tracey Robb (née Menzies) helped by supplying material on the introduction of the Girls to the School.

We also wish to acknowledge the kindness of Graham Legge, the present Rector, and his Deputy Helen Innes in giving up their time to answer our many queries and to welcome us when we sought their help. Moreover, we called on former colleagues to confirm and help with inquiries and we have to thank Jean Downie, Sandra Ramsay, Moya Cromar and Russell Gray for their patience in dealing with our questions on many different topics.

The authors also appreciated the help of the publishers, Birlinn, and Mairi Sutherland in particular.

Finally, we thank Elizabeth W. McCombie for her contribution to the proof-reading of the book.

NOTE ON STYLE AND ABBREVIATIONS

Spelling and punctuation are as in the original, where this is quoted in the text and in the endnotes. Reference to 'the School' (with capitals) and 'the Grammar' always refers to Aberdeen Grammar School. You can assume that if reference is made to a University after 1860 it is always Aberdeen. Normally, other than when indicated otherwise, figures for money are given in sterling. The conversion rate of pounds sterling to Scots pounds was 1:12, while that of pounds sterling to Scots merks was 1:18.

The following abbreviations have also been used in the text and endnotes:

ACF	Army Cadet Force
APS	Aberdeen Philosophic Society
ARI	Aberdeen Royal Infirmary
ARP	Air Raid Precautions
ARSA	Associate, Royal Scottish Academy
ATC	Air Training Corps
BBC	British Broadcasting Corporation
BD	Bachelor of Divinity
BMA	British Medical Association
BP	British Petroleum
CA	Chartered Accountant
CB	Companion, Order of the Bath
CBE	Commander, Order of the British Empire
CC	County (City) Council or Cricket Club
C-in-C	Commander-in-Chief
CCF	Combined Cadet Force
CMG	Companion, Order of St Michael and St George
CO	Commanding Officer
Col.	Colonel

Debr.	Debrett's *People of Today*
DL	Deputy Lieutenant
DPH	Diploma in Public Health
DSC	Distinguished Service Cross
DSO	Companion of the Distinguished Service Order
EA	Educational Authority
EIS	Educational Institute of Scotland
FC	Football Club
FCH	First Class Honours
FCO	Foreign and Commonwealth Office
FP	Former Pupil(s)
FRCP	Fellow, Royal College of Physicians
FRCSE	Fellow, Royal College of Surgeons of England
FRS	Fellow, Royal Society
FRSE	Fellow, Royal Society, Edinburgh
FSAScot	Fellow, Society of Antiquaries of Scotland
GA	General Assembly
GCMG	Knight (Dame) Grand Cross, Order of St Michael and St George
GMC	General Medical Council
GS	Grammar School
HAS	Headteachers' Association of Scotland
HMCI	Her (His) Majesty's Chief Inspector
HMI	Her (His) Majesty's Inspectors
HS	High School
HSOG	High School of Glasgow
ICI	Imperial Chemical Industries
ICS	Indian Civil Service
ILO	International Labour Organisation
IMS	Indian Medical Service
JP	Justice of the Peace
KC	King's Counsel
KCB	Knight Commander, Order of the British Empire
KCIE	Knight Commander, Order of the Indian Empire
KCMG	Knight Commander, Order of St Michael and St George
KCSI	Knight Commander, Order of the Star of India
KCVO	Knight Commander, Royal Victorian Order
Kt	Knight
LMC	Local Medical Committee

LMS	London Missionary Society
LSE	London School of Economics
Lt	Lieutenant
LTA	Lawn Tennis Association
Lt Col.	Lieutenant Colonel
MAFF	Ministry of Agriculture, Fisheries and Food
MC	Military Cross
MO	Medical Officer
MOH	Medical Officer of Health
NHS	National Health Service
NP	Notary Public
OBE	Officer, Order of the British Empire
ODNB	*Oxford Dictionary of National Biography*
PE	Physical Education
P & O	Peninsular and Oriental
POW	Prisoner of War
PPE	Philosophy, Politics and Economics
Prep.	Preparatory
QC	Queen's Counsel
RA	Royal Academy or Royal Artillery
RAF	Royal Air Force
RAM	Royal Academy of Music
RAMC	Royal Army Medical Corps
RAOC	Royal Army Ordnance Corps
RC	Roman Catholic
RCA	Royal College of Art
RCCM	Research Council for Complementary Medicine
RCM	Royal College of Music
RCOG	Royal College of Obstetricians and Gynaecologists
RCPE	Royal College of Physicians Edinburgh
RCP	Royal College of Physicians London
RCSE	Royal College of Surgeons Edinburgh
RE	Royal Engineers or Religious Education
RGC	Robert Gordon's College
RGH	Robert Gordon's Hospital
RGIT	Robert Gordon's Institute of Technology
RGS	Royal Geographic Society
RGU	Robert Gordon's University
RIAS	Royal Institute of Architects (Scotland)

RM	Royal Marines
RN	Royal Navy
RSA	Royal Scottish Academy
RSE (= FRSE)	Fellow of the Royal Society of Edinburgh
SA	South Africa
SAS	Special Air Services
SB	School Board
SCE	Scottish Certificate of Education
SED	Scottish (Scotch) Education Department
SHHD	Scottish Home and Health Department
SRC	Students' Representative Council
SRU	Scottish Rugby Union
TA	Territorial Army
TAA	Territorial Army Association
TC	Town Council
UN	United Nations
UNESCO	United Nations Educational, Scientific and Cultural Organisation
UNRRA	United Nations Relief and Rehabilitation Administration
VC	Victoria Cross
VSA	Voluntary Service Aberdeen
WHO	World Health Organisation
WS	Writer to the Signet
WW	*Who's Who*
WWS	*Who's Who in Scotland*
WWW	*Who Was Who*
WWI	First World War
WWII	Second World War
YMCA	Young Men's Christian Association

ONE Beginnings

This chapter describes the evolution of school education in Scotland from its origins and, within that general context, in Old and New Aberdeen. Unfortunately sources are fragmented and incomplete and it is not possible to be precise on the details of the Grammar School's historic antecedents. Certainly our survey of early schooling in Aberdeen confirms the existence of four grammar schools. In chronological order of foundation these were – the grammar school of Old Aberdeen; the Dominican school at Schoolhill; the grammar school of New Aberdeen and the grammar school at King's. Of these it seems most likely that it was the burgh grammar school of New Aberdeen which was the precursor of the modern Grammar School. If so, this would date the foundation of Aberdeen Grammar School as before 1418. It is still possible that its foundation could date back further, perhaps even to 1256 or before, but that seems less plausible given that the documentary references to the mid-thirteenth century refer to the grammar school of Old Aberdeen.

FOUNDATION

Aberdeen Grammar School has had a long and distinguished history but, when one tackles the question of how long, many problems arise. In 1906 the School celebrated its 650th Anniversary based on information which the then Rector, Morland Simpson, had discovered in various sources. By the time of the 1920s, claims that the School was the oldest in Britain were being championed particularly by W. Keith Leask who highlighted the 'myths' of many of the early English school foundations.[1] And so matters rested until the beginnings of discussions on the forthcoming 700th birthday arrangements planned for 1956. In an endeavour to settle the thorny issue of the foundation date Professor G.O. Sayles of Aberdeen University was asked for his opinion. As a specialist in Medieval History, he produced in September 1954, a memorandum holding that whereas the evidence about Old Aberdeen came from the thirteenth century, the earliest evidence for the burgh school of New Aberdeen, the Grammar School, came from the early fifteenth century. Other expert opinions concurred.

One is inclined to dismiss the early medieval period as the Dark Ages but modern research indicates that that period was becoming increasingly complex and sophisticated and the need for an educated work-force to deal with religious duties and administration of many kinds was provided by the setting up of many education bodies in Scotland and elsewhere, and it was among these that the beginnings of Aberdeen Grammar School are to be sought.

THE ORIGINS OF ABERDEEN

The modern city of Aberdeen evolved mostly from two medieval burghs: Old Aberdeen, the smaller religious settlement beside the river Don to the north, and New Aberdeen, the commercial town on the river Dee to the south.

Old Aberdeen developed around religion and education. It was dominated by St Machar's Cathedral, founded, as tradition relates, by St Machar, a companion of St Columba, who had set out from Iona in the second half of the sixth century to preach the Gospel to the Picts. He had built a church on or near where the Cathedral now stands because he was told to build it 'where the river curves in the shape of a bishop's crosier just before it enters the sea'. However, its 'real' history began, confirmed by documentary and physical evidence, with the transfer of the bishopric to it in the twelfth century and the later establishment of a cathedral ruling body, a chapter, which created a demand for a work-force of stone-masons, joiners and other craftsmen and the regular services of food suppliers. Although they helped its viability it was not until December 1489 that Old Aberdeen received formal status as a burgh of barony, under the authority of the bishop. This allowed its inhabitants to elect their own magistrates and other officials, so ensuring that Old Aberdeen would no longer be politically or economically dependent on the royal burgh of Aberdeen. Its weekly market was held on Mondays and was only a short distance from King's College, founded in 1495. Its population, even as late as the beginning of the seventeenth century, had not reached a thousand, but despite being tiny it had the unusual distinction of possessing both a Cathedral and a University.

Early on, New Aberdeen became the centre of an important regional trade and by the reign of Alexander I (1107–24) it was one of only three important trading centres of Scotland north of the river Forth, the others being Perth and Inverkeithing. Its achievement of burgh status under David I (1124–53) set the formal seal on the potential commercial success of the town. Its focal point became the broad Castlegate, while other imposing features included the parish church of St Nicholas, the Mither Kirk, dating from about 1157, and the friaries of four different religious orders. Its population, by 1488, was in the order of four to five thousand.

THE DEVELOPMENT OF EDUCATION

Although early records on schools are sparse, most standard histories regard the advent of Christianity as the starting point of Scottish education. The first missionaries founded settlements, which were not only places of Christian communion and devotion but also schools for training their successors. The instruction focused on Latin, the language of the Church, thereby enabling future ecclesiastics to read and copy the books of Scripture.

From the sixth century onwards the Church, which St Columba in Iona represented, established a network of monasteries in Scotland with seminaries attached to a number of them. However, Christian practices introduced by Columba were soon challenged. In 597 St Augustine arrived in Kent as an emissary of the Church of Rome, and a prolonged conflict between the two monastic churches began. The result was inevitable. A church relatively poor, small in numbers, and ruled from a remote fringe of Europe could not prevail against the resources and missionary power of the Church of Rome. Thus when England went over to Roman observances, Scotland followed suit. The marriage of the Scottish king, Malcolm III, to Margaret of England, helped complete the conversion of Scotland.

However, it seems that three scholastic offices of the early Scottish Church survived the revolution of Margaret and her sons.[2] Schools were conducted by *scolocs* – scholars – who were young churchmen in training. They were to be found at St Andrews in 1120 while in the following century the parish church of Ellon, the capital of the earldom of Buchan, was endowed to maintain four of them, and further documentary evidence confirms their presence at Arbuthnott in the Mearns. They assisted *rectors* – masters – who were in charge of the educational work of a monastery and who were frequently mentioned in the medieval manuscripts of the religious houses. Master Berbeadh was rector of the schools of Abernethy as early as 1124, while rectors are also mentioned in the documents of a number of burghs, including Aberdeen, in succeeding years. They were officers of high dignity: in early records they were classed with some of the highest in the land and as such were liable to be involved in judging and settling important disputes.

David I determined to establish the integrity of his kingdom. As a younger son of Malcolm III and Margaret, and with little apparent prospect of succeeding to the throne, he spent a great deal of his time at the court of his brother-in-law, Henry I of England.[3] There he became aware of how the Church was being reformed and developed. This led him to reorganise Scottish dioceses in a more systematic way, both before and after becoming king, moving the site of the north-eastern see to Old Aberdeen in about 1131.

The organisation of cathedral chapters tended to be based on English models, which increasingly made provision for the establishment of grammar and song (music) schools for cathedral cities and nearby villages. The development of schools also was encouraged by Rome especially following the decree promulgated by the Third Lateran Council of the Western Church in 1179 to the effect that each cathedral had to provide a teacher charged with free instruction of not just clergy of that church but also of the poor scholars. Although there was a time lag before some fell into line many continental cathedrals had schools attached to them particularly after the further urging of the Fourth Council of 1215.

SCHOOLING IN OLD ABERDEEN: THE ST MACHAR CATHEDRAL SCHOOLS

By the mid-thirteenth century the Aberdeen chapter had 'a sophisticated corporate character'.[4] Its four principal members, known as dignitaries, were the dean, the administrative head, who took the bishop's place at the weekly meetings of the chapter where diocesan problems were discussed; the treasurer, the custodian of the furnishings, ornaments and treasures of the Cathedral, and in charge of heating and lighting the Cathedral and also maintaining a constant supply of oil and wine for the daily services; the cantor, who was responsible for the liturgy at the Cathedral, looking after the choir, arranging the music for the services and in charge of the song school; and the chancellor, who dealt with the charters, documents and correspondence and was responsible for the Cathedral grammar school.

Although all these posts had appeared by 1240, the Aberdeen establishment, with only the four dignitaries and seven ordinary canons,[5] was still small. When the total chapter number reached thirteen in 1243 the first formal recorded constitution was promulgated by Bishop Ramsay and, significantly, was followed by more detailed statutes in 1256. In the latter, duties were spelled out further with the chancellor to supply both a suitable teacher to direct its schools and instruct the boys in grammar and logic[6] and a rector of schools to supervise the attendance of four choir-boys at matins and high mass on all the great festivals: two were delegated to carry tapers, and two bore the incense.[7]

The documentary evidence confirms then that behind its enclosed walls the Cathedral supported a song school and a separate grammar school in the Chanonry of Old Aberdeen in 1256. Indeed it is difficult to see how the services of the Cathedral could have been adequately maintained without them. There had to be instruction in song so that choristers might chant in accordance with liturgical requirements which demanded continual practice in both Gregorian and polyphonic chant. It was the cantor's task to see that the choristers were duly taught how to sing. However, the chorister also had to know (and understand to some extent) the words being sung which necessitated him having at least an elementary education in Latin. This was left to the rector scholarum (the teacher of classes in one school). The elements of rudiments of "grammar subjects" were expected to be mastered to some degree before entry; the other subjects of the *trivium* (rhetoric with versification, and dialectic) were often added. The length of course varied, but it was usually longer than two years.

Examining the legends of those saints associated with the North-East it is clear that monks such as Machar were literate and widely travelled and it is more than likely that the monks had established schooling at St Machar's as early as the tenth century. If this likely scenario is accepted then the development of schooling in the thirteenth century was not new but a refinement of previous practice. The example of Glasgow Cathedral, which had formed song and grammar schools in this period, and the creation of the post of chancellor in Aberdeen in 1240, both suggest that Aberdeen was falling into line with contemporary practice. Certainly the chancellor followed his statute instructions, as an ordinance of Richard, Bishop of Aberdeen, regarding the village of Buthelny, in 1262, was witnessed by Master Thomas de Bennum, described as 'rector of the schools of Aberdeen'[8] and a further reference is made to an anonymous rector in 1281.

Unfortunately, after 1281 little more is documented about the Cathedral school. The chapter records are unhelpful, perhaps because the appointment of a schoolmaster was a matter for the chancellor who made his own arrangements. However, it seems reasonable to deduce that the school continued to exist in Old Aberdeen in the next few centuries.[9] It gave choristers and would-be priests their basic training in Latin grammar, the liturgy, and perhaps some philosophy. It is not known whether it had a special building set aside for teaching purposes but given the small number of pupils involved it is likely that the would-be-choristers were being trained by the cantor in his house, while the grammarians were taught in the chancellor's or schoolmaster's manse.

St Machar's Cathedral grew in wealth in the years leading up to the Reformation, the result of extensive gifts of land. By 1445, the twenty-eight canons employed were supported by a team of procurators, lawyers, surveyors, bailies and clerks to monitor the income, collect its rents and watch for problems with its property. It has been estimated that by 1560 – the date of the Reformation in Scotland – the Cathedral's income in cash and kind must have amounted to well over £1,000 per annum, a very large sum in those days.[10] Of course, the Church had much to spend this on. There was the upkeep of the twenty members of the vicars' choral, the professional adult singers, the chaplains and the choir boys, who sang the Divine Office daily in the Cathedral on behalf of the whole community. The costs of the song school would come under this heading: at the end of the fifteenth century its master, John Malison, and six members of the vicars' choral, resided in the Chaplains' Court close by the Cathedral and its curriculum offered reading, writing and arithmetic to meet the needs of rural Old Aberdeen. Next came the care of the widows, orphans, the destitute and the sick, who were a constant obligation; then there were the educational needs of the diocese, chiefly the maintenance of boys and young men aspiring to the priesthood and those attending and being trained at the Cathedral grammar school. Other heavy costs included law suits, Papal taxation, the upkeep of the Cathedral fabric and the building programme.

The grammar school appears to have suffered from the development nearby of the new grammar school associated with King's and after the Reformation the Cathedral and the burgh of Old Aberdeen saw a steady decline. Most of the Church's wealth was diverted to other purposes and, while this tended to enrich local lairds and the aristocracy, it impoverished the new ministers and left little for the upkeep of the fabric and the song and grammar schools. As far as the latter were concerned they were also soon over-shadowed by a burgh school taught by a qualified master.

SCHOOLING IN NEW ABERDEEN: THE DOMINICAN SCHOOL AT SCHOOLHILL

At the edge of New Aberdeen at a place later known as Schoolhill, between 1230 and 1249, Alexander II of Scotland (1214–49) granted his 'palace and garden' to the Dominicans (or Black Friars) so that they might extend their educational work in the North-East. The Dominican Order had been founded by a Spanish priest, Dominic de Guzman, in 1216, and spread quickly, helped by permission from the Roman Catholic Church to preach (previously reserved for bishops) and the power to move around.

The Order emphasised teaching and soon developed a sound educational structure, with the most talented students at priory level being sent to provincial centres which in turn sent on their brightest to universities in Europe to study theology and, increasingly, arts subjects.

From the first, facilities were provided at the Schoolhill priory for grammar teaching and, for a time at least, the bishops of Aberdeen may have encouraged their flocks to attend the Dominican school, despite the priory having been situated some distance from the Cathedral of Old Aberdeen. Unfortunately we have little direct evidence about the schooling but it seems likely that the emphasis was on the teaching of novices and younger friars who improved their Latin and learned skills for further study. Nonetheless, such a curriculum was intellectually somewhat higher than that offered elsewhere in the area.[11]

The Dominicans were to play an important part in encouraging the foundation and development of education in Scotland. They were numerous enough to teach in schools in Ayr in 1436 and in Glasgow in 1478, while their contribution at university level was probably even more significant. The chapter room of the Dominican Order in Glasgow was not only the friars' classroom but was also where the newly founded Glasgow University held some classes. Bishop Elphinstone, the founder of Aberdeen University, was an early graduate of Glasgow and, having been brought up near the Black Friars' priory in Glasgow, was particularly sympathetic to that Order.

It was only after the Reformation that the Dominican house at Schoolhill fell into disuse. By the time of James Gordon in 1661 all that was left was a ruined precinct wall. The Order's legacy was important but more for higher education and Scotland's universities than for more local and general schooling.

SCHOOLING IN NEW ABERDEEN: THE GRAMMAR BURGH SCHOOL UNTIL THE REFORMATION

In chronological order, according to documentary evidence, Aberdeen's next grammar school was in existence by the early fifteenth century. St. Nicholas Church dates from at least 1157, although there is no certain record of an associated school until 1418. It was in October of that year that the burgh records of New Aberdeen relate the death of Andrew de Syves and his replacement as 'rector of the schools' by John Homyll. The appointment was for life, a common procedure at the time, and followed an 'examination of his sufficiency' in which he was found to be 'of good life, praiseworthy conversation, and skilled in literature and science'. Homyll had achieved an arts degree 'gained by his own deserts' and was instituted in his new office by Duncan, chancellor of St Nicholas, who gifted his own cap or biretta to commemorate the event.[12] However, significantly, Duncan had not chosen Homyll personally: he had been chosen by the Provost and Corporation of the burgh. This decisive action was an early example of the growing influence and power of burgh representatives in areas of jurisdiction and responsibility at the expense of the Church.

However, in June 1479, the then chancellor, Alexander Inglis, was involved in the ceremony of the appointment of the Rector, Thomas Strachan. The burgh still accepted that all such appointments would be given to churchmen but his salary of five pounds Scots, which came from the Town's Common Good coffers, was expected to be supplemented by payment from a chaplaincy to St Nicholas.[13] But circumstances were different in June 1509, when John Marshall seems to have been both presented and appointed as Rector by the Provost and Corporation, the occasion being marked by a gift of two rosaries.[14] As this was the first such appointment without the Chancellor being involved, unsurprisingly it was questioned and Marshall appealed to Rome for support. When this was forthcoming he was questioned by the burgh representatives in January 1521. He gave way and accepted their jurisdiction, but perhaps only grudgingly, for in November 1523 he prayed for pardon and reaffirmed burgh patronage of the grammar school.[15]

The grammar school was situated in the vicinity of St. Nicholas on Schoolhill, and the expense of keeping the building in repair fell to the Town Council. In October 1527, Marshall reported on the deterioration of the building, which he claimed was near collapse. The Council responded immediately charging the master of the kirk-work to begin work without delay at the Town's expense,[16] although there is no evidence that this was carried through at this time. Marshall was succeeded by John Byssat (Bisset), whose salary was increased in 1529 from ten merks to ten pounds Scots per annum to compensate for the lack of pupils, given the successive epidemics of plague the town had suffered. Poor wages were still an issue in 1538 when Byssat decided to give up the post of Rector and become instead a regent[17] at King's.[18]

The battle between Town and Church over the appointment of the Rector was not quite over. In January 1539 the Provost and Council elected Hugh Munro, unusually a layman, married and with a family and servants, as Rector, and instructed him to make a formal visit to the chancellor. The latter reacted by promoting his own candidate – a Robert Skene – whom he deemed 'able, suitable and discreet'. Appreciating, however, his weak position, the chancellor declared he was willing to propose an alternative if Skene was not acceptable to the Town. It appears that the Church still held the belief that *it* was the proper authority for presentation, but the Town was in no mood to compromise. In July 1544 the Council unanimously granted Rector Munro an annual salary for 'his diligent labours . . . for the instruction and learning of the bairns' of the grammar school of New Aberdeen who were to be instructed in "science, manners, writings, and other such virtues".

Significantly, in April 1550, Munro handed in his resignation to the Town for it to dispose of as it thought fit.[19] In return the Town bought him out, agreeing to pay him forty pounds Scots. The Town then proceeded to elect James Chalmers as Rector 'during its will' with ten merks salary: the more cautious conditions were to avoid a future buy-out. Chalmers was presented to the Chancellor for formal approval which followed without incident or dispute. The new Rector remained in office until appointed a regent in King's College in November 1557.[20] The next master, John Henderson, succeeded to the chaplaincy of St Michael in July 1559 and had his salary increased to fifty merks in March 1560.[21]

Originally, education was free to any boy who attended classes at the Grammar School but as more and more families began to appreciate the value of the teaching on offer the numbers increased. Accordingly, an annual fee of 4s Scots was charged for each boy with the expectation that more would be paid if it could be afforded. Refusal to pay fees resulted in a fine of 8s Scots plus the original fee, with the fine going to the Magistrates rather than the School.

Pre-Reformation there had grown up in monasteries, especially in England, the custom of electing a boy bishop for the entertainment of the younger inmates and this practice had spread to universities and schools. In Aberdeen annually on 6th December – the festival of St Nicholas – the Rector of the burgh grammar school visited in their homes the parents of boys under his charge, accompanied by one of the boys, elected for the occasion and dressed in a bishop's vestments representing St Nicholas, the patron of schoolboys. They collected the annual fees from 'every honest freeman' both merchant and craftsman.[22] The boy bishop held 'office' until Innocents' Day, 28th December. This tradition was still adhered to in the 1540s.

By the time of the Reformation the burgh School of New Aberdeen was well-established in the community, providing a social as well as an academic function. The curriculum was dominated by the learning of Latin but other preparation for the priesthood was undertaken, including practical instruction on the celebration and administration of the sacraments, on the groundwork of their faith and with receiving the basic psychological and ethical instruction they would require to hear confessions and, if they had not already received it in the song school, gaining some musical competence for the performance of the liturgy.[23] This grammar school was to continue flourishing in the years to come.

The song school of the Town had a much more chequered existence. It was also situated close to St Nicholas's Church being sited at the west wall of the kirk yard, on the east side of what would later be called Back Wynd. It first turns up in documents in 1483 but it was probably much older. In October 1558 the Town Council agreed to pay a yearly salary of twenty-two merks to John Black, the rector of the song school. However, the major problem for the school was being associated with the discredited medieval Roman Catholic Church. The Reformation made it an immediate target in 1559–60 when its building was sacked and its Rector fled to France. When it reopened in 1570 it embraced the new Protestant faith and survived for a while as a shadow of its former self. By the seventeenth century its master was restricted to instruction in music, singing and playing.

SCHOOLING IN OLD ABERDEEN: THE GRAMMAR SCHOOL AT KING'S

Old and New Aberdeen together thus already had three grammar schools when Bishop Elphinstone founded King's College in 1495. Anticipating that young men and boys would come to the university seeking to improve what

Latin they had already acquired elsewhere, so that they could soon enter the Faculty of Arts, or simply to expand their grammar education hoping perhaps for future study at his university, Elphinstone decided to create a grammar school. In doing so he had the further intention of providing a more 'modern' type of grammar education in line with the latest views of more radical scholars. This explains why from its earliest days King's appointed a Grammarian whose duties were 'to hold a grammar school in his own manse, and teach the scholars in it, to instruct them in grammar, poetry and rhetoric as well as in discipline, morals and behaviour, and to punish offenders as appropriate'.[24]

Elphinstone's Grammarian lived outside of King's in a manse of his own, as the mixture of schoolboys and arts students put pressure on space and produced a clash of interests. Originally the Grammarian was expected to teach there but this idea was abandoned and a separate grammar school was later built at the front of King's, abutting, but outside the College, as can be seen in Parson Gordon's picture of about 1661.[25] It is probable that the Old Aberdeen 'song school' boys lived in the cantor's house.

At the very time when Elphinstone's plans for the establishment of a University at Aberdeen were well advanced he seems to have been influential in persuading James IV in 1496 to introduce an Education Act. This ambitious legislation required all important Scottish noblemen to provide a grammar school education for their eldest sons and then to send them to a University to study arts and law for three years. Clearly Elphinstone was keen not just to cater for the merchant class but also to promote the movement of the sons of the higher gentry and nobility into the universities. Unfortunately, military disasters and consequent internal disorder ended any thought of implementing the Act as it was the Scottish nobility that was decimated in early sixteenth century battles such as Flodden Field.

The burgh of New Aberdeen does not seem to have been jealous of the siting of the University in the neighbouring burgh. Its Town Council had no resources to fund such a project and may have been dubious at first about its viability. The benefits of the scheme to a commercial sea port were not obvious and there were fears of clashes between groups of young students and gangs of sailors.

In fact, relations between New Aberdeen and Elphinstone were cordial and individual citizens made donations to King's in its early years. It was to be a full century before New Aberdeen actively supported another project to establish a further university in this burgh. By that time, King's had come to represent the conservative forces of the Catholic religious interest from which the town councillors of New Aberdeen wished to distance themselves.

In 1553 Theophilus Stewart published the third edition of Vaus's Latin textbook.[26] In it he included the Statutes and Laws of the Grammar School of Old Aberdeen. John Vaus[27] had been chaplain of the Holy Name of Jesus altar at St Nicholas parish church and was employed by King's College as the Grammarian to teach Latin there. On his death around 1539 Stewart followed him into the latter post and drew up a code of management for the school. His rules appear somewhat 'quaint'[28] but were produced to ensure that the pupils could not plead ignorance of the Statutes.

The boys had to acquire a basic knowledge of Arithmetic and they were to be taught from Terence,[29] Virgil,[30] Cicero,[31] and Quintilian.[32] Only boys in their first year were able to use the Scots tongue as their Latin was deemed inadequate to converse with older grammarians but remarkably they had a choice of using instead Greek, Hebrew, French or Gaelic, the first of which was probably taught in the School. The Statutes bear this out through the inclusion of a number of Latinised Greek words – gymnasium for school; gymnasiarcha for head; and hypodidascalus for under-master or doctor. As Montrose grammar school taught Greek in the 1530s it seems plausible that a more liberal curriculum had been introduced into Aberdeen schooling by 1553 and King's College some time before this. This would explain the proficiency of students in Aberdeen in 1540 when James V was welcomed in the town with 'diverse orations made in Greek, Latin, and other languages, quhilk was mickell commendit be the king and queen and all thair company'.[33]

The Statutes give a picture of daily life in school in pre-Reformation times. On arrival boys prostrated themselves on the ground and on bended knee prayed to Christ and the Virgin Mary. Latin grammatical analysis began at 7 a.m. and when completed any delinquents were punished by chiding or beating. When the punishments were over, a public lecture was given at 8 a.m., after which the boys hurried to breakfast. Thereafter at 10 a.m., the boys broke up into classes taken by the doctors.[34] These ended by 11 a.m. when the youngest scholars were allowed to go into town while the Rector lectured on Terence, Virgil or Cicero to the older pupils. Lunch-time followed with all having to be back by 2 p.m. when classes began again. At 4 p.m. the boys gave an account to their tutors of the work of that day. Between 5 and 6 p.m. disputations – defence and discussion of a theme conducted in Latin – were held, and then the boys attended evensong and joined in prayer. There was always one assistant master on duty correcting and noting errors, mistakes in writing Latin and dealing with the idle. Only two pupils at a time were allowed to leave the room and took with them the tally or stick. No others were allowed out until the return of those who had had leave.

This invaluable description of life in the grammar school of Old Aberdeen is likely to have been similar in most aspects with that of the routines of the Grammar School of New Aberdeen, apart from evensong which would have been held in St Nicholas Church, where the pupils had their own special seats.

In the later sixteenth century the Grammarian remained and continued to divide his time between University teaching and running the grammar school of Old Aberdeen. The Grammarian was still situated outwith King's which showed Elphinstone's desire to combine under one roof the teaching of University students needing revision in their Latin together with those senior boys studying for the priesthood but not destined for further studies, who until then had been taught in the nearby Cathedral grammar school. In the longer term this meant the decline of the latter. A song or music school also continued to function with the cantor's manse situated at the north-west of King's College.

THE GRAMMAR BURGH SCHOOL AFTER THE REFORMATION

In New Aberdeen, John Henderson (1557–73) was Rector of the Grammar School while the Reformation was in full swing. The friars came under attack with the Blackfriars and Whitefriars destroyed and the Greyfriars saved only by the vigorous action of the authorities, encouraged by the Earl of Huntly, and by the Provost, Thomas Menzies of Pitfodels, part of a family of staunch Roman Catholics.[35]

The wrath of the scholars, however, was only unleashed when Henderson and the Town Council, following the reform programme, interfered with the School holidays, which were regarded by the boys as a matter of right rather than privilege. Faced with the threat of significant disorder, in January 1569 the Town determined to compromise, at least meantime, and agreed to re-introduce holidays around Christmas (or Yule) from 21st December until 7th January. The pupils remained dissatisfied that their holidays continued to be under threat as the Reformers strove to remove Saint Days, and even Apostle Days and the commemoration of Christ's Epiphany, from the calendar.[36]

Henderson was a Roman Catholic and graduate of King's. He found his position increasingly difficult especially when parents were threatened by the kirk session if they kept their children away from School when they were expected to be in attendance. He departed to France in 1573 to avoid further problems. He was succeeded in December 1575 by William Carmichael, who inherited the annual salary of fifty merks 'for bringin up, teching, and instructing of the barnes and schollaris . . . in vertew, lerning, letteris, and guid manneris'.[37] Within a fortnight of his appointment the Council, stimulated by the manifestations of popery exhibited at Christmas and the New Year, determined to end the Yule holidays again. The grievance of the boys smouldered for a while. Carmichael meantime, in October 1579, successfully petitioned for a higher salary and the fees were raised to 3s 4d each quarter (the poor being exempted).

Carmichael resigned in July 1580 and Thomas Cargill was appointed on the same terms as his predecessor. He inherited the problem of the Yule holidays and the boys committed 'enormities' by occupying the school building and 'usurping aganis the maister and magistrates'. On 21 December 1580 the authorities reacted by insisting that any boy being educated in the burgh had to produce a burgess cautioner who would forfeit ten pounds Scots if the scholar broke the rules. Any refraction would be registered in a special ledger and details read out from the church pulpit on the next Sunday.[38]

Cargill continued to experience discipline problems every year around Yule-time. On 26 December 1581 the scholars seized the Grammar School in a demonstration of how unhappy they remained about their loss of holidays. The Council reiterated its determination not to give way and allow Yule holidays. However, as a compromise it agreed to give the scholars three days' holiday at the beginning of each of the four quarters in the year, in the belief that twelve days was a generous arrangement.[39] Although this quietened matters for a time there was always the possibility of another flare-up. On 12 December 1589, as a precaution, the Council reaffirmed that all scholars needed a cautioner to be admitted to the School and he would be liable to pay for any and all damage done to buildings and furnishings.[40]

Unlike his predecessors Cargill was not preoccupied with the poor salary he received as Rector. Instead he was more concerned with threats to his monopoly of school education in the burgh. In April 1586 he complained about the teaching of boys without his consent or a licence from the Council, and did so again in March 1593. His exclusive privileges were spelled out in August 1597: no schools, other than the song school, could be set up or masters employed, without the express permission of the Rector of the Grammar.[41]

Cargill had inherited a building in a ruinous and dilapidated state. Despite fears being expressed half a century earlier it was not till 1581/2 that attempts were made to shore it up, but in September 1589 the Dean of Guild was instructed to mend the heather roof and windows. However, the work done was piecemeal and unsatisfactory and the Council spent six pounds Scots in December 1598 'to repair the Grammar Schule presentlie ruinous and decaying'. Problems persisted and the roof blew off in 1612.[42]

Cargill was a noted Latinist. His commendation in verse of the Earl Marischal for erecting his College in Aberdeen was printed and published by the Town Council in 1593. Even more significant nationally was his contribution in thanksgiving for the safe delivery of James VI from a kidnapping conspiracy in August 1600. The Aberdeen Town Council voted Cargill twenty pounds Scots for his Latin treatise commemorating the occasion and was pleased that it contained positive statements about the burgh's antiquity and privileges.

From an early stage Marischal took many of its students from the Grammar School of New Aberdeen where they had been drilled in Latin grammar and the principles of rhetoric. Before they had arrived they had become familiar with the ancient authors of Virgil, Ovid, Terence, Homer, Livy and Cicero, and introduced to the modern texts of Buchanan, Erasmus and Vives. Given such a good grounding it is understandable why, unlike King's, Marischal did not employ a Grammarian until the nineteenth century.

SCHOOL TEXTBOOKS

Grammar schools used the popular Latin class books of the time. The longest lasting was that of Aelius Donatus, a fourth-century AD Roman grammarian and teacher of rhetoric. His *Ars minor* in the form of question and answer was aimed at younger learners and provided elementary instruction in parts of speech. It was used widely in Scotland and England in the Middle Ages.[43]

Another famous work used was that of Johannes Despauterius, a Flemish grammarian (1460–1520). When the Scottish government made its first attempt to create a national curriculum for education in 1559 the schoolmaster and grammarian William Niddrie was awarded a ten-year licence to publish a variety of school texts which included Despauterius's grammar.

In England, William Lily's *Grammar*, written in 1513 and published in its final form in 1542, became a prescribed textbook in English schools for over two centuries. In Scotland, and in Aberdeen in particular, the work of John Vaus became popular following his translation of the *Ars minor* into Scots (1508) and similar work with the *Doctrinale* of Alexander de Villedieu (1522) and his grammar texts of 1531 and 1553.[44] Generally, books called *Vulgaria* were devised to help pupils master vocabulary and rules. From composition the boys went on to imitate classical stylists and to write themes, or formal argumentative essays, and verses in Latin. It was taught as a spoken language via colloquies, orations and disputations, though, in due course, the spoken element declined.

In December 1575 the Privy Council of Scotland, under Regent Morton, decided that there should be only one form of grammar-teaching in all Scottish grammar schools. George Buchanan, the learned Latinist, was asked to convene the leading schoolmasters in the country and to obtain agreement on the best grammar available. However, he reported that there was no existing grammar which could be recommended as perfect in all parts. The schoolmasters were then instructed to produce such a grammar themselves. To this they responded with a division of labour, which resulted in two books of Latin etymology, at simple and advanced levels. They then produced the rest of the Latin grammar in manuscript form. By an Order in Council the printed books were to be used immediately, followed by the manuscript once it was available in book form. No schoolmaster in Scotland was to teach grammar from any other textbooks, on the pain of dismissal.

The first two parts of the long-awaited authorised Latin Grammar were published in 1587. By then free competition in grammar books had taken over again and, although this led to progressive improvement, many pupils were still being subjected to poor material. In December 1593 the Scottish Government, under Chancellor Thirlestane, condemned the inconvenient and injurious multiplicity of grammar books used in schools, and encouraged the use of one authorised grammar only. This, however, as before, proved difficult to enforce. A further attempt to establish a common grammar failed in 1607.

SCHOOLMASTERS

In burghs the schoolmaster or dominie was quite frequently a Master of Arts: AM, which in the nineteenth century became MA. However, a cleric styled Dominus was generally someone in sacred orders who had not fully graduated in any subject. The commonest class of schoolmaster were chaplains but burghs were reluctant to employ a permanent chaplain or appoint for life, perhaps fearing that such tenure would lead to complacency and neglect of work. Often they appointed a stipendiary chaplain with an annual fee or pension, which resulted in complaints that the income was insufficient. However, payment was augmented by entry silver from new boys; book silver was collected when the master started a new book; bent silver was paid when rushes were being collected to strew the floor and candle silver was paid at Candlemas. Scholage, a fee that may have originated as a charge towards the upkeep of the school building, appears to have become a prerogative of the schoolmaster. Given such variations teachers appear to have moved around in the quest for better rewards: Sir John Fethy, master of Aberdeen song school from 1544 to 1546, worked in Aberdeen, Dundee and Edinburgh. The provision of a rented schoolhouse was usually an additional attraction.

Until the Scottish Reformation in 1560 the Rector of Aberdeen Grammar School remained a priest and the Church 'continued to watch civic activity with a jealous eye'.[45] Clerical influence, then, remained strong and the founders of the three fifteenth-century Scottish universities – Henry Wardlaw at St Andrews in 1412, William Turnbull at Glasgow in 1451 and William Elphinstone at Aberdeen in 1495 – situated their university in their cathedral town.

Contemporary observers were often dissatisfied with what had been achieved. Ninian Winzet, the religious controversialist,[46] held that rich endowments had been given to religion and learning but not to grammar schools, while John Mair[47] in his History of 1521 maintained that the Scots gentry failed to educate their children in letters and morals. The bishops of the period were accused of failing to provide for poor scholars and men of talent, while many schoolmasters continued to charge book fees for the copying of their master copies of textbooks, when printed books were becoming more widely available. The provision of a Grammarian for the teaching of Latin in Old Aberdeen was a mark of dissatisfaction with the quality of school pupils and university students.

Nonetheless, there is plenty of evidence suggesting a widespread provision of a basic education, in reading, if not in writing. Certainly the impact of the printing press, which from 1507 created a much wider reading public, and the extensive presence of schoolbooks in the inventories of booksellers, both also point to a growing level of literacy. This, however, was not a priority for a grammar school.

As far as grammar schools were concerned, provision nationally was extensive, offering an exclusively Latin curriculum and for the most part aiming at sending their pupils to university. In 1539 well over a hundred boys from grammar schools attended University which, given the country's small population, appears a creditable number.[48]

SCHOOL PUPILS (UP TO 1600)

Educational commentators have long stressed the 'unique influence exerted by Aberdonians on the Continent'.[49] A significant number of Grammar School pupils in this period studied and taught at universities in Protestant Europe, particularly in Germany, Switzerland and Holland. Some of those students remained abroad long enough to visit usually three universities for more than one year, and then undertook a more extended tour of the Continent before returning to Scotland to make a significant contribution to the academic, ecclesiastical or professional life of the country. Others decided to remain abroad for a much longer period engaged in academic teaching and in pursuing higher, usually medical, qualifications. For the most part they had an abiding attachment to their school, university and home town, which was reflected in bequests in their wills and testaments.[50]

The following short biographical profiles – in chronological order of birth – bring home the quality of Latin teaching going on in the burgh Grammar School in the sixteenth century which laid the basis of subsequent careers.

Gilbert Skene (1522–1599) was educated at the Grammar and King's. Appointed Professor of Medicine at King's in 1556 and James VI's physician in 1581, he produced the earliest medical work to appear in the vernacular in Scotland in 1568.[51]

(Sir) John Skene of Curriehill (1540–1617) was the younger brother of Gilbert. He was at the Grammar in 1549 and thereafter at King's. He studied Law in Paris and after becoming an advocate in Scotland in 1575, he was involved in a project reviewing the laws of Scotland and was appointed joint Lord Advocate in 1590. Four years later he became Clerk Register and a Lord of Session. He produced the first Dictionary of Scots Law and in 1609 *Regiam Majestatem,* which included legal texts or statutes attributed to monarchs from Malcolm II to Robert III.[52]

Duncan Liddel (1561–1613) of Pitmedden attended the Grammar and King's. He then studied at Frankfurt under the Scot John Craig (later James

VI's physician) and Rostock, where he lectured on Copernicus's theories to leading German astronomers. He became a Professor of Mathematics at the University of Helmstedt and by 1600 had become a Professor of Medicine. He produced three principal medical works, one completed by one of his pupils, Patrick Dun (also a Grammar boy). He generously endowed six bursaries and the first chair of Mathematics, as well as his books and mathematical instruments, to the newly founded Marischal College.[53] Some surplus funds in his mortification were designated for poor scholars at the Grammar. He was the most outstanding of Grammar scholars in this period.[54]

James Cargill (1565–1616) probably was educated at the Grammar and King's College, where he qualified in arts, before going on to study Medicine at the University of Basel graduating 'magna cum laude' in 1598. In his Will of 1614 he bequeathed to the Town Council four thousand merks for the maintenance of four poor scholars and smaller sums to the Grammar and the Hospital.[55]

Robert Howie (1565–1645) attended the Grammar and King's, before further education at Rostock, Herborn and Basel. In 1592 he became a minister in Aberdeen supporting the Presbyterian form of church government. Becoming Principal of the newly founded Marischal College in New Aberdeen in 1594 he is credited with its successful launching. He moved to a pro-Episcopal stance and as a reward James VI chose Howie as the Principal of St Mary's College, St Andrews. He furthered royal interests until Charles I's ecclesiastical policy led him to support the National Covenant.[56]

John Johnston (1565–1611) was educated at the Grammar, King's and Rostock before becoming the first Scottish student to matriculate at the Universities of Helmstedt and Heidelberg. On his return he became the ally of the Presbyterian theologian, Andrew Melville, in Scottish ecclesiastical and educational policies, but both were disappointed by James VI's move to Episcopalianism. He became a Professor of Theology at St Mary's College, St Andrews. His bequests included a thousand merks to Marischal to fund a scholarship.[57]

(Dr) Alexander Reid (1570–1639), brother of Thomas Reid, Latin Secretary to James VI, was taught by his minister-father before attending the Grammar and King's, from which he graduated before 1600. He travelled and studied abroad in France and Germany before practising as a surgeon in London. He published *A Description of the Body of Man* in 1616 and further surgical writings aimed at providing clear introductory explanations for the newly qualified and student anatomists. He gave generous gifts to both King's and Marischal for poor scholars and included the grammar schools of the burghs of Old and New Aberdeen in a share of a debt owed by the Earl of Annandale. Unfortunately for the schools, the latter debt was not recovered.[58]

Patrick Copland (1572–1651), philanthropist and Presbyterian chaplain to the East India Company, went to the Grammar and was an early graduate of Marischal. He campaigned for funds to educate children in the new colony of Virginia and later Bermuda, but failed in his efforts to found a College at Henrico for educating Native Americans. In three instalments made in 1616, 1622 and 1627 he contributed six thousand merks[59] to found a chair of Divinity at Marischal, proving a tireless campaigner in the cause of charitable support for education.

Walter Donaldson (1574–?) probably attended the Grammar and King's. He accompanied the Bishop of Aberdeen in 1598 on an embassy to Denmark and the German protestant princes. He studied Law at Heidelberg in 1599. He was appointed Professor of Natural and Moral Philosophy in 1603 at the Protestant Academy of Sedan, where he also lectured on Greek and political theory and stayed for sixteen years before becoming the Principal of the Academy at La Rochelle.[60]

Gilbert Jack (1578–1628) attended the Grammar and Marischal, before going on to the Universities of Helmstedt, Herborn and Leiden. He gained posts in Rhetoric and Ethics, before taking a Medical degree in 1611. Having produced several philosophic textbooks he became a Professor of Physics in 1617.[61]

Thomas Dempster (1579–1625) was educated at the Grammar and Pembroke College, Cambridge before further study at Louvain, Rome, Douai and Paris. He became Professor of Humanities at Toulouse, then Professor of Eloquence at Nimes prior to being employed in Paris as a regent. James VI and I appointed him Historiographer Royal, but Dempster's Catholicism led to criticism and he became Professor of the Pandects (= body of Roman Civil Law) at the University of Pisa in 1616. Fluent in Latin and Greek his scholarly approach and writings led to his appointment as Professor of Humanities at Bologna, at that time the most prestigious seat of learning in Italy, where his career flourished.[62]

Arthur Johnston (1579–1641) attended school at Kintore, the Grammar[63] and probably King's, where he was later Rector. He studied further at Heidelberg, and Sedan, where he became Professor of Logic and Metaphysics in 1604. He received a medical qualification from Padua and became professor of Physic at Sedan, both in 1610. Returning to Aberdeen he wrote a substantial amount of Latin verse. His fame as a Latin poet continued in the next few centuries.[64]

(Dr) Patrick Dun (1581–1652) probably attended the Grammar and Marischal and was taught Medicine by Liddel at Helmstedt. He studied further at Heidelberg, Nimes and finally Basel, where he qualified in Medicine. About 1610 he became one of the three regents in Marischal and taught all seven subjects of the curriculum, taking his class through the first three years – bajans, semis and tertians. He was appointed Rector of Marischal and Professor of Medicine (Mediciner) at King's. He was then the first lay Principal of Marischal from 1621–49, teaching the fourth and final year – the magistrands. He bought land in Ferryhill to endow the Grammar School. He became Dean of Medicine at King's in 1634. A portrait of him by George Jamesone hung in the hall of the Grammar until it was destroyed in the fire of 1986, but copies survive in print.[65] One of the Houses in the modern School was named after him.

Andrew Cant (1584/90–1663), Church of Scotland minister, was probably educated at the Grammar and at King's, from which he graduated in 1612 and was appointed Humanist in 1614. He was minister at Alford for over a decade before being tutor to the Forbes of Pitsligo family and minister at Pitsligo. Unlike most ministers in the North-East he supported the Covenants and argued the Presbyterian cause in Aberdeen, the scene of the only organised opposition to the National Covenant. He became minister of Newbattle, chaplain to the covenanting army and minister of St Nicholas in Aberdeen. He was elected Moderator of the General Assembly in 1650 and in the following year Rector of King's.[66]

William Forbes (1585–1634) attended the Grammar before going in 1597 to Marischal, graduating MA in 1601. He was appointed a regent in the University, resigning in 1616 to travel on the Continent. He was minister successively of Alford and Monymusk, and the Aberdeen Town Council selected him as Principal of Marischal in 1620. He became the first Protestant Bishop of Edinburgh in 1634, shortly before his death. His attempts to reconcile different doctrines were unpopular with many Presbyterians.[67]

(Rev. Dr) William Guild (1586–1657), Church of Scotland minister and benefactor, attended the Grammar and was an early student of Marischal between 1598 and 1605. His first charge was King-Edward in the presbytery of Turriff. He joined other ministers protesting against royal control and certain innovations of James VI in the Scottish Church. In 1640 he became

Principal of King's College, but was deposed in 1651 after General Monck's visit to Aberdeen. He wrote extensively. During his lifetime and in his Will he exhibited a significant degree of philanthropy to Aberdeen and its citizens.[68]

George Jameson (1589/90–1644), portrait painter, attended the Grammar between 1597 and 1601 and undertook an eight-year apprenticeship as a painter in Edinburgh. From 1620, when he painted Sir Paul Menzies, Provost of Aberdeen, he established a substantial practice which earned him wealth and fame. In 1633 he was commissioned to decorate Edinburgh for the visit of Charles I. His death was commemorated by David Wedderburn in Latin verse, indicating Jameson's national success in his own lifetime.[69] He lived on the north side of Schoolhill: a plaque commemorating him can be found at No. 22.

David Chamberlaine (1590–1619) spent part of his childhood in Aberdeen and most likely attended the Grammar. His father was the obstetrician to Anna of Denmark (consort of James VI) and such royal connections may have been the reason behind his appointment as surgeon in the first ship of the East India fleet.

Alexander Ross (1591–1654), Church of England clergyman and writer on philosophy, attended the Grammar. After an unsuccessful spell as master of Southampton GS (1616–20) he found other sinecures in the Church especially All Saints' in Southampton in 1628. He devoted himself to building a literary career and produced a large and diverse body of writings.[70]

By the end of the sixteenth century the burgh Grammar School had had a continuous history of around two centuries and had built up a strong intellectual reputation, based on a curriculum geared as a preparation for university study and public life. It appealed to the aristocratic and gentry classes of the North-East of Scotland as an institution aimed not at literacy but at training the leaders of society. For the time being at least the Town was able to raise its fees for pupils without parental reaction. The verdict appeared to be that the School was giving value for money.

Of the four grammar schools surveyed in this chapter, two continued until recent times, but the closure of the Barn (the grammar school of Old Aberdeen) late in the nineteenth century left only Aberdeen Grammar School operating. It seems unfortunate that the focus on the controversial issue of the foundation of the School has obscured the fact that the traditions and values of all the grammar schools in Aberdeen are now carried forward in the one remaining School. It seems reasonable that in doing so the Grammar School can lay claim to a precursor in Old Aberdeen with a history going back to 1256 and earlier. Seen in this perspective the foundation saga of our burgh School may need to be revisited as the claim that the Grammar School of New Aberdeen was 'founded prior to 1256' no longer seems to be so unhistorical when viewed in the context of the histories of the other grammar schools of medieval Aberdeen.

TWO Limited Progress and Generous Bequests

This chapter concentrates on the burgh Grammar School of New Aberdeen, which, since the fifteenth century, has had a continuous and uninterrupted documentary history up to the modern period. Already by early in the seventeenth century the post of Rector of the Grammar was able to attract the best Classical scholars in Scotland and David Wedderburn set a high standard, at least in scholarship, for his successors to maintain. To ensure they did so the Town Council began a rigorous inspection regime by means of regular and thorough 'visitations'. This proved necessary as the under-paid and over-worked teaching staff remained dissatisfied with their conditions of service and the promises of Dun's mortification remained unfulfilled. At least the *raison d'être* of the Grammar did not change and the School continued to fulfil its over-riding function – to prepare scholars for University entrance – so the chapter ends with details of a selection of the pupils of the School of this period who go on to illustrious careers.

MASTERS AND UNDER-MASTERS

Co-Rectors: Reid and Wedderburn, 1602–1603

On 6 February 1602 Thomas Reid (1583–1624) and David Wedderburn (1580–1646) were appointed co-Rectors of the Grammar School of New Aberdeen. Having been examined for four days on oratory and poetry and on composition in prose and verse the Council decided that there was nothing to choose between the contenders; both were probably the best Latinists of their day in Scotland. They were charged with instructing the youth in the 'art of grammar, gude letters and manners' and were to receive the same salary as Cargill viz. eighty pounds Scots per annum and schoolage of six pounds eight shillings per pupil per quarter. They were to continue to employ a teacher or doctor who would be paid three shillings and four pence per pupil per quarter.[1]

Thomas Reid, philosopher, translator and founder of the first public reference library in Scotland, was educated at the Grammar and Marischal, from where he graduated MA about 1600. However, he did not remain long as a Grammar master, for he resigned the post after only eighteen months on being appointed one of the three Regents of Marischal. After some four years there he pursued his studies in France and Germany, teaching Philosophy and Humanity in Rostock and producing a number of works on Metaphysics. Later in 1618 Reid became Latin secretary to James VI and I, producing Latin translations of the King's collected works. He left his collection of books and manuscripts to Marischal and they still form an integral part of the University library today.[2]

Rector: David Wedderburn, 1603–1640

David Wedderburn, poet and Latin grammarian, probably attended the Grammar and King's. He also was tempted away from his post as co-Rector of the Grammar but in his case he changed his mind and stayed. That was in 1603 when he resigned with the intention of pursuing a clerical vocation. He did not do so, earning the label of being a 'stickit minister' – one of those unsuccessful in gaining a minister's charge.[3] Instead he abandoned this aim and returned to the School, perhaps because Reid's departure meant that Wedderburn could expect an increase in salary. He hoped that this would solve his financial difficulties which were at the root of most of his problems at this time.

Unfortunately this was not the case. Despite being given the whole stipend Wedderburn was to suffer at the hands of inflation throughout his tenure. Within a year, in October 1604, this had led to him being accused by a number in the community of charging extortionate fees in the School. On investigation the Council found that Wedderburn had proceeded upon 'auld use and custome' and had continued to extract additional payments collected by his precedessors. It immediately restricted Wedderburn to the terms of his contract and insisted that the details were to be 'writtin in gryt letteris on a brod' and hung on the wall of the School. At the same time, to ensure the Council's policies were strictly adhered to, a Visiting Committee, headed by the Provost, was set up to visit the School quarterly 'to censure and tak tryell baith of doctrine and discipline' and to deal with any abuses which had cropped up.[4] Such measures were partly to assure the local gentry and ensure that they were not tempted to take their sons away.

Wedderburn's time as Rector was far from uneventful. In his time the Grammar boys were divided into town boys and 'landward' boys, the latter made up of the sons of the old families of the Northern Counties who lived in lodgings and were relatively free of effective supervision. This was a recipe for disciplinary problems, which surfaced again over the Yule holidays in 1604 when the pupils occupied the School and held it against the Rector with 'swordis, gunnis, pistollis, and utheris wappynis, spuilzeing, and tacking of puir folkis geir, sic as geisse, foullis, peittis, and utheris vivaris'. The Council ordained that the Rector should receive no pupil into the School without some friend standing surety for his behaviour to the extent of twenty pounds Scots (a doubling of the previous caution). Despite this precaution trouble arose again in August 1609 when the scholars exhibited disorderly and riotous behaviour – the caution sum being doubled again – and in December 1612, when seven young men, sons of country gentlemen, seized the Song School and held it for three days with 'hagbuttis, pistollis, swordis, and lang wappynnis'. In this last instance, twenty-one scholars from burgh schools were expelled although the Provost and Council thought the masters were partially responsible for the problems because of their slack approach to discipline.

Matters, however, did not end there for, shortly thereafter, Gordon of Birsmoir, a close relative of two of the expelled boys, attacked the Rector of the Writing School (Gilbert Leslie) with swords in the street and wounded him. Gordon admitted his fault and, faced with the authority of the Privy Council, produced the surety that he would not molest the Rector in future. The Town Council, however, now put the ongoing problems firmly at the door of the masters – Wedderburn, Gilbert Leslie and Patrick Davidson of the Song School. Their 'negligence' had encouraged indiscipline and their correction and chastisement of pupils had to be more severe. The masters were called in to hear their censure and accepted that they would be answerable for all damage done in future by their students.[5] This seems a harsh verdict given that the Council had introduced regular visitation by councillors presumably to head off disorder and that Edinburgh had experienced similar disturbances climaxing in 1595 when a town bailie had been shot by High School pupils.

However, only two months later, the brother of Gordon of Birsmoir, along with the brother of the laird of Cowbardie and other accomplices, sought out the Writing School Rector and beat him with 'durkis and battounes' resulting in such loss of blood as to endanger his life. The two attackers were arraigned along with Birsmoir, and only got off through the intervention of Alexander Gordon of Cluny. Birsmoir paid a fine of two hundred merks, and the three were ordered to attend a St Nicholas' Kirk service and, immediately after the sermon and before the blessing, they had to 'ryis out of thair seat in the ruid lift and compeer befoir the pulpit, and thair in all humilitie ilk ane severallie efter either, crave pardon'.[6]

Wedderburn had a national, even international, reputation as a Latinist. On various occasions the Council and the North-East community were reminded of this. In 1612, on the premature death of Henry, Prince of Wales and heir to the throne, Wedderburn composed a Latin poem; five years later he was paid five hundred merks by Aberdeen Town Council for his poem on James VI and I which was read to him at Falkland Palace. He was appointed Poet Laureate of Aberdeen in 1620 and was paid an annual sum of eighty merks, and later that same year he was awarded the Freedom of the City. He also produced poems on the death of James in 1625 and the visit of Charles I to Scotland in 1633. He further contributed to verses in memory of Patrick Forbes, Bishop of Aberdeen, and of his school-friend and fellow classicist, Arthur Johnston and in celebration of the life of George Jameson in 1644.

Following failed attempts to produce a common or universal grammar for schools Wedderburn produced a *Short Introduction to Grammar* in 1632 for which he was paid one hundred pounds Scots by the Council. Partly through its own merits and partly through the support it received from the Convention of Royal Burghs, it became the standard text on Latin in grammar schools throughout Scotland and was reprinted several times.[7] In time, however, others were produced and Wedderburn himself produced *Institutiones Grammaticae* and *Vocabula,* first published in 1633 and 1636 respectively. In practice, grammar schools almost always followed similar courses and made few adjustments to their teaching methods and content. In New Aberdeen Grammar School these remained very much unchanged throughout the sixteenth and seventeenth centuries.[8]

Throughout his long period as Rector the poor remuneration on offer resulted in the sharing of classes which was not conducive to effective teaching and learning. As early as 1614 in an effort to keep him Wedderburn had been allowed to take on a professorship (Grammarian) and taught Humanities in Marischal. This continued for a decade but the under-staffing and over-stretched resources in the School led to complaints about the quality of teaching and the 'slaknes' of the staff in matters of time-keeping and discipline. The Council decided that he had to give up his university commitments and concentrate solely on raising standards in the School.[9]

Wedderburn responded by successfully petitioning the Council in

February 1628 for Andrew Howat to be appointed to teach Writing and Arithmetic in the Grammar. This was a significant change and the development of the curriculum in this manner suggested that the Council feared that the School's position was in danger of being usurped. After all, the grammar school of Old Aberdeen had been doing something similar since at least 1553.

Five months later, in July 1628, for the 'godlie and virtuous education and teaching of the youth in pietie, gude letters, and gude maneres' Alexander Fraser was added to the teaching staff after an anonymous benefactor bequeathed five hundred merks for that purpose. Wedderburn's own salary was increased by eighty merks in 1629 and on his retirement as a result of ill-health in 1640 he received a pension of two hundred merks in recognition of his service to education in the Town.

William Wedderburn (1582–1659/60), Church of Scotland minister and younger brother of David, taught alongside his brother as the doctor or under-master in the Grammar School in 1616–17. He found the going tough and was at the receiving end of 'ane cuff' from Alexander Forbes of Towie in June 1617. It was deemed a serious offence by the Council who forced Forbes to return to the School and apologise on his knees for his misdemeanour.[10] Shortly afterwards Wedderburn took up an appointment as a Regent in Marischal.[11]

Alexander Fraser of Finzeauch had gained his MA from Marischal in 1627 and was appointed doctor in the School at a salary of one hundred pounds Scots the following year. When Fraser moved on he was replaced by Thomas Chalmers in 1630. Chalmers had been Liddel bursar at Marischal and won a prize for poetry in 1624; he took his MA in 1628 and between 1633 and 1637 was Johnston Divinity bursar. When Chalmers demitted office in 1636 James Boyd was appointed as doctor. He had been Cargill bursar in 1627 and gained his MA in 1631. Meantime Chalmers, after a break from 1636 to 1640, returned as Rector.

STAFFING IN THE GRAMMAR SCHOOL, 1640–1717

Rector: Thomas Chalmers, 1640–1655

1640 July 15 – With Wedderburn retiring owing to "bodily infirmity" he was replaced as master by Thomas Chalmers at a salary of 200 merks.

1641 June 16 – Robert Moreson replaced James Boyd (as doctor) who had gone abroad for university study. Moreson had been Liddel bursar, 1635–7. He took his MA in 1639 and an MD from Angers in 1648. He was to become physician to Charles II and Professor of Botany at Oxford in 1669 and is regarded as one of the fathers of Science in England.

Rector: Alexander Strachan, 1655–1663

1655 Sept. 12 – Alexander Strachan became Rector in place of Chalmers who demitted office. Strachan had gained his MA in 1644.

1655 Oct. 4 – John Cassie became a doctor. He had taken his MA from King's as early as 1629.

1656 July 16 – Patrick Strachan was appointed a doctor. He had graduated MA from King's in 1656 and left to become minister of Maxton in 1683.

1657 Aug. 26 – Alexander Reid, who was a Liddel bursar in 1651 and graduated MA in 1655, became a doctor. He 'desertit his charge' in 1659.

1658 May 5 – James Lundie was made second doctor, justified to the Council on the grounds that the Grammar School 'was in use to have two'; each with a salary of 100 merks. He had taken his MA from King's in 1657 but soon 'desertit his charge'. He was to become a minister in Edinburgh in 1663.

1658 Dec. 29 – Walter Alexander, schoolmaster at Bellie, became second doctor. He had a Crombie bursary in 1651 and took his MA at Marischal in 1655. He won a Johnston Divinity bursary, 1658–62 and ultimately became minister at Echt in 1666.

On 18 January 1659 the books, which had been left to the Grammar by George Robertson in his Mortification of December 1644, were finally delivered up. This was the beginnings of the School Library, which by 1820 had over two thousand volumes.

1659 Aug. 10 – William Saunders, student of Divinity, became a doctor. He had just gained his MA in 1659. He was appointed Professor of Mathematics at St. Leonard's College, St Andrews in 1672 and Rector of Perth Grammar School in 1690. He published a textbook in Edinburgh: *Institutiones grammatiae succinctae ac faciles.*

Rector: John Forbes, 1663–1670

1663 June 3 – John Forbes, Humanist Professor at King's, became Rector. He had taken his MA from King's in 1660 and later he became Sheriff-depute of Aberdeen.

1663 Dec. 12 – John Barclay, student of Divinity, became one of the doctors. He was a Liddel bursar in 1655 and took his MA at Marischal in 1659. He resigned in 1664 to become minister of Monquhitter and in 1678 he became minister of Cruden.

1664 Nov. 16 – John Findlater, another student of Divinity, became a doctor (replacing Barclay). He was a Crombie bursar in 1660 and took his MA at Marischal in 1664.

1666 Jan. 16 – Alexander Innes was appointed as a doctor. He had graduated with an MA from Marischal in 1663. He demitted office in 1670.

1667 Mar. 20 – Under Patrick Dun's mortification, the master was to receive a salary of 600 merks, and the fees of his own class, together with an 'eik' of £200 in full satisfaction of 'candle and bent silver' fees. The doctors were to receive salaries of 300 merks each, and the fees of their own classes, and a third doctor was appointed. He was Patrick Innes, the Liddel bursar in 1659, who had graduated with an MA from Marischal in 1663. He received a Johnston Divinity bursary, 1665–9, and became minister of Deskford and of Banff, 1679.

Rector: Robert Skene, 1670–1676

1670 Mar. 30 – Robert Skene, schoolmaster at Banchory-Ternan, was appointed master 'ad vitam aut culpam' (for life or until fault) for at least eight years. He was a Crombie bursar in 1652 and took his MA in 1656. He died in 1676.

1670 Nov. 9 – John Alexander became a doctor, replacing Innes. He was a Ross bursar in 1665 and graduated MA from Marischal in 1669. He demitted office in 1679.

1672 Feb. 28 – Robert Alexander became a doctor. He was a Liddel bursar in 1666, and graduated from Marischal in 1670.

Interregnum – Acting Rector: John Findlater, 1676–1679

1679 Nov. 19 – Alexander Thomson became a doctor. He took his MA from Marischal in 1674. He demitted office in 1684.

Rector: John Findlater, 1679–1717

1679 Nov. 19 – John Findlater, one of the doctors, became Rector (following the death of Skene in 1676), but at a doctor's salary of 300 merks. The post had been kept vacant for three years to allow Dun's mortification to augment, Findlater having charge of the master's class and some authority over the other doctors.

1679 Nov. 19 – Gilbert Ramsay became a doctor (replacing Findlater, now Rector). He was a Ross bursar in 1673 and graduated MA from Marischal in 1677. He left to become minister of Dyce in 1682, remaining there until 1717.

1682 Sept. 2 – James Troup became an under-master (replacing Ramsay). He was a Cargill bursar in 1676 and graduated MA in 1680. In the Records the term *under-master* is henceforth used increasingly instead of *doctor.*

1684 Dec. 5 – Andrew Mitchell became an under-master. He had taken his MA at Marischal in 1683.

1684 Dec. 5 – Gilbert Black became an under-master having taken an MA the same year.

1692 William Gellie was appointed an under-master after taking his MA the same year. He was to become Dean of Guild in 1712 and a bailie of Aberdeen in 1716.

1696 Sept. 10 – William Carnegie became an under-master. He took his MA at Marischal in 1696.

VISITATIONS

An important record of the thoroughness of visitations is preserved in the Town Council records. On 15 June 1659, the Council, believing that the quarterly visitation of the Grammar and music schools appointed by former acts would, if conducted properly, promote the learning of the youth, approved the following regulations, together with the 1636 *Leges Scolae* (now lost):

> 1. There shall be four visitations of the GS every year at the beginning of each quarter, when the scholars are to be tested in making themes, interpreting and analysing authors and compiling verses.
>
> 2. The Master of the GS shall keep a record of visitations and details on the scholar who gains the premium (only awarded when confirmed by examination that it was scholar's own work). This was the first mention of premiums or prizes in the history of the School.

3. Each scholar is to be teamed up with another scholar of like ability to stimulate competition and to encourage 'sneaking' on each other.

4. The Master is to be given the results of the current visitation so he can track progress of scholars at future visitations.

5. It was recommended that the master choose material short and easily performed – the colloquium of Erasmus, or recitation from Cato Sulpitius, a psalm of Buchanan, an epistle of Ovid, a satire of Juvenal or Persius, or an ode from Horace. The highest class should include declamations as acting in public develops in scholars 'boldness and a vivacity in public speaking'.

6. Visitors were encouraged to commend not just winning a premium, but also the runners-up. They were to take their responsibilities seriously so encouraging others to support learning.

MORTIFICATIONS

Aberdeen did well economically in the first four decades of the seventeenth century with New Aberdeen reaching a peak of population and prosperity that was not to be matched for almost a century. This advance came from merchants who manufactured and exported the coarse cloth of plaiding, a speciality of the North-East. The resulting prosperity was accompanied by an unprecedented number of charitable legacies or mortifications and led the Council to create a new office of Master of Mortifications in 1632. The Grammar School was the recipient of a significant number of legacies although they took the form of mortifications entrusted to the Town Council.

Successful former pupils, such as Duncan Liddel in 1613 and James Cargill in 1616 and 1622, aimed at helping the poor while Robert Ferguson in 1625 gifted a bell. A 'neighbour of the burgh'[12] bequeathed five hundred merks Scots to pay for an extra teacher in the school in 1628, while the following year Alexander Irvine of Drum left ten thousand pounds Scots to maintain bursaries at the Grammar School and Marischal. Also in 1629 another former pupil, Patrick Dun, bought the lands of Ferryhill to the south of the burgh, with a view to gifting them in perpetual trust to the

Town for the endowment of the School. In his Deed of Mortification of 1631 he stated his intention that after his death the profit from the lands should be used to support four full-time teachers at the School. Poor scholars were to be educated free, and Dun hoped that sufficiently endowed posts would improve the quality and commitment of their teachers. The importance of this bequest can be gauged by the fact that one informed commentator has described it as being practically a refounding of the School.[13]

In 1644, George Robertson, a lawyer and burgess of Aberdeen, left a thousand merks Scots, and in 1657 Dr William Guild, Principal of King's, bequeathed seven thousand merks Scots, both seeking to extend educational opportunity for the sons of craftsmen. Catharine Rolland, widow of Guild, in 1659, made provision for the support of four bursaries at the School provided they were sons of decayed burgesses, and she also included help for poor scholars. In 1677 James Milne bequeathed two thousand, five hundred merks Scots to maintain two bursary scholars at Marischal, who must 'have learned ther courses in the Grammar School'. As with a number of the other mortifications preferential treatment was to be given to his relatives, for nepotism was generally a more important criterion than poverty for charitable support.

Such generous benefactions should have made a significant difference. That they did not was nothing less than a scandal. In 1704, the monies belonging to various mortifications including those of Liddel, Cargill and Guild, were invested by the Council in the purchase of half of the lands and barony of Torry. There is no evidence that the mortifications were credited with any of the profits of these transactions. In the case of the 1628 arrangements they were followed until about 1667 when no more notice was taken of them.

However, what happened to the most significant and important mortification – that of Patrick Dun – which should have relieved the Town of its financial support of the School, as well as ensuring a free education of quality for poor children who were capable of studying there?

The Trust had an unfortunate beginning and an alarming deficiency was produced as the masters were paid the salaries provided by the Deed even before the stock had accumulated sufficiently to bear the burden. Nonetheless, by 1666, the Council accepted that the Trust was now in a position to invest in land with the funds available reaching some 12,000 merks.[14] However, instead of buying land, as it was legally bound to do, the Council began to lend the money out without adequate security to, amongst others, some of its own members. As they all became insolvent the

Trust sustained a heavy loss. Moreover, the legal costs incurred in recovery efforts were also charged against it. A further issue – increasing substantially a large floating balance to facilitate transactions – lessened the interest being accumulated. Had such bad management not taken place the Trust fund could have reached some 36,000 merks by this time.[15]

Things went from bad to worse for in 1677 the Council purchased for the Town the lands of Gilcomston and paid for them with money from the Dun Trust and two other mortifications, which was an illegal act, for the capital of the Trust belonged to the Grammar School masters. The sad state of the stock was revealed in the returns for 1681: the total of the Trust amounted to £470 sterling of which more than half was gaining no interest and of this latter sum a half was in the event wholly lost.

In 1752 the tacksman of the Ferryhill lands resigned his tack in exchange for an annuity, and at last, more than a century after Dun's death, the Council took full possession of the property. Unfortunately, this only prepared the way for further mischiefs, for instead of letting out the lands to rent, the Council proceeded to feu them off by public roup, to the great ultimate loss of the Trust.

It was at this time in 1753 that the masters, patience exhausted, presented a petition to the Council for an increase in salary, basing their claim on the contention that the funds must now be sufficient to carry out the intentions of the founder and adequate to yield a considerable increase to the petitioners. Following much haggling the dispute was given over to arbitration. Each party provided one arbiter, but, extraordinarily, no independent chair was provided for. The resulting award of November 1754 ordained that the Council pay the masters £164 sterling yearly – the value of the Ferryhill feu-duties – in the proportion set out in Dun's will; that, to recompense the Common Good Fund for the payments toward the salaries made up to date, the Town's debt to the Trust (calculated by the Town Treasurer at £427 sterling) should be cancelled; and that the balance should be applied to building a new Grammar School and establishing an endowment fund for its maintenance. Both sides accepted these arrangements despite their illegality. Presumably the masters concurred to avoid a legal wrangle with their employer. This whole Award 'contributed disastrously to the further dissipation of the Trust'.[16] The stock which stood at over £250 in 1759 had dropped to £100 by 1770.

Contemporaneously, Town Councils elsewhere in Scotland but particularly in Edinburgh and Glasgow were also guilty of putting their own personal interests and those of the Council they served before mortifications they had been entrusted with. However, in the case of Aberdeen the blatant dishonesty seems on a different scale. In 1811 Walter Thom published his *History of Aberdeen* and was the first to draw attention to the scandalous misappropriation of the Dun Bequest.[17] His account has stood the test of time well.

Yet nothing had been done to change or redeem the position until the School Board took over the administration of Aberdeen's educational endowments. A special committee was set up to investigate the Bequest, the capital of which amounted to £3,625 in 1872. The result was a settlement in 1874: the Town Council agreed to pay £164 annually to the Board for the GS (being the annual value of the feu-duties payable from the Ferryhill lands). By 1934 the Council was back in control and a commission awarded the school £300 to provide for free education for those who could not afford the fees and £150 as the Dun 'benefit' to help group activities in the School. When fee-paying ended, instead of losing this sum the Secretary of State for Scotland decided that the Dun money should be increased to £300 per annum.

ARCHERY MEDALS

The need to train young men in self-defence was realised early in Scotland. In 1425 laws were enacted to ensure all yeomen were provided with a bow and by 1457 wapinschaws were to be held, four times a year, while football and golf were forbidden. These laws were confirmed in 1471, 1491 and 1535. Specifically, archery was a favourite sport with the students of St Andrews University in the sixteenth century and they arranged a Silver Arrow competition early the next century. Archery contests were also encouraged at the Grammar School: the winners gave a medal to the Rector who had to sign a receipt for them, witnessed by two of the town's bailies. The medals bore the arms, initials or motto of the winner and were attached by a chain to the arrow.

In 1881 when Rector Moir was appointed, a silver arrow and fourteen medals were discovered hidden among a heap of lumber and books which had lain undisturbed from the time of the School's removal from Schoolhill in 1863. The discovery was not altogether a surprise for William Kennedy had described the medals in his work *The Annals of Aberdeen*[18] written in 1818. Moreover, Rector John Findlater had signed for the arrow and thirteen medals when appointed in 1679 and he acknowledged another additional medal in 1699. John Milne also signed for these in 1717, and a similar signed declaration was made by Rector James Dun in 1744.

The Arrow and medals are still in the possession of the Grammar today. The date of the archery contest and the winners are as follows:

1664 George Mackenzie who went on to Marischal College.
1665 Thomas Fraser.
1666 John Bannerman of Elsick.
1667 Andrew Skene of Ruthrieston, the son of the Dean of Guild.
1670 Adam Gordon of Glenbucket who went on to Marischal College.
1672 John Gordon of Brachlie who went on to Marischal College.
1673 James Moir of Stoneywood (1659–1739). He was to become MP for the County for fifteen years and one of the Commissioners on the Act of Union of 1707 with England.
1674 John Skene (b. 1658) was the fourth son of James Skene of Newtyle. He went on to Marischal College.
1675 Walter, Lord Deskford was the eldest son of the third Earl of Findlater. He went on to Marischal College in 1675 but died before 1698.
1676 John Udny of Udny. He became MP for the County from 1703 to 1736. In 1701 he married Lady Martha Gordon, daughter of George, first Earl of Aberdeen and High Chancellor of Scotland.
1677 William Keith, 9th Earl Marischal, attended Marischal College. He succeeded to his title in 1694. He died in 1712 aged about fifty-two. A strong Jacobite and anti-Unionist, his two sons – George and James – also attended the GS.
1678 Alexander Fraser of Strichen was the eldest son of Thomas Fraser, fourth of Strichen.
1679 (Sir) John Ogilvy of Inverquharity, third baronet, came from a family of Forfarshire Royalists. This was the only medal given by a pupil who came from outwith Aberdeen and the County.
1699 Theodore Morison of Bognie (b. 1685) was the son of George Morison and Viscountess Frendraught. He attended Marischal College. He died in 1766.

The wapinschaws took place on the Links. Although it would have been handier for the Grammar boys to use the open slopes of Schoolhill, it is significant that the medal donors came from noble or county families: the best known of whom would be Skene of Skene; Udny of Udny; Moir of Stoneywood; the Earl Marischal and Morison of Bognie. This suggests that the social base of the pupils was particularly high at this period.

PUPILS (INCLUDING THOSE STUDYING AT THE GRAMMAR BETWEEN 1600 AND 1700)

Grammar School pupils, from the seventeenth century on, furthered their education by studying usually at King's College founded in 1495 in the Old Town of Aberdeen or at Marischal College, founded in 1593 in the New. Both had introduced new constitutions modelled on those created for the universities of Glasgow and St Andrews by the reformer, Andrew Melville. Under the chancellorship of Patrick Forbes, Bishop of Aberdeen (1619–35) King's taught an arts course centred on the works of Aristotle, reinterpreted in the light of new ideas and methods from the Continent. Marischal, which had been founded as an assertion of Protestant supremacy in the still resistant North-East, matched King's under the vigorous leadership of their principals – Gilbert Gray (1598–1614) and Patrick Dun (1621–49).

To gain entry to these universities Grammar boys were tested on their Latin and only the proficient admitted. Competitors for bursaries were judged by even higher standards. They were tested on their Latin, their conduct and their means and only the most deserving selected. At King's scholars consolidated their Latin for the first six months before going on to Greek; at Marischal they followed a similar course but were pushed harder and introduced to the basics of eloquence and rhetoric at the same time. The students were also required to develop transferable skills and, to encourage these, Duncan Liddel began an annual composition competition with a money prize in 1623 open to learned scholars of the colleges and grammar schools. But the students spent most time on declamation and disputation, seen as essential to a career in the church, teaching or public office.

A number of scholars enrolled at university toward the end of the first year to save time and money, but this was opposed by both King's and Marischal which already were unhappy about the limitations of their entrants. Indeed in 1690 sub-Principal George Fraser of King's was complaining bitterly about grammar schools in the North being 'so farre degenerit' that they produced few good Latinists and no Grecians at all.[19]

Although Aberdeen maintained close connections with Europe in the seventeenth century, from about the 1610s onwards the established patterns of cultural exchange were disturbed by the Thirty Years' War and Scotland became involved in the political and religious affairs of England during the Civil War. The Restoration of Charles II in 1660 led to further turmoil with the establishment of Episcopalianism in the Kirk, but its strength in the North-East helped foster strong religious ties with England. Increasingly, Aberdonians carved out successful careers for themselves especially south of the border with the founding of the Royal Society of London in 1660.

Nathaniel Welsh was the son of Elizabeth (1570–1625), daughter of John Knox, the Protestant reformer, and Rev. John Welsh (1568–1622), Church of Scotland minister at Ayr. Shortly after his father's death in April 1622 he boarded with Rector Wedderburn and attended the Grammar, with his fees and lodging being paid for by the Town Council from capital of two thousand merks gifted by Patrick Copland. Unfortunately Welsh was shipwrecked and died young.[20]

Alexander Jaffray (1614–1673), son-in-law of Dr Patrick Dun, attended the Grammar and Marischal, before studying Law at Edinburgh. A supporter of the National Covenant Jaffray represented Aberdeen in the Scottish Parliament (1644–50). He was one of the Commissioners who successfully negotiated the return of Charles II to Scotland in 1650. He was wounded at Dunbar but on returning to Aberdeen he again became Provost and was able to surrender the City on generous terms. He gained favour with Cromwell which led to imprisonment (1660–1) on the Restoration. In his last years Jaffray converted to Quakerism.[21]

Donald Cargill (1627–81), field preacher and insurgent, attended the Grammar and St Andrews where he studied Divinity. In 1655 he became the minister of the Barony Church in Glasgow and built a sizeable following. He lost his charge following attacks on Charles II and the re-establishment of prelacy. His unauthorised preaching led in 1674 to him being outlawed and spending the rest of his career as a hunted fugitive. He was badly wounded at Bothwell Bridge in 1679 but led the Cameronians before his final capture and beheading.[22]

Robert Ferguson (1637–1714) probably attended the Grammar and Marischal in the mid-seventeenth century. He supported himself by teaching and wrote religious tracts supporting Nonconformity. He also wrote political pamphlets against Roman Catholicism and the claims of James, Duke of York, to the throne. He was a supporter of Monmouth's failed rebellion in 1685 and aided William of Orange's cause with his pen. Disappointed by the fruits of the 'Glorious Revolution' of 1688–9 he sided with the Jacobites and his fortunes declined.

(Prof.) James Gregory (1638–75) left the Grammar in 1651 and graduated from Marischal in 1657 before studying in Padua. He invented, in 1661, the reflective telescope (the 'Gregorian' telescope), and in 1668 he was elected a member of the Royal Society. He was the first Professor of the new chair of Mathematics at St Andrews (1669–74) and first Mathematical Professor at Edinburgh University (1674–5).

(Sir) Patrick Dun (1642–1713), great-nephew of Dr Patrick Dun, attended the Grammar and Marischal before studying at Valence, and graduating from Dublin University. He was president of the Irish College of Physicians (1681–7) and a founder member of the Dublin Philosophical Society. He became physician to William III's army in Ireland, dominated the College of Physicians until 1706 and was elected to the House of Commons. He left generous medical endowments in Ireland.[23]

David Gregory (1659–1708), mathematician and astronomer and brother of James (see above), attended the Grammar and Marischal. He came from a line of mathematicians and medical men and continued this tradition. He studied at Leiden and was elected to his uncle's chair in Mathematics at Edinburgh University in 1683. As an Episcopalian with Jacobite connections his position was precarious for a time after 1688. However, backed by powerful friends, including Isaac Newton, he became Professor of Astronomy at Oxford. He was elected FRS in 1692 and published mathematical papers. Significantly, he taught Newtonian mechanics at Edinburgh before the teaching of it was undertaken at Newton's home university of Cambridge.[24]

Simon Fraser, Eleventh Lord Lovat (1667–1747) attended the Grammar (according to a pamphlet of 1767) before going on to graduate from King's in 1683. As Highland Chief he supported the Hanoverians in 1715 but fought with the Jacobites at Culloden in 1746 and was executed at Tower Hill for treason.

(Prof.) James Gregory (1674–1733) attended the Grammar and Marischal and Edinburgh Universities. He graduated in Medicine from Rheims in 1698 and became a general practitioner in Aberdeen. He was elected Professor of Medicine in Aberdeen University in 1725.

Robert Keith (1681–1757), Scottish Episcopal bishop and historian, attended the Grammar, between 1692 and 1696, and Marischal, before becoming a domestic chaplain and a minister in Edinburgh. He continued to promote the Jacobite cause but his prudent and moderate actions helped resolve disputes and he was made Bishop of Edinburgh and then *primus episcopus inter pares.* In his final years he gained the reputation of a scholar displaying original research.[25]

James Gibbs (1682–1754), architect, attended the Grammar and Marischal, and became 'the first Briton to receive a professional architectural training abroad'.[26] His Roman Catholic faith, which he retained throughout his life, led to early setbacks in his career but the failure of the Jacobite rebellion brought him into vogue and his rebuilding of St Martin-in-the-Fields was seen as an influential masterpiece. He became FRS in 1729. In Aberdeen his 1741 design for rebuilding St Nicholas West Kirk was executed in 1751–5 by James Wylie. Interest in his buildings has never flagged. A commemorative plaque can be found on the west wall of St Nicholas Kirk, Union Street.

Donald Andrew Brockie (1687–1755), Benedictine monk and historian, attended the Grammar and King's. As a Roman Catholic he went to the Scots abbey at Regensburg and was ordained a priest in 1713. He completed his theological studies at Erfurt, where he was appointed Prior to the Scots Monastery. He produced volumes on the rules of religious orders and monasteries.[27]

In retrospect Dun's mortification of 1631 was the most important event relating to the Grammar during the seventeenth century. It did not solve the financial problems of the School but without its existence matters would have been worse. Dun aimed at improving the quality and efficiency of teaching and his mortification laid down what salaries were appropriate for masters of the School. Unfortunately, the warfare of the middle decades led the Town Council to uplift monies belonging to mortifications that it could never realistically hope to pay back in full. Councillors could and should have arranged things better but in some instances the mismanagement was forced upon them by outside agencies and circumstances.

The Town did not follow the mortification to the letter but neither did it completely ignore it. This ensured that the advances made by the Grammar School were limited. Lack of resources impinged on many decisions. The filling of posts took longer as the century progressed until 1676 when the state of the mortification was in such a poor state that the Rector's post was left unfilled for three years. Fortunately, the next century was to bring advance on a number of fronts.

THREE The Contribution to the Scottish Enlightenment

This chapter details the Statutes of the Grammar in 1700 which were more comprehensive than those in 1553 (see chapter 1). They are important not just in showing how far the School has developed but because they set the framework for the next century. The chapter also examines the reaction in the School to the Jacobite Risings and ends with information on its staffing and the significant pupils who play an important role in raising the status of the Grammar especially during the period of the Scottish Enlightenment.

VISITATIONS

In 1700 the Town Council returned to the matter of Visitations. The 1636 *Leges Scolae* had been lost and the 1659 Laws on Visitations had not given specific guidance and instructions to the Rector. Hence the belief that the Grammar School had 'no fixt rules set down and enjoyed this long tym bygone' for its regulation. The Council determined to rectify this and took advice from local ministers and the Principal and Regents of Marischal College. The result was the following:

> Laws and Maner of Teacheing to be observed in the Grammar-School of Aberdeen as agreed by the Town Council, 23 October 1700:
>
> 1. That there be one Solemne Visitatione of the Grammar School in the begineing of October yeirly, at which the severall classes are to be tryed and examined by makeing of Thems, interpretatione of authors, and analyzing the same, makeing of verses, &c. At which visitation allenarly, praemiums are to be given to the most deserve-ing and best qualified Scholars; and the names of those who gains

the praemiums at each visitation yeirly, are to be insert in the said School Register of Laws, and upon what poynt of tryall each scholar gains his praemium. As also, that beside the forsaid Solemne visitatione yeirly in October, Ther be three other visitations of the said school, by such of the Counsell as they shall appoynt, and by any two of the ministers of this Burgh, and any two of the masters of the said Marischall Colledge whom the Counsell shall name; and that the first of the saids three visitations shall be yeirly, upon the first Thursday of Februarie. The second upon the first Thursday of May, and the third upon the first Thursday of August, in all tyme comeing; and that beside the saids four yeirly visitations, two or more of the Magistrats and Counsell of the said Burgh visite the said schooll the first Tuesday of every month, and enquyr how the laws and rules of the school and discipline thereof are observed.

2. They appoynted the method of teaching the Grammar and Classick authors to be diligently observed in maner following:

a. The entrants to be keept reading Latin the first quarter or longer, as shall seem good to the masters.
b. After reading they are to learn the declinations, comparisons, pronouns, conjugations, with the rest of the Rudiments to the constructions. As also, they are to have the first four sections of Wedderburn's Vocables [of 20th July 1636], not only to get by heart, but to decline and conjugat the same conform to ther progress.
c. With the constructions they are to have the two last sections of the saids Vocables, Dicta Sapientis and Rudimenta Pietatis.
d. With the first pairt of the Grammar, they are to have Lilly, Sulpitius, Disticha Catonis, Ovid's Epistles, Virgil's Epigrams, Moretum, Terentii Andria; and for prose authors, Corderius, Minora Erasmi Colloquia, Lodovici Vivis Dialogi, Minores Ciceronis Epistolae; and for sacred pense, Ursino Catechism, Dialogi Sacri Sebastiani.
e. With the second part of the Grammar, Virgil's Eclogs, Ovid's Metamorphosis, Virgil's fourth book of Georgeicks; and for prose authors, Curtius, Salust, Caesar's Commentares; and for the sacred pense, Buchanan's Paraphrase one the Psalms.
f. With the third part of the Grammar, Virgil's second and sixth Aeneods, Horas Ods; and for prose authors, Cicero's Offices,

Colloquia Erasmi Majora, Sueton; and for sacred pense, Buchanan's Paraphrase continued.

g. With the fourth pairt of the Grammar, some of the select Satyres and Epistles of Horas, the tenth and thirteenth Satyres of Juvenall, some of Persius' Satyres; and for prose, Florus, Livius first Decad, and Buchanan's Chronicle, together with the turneing and makeing of vers, dictats of Rhetorick, and rules of Elegancie; to which is to be added, some practice in composeing and resolving orations conform to the rules of Rhetorick.

h. After Dispauter's Grammar is taught, that Kirkwood's Thographie and Syntax be learned, with his Tractat de Variis Carminum Generibus.

i. From Vivis Dialogs all allong throw the rest of the prose authors, the choicest sentances of each daye's lessons be dictat in Latine and English, together with the versions of each daye's lesson; and for each lesson throughout the severall factions, there be a dayly conference appoynted.

j. As to composition of Thems, the publick argument be dictat three tymes in the week, and besides these, the high class to have fyve arguments more.

k. That on Saturday's foirnoon, there be Disputs repeating of rules and authors, publickly, out of the severall classes by course; and once a-week all the rules and questions of the Shorter Catechism are to be repeated publickly.

l. In the winter quarter each scholar (of the higher class) repeat a fable of Aesop, from the publick dask, before the whole school.

3. That the masters and doctors of the Grammar School shall give due attendance the tyme of Crismas, at the usuall hours every day, and shall suffer none of ther scholars to withdraw att that tym; unless such whose parents and friends shall desire it of the master. And that if any scholar shall at his own hand absent himself without leave asked and given, the master shall not receive him again into his school without punishment conform to the discipline of the schooll, in the case of absents, of whom he is to give account at the visitation every first Thursday of Februarie thereafter.

4. That the hebdomader be present dayly in the school at seven a cloak in the morneing, both in winter and summer tyme; except betwixt Hallowmass and Candlemass, when the scholars are only to conveen at nyne in the morneing.

5. That upon every play-day, the hebdomader for that week, shall goe allong with the scholars to the hill, when they get the play, and shall be careful that ther be no disorders nor abuses amongest them, and bring them back to the schooll at reigning of the bell.

6. That the hebdomader shall, every Sabbath day, sitt in the little dask befor the loft door of the Church, to notice that noe scholar goe out of the Church without his leave.

7. That the disciplin of the School be observed as follow:
   a. That public prayers be said every morning and every evening.
   b. On the Sabbath day, after prayer being said at the second bell, that the questions of the Shorter Catechism be examined in the severall classes and in the afternoon from the second bell to the third bell, the high class to give an account of the catechism, with the scripturall proofs, together with the exposition of a chapter of the Latine New Testament. And after sermon, that they conveen (prayer being said) and give account of ther notes, and shutting up all with prayer, be dismissed.
   c. That in making of thems and Disputs, each have his adversary for stirring up aemulation.
   d. That there be chosen out of the high class, whom the masters judg most fitt for their observance and faithfulness, so many as may have inspectione of the rest of the schooll under the masters, called Decurios, of whom each hath six committed to his charge, who take ane account if they have prayed and read a portione of Scripture, of which they are to give a vers. As also to notice that ther hands be washen, their head combed, and ther cloaths neat, and to take ane account of two questions of the Shorter Catechisme each day. And at ten o'clock the Decurios to give up ther lists of such as are faultie, together with the absents of the morneing and preceeding day. As also censors of such as speak English prophain talk, or

swearing throughout the severall factions be taken account of.

e. In tyme of pryer that each Decurio go to the factions under his inspectione.

f. That on each Monday the perturbers of and absents from the Church be called to ane severe account.

g. That on each Saturday the publick tables be exacted.

8. That the master pitch upon some fitt persone to be janitor who is to officiat instead of the publict Censor, and doe all other dutyes incumbent on a janitor, and have for his pains from each scholar twelve pennies Scots money quarterly.

9. That the first three laufall days of Januarie be allowed to the scholars for play-days, instead of the Yooll Vacance, and so furth quarterlie through the whole year.

10. That in absence of the principall master, any of the other masters present may exercise School Discipline upon any of the scholars offending.

11. That the master shall use his endeavours to cause all the scholars repair to the school each Sabbath day after the afternoons sermon, and give ane account what they have heard that day and in what churches And the visitors at ther quarterly visitations, are strictly to inquyre into the observance of this.

12. If parents complain on the master for correcting of ther children, the master shall not be called befor the latron [= lectern or reading-desk in the church] on that account, till that the quarterly visitors have examined the whole mater privatly and heard both partyes and taken informatione and report if need bees and if any parent be found to complain without cause they shall be fyned or otherwayes censured, as the magistrats shall think fit and that the child be chastized for his unjust complaint.

13. That the severall classes in the schooll be called to the church per vices, as the ministers shall find convenient, (they acquainting the masters therwith twenty-four hours befor) where they are to be examined anent the principles of Religione.

14. That for the winter quarter, (from the first of November to the first of Februarie) the scholars are not to convene till nyn in the morning, and are to stay till twelve o'clock befor noon.

15. That every scholar pay his school-dues at the beginning of each quarter.

16. That ther be two of the scholars appointed to goe to each of the two churches [St Nicholas and Greyfriars] every Sabbath day at the second bell afternoon and betwixt that and the last bell to repeat such ane portione of the Shorter Catechisme as shall be appointed to them from tyme to tyme, and this to begin after the next quarterly visitatione.

17. That those in the Grammar School who are learning to write shall only be taught by the masters of the high English School and that they write only in the loft above the Grammar school, betwixt eleven and twelve befoirnoon, and that the master of the Grammar School notice their writeing, and complain if the masters of the English school give not due attendance.

In summary, specific dates in October, February, May and August were set aside for visitations and they were to be carried out by Council representatives, two burgh ministers and two masters from Marischal College. Further, two or more of the magistrates and Council were to visit the School on the first Tuesday of every month to inquire how its discipline is observed.

The document was signed by Provost John Allardes but proved a basis for further refinement. Following the Visitation of October 1710 by a group of ministers and masters from Marischal College amendments to the rules were introduced, coming into effect on 6 February 1711. All scholars were to be taught Kirkwood's last edition of Despauterius and the School was to be reduced to four classes learning the same lesson, apart from the 'elementarians' who were to be taught by William Meston, a master since 1701. It was now expected that boys joining the first class would be proficient in reading English otherwise they would continue in the first class for another year to achieve this. Each doctor was to take his class until handed over to the Rector. In the second class and above, scholars who did not sufficiently master their grammar were now expected to take the class again. With regard to the visitation, the master was to provide two catalogues, with

The last Grammar School in Schoolhill, 1758–1863.

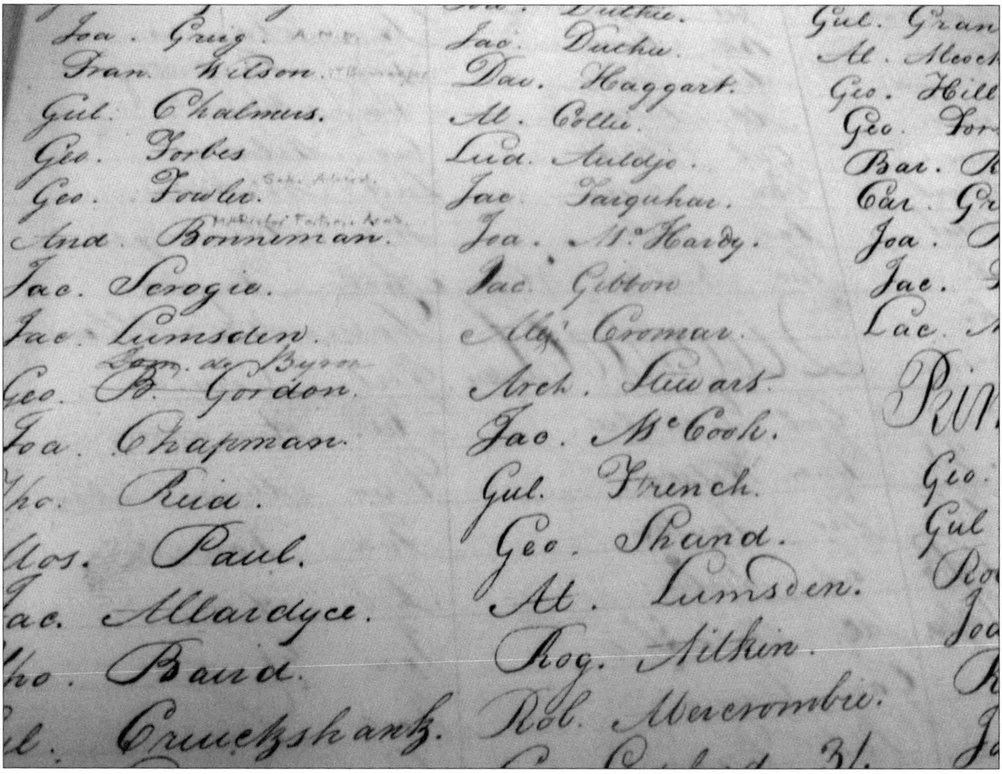

George Byron Gordon – Lord Byron – School register amendment, 1798 'Dom de Byron'.

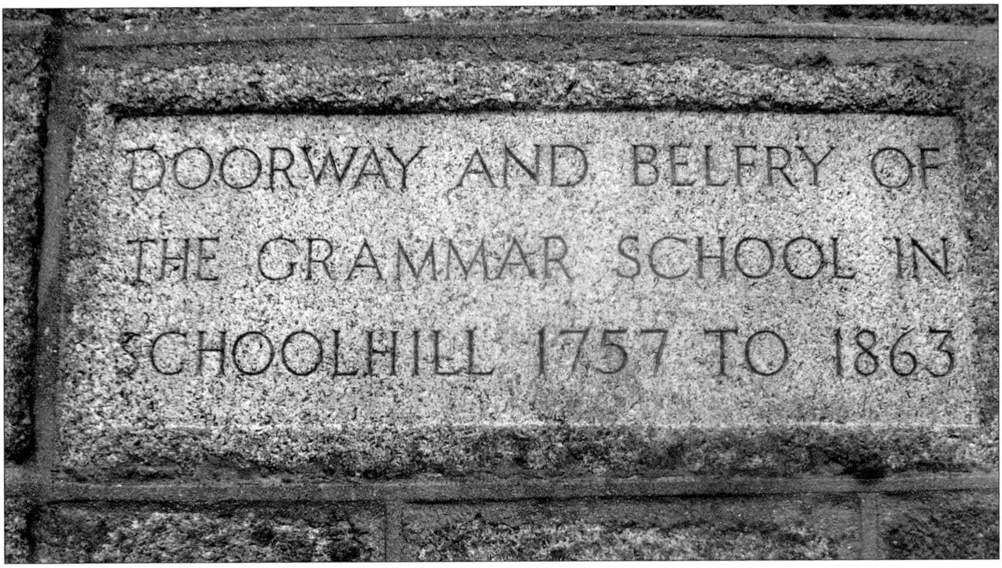

ABOVE. Plaque of Doorway and Belfry from Schoolhill.

RIGHT. The Doorway and Belfry is now situated at Skene Street.

ABOVE. Plaque on the present School wall commemorating Sir James McGrigor, a very distinguished medical soldier and former pupil.

LEFT. The McGrigor obelisk was moved from Marischal College to Duthie Park in 1906.

RIGHT. Dr John Gregory was a famous former pupil remembered as a Professor of Philosophy and the Practice of Medicine. (With permission of the University of Aberdeen).

BELOW. Parson James Gordon's View of King's College from the South-West in 1660. His key to the College identifies its separate Grammar School (9) and close (14).(University of Aberdeen).

George Keith, Earl Marischal, was a famous former pupil remembered as a Jacobite exile who won fame in Europe as a diplomat. (University of Aberdeen).

Thomas Reid was a famous former pupil remembered as a founder of the Aberdeen Philosophical Society, 1758–73. (University of Aberdeen).

George's brother, James, another famous former pupil, was killed at the Battle of Hochkirk in 1758. (University of Aberdeen).

The School in 1863 with the Denburn open and before the building of Esslemont Avenue.

The arrow and medals from the archery contests held in the later seventeenth century still remain in the possession of the School.

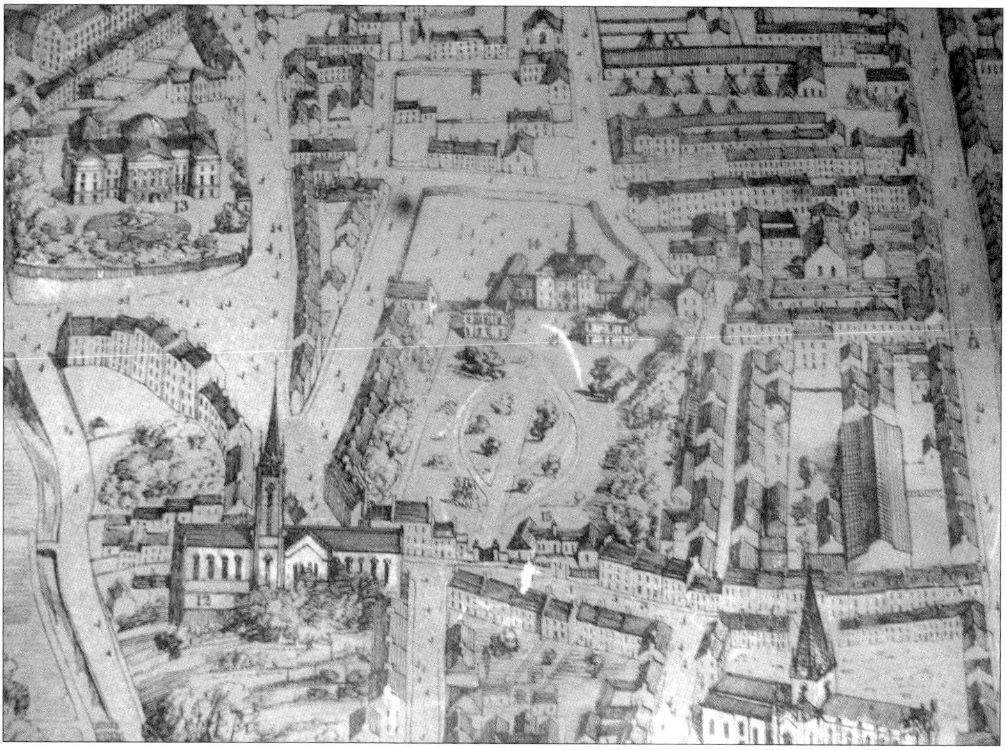

ABOVE. The map of Aberdeen in 1850 drawn by Washington Wilson shows the exact position of the School in Schoolhill.

LEFT. Patrick Dun, Principal of Marischal College, was the former pupil who left the lands of Ferryhill to the School in 1631.

James Dun, Rector, 1744–98, served some sixty-six years on the School staff.

James Melvin, Rector, 1826–53, was the greatest Latinist of his day and a famous teacher.

Rector Melvin's Snuff-Box, which was presented by the FPs in 1853 acknowledging their debt to him.

names of scholars, the author and grammar they were learning and what they had been taught since the last visitation.

The 1700 Laws and the subsequent changes remained substantially in force until the middle of the nineteenth century.

THE GRAMMAR SCHOOL AND THE JACOBITE REBELLION OF 1715

The Jacobites were the supporters of the deposed and exiled King James VII of Scotland, who took their name from the Latin form of his name: Jacobus. An active cause since the Revolution of 1689, when William III and wife Mary (King James' Protestant daughter) took the throne from the Roman Catholic King James, Jacobitism sought a return of the monarchs from the House of Stuart. Although it was associated with Catholicism many Episcopalians were also Jacobite.

In early September 1715 the Earl of Mar and other Jacobite leaders, including the Earl Marischal, raised the standard at Braemar, thereby beginning the abortive Jacobite Rising of 1715–16. Two weeks later the Earl Marischal proclaimed James VIII sovereign in Aberdeen and he repeated his proclamation in Old Aberdeen the next day. Shortly after, a new Jacobite Town Council was elected in Aberdeen and James, safe at the Earl Marischal's family seat at Fetteresso, received addresses from Provost Bannerman on behalf of the burgesses of Aberdeen, as well as from Aberdeen's Episcopal clergy and from Principal Middleton of King's College and William Smith of Marischal. It is clear that many prominent Aberdonians were deeply implicated in 1715 and a large portion of the local elite, including most of the masters of King's and Marischal and some of the Grammar masters, were involved.

With the Rebellion defeated George I appointed a Royal Commission in July 1716 to examine the conduct and behaviour of the university men. It met in Aberdeen and, having interviewed the masters, quickly came to the conclusion that both Aberdeen Colleges were a haven for Jacobites. The Hanoverians included the Grammar School in the remit of a second Royal Commission in March 1717 which was briefed to remove all guilty of disloyalty from their posts, probably because of its connections to William Meston, who had taught at the School and was seen as one of the most extreme partisans who used 'scandalous and criminal' language against George I.

Of the masters in the Grammar five were declared Jacobites:

1. The veteran, John Findlater, who had been appointed an under-master in 1664 and Rector in 1679. He was deposed by the Royal Commission of 1717 on the grounds of his Jacobite sympathies. It was held that he intimated to the scholars that 'the King had returned, which was an occasion of joy and therefore the School would not meet on Thursday'. He further encouraged the scholars to hiss at some of the other masters when praying for George I. He also, with Patrick Thomson, 'carried the schoolboys into the church, where the Pretender was prayed for by some of the Episcopal intruders under the name of James VIII, and gave them the play upon festival days!'

2. Patrick Thomson was deposed on same grounds.

3. Gilbert Ramsay, under-master since 1679, was deposed from his living of Dyce in 1717 'because he had prayed for the Pretender during the rebellion'.

4. Gilbert Black, under-master, was deposed because of his Jacobite sympathies.

5. William Meston, under-master from 1701 until 1713 when he became a Regent at Marischal, following a treasonable address, was also accused of riding in with the Earl Marischal to proclaim the Pretender and did so with sword in hand. He, with others, delivered an address to the Pretender at Fetteresso under the title of King James. He fled to avoid the repercussions of his actions, undoubtedly a prudent move.

THE GRAMMAR SCHOOL AND THE JACOBITE REBELLION OF 1745–1746

The following extracts are from the diary of Rev. John Bisset of Aberdeen (as found in the *Spalding Club Miscellany*, i, 353, 354, 357). His Diary was written from the stand-point of a strong supporter of the Hanoverian Government.

1st November 1745 – Although the masters of the Grammar School drop King George name out of their prayers, it rather inflamed many of the young people, who, when Mr. Howieson [Master appointed in 1718] was praying this week, upon his omitting the King's name, cried out King George; and one of the boys, after prayer was ended, cried out, None pray for King George, God bless him; but when it comes to the turn of one of the doctors to be hebdomader [master on weekly duty], if he resumes not King George's name, I shall offer him no more advice . . .

November 5th – Mr. Charles Dun [Master appointed 1736], being at present hebdomader, prays stoutly for King George by name, and against his enemies. I hear Pitna [John Smith, Master appointed January 1745] doth so, very much, and I am told that Mr. James Dun [the rector] hath prayed this morning *nominatim*, it is like after the example of another . . .

November 28th – The masters of the Grammar School now continue praying *nominatim* for King George, excepting the old Doctor [Andrew Howieson], who was lately, in his own conceited opinion, on the road to heaven, with such full assurance. I hear he hath been bullying some of the rest, as a man not to be put out of his measures. Whatever be the issue of matters presently in dependence, I shall not expect to see good days, unless the churches and schools be purged of such miscreants.

Omitting King George from their prayers was as far as sympathisers at the Grammar went; they did not join the Rising as the School had been too badly affected by the purges following the 1715 Rebellion. This reflected the position in the North-East, which was cooler towards the Jacobites than in 1715.

STAFFING IN THE GRAMMAR SCHOOL

(Prof.) William Meston (*c.*1680–1745), poet and teacher, studied at Marischal as the Rolland bursar (1694) and graduated in 1698. He taught at the GS (of New Aberdeen) from 1701 to 1713, becoming a Regent at Marischal in 1713. He supported the Jacobite rebellion of 1715 and was appointed Governor of Dunnottar Castle. Later he set up a number of private schools before becoming tutor to a Jacobite family, Oliphant of

Gask, in 1736. He wrote poetry about Jacobite politics and directed his satire against the Whigs and Presbyterians.[1]

Appointing an under-master in 1713

On the resignation of William Meston in 1713 his post was advertised in Latin and candidates were invited to come to Aberdeen for a 'comparative trial'. The examination consisted of Latin Grammar and Literature, and the examiners were two ministers of the Burgh and the Principal and four Regents of Marischal College. In due course the Principal and Regents recommended John Leslie, tutor to the children of John Sandilands of Countesswells, to the Town Council, the appointing body, while the ministers recommended David Couper of Perth GS, given his judiciousness in his exposition. The Council decided on Couper and appointed him. Leslie took legal action: he had been the choice of the majority and he was preferred for his promptness, which included judiciousness, whereas judiciousness did not include promptness. The Council claimed discretionary power in all appointments, irrespective of the recommendation of examiners.

Leslie was to claim that Couper was being treated for madness and was unfit for the post and then claimed damages resulting from the illegal action of the Council. The Council responded by debarring Leslie from applying again and, holding that neither of the reports of the examiners were in conformity to Dr Dun's mortification, went ahead and re-advertised the post.

The Court rejected Leslie's appeal in July 1714 and in December of that year William Mackie was appointed under-master.

In retrospect it seems unfortunate that the Grammar missed out on John Leslie. He remained a tutor until 1720 when he became Rector of Haddington GS and then between 1731 and 1739 Rector of Dalkeith GS. In the *First Statistical Account of Scotland* Leslie is described as 'one of the ablest teachers in Scotland'. Ruddiman presented him with a copy of his famous textbook and inscribed it in Latin 'to a man most distinguished for his remarkable erudition and for his ability and diligence in teaching'.

The selection of the Principal and Regents was sound, given that they were teachers themselves but the Council yielded to ecclesiastical wire-pulling and accepted the minority recommendation of two ministers.

Rector: John Findlater, 1679–1717

1709 Nov. 10 – John Milne, schoolmaster at Skene, was appointed under-master. He had been a Milne bursar in 1702 and graduated MA in 1706.

1713 Sept. 12 – David Couper, teacher in Perth GS, became under-master. He had taken an MA at King's in 1705.

1714 Dec. 15 – William Mackie appointed under-master. He was a Rolland bursar in 1707, gaining an MA in 1711. He died in office in 1725.

1717 Aug. 16 – Charles Kay, schoolmaster at Banchory-Devenick, was appointed as under-master. He had gained his MA in 1715. He went insane in 1736.

1717 Aug. 28 – John Findlater, who had been Rector of the GS since November 1679, was deposed by the Royal Commission set up after the Jacobite rebellion. He was replaced as Rector by John Milne.

Rector: John Milne, 1717–1744

1718 Feb. 5 – Andrew Howieson was made under-master. He was a Rolland bursar in 1699, graduating MA in 1703. He remained on the staff until 1747.

1725 Apr. 14 – William Stephen became an under-master. He was a Liddel bursar in 1721 and gained his MA in 1725. He died in office in 1732.

1732 Apr. 14 – James Dun was made under-master. He was a Turner bursar in 1728 and gained his MA in 1732. On the death of John Milne he was appointed Rector in September 1744. He was awarded an LLD, from Marischal in 1772 'as a proof and testimony . . . of the services he has done to Literature during the space of forty years in which he has acquitted himself as a teacher of the Latin tongue with great credit to himself and advantage to the Town and University of Aberdeen, as well as to the country in general'.

1736 June 28 – Charles Dun was appointed under-master. He had taken his MA from King's in 1734.

Rector: James Dun, 1744–1791

1744 Sept. 29 – James Dun made Rector on the death of John Milne.

1745 Jan. 15 – John Smith made under-master. He was a Guild bursar, 1735–7 and Liddel bursar, 1737–9, and gained his MA in 1739. He died in office in 1757.

1747 Aug. 25 – Alexander Reid was made under-master. He was a

Rolland bursar in 1728 and gained his MA in 1732. He left to become minister of Kemnay in 1758.

On 24 September 1753 the Town Council agreed on augmentations to the salary of the Rector and under-masters. James Dun received four hundred merks, while Charles Dun, John Smith and Alexander Reid received two hundred merks each.

1757 Nov. 26 – James Smith became an under-master but died in office in 1760.

(Prof.) James Beattie (1735–1803), poet and philosopher, attended Laurencekirk parish school, which had a reputation for Classics, and as First Bursar won a Milne bursary to Marischal in 1749. He shone academically, especially at Greek, and after graduating in 1753 he became schoolmaster at Fordoun for five years. He then was chosen as under-master at Aberdeen GS, a post he retained for two years when in 1760, much to his surprise, he was appointed Professor of Moral Philosophy and Logic at Marischal. He was a founder member of the RSE and became a member of the Aberdeen Philosophical Society. He produced many philosophical and poetical works, the most celebrated in the later 1760s: *Essay on the Nature and Immutability of Truth* and his influential poem *The Minstrel*.[2]

PUPILS
(INCLUDING A SELECTION OF THOSE EDUCATED AT THE GRAMMAR BETWEEN 1700 AND 1757)

For much of this period Aberdeen's two universities – King's and Marischal – sought to survive in an increasingly competitive academic market by providing the learning required by a Hanoverian-Whig-Presbyterian establishment, together with the skills and knowledge needed in commerce and industry. Fundamental to the strategy of both Colleges was the reform of the Philosophy curriculum. At King's this came in 1753–4 from Thomas Reid, while at Marischal innovations in the teaching of Mathematics and experimental Science preceded the reform of the curriculum itself in 1752.

Although the age at entry to University varied greatly, usually between ten and nineteen years of age, with a number at age twelve, the general view was that a great many arrived too young. Their social origins remained from noble or landed families, professional classes and farmers, merchants and craftsmen and new bursaries enabled more entrants from the 'middling sort', either genuinely in need, or fortunate in their connections. Their fathers (where known and not deceased) tended to be ministers, merchants, craftsmen or civic officers. Geographically previous trends continue, with Marischal serving Aberdeen and its immediate hinterland, while King's drew strongly from the northern counties.

The age, social origins and geographic background of university students continued to affect directly the Grammar which was preparing pupils for entry to higher education. Its scholars could be as young as seven or eight years of age; generally they came from the relatively affluent middle class, although some bursars were of more humble origin; and the majority of them aimed at attendance at Marischal.

George Keith, tenth Earl Marischal (1692/3–1778), and his younger brother, James Keith [known as Marischal Keith] (1696–1758), seem to have been tutored by a kinsman, Robert Keith, who had left the Grammar about 1696, and William Meston (see above), who at the same time was teaching at the School. It seems likely that Meston's tutoring and teaching became inter-linked and hence the claim that the Keiths attended the Grammar appears plausible. Before the Union of 1707 Scottish nobles still had confidence in their burgh schools, unlike in England where increasingly exclusive schools had become available.

Both George and James participated in the 1715 Jacobite Rising, including the defeat at Sheriffmuir, following which they were forced into exile in Europe. George Keith remained a devoted Jacobite and led the unsuccessful 1719 rising which gained Spanish help. Although he was the prospective leader in 1745–6 his poor relationship with Charles Edward Stuart ensured that he took no part in the events of these years. He joined James in Prussia in 1747 and became Frederick the Great's Ambassador to France. However, he converted from Scot to Prussian after 1753 and divulged to Britain (Frederick's ally) the Spanish intention to wage war against France. For this the House of Hanover, in the person of George II, pardoned George but he lived out his days in Prussia as Frederick's close and valued friend.[3]

James Keith served in the Spanish army before leading Russian forces. In 1747 he became a Field Marshal under Frederick the Great of Prussia. However, James was killed at the battle of Hochkirch in 1758. George supplied his epitaph which appears on James' statue in Peterhead, near where he was born: *Probus vixit, fortis obit* (He lived honestly and died bravely).[4] One of the modern School Houses was named after James.

Alexander Cruden (1699–1770), biblical scholar and eccentric, left the Grammar in 1713 and attended Marischal. He worked as a private tutor until he became a proof-corrector and bookseller at the Royal Exchange. He produced his celebrated *Complete Concordance to the Holy Scriptures* in 1737 which was revised in 1761 and 1769. It remained the most authoritative work of its kind until well into the next century.[5] He suffered from periods of insanity. A commemorative plaque can be found in Cruden's Court, off Concert Court, Broad Street.

(Prof.) Thomas Blackwell (1701–1757), classical scholar and historian, attended the Grammar and studied Greek and Philosophy at Marischal, of which his father had become Principal in 1717. He became Professor of Greek in 1723 and then Principal in 1748. He modernised the curriculum of the University and promoted a Union with King's. His main fame is as a writer of books published between 1735 and 1763 which were pioneering studies and made him a major figure in the Scottish Enlightenment. He was awarded an LLD from Aberdeen University in 1752. In his short period as Principal he gave the University and Aberdeen a new impetus.[6]

(Dr) Alexander Blackrie (1702–72), surgeon-apothecary, attended the Grammar and, between 1718 and 1722, Marischal. After working as surgeon-general in India he practised in Bromley, Kent.[7]

(Sir) Andrew Mitchell (1708–71) attended the Grammar before studying Law at Edinburgh University and being articled to an advocate in 1725. On the Grand Tour he studied further at Leiden and Paris. He was elected to the RS in 1736, and was admitted to the Faculty of Advocates in the same year. He was Under-Secretary for Scotland and served as MP for Aberdeenshire. He was a Trade Commissioner in Brussels and then minister in Prussia. He was "the most successful British representative in Berlin during the entire eighteenth century".[8]

Alexander Blackwell (1709–1747), brother of Thomas, attended the Grammar and the Universities of Aberdeen, Edinburgh and Leiden. His work on soil fertilisation was noticed in Sweden. He found royal favour for a time as an agricultural and animal husbandry improver, however he became involved in the political intrigues of the Swedish Court, with disastrous consequences. He was executed for treason in 1747.[9]

Thomas Reid (1710–1796), natural and moral philosopher, attended the Grammar in 1722 before entering Marischal. Having studied Divinity he did some preaching before becoming Librarian of Marischal (1733–6). He kept abreast of Mathematics and the Natural and Moral Sciences and in 1751 became Regent at King's, teaching the whole of the three-year Philosophy course. He was a founder of the Aberdeen Philosophical Society, 1758–73. He published his *Inquiry into the Human Mind* in 1764 and later the same year succeeded Adam Smith as Professor of Moral Philosophy at Glasgow

University. His *Essays on the Intellectual Powers of Man* (1785) and *Essays on the Active Powers of Man* (1788) shaped the teaching of Moral Philosophy in Britain and America well into the nineteenth century.[10] A commemorative plaque can be found at the Pend of King's College Quadrangle, Old Aberdeen.

(Prof.) David Fordyce (1711–1751), university teacher and writer on education, entered the Grammar in 1720 and Marischal in 1724. He studied for the ministry and became a preacher before his appointment as Professor of Moral Philosophy at Marischal in 1742. He proved a successful lecturer on General and Natural Philosophy and his writings sold well. He was important in the early Scottish Enlightenment but is now largely forgotten.[11]

(Prof.) William Duncan (1717–1760), natural philosopher and classicist, attended the Grammar and Marischal. He published *The Elements of Logic* in 1748 whose success led to his appointment as a Professor of Philosophy at Marischal specialising in Experimental and Natural Philosophy. He produced popular translations of the Classics.[12]

(Rev. Dr) George Campbell (1719–1796), Church of Scotland minister and college head, attended the Grammar between 1729 and 1734 and then Marischal where he learned Greek. He studied Divinity and was called as a Church of Scotland minister to Banchory-Ternan. He became Principal of Marischal in 1759 and Professor of Divinity in 1771. He was an original member of the APS and a founder member of the RSE in 1783. His work on Miracles (1762) established Campbell as one of Christianity's leading apologists, while his work on Rhetoric (1776) became a bestseller in the nineteenth century, when it was established as a standard text in the American College curriculum. His work on the Gospels (1789) was seen by contemporaries to be a scholarly masterpiece.[13]

(Dr) James Fordyce (1720–1796) attended the Grammar and Marischal. He was licensed by the Aberdeen presbytery in 1743, and was minister at Brechin and then Alloa. His sermon at the 1760 General Assembly of the Church of Scotland stamped him as a pulpit orator of the first rank. He soon moved to Monkwell Street, London, and, for over a decade, proved a celebrated and fashionable preacher.[14]

John Skinner (1721–1807) attended Echt parish school, the Grammar and Marischal, graduating AM in 1737. He worked as an assistant teacher at Monymusk. He became a minister in the Episcopal Church and had the charge of Longside, near Peterhead, for sixty-four years. He wrote extensively and of particular significance was his two-volume *Ecclesiastical History of Scotland* (1788). He wrote poetry and was admired by Robert Burns.[15]

(Brig. Surg. Sir) William Fordyce (1724–1792; Kt. 1787) was the brother of Alexander the banker, James the divine, and David the academic. He attended the Grammar and Marischal, and served a medical pupillage. He obtained an appointment in the Guards and served in a number of campaigns. He set up a general practice in London, was admitted to the College of Physicians in 1786 and became FRS in 1789. He won a Gold Medal from the Society of Arts and was Rector of Marischal, to which he left his medical library.[16]

(Prof.) John Gregory[17] (1724–1773), physician and writer, attended the Grammar and King's between 1736 and 1740 before studying medicine at Edinburgh and Leiden universities. He was elected Professor of Philosophy at King's and began to practise Medicine. He was a member of the APS and in 1756 elected a Fellow of the RS. In 1766 he became Professor of the Practice of Physic at Edinburgh and first physician in Scotland to George III. His writings stressed the importance of experiment and observation, holding Medicine as a practical art acquired by extensive experience, and developed the first philosophical, secular medical ethics.

(Very Rev.) Alexander Gerard (1728–1795), Church of Scotland minister and philosopher, attended the Grammar between 1738 and 1740 and then Marischal where he studied Divinity and became a minister. He was appointed a Regent at Marischal in 1752 and reorganised its curriculum, becoming the first Professor of Moral Philosophy and Logic. The changes later influenced pedagogical thinking in Germany and the American colonies. Gerard was an early member of the APS. He transferred to Marischal's chair of Divinity and became Moderator of the General Assembly in 1764. He was then elected Professor of Divinity at King's and became a founder fellow of the RSE in 1783.[18]

Alexander Garden (1730–1791) attended the Grammar and Marischal, where he pursued Medical Studies until 1748. He studied further at Edinburgh University and took up a medical practice in South Carolina, where he became interested in botany. He sent samples home and his work was acknowledged by Linnaeus, which led to his election to fellowship of the Royal Society. His estates were confiscated when he took the British side during the American War of Independence.[19]

(Dr) David Skene (1731–1770), physician and naturalist, attended the Grammar and Marischal, emerging as a polymath. In 1753 Skene joined his father in his Aberdeen medical practice and established Midwifery training in Aberdeen. He managed the Aberdeen Infirmary and acted on behalf of sick and wounded seamen. He was a founder member of the APS and became its president in 1766. He was elected annually Dean of Faculty at Marischal (1767–70). He gained a reputation as a classifier and arranger of scientific material.[20]

John Ogilvie (1732–1813) attended the Grammar and graduated from Marischal in 1750. He became a minister in the Church of Scotland, having the charge of Midmar, Aberdeenshire, for fifty-three years. A prolific writer in poetry and prose, he spread his talents on too many and too varied works to make any lasting impact.[21] He was admitted to the RSE in 1789.

James Mercer (1734–1804), poet and soldier, attended the Grammar and, in 1748, Marischal. He followed a military career, reaching the rank of major before leaving in 1772, returning to take a commission during the American War of Independence. An edition of his lyric poems was published in 1795.[22]

(Sir) William Forbes of Pitsligo (1739–1806; Baron 1781) attended the Grammar between 1749 and 1753. He was articled to the Coutts brothers, bankers, in London in 1754 and was fully admitted in 1763. He was a prudent and influential banker and became a leading member of the Merchants' Company of Edinburgh. He advised the Lord Advocate on the terms of the Bankruptcy Act of 1772. He accumulated significant wealth and was involved in all charitable institutions in Edinburgh, which benefited from his exceptional philanthropy. He was responsible for the development of New Pitsligo in Aberdeenshire. He advised PM Pitt the Younger on monetary matters.[23]

Francis Masson (1741–1805) was probably educated at the Grammar. He gained a gardening appointment at the Royal Botanic Gardens, Kew. He was sent to the Cape Colony to collect plants and bulbs, sailing with Captain Cook. Success as Kew's first collector led to his despatch to the Canaries, Azores, Madeira, St. Kilda and Portugal. His book on *New Species . . . in the interior of Africa* was published in 1797. A commemorative plaque can be found in the Cruickshank Botanical Gardens.

George Chalmers (1742–1825) attended the parish school of Bellie and in 1753 the Grammar. He studied further at King's before reading Law at Edinburgh University. He practised in Baltimore, Maryland but as a Loyalist he travelled home as the American War of Independence loomed. He wrote attacking Edmund Burke's pro-colonist views. In 1786 he became Chief Clerk to the Privy Council Committee on Trade and Foreign Plantations, which gave him time to pursue other interests. He was elected FRS in 1791. He published three volumes of *Caledonia*, a survey of Scottish history and antiquities and wrote extensively on the political topics of the day.[24]

(Prof.) Patrick Copland (1748–1822) attended the Grammar gaining a minor bursary to Marischal in 1762, graduating AM in 1766. He was appointed Professor of Philosophy in 1775 and continued as a professor till his death. He was also Professor of Mathematics from 1779 to 1817. He introduced into university teaching the large-scale use of demonstration apparatus and was acknowledged to be the best teacher at Marischal in his day. He gained a national reputation. He was one of the founding members of the RSE in 1785 and bought Fountainhall House as his family home in 1803.[25]

John Farquhar (1751–1826) of Fonthill Abbey, attended the Grammar and gained a bursary in 1766 to attend Marischal. After completing his MA he migrated to India where the Governor-General of Bengal, Lord Cornwallis, contracted him to conduct chemical experiments. The result led to him becoming the sole agent for gunpowder. His resulting wealth bought estates. Unfortunately, on his death, his Will, which it was believed left a large bequest for educational purposes in Scotland, could not be found.[26]

It was in philosophy that Aberdeen achieved eminence in the Enlightenment period in Scotland and the Grammar School played a part in this development. To counter David Hume's scepticism Thomas Reid established the Scottish philosophy of 'Common Sense' and he was educated at the Grammar and Marischal, as were George Campbell, John Gregory, David Skene, and Alexander Gerard, while, after attending Marischal, James Beattie taught at the Grammar. Networking at the School and University led them to meet regularly, forming the successful Aberdeen Philosophical Society which, between 1758 and 1773, was the centre of 'discourses' in the Lemon Tree or the Red Lion.[27]

As a result of its contribution to intellectual productivity the reputation of the Grammar soared to new heights as it produced professors, lawyers and preachers who participated in the Scottish Enlightenment. This conclusion is borne out by a study of the Scottish schooling of the 297 individuals included in the *ODNB* in the period 1685–1785. The High School of Edinburgh headed the list but comfortably in second place was Aberdeen Grammar School already producing a significant number of boys who were earning reputations of national prominence.[28]

FOUR The School, the Bursary Competition and the Universities

One of the most distinguished Former Pupils of the Grammar School, Professor David M. Masson, Historiographer-Royal, attended the School between 1831 and 1835. He wrote an article published in January 1864 which clarified the *raison d'être* of the School through the centuries:

> The Schoolhill in Aberdeen, a street of oldish houses, derived its name from its containing the public Grammar School of the town. There had been a grammar school in the burgh, on or near this same site, for centuries; and in the records of the town frequent mention is made of this School, and of the names of its masters. Its most noted benefactor, in later days, had been Dr. Patrick Dun, Principal of Marischal College, in the first half of the seventeenth century. How many successive buildings of older make had served for the School before Dr. Dun's time, or what sort of building it was lodged in when he took interest in it, I can only vaguely guess through fancy, and through such occasional entries in the burgh accounts as that of a sum of £38, 5s. 6d., in or about the year 1597, for 'thecking the Grammar School with hedder'.
>
> The School in my time was a plain, dingy building, which had been erected, I believe, in 1757, and which, if it was superior to some of its predecessors in not being thatched with heather, but slated and quite weather-tight, was certainly nothing to look at architecturally. Within a gateway and iron-railed wall, separating the School from the street, and forming a very limited playground in front, you saw a low main building of a single storey, parallel with the street, and having a door with stone steps in the middle, and windows at the sides; and from this main building there projected towards the street two equally low wings, forming the two junior class-rooms. Two similar wings, which you could not well see from the street,

projected from the main building behind, and accommodated the senior classes. The only entrance to the two back class-rooms was through the public school; the two front class-rooms might also be entered through the public school, but had separate doors from the front playground. The arrangements inside were simple enough. Each of the four oblong class-rooms had a raised desk for the master in one angle, and two rows of 'factions' as they were called – i.e. wooden seats, with narrow sloping writing benches in front of them – along the two sides of the oblong, so as to leave a free passage of some width in the middle for the master, when he chose to walk from end to end. Each 'faction' was constructed to hold four boys, so that the look of a full class-room was that of a company of boys seated in two parallel sub-divisions of fours along the walls. In the public school, where meetings of all the classes together took place for general purposes, the main desk, a wooden structure of several tiers, was in the middle of the long side of the oblong, immediately opposite the main door, and there were four sets of somewhat larger 'factions' where the several classes sat on such occasions, all looking inwards.

The entire accommodation internally, as well as the look externally, was of the dingiest; nor was it, perhaps, very creditable to the Town that, even in the middle of the eighteenth century, they should not have risen to a somewhat loftier idea of the sort of building suitable for a School that was already historical among them, and was still likely to be of importance. But boys think little of these things; and the low dingy building had for them many snug, and some venerable, associations. In these rows of 'factions', which they thumped energetically with sticks and fists at every meeting, making an uproar till the masters appeared, and over which at other times they leaped in a thousand fashions of chase and mutual fight, roaring out tags of traditional school-doggerel . . . They could not but have a dim idea that generations of young Aberdonians, either long defunct and in their graves, or scattered abroad in mature living manhood, had sat and made uproar before them. The very tags of doggerel they shouted had come down to them from those predecessors; and in the appearance of the 'factions' themselves, all slashed and notched and carved over with names and initials of various dates, deeply incised into the hard wood, there was a provocation to some degree of interest in the legends of the school. It was not in the nature of boyish antiquarianism to go back to the times of those older heather-thatched school-buildings, ancestors of the present, in which the Cargills and Wedderburns, and other early Scottish Latinists of note, had walked as masters; but some of the traditions of the existing fabric in the days of recent masters, whose names and characters were still proverbial, were within the reach of the least inquisitive . . .

The School was a grammar school in the old sense of the term as understood in England as well as in Scotland. It was exclusively a day school for Classical education in preparation for the University. In fact, down to my time, it was all but entirely a Latin school. The rudiments of Greek had recently been introduced as part of the business of the higher classes;[1] but, with this exception, and with the further exception that, in teaching Latin, the masters might regale their classes with whatever bits of history or of general lore they could blend with their Latin lessons, the business of the School was Latin, Latin, Latin. Since that time there have been changes in the constitution of the seminary to suit it to the requirements of more modern tastes in education. There is now more Greek, and express instruction in Geography, History, and I know not what all; but in those days it was Latin, nothing but a four or five years' perseverance in Latin, within those dingy old walls. Although the usual age at which boys entered the School was from eight to twelve, it was assumed that the necessary preliminary learning in matters of English, and in Writing and Arithmetic, had been gone through beforehand; and, though there were public schools for Writing, Drawing and Mathematics, equally under the charge of the city authorities with the Grammar School, and which the pupils of the Grammar School might attend at distinct hours for parallel instruction in those branches, these schools were not attached to the grammar school, and attendance at them was quite optional. So, on the whole, if you were an Aberdeen boy, getting the very best education known in the place, you were committed, at the age of from nine to eleven, to a four or five years' course of drilling in Latin, five hours every day, save in the single-vacation month of July – tipped only with a final touch of Greek; and, this course over, you were expected, at the age of from thirteen to sixteen, either to walk forward into the University, or, if that prospect did not suit, to slip aside, a scholar so far, into the world of business. A four or five years' course, I have said; for, though the full curriculum was five years, it was quite customary for readier or more impatient lads to leap to the University from the fourth class.

This exclusive, or all but exclusive, dedication of the School to Latin was partly a matter of fidelity to tradition; but there was a special cause for it in the circumstances of the intellectual system of the town, and, indeed, of that whole region of the North of Scotland, of which the town was the natural capital. The School was the main feeder of the adjacent Marischal College and University of the city of Aberdeen, and it also sent pupils annually, though not in such numbers, to the other neighbouring University and King's College, Old Aberdeen. These two Universities, now united in one,[2] were the Universities to which, for geographical reasons, all the scholarly youths of that northern or north-eastern region of Scotland which lay beyond the ranges of attraction of the other three Scottish Universities of Glasgow, Edinburgh, and St Andrews, were naturally drawn. Whatever young man looked forward to a University education in this extensive region – of which Aberdeenshire itself and the adjacent county of Kincardine formed the heart, but which had Forfarshire, Banffshire, Morayshire, Inverness-shire, Ross-shire, and even more distant northerly parts, for its fringes – thought of Aberdeen, and of one or other of its two Universities, as his destination while that education should be going on. The tendency from the Highland, and generally from the more northerly districts, was rather to King's College, while from Aberdeen itself, the eastern and lowland parts of Aberdeenshire, and from Kincardineshire and Forfarshire, the tendency was rather to Marischal College. But, to whichever of the two Universities the predisposition might be, the possibility of giving effect to it was, for many who cherished it, a matter of long preliminary anxiety. There were in that region of North Britain many well-to-do families, perfectly able to send their sons to either of the two Aberdonian Colleges, or even, if they so preferred, to Edinburgh, or either of the two English Universities; but in that region, more perhaps than in any other even of North Britain, there has always been a numerous class of whom it may be said, *Musam tenui meditantur avena.* 'They cultivate the Muse, or the best rough Muse they find accessible, on a little oatmeal.' In other words, the ambition after a University education existed among a wider and poorer class in that region than is found to cherish a similar ambition elsewhere. The Town of Aberdeen is included in this statement. The notion of a University education as possible descended very far down indeed among the ranks of that community – far below the level of those families who could sustain by their own means the very moderate expense that was necessary with the University actually at their doors. To what is this to be attributed? Partly, if you so choose, to the breed of the folk; but considerably, at least, to a more palpable social cause. This desire for a University education exists there so widely, penetrates there so deep down in society, because in that region, more than any other part of Great Britain, the means have existed from time immemorial for gratifying the desire.

That part of Scotland has long had a peculiarity, of which I have often thought that the whole British world ought to hear, despite its natural antipathy to over-abundant information respecting uncouth Scottish matters. That peculiarity is its Bursary System: I say *is*, for I hope it still exists. But what is a bursary, and what is or was the Bursary System of that Aberdonian region of Scotland? A bursary, in Scottish academic phraseology, is what a scholarship or exhibition is in English – a small annual stipend granted to a young man going to College out of funds bequeathed for the purpose, and tenable by him while he is at College. All the Scottish Universities have such bursaries at their disposal, founded by lovers of learning in past centuries; but the two Aberdeen universities were peculiar in this (St Andrews alone, I think, coming near them in the practice), that the greater number of the bursaries were put up annually for open competition to all comers. There were more private bursaries in the gift of certain families, or of the professors, and bestowable by favour, or on the bearers of certain names; but each of the two Colleges – King's and Marischal – had about twenty public bursaries to be disposed of every October by open competition. The bursaries were of small amounts, ranging from £5 a year to £20 a year; but, invariably, by the terms of the foundation, each bursary more than covered all the expenses of the College classes. Now it was this Bursary System – as familiarly known over the whole region concerned as the Aurora Borealis in its nightly sky – it was this Bursary System that had generated and that sustained there a habit of looking forward to a University education among classes in which otherwise such a habit could have hardly been possible.

Though the well-to-do youths in the town or in the country around might not care for a bursary, save for the honour – and it *was* reputed an honour, and, when obtained, was kept as such by many to whom it could have been of no substantial consideration – yet for a scholarly boy of poor family in one of the third-rate streets of Aberdeen, or for a poor farmer's son on Donside, following his father's plough and dreaming of a College life as the furrow came to the field's edge, the thought that would murmur to his lips would still be 'A bursary: O for a bursary!' With many their going or not going to College depended on their winning or not winning, at the proper time, this coveted prize.

One can see what influence such an agency might have been made to exercise over the schooling and intellectual activity of the region within which it operated – how, just as the India and Civil Service Competitions have affected the education of the whole country in these days, and swayed it in particular directions according to the subjects set for the competitions, so, on a smaller scale, even the frugal Bursary System of the North-East of Scotland might have been managed so as to stimulate, within its range of action, not one but many kinds of study. After the time of which I now speak, there *was* a change to this effect in the administration of the bursaries, and they were conferred after an examination testing proficiency of different kinds. But down to the time with which I have here to do the competition for bursaries at both Colleges was solely in Latin, and even mainly in one particular practice of Latin Scholarship – that of turning a piece of English into Latin. The Competition took place with great ceremony every October in the halls of the two Colleges. All who chose might come, and no questions were asked. A lad from Cornwall or from Kent, who had never been to Aberdeen before, might have entered the hall on examination-day, taken his place with the rest, and fought for a bursary with whatever force of Cornwall Latin or of Kent Latin was in him. The temptation was not such, however, as to attract many such outsiders; and it was generally some forty Aberdeenshire, Kincardineshire, Forfarshire, Banffshire, or Highland lads, out of about one hundred and sixty who had assembled in Aberdeen for the Competition, that were made happy by obtaining the bursaries of the year. But, as it was skill in Latin that the feat was to be done, one can see what a powerful premium was thus put on Latinity all over the territory interested. Even the common parish schools of the region gave some attention to Latin, and any parish school that had within twelve years or so sent two or three lads to Aberdeen who had been successful in obtaining bursaries had celebrity on that account. Naturally, however, even if a country lad began his Latin with his own parish schoolmaster, he would, if possible, finish with a year or two at the grammar school of the nearest town. There were several such grammar schools of some distinction in the far-north region; and Old Aberdeen had a grammar school of its own, acting more expressly as a feeder to King's College. But Aberdeen Grammar School proper, the Grammar School of the main city, was the School of greatest note. And so, on the whole, if the School had been aboriginally a Latin School, this influence of the bursary system, in the centre of which it was situated, had helped to make it more and more tenacious of its original character. It was a case, I doubt not, partly of cause and partly of effect.

How far back in time the influence of the bursary system had been in operation in the territory I do not know; but I should not wonder if it were to turn out, on investigation, that some form of the influence had to do with what is, at all events, the fact – that for more than two centuries Aberdeen and the region around had had a special reputation in Scotland for eminence in Latinity. The greatest Scottish Latinist, or at least Latin poet, after Buchanan, had been Arthur Johnston, born near Aberdeen in 1587, and educated at Marischal College; his *Parerga, Epigrammata,* and other Latin poems were first given to the world, between 1628 and 1632, from the Aberdeen printing-press; and among his fellow-contributors to the famous *Delitiae Poetarum Scotorum,* or collection of Latin poems by living or recently deceased Scottish authors, printed at Amsterdam in 1637, several of the best, after himself, were also Aberdonians and Marischal College men. From that time Aberdeen had kept up the tradition of Latin scholarship.

My readers may like to know what was the expense of education at this Grammar School: ten shillings and sixpence a quarter for each boy. Even that was grumbled at by some as too dear, and it was a rise from what had formerly been the rate. Ten shillings and sixpence a quarter for the very best Classical education that was to be had, for love or money, in all that area of Scotland! The wealthiest and most aristocratic parent, if he had kept his son on the spot, could not, by

> any device, do better for him in the way of schooling than send him to precisely this School – the historical School of the place. The sons of all classes, from the highest to the lowest, were there mixed – all on the equal platform of ten and sixpence a quarter; save that, if a boy was lucky enough to be called Dun, he paid nothing. Add six and sixpence a quarter at Mr. Craigmyle's Writing School and six and sixpence a quarter for attendance at Mr. James Gordon's Mathematical School – at which two public schools it was usual for the Grammar school boys to take instruction at separate hours – and you have the almost total school expense for each boy as under five and twenty shillings a quarter. Extras, such as French, German, Fencing, Music, and other kickshaws,[3] were then very rare in Aberdeen; they were to be had, I know, but it was as turtle and champagne were to be had. As for Dancing, Heaven only knows how Aberdeen boys, whom I have since seen reel-dancing magnificently as full-grown men in Hanover Square Rooms, came by the rudiments of that accomplishment. I believe it was done by many at dead of night, on creaky floors in out-of-the-way places in the Gallowgate, with scouts on the look-out for the clergy. The only difference, in the matter of expense, between the wealthier and the poorer boys attending the Grammar School was that the former generally had private tutors, who went to their houses in the evening to assist them in preparing their lessons. Such supplementary tuition was cheap enough. A guinea a quarter for each evening hour so spent was what many a Divinity student was glad to get; and two guineas a quarter was the maximum . . .

A modern educational historian, R.D. Anderson (Oxford 1983), illustrated the development of a Scottish educational tradition and the part played in this by parish schools and burgh schools like the Grammar School:

> Historians of Scottish education rightly see its founding charter in the document of 1560 known as the First Book of Discipline, which outlined a national system of schools and put special emphasis on helping the poor through scholarships and on the benefit which the community as well as the individual derived from a wide recruitment to the professions – medicine and law as well as the ministry. The proposals of 1560 envisaged three types of school below the level of the universities, but they were not put into effect

> at the time, and when expansion of education was seriously undertaken in the seventeenth century it concentrated on the provision of a school in every parish . . .
>
> Only in the largest towns did burgh schools give an education of a mainly secondary type. This led universities to admit boys at fifteen or even younger. For boys with talent but no resources, bursaries for university were quite widely available, and many of the men thus educated returned as schoolmasters to carry on this educational cycle. But some were older as universities were open to anyone who could scrape together a little Latin and Mathematics. However, with industrialisation and urbanisation strains appeared [in the parochial tradition]. The middle class required more formal qualifications in a society which was becoming more complex and more achievement-oriented, but it also valued education for reasons of status . . . rural and small-town communities survived alongside the new urban society.

Anderson gives two examples to illustrate how the "mechanisms of mobility" worked: the first from the countryside: Alexander Gray was born at Tarves in Aberdeenshire in 1822 and by the age of twenty was celebrated as a champion ploughman. At twenty-two he entered the Fourth Class of the Grammar School and having been taught by Rector Melvin between 1845 and 1847 he went on to University, and became a rural clergyman.[4] The second from Aberdeen itself: Alexander Bain was the son of an Aberdeen weaver and left school at eleven because his parents could not afford to keep him on. From thirteen to eighteen he worked at the loom while educating himself. With some like-minded friends he revived the Aberdeen Mechanics' Institute and profited from its library and from a 'mutual instruction class' based on it. Bain was eventually taken up by a local clergyman, who coached him in Latin and interested the university professors in his case. He was given a free place at the Grammar for a few months to complete his preparation, and after that a bursary at Marischal College. Thus when Bain went to university at the age of eighteen, it was as an adult with experience of work and life. After a career spent partly in teaching and partly in the London literary world, he returned to Aberdeen in 1860 as Professor of Logic.

> The parochial tradition came nearest to its ideal form in the North-East, the region dominated by Aberdeen, where the schools had a

symbiotic relationship with the city's two universities, King's College and Marischal College. The cultivation of the 'university subjects' in the North-East was encouraged by the local social structure – there were many small farmers in this region who were prosperous enough to afford school fees, but whose sons needed to look to the towns or the professions for their future – and by the unusually large number of bursaries at the Aberdeen universities, mostly awarded by open competition, which extended interest in higher education downwards from the farmers to labourers and rural artisans. The annual Bursary Competition was the target to which the schoolmasters directed their most promising boys, and it became a part of local folklore. Since the examination was based almost entirely on Latin prose composition, it had the effect of keeping the Classics somewhat artificially alive, and of diverting to the University and the professions boys who in other parts of Scotland might have studied some more modern subject and found an outlet in commerce.

Most of the schoolmasters were themselves Aberdeen graduates and from the 1830s their quality was maintained by an important charitable endowment, the Dick Bequest. James Dick was a West India merchant from Forres, who left his money 'to elevate the literary character of the Parochial Schoolmasters and schools' in the counties of Aberdeen, Banff and Moray. The Trust gave a substantial supplement to the salaries of schoolmasters who passed its special examinations, and its inspector ensured that the schools kept up to the mark. In the North-East, therefore, the university-qualified schoolmaster survived in strength, and the importance of University preparation was itself an attraction, allowing the teacher some relief from the drudgery of elementary teaching through keeping his scholarship alive and the pleasure of working with one or two enthusiastic pupils . . .

The special feature of the Scottish system was that although its different parts were linked by the teaching of Latin as the essential university subject and by the presence of university-trained schoolmasters in both parish and burgh schools, the articulation was a loose one. Students could go to the University from either sort of school, or direct from adult life, and the level of Classical teaching in a traditional burgh school did not put boys from parish schools at a disadvantage when they had to compete at the University. But if the secondary schools taught to a higher level, and became more Classically oriented, the Universities would be under pressure to raise their age of entry and drop more elementary teaching, which would imperil the direct link between parish schools and universities and drive a wedge between students of different backgrounds. The logical outcome was that entry to the universities should only be via true secondary schools, and this was what came about by the end of the nineteenth century after seventy years of controversy centring on the issue of a compulsory examination for university entry. Whether or not this reduced opportunities for individuals depended on the arrangements made for scholarships and for the transfer from primary to secondary schools. Such arrangements might help [the Grays and] the Bains of later years, and save much energy painfully if heroically spent on self-education. More important, perhaps, they might save wasted potential by giving more systematic help to those of average talent, as well as to the exceptional men who were likely to win through whatever the circumstances.[5]

FIVE From Melvin to Barrack: The Grammar School to 1863

This chapter has three major sections. The first is a chronology of the Grammar School in its new building at its site in Schoolhill from 1758 until its move to its modern situation in 1863: it is also a history of the Rectors of the period – with James Melvin the dominant figure of the time. The second gives details of the early Rectors and their staffing. The final part consists of biographical details of the later careers of over two hundred boys who attended the School before 1863: they are presented here, as indeed throughout the book, in chronological order of birth year within their professions. As a snapshot of a far larger cohort such information gives a general indication of the sort of education being offered and the status of particular occupations for the middle-class before the middle of the nineteenth century. Hence the ranking of careers for this period is: Churchmen (50); Academic, usually University Professors (41); Medical (29); Legal (18); Merchants covering industrialists and later businessmen (17); Military (16); Administrative and Political, many abroad (15); Writers including newspapermen (13); the Arts (11); Finance (7); and Sport (1). A number could have been placed in several categories.

THE YEARS AT SCHOOLHILL, 1758–1863

Although Parson Gordon's map of 1661 gives an idea of what sort of building was in use as the Grammar it is only in 1757 that we get an accurate picture of what the school building was like because the Town Council decided to replace the former building by a structure which was used as the School until 1863.

On 25 October 1754 the Town Council recorded its view about the then School buildings, commenting on 'the insufficiency of the present Grammar School and the necessity of building a new one'. The magistrates then further recorded that they had 'visited the present School and ground round the same' and 'found that there was no convenient stances there for a school and having also visited the malt barn belonging to Jean Guild's Mortification, with the back close thereof and Mr Bissett's garden, they are unanimously of the opinion that the said barn, close and garden would make a very good stanse [sic] for a new School, and appointed Mr James Dun, Rector of the said School, Mr. Wyllie's mason and the Clerk to meet together and concert a proper plan of a school to be laid before the Council'. No trace of the original buildings or site remains but the early photographs of the building clearly show the top of the central block of Robert Gordon's in the background and a plaque on the building at the right hand side of the main gate into Gordon's, which originally housed Gray's School of Art, indicates the location of the old Grammar School.

Even then planning took time and not till January 1757 did the Council settle on a plan submitted by Charles Beveridge for the new School building. In the course of time this modern building was to gather its critics but, by the standards of the mid-eighteenth century it was, with a hewn belfry, pallisaded entry and hewn stone surbase, a fairly substantial structure. As often happens the cost was underestimated and in February 1758 £80 sterling more was paid to the contractors and the old building it replaced was put up for roup at £60. The advent of photography in the nineteenth century has left an accurate picture of what this building was like. It had four classrooms and a central hall which formed the cross-bar of a ground plan in the shape of a capital H.

In the late nineteenth century James Valentine produced an account of his recollections of the days he spent as a pupil at Schoolhill from 1858–62, entering Class II. By then the building was suffering from years of neglect and was in a very dilapidated state. Facing the street, the right-hand room was used by the First Class and the left-hand was used by the Second Class. The rear left-hand room was used by the Third Class and the last room, on the right, was used by the composite Class of Four and Five taught by the Rector. The three under-masters in turn took a Class from the First year through till the Third, before handing over to the Rector. They then started again with the First year group and repeated the process.

The only playground was the small area in front of the School. There was a space at the back but Valentine tells that it was left to 'giant dockens and nettles' and also contained the 'kits' – toilets or latrines which 'would have disgraced the precincts of the residence of the unspeakable Turk' – suggesting that they were very unpleasant. But then he also says that the

School itself did not enjoy too much cleaning and the main public school (central hall) was washed only once a year. This lack of cleaning allowed the pupils the delight of 'ruffing' – stamping their feet – when a Visitation of the Town Council took place for inspection and prize-giving, so that great clouds of dust from the 'worm-eaten and half rotten floors' enveloped their distinguished visitors.

From time to time voices were raised about the state of the old building in Schoolhill. At the inquiry into the state of the Town's Schools, in 1834, suggestions were made that the site there could be developed by adding an additional storey and introducing girls whose education was 'too much overlooked bearing in mind their own happiness and their opportunity for influencing future generations'. It was, however, another century and a half before girls were to be admitted as Grammar pupils.

Meantime, the end of the eighteenth century saw the departure of George Gordon, Lord Byron, to England and Harrow School and also the ending of the long career as master and Rector – sixty-six years – of James Dun by his death in 1798. The practice of making appointments 'ad vitam aut culpam' allowed incumbents enjoying this arrangement to continue to hold an office even when old age prevented their active participation in its duties. In such cases it was the practice to employ an assistant to carry out such duties under agreed financial arrangements.

Faced with the burden of ageing, Dr Dun arranged that his teaching should be assumed by a co-Rector, so in 1791 he proposed the appointment of his nephew, James Cromar Snr. This was challenged by Andrew Dun, an assistant master, on the grounds that under the terms of the Dun bequest, being a Dun he was entitled to preference. A wrangle ensued, which went as far as the Court of Session to settle the issue. Cromar was confirmed in his appointment and held it until 1796 when he mysteriously left Aberdeen without explanation.[1] An investigation by the Town Council into the situation at the School followed and the outcome was the appointing of Andrew Dun as co-Rector and the termination of Dr Dun's son's position as assistant master, as he had been mentally ill and had not attended the School for many years. The vacant rectorship was filled by Andrew Dun until his death in 1803: his successor, James Cromar Jnr, was as usual already a member of staff.

Although the early nineteenth-century world showed remarkable changes since 1758 and the opportunities for careers in many new fields were on offer to the pupils of that period, the School itself was not directly affected. The curriculum in the School remained based on the study of Latin even though the Industrial Revolution was already in full force at both local and national levels. Moreover, since 1758 the overseas world had seen, by conquest and exploration, a vast expansion of opportunity for well-educated, adventurous and ambitious young men. It was not long before the limited horizons of earlier times were widened to offer opportunities for employment not only at home but also in India, the Far East, America and Africa. Grammar former pupils spread everywhere following occupations of every kind, in business, government service, teaching and the armed forces as well as the traditional professions of medicine, law and the church. Such varied careers were well documented in the reminiscences which filled the pages of the Former Pupils' Magazine after 1885.

The internal organisation of the School remained unchanged as long as it remained at Schoolhill. The annual inspection, the Visitation, was carried out by the town councillors and other local dignitaries but that apart there was no outside interference except when an emergency arose like the dispute over the rectorship. However, as the nineteenth century wore on the London government began to take an interest in the provision of education and it is clear that there was great ignorance at first about the whole subject. To remedy such a situation the Victorian practice was to provide a list of questions to local authorities and require them to gather answers. This procedure was followed throughout the century at both local and national levels and thus provides an enormous amount of information.

Strangely in his book of records about the Grammar, *Bon Record,* Morland Simpson never offered any examples of the material which was gathered in such surveys and, in fact, never made mention of, or reference to, the wealth of information about the School which existed in these reports. As early as 1834 the government had set out a list of searching inquiries about the number of schools. In 1838 questions were asked about religious affiliation, their financial basis, the qualifications of the staff, their salaries, any cultural offering and the forms of reward and punishments practised.

DR JAMES MELVIN: RECTOR, 1826–1853

The Rector whose task it was in 1838 to provide answers on behalf of the Grammar was Dr James Melvin, who had become Rector in 1826 after being appointed assistant master five years earlier. Having already taught in both Udny and Old Aberdeen Grammar School, this was the man who dominated the education scene in Aberdeen in the first half of the nineteenth century. He was an outstanding former pupil of the Grammar who had been the First Bursar at Marischal in 1809. After graduation he began a career which was to win wide recognition as the greatest Latin scholar of his time. Not only did he serve as Rector of the School but he also held the post of lecturer in Humanity (Latin) in his old University at Marischal, but twice he personally suffered disappointment when the position of Professor of Humanity was filled by others.

Nevertheless, as a school-teacher, Melvin built up a huge reputation not only locally but throughout Scotland. This was demonstrated by the increasing number of 'extranei' who came to swell the number of pupils who filled the Fourth and Fifth classes in the School. These 'extranei' were the boys and young men who came to sit in Melvin's classes in order to acquire the polish on their knowledge of Latin which would improve their chances of success in the Bursary Competition, the annual examination for bursaries awarded by the Universities. In Melvin's heyday, in 1850, of the 111 members of the Fifth class, 69 were 'extranei' and only 42 were 'alumni'.[2]

The key to success in the Competition was the 'Version': the ability to translate a passage of English into Latin. In this field Melvin was the great expert in preparing his pupils for the challenge. Essentially his method was punctilious. He concentrated on a limited range of classical authors and analysed in meticulous detail the general scope and subtleties of the text being studied. Later ages were to cast some doubts about the narrowness of the curriculum and the methods of preparation but the system produced results – great success in the Competition. The standing of Melvin as scholar and teacher soared and the School's status rose as well.

Another string to Melvin's bow was his ordination as a minister in the Church of Scotland but in keeping with his quiet unassuming personality this was not a field that he entered very frequently and he apparently played little part in the religious turmoil which led to the Disruption of 1843 when all the ministers in Aberdeen left the Established Church and joined the Free Church. In Gammie's *Churches of Aberdeen* Melvin's name does not appear nor does it in McLaren's *Religion and Social Class: The Disruption Years in Aberdeen,* though he is mentioned in its biographical notes as an elder of the West Church.

On a more personal level, his portrait by Cassie (sadly lost in the 1986 fire at the School) suggested a small man but he was over six foot and badly marked on his face by smallpox. He lived, in 1831, at 209 Gallowgate but latterly (by 1841) at 41 Belmont Street and solemnly, accompanied by a Newfoundland dog, Caesar, he made his way daily across to the School to be greeted by a respectful gathering of the pupils. His arrival was heralded by the warning that 'Grim Pluto' (or just 'Grim') was on his way. But his rather unflattering nickname did not indicate either lack of esteem or even affection among pupils, old and new, and the citizens of Aberdeen, who accepted him as something of a local celebrity. His dry sense of humour allowed him to poke fun at the local dignitaries in his Latin address of welcome at the Annual Visitation by alluding to the declining state of the premises in which they gathered. Unlike the majority of the Scottish teaching profession he did not use the tawse very much and maintained discipline by the strength of his personality and reputation.

It would be remiss not to mention his great love for his books, particularly Latin works which numbered close to seven thousand. They were later gifted to the University Library where there was established the memorial window depicting four great Scottish Latin scholars (which included Melvin).[3]

In his answers to the Inquiry of 1838, Melvin stated quite bluntly that the purpose of the Grammar School was 'to prepare young men for College (i.e. University)' and described the School as a 'Classical seminary'. With these guiding principles it is not surprising that there was little attempt to widen the curriculum although reference was made to some teaching of Arithmetic, and a little Greek was added for the more senior classes. However, the Town Council was aware that modern times required a wider choice of subjects as well as better facilities to accommodate them.

(SIR) WILLIAM D. GEDDES: RECTOR, 1853–1855

When Melvin died unexpectedly in 1853, probably from over-work, the Town Council took little time to appoint as his successor one of his assistants, Geddes, who was also to play a prominent part in Scottish education not so much for his role as Rector but more for his subsequent role as Principal of the University of Aberdeen. Geddes was Rector for only a short time before he rather fortuitously became Professor of Greek at King's in 1855.

William Geddes (1828–1900; Kt. 1892) was educated at Elgin Academy and King's, graduating in 1846. He was parish schoolmaster of Gamrie at the age of seventeen, before becoming Classical master at the GS in 1848. He was appointed Rector of the Grammar in 1853 and two years later was elected Professor of Greek at King's. In the same year he published a *Greek Grammar*, which reached a seventeenth edition in 1883. When the fusion of the two Aberdeen Universities took place Geddes became Professor of Greek in the united College. He held this post until 1885 and was largely responsible for reviving and reforming the study of Greek in Scottish Universities. In 1885 he was elected Principal and Vice-Chancellor of Aberdeen. His chief achievements were the restoration of the chapel in 1891 and the extension of the buildings of Marischal to house the Faculties of Science and Medicine.[4] He was the first Honorary President of the FP Club formed by Rector Simpson in 1893.

His first task as Rector was to draw up a set of proposals for a new curriculum and a review of the School organisation. When this report was offered in June 1854 it was quite cautious in its suggestions. First he felt that an English master should be appointed. Perhaps the most radical change, he suggested that Natural History should be introduced with the emphasis to be on the practical rather than the theoretical side. He felt it was time to raise the salaries of the teachers to ensure that the calibre of the staff would be maintained. One of the problems created by introducing new subjects to the curriculum was the need to be able to recruit suitably qualified teachers.

One difficulty that faced the School for much of its earlier existence was the uneven levels of education which incoming pupils could offer as this led to classes often having a long tail of non-achievers. Geddes suggested that promotion from one class to the next should depend on performance though this was not something which attracted much enthusiasm from a staff which depended for much of their income on the number of fee-paying pupils in their classes. Geddes also suggested that Greek should be given more prominence, not surprising perhaps when his nickname was 'Homer'. He wanted to encourage more reading by establishing a library and lastly he proposed that a Mathematics teacher should be appointed to avoid the need for pupils to leave the School to attend the Town's Schools in Little Belmont Street.

So the need for change was recognised, but before anything could be done Geddes was gone, rewarded by the gift from the Town of a large silver punch-bowl (which was another victim of the 1986 fire).

The Town Council again faced the responsibility of finding a new Rector. They followed the usual practice of advertising the post in the press and then facing the candidates with a series of examinations to ensure their competence. But events were to emerge to question whether this procedure was to ensure competence in teaching or whether it was to identify the best Classical scholar. The list of Rectors up to 1855 indicates that appointments almost invariably had come from the existing staff, but on this occasion a shock was in store.

JOHN KELMAN: INTERIM RECTOR, NOVEMBER 1855 – JANUARY 1856

With no Rector the Town turned to John Kelman for help. A young man from Keith with academic ambitions, he had attended Melvin's highest class in the Grammar in 1846–7 to prepare for the Bursary Competition. Within a short time he became Melvin's best Latin scholar and it was a surprise and disappointment when he was low down the Bursary list. Although he redeemed himself somewhat in his first year at King's by being top scholar he was outshone in his MA results in 1851 by Robert Machray, another former Grammar pupil. Thereafter Kelman determined to devote himself to the Free Church. However, he filled the gap as temporary Grammar Rector for three months. Following his time at the School Kelman was Free Church minister at Port Glasgow, 1858–63, transferred to Dundonald and then served St John's West in Leith. He was responsible for organising the evangelical Moody Revival in Edinburgh in 1874 and his son, John, minister of Free St George's in Edinburgh, became a prolific biblical writer.

THOMAS WALLER EYRE EVANS: RECTOR, 1856–1859

Seven candidates applied for the rectorship: two members of staff, Brebner[5] and Beverly,[6] and Martin (who later joined the staff and later still became Rector) were strong local candidates but there were also two other serious applicants. One was also a 'local' candidate: James Donaldson, a former pupil, a brilliant Classical scholar who was already Rector of Stirling HS and later of the Royal HS in Edinburgh. His career took him back to Aberdeen as Professor of Humanity and finally to St Andrews as University Principal. The other contender was an Irishman who was Head Classical Master at Belfast's Royal Academical Institution.

There were no Duns or 'Ferryhill loons' to complicate the procedures and the candidates duly sat the examinations set. To the astonishment and dismay of the Town, the person selected for the post was Thomas W.E. Evans (b. 1826), Welsh by name but the son of a doctor from Cork, who had studied at Trinity College, Dublin. It was not a unanimous decision because there was a minority who had supported Donaldson but his drawback was his close connection to a Congregational Church in Blackfriars Street whose views were unacceptable to the Free Church majority then controlling the Town Council of Aberdeen.

However, Evans also suffered from a major handicap. He was Irish, at a time when the great influx of Irish emigrants had landed on Britain's shore and thereby incurred great hostility and resentment in much of central Scotland, though Aberdeen was not much affected.[7] On his initial introduction Evans got off on the wrong foot by failing to secure the holiday which pupils felt they were entitled to enjoy. Thus began a most unhappy four years in the School's history.

In his book *Reporting Reminiscences*[8] the local worthy William Carnie drew the charming sketch of a kind-hearted, hospitable man who was 'different'. He was without doubt a great Classical scholar even though inquiries at Trinity revealed he had never actually graduated there. It was then not especially uncommon for University students not to bother to graduate and there was no body existing to examine teaching qualifications. However, he was not nearly so much in awe of Melvin's scholarship as many of Aberdeen's citizens had been and was not above reminding his pupils how he had beaten the locals to win his post.

When settling into Aberdeen he and his wife, Emily-Mary, took lodgings with Mrs Yule just west of the Music Hall in Union Street, but by 1858 they had bought a property at 24 Union Place, just west of Rose Street. In November 1857 Evans became a Fellow of the Society of Antiquarians (Scotland).

However, it was his teaching methods which were controversial. Instead of playing the role of the supreme authority on Latin, he was quite happy if pupils dug deeply to find points on which they would challenge his scholarship. This unfamiliar attitude to teaching, both the parents and pupils found hard to stomach and the unruliness and indiscipline which arose through Evans' inability to maintain order, partly because of his very bad eyesight and partly because of his short temper, led to a rapid decline in the School roll as many pupils departed to Old Aberdeen GS. The numbers in the Fifth Class fell to four boys in April 1859.[9]

As relations between Evans and the School authorities declined it was decided, after only a few years, that steps should be taken to dismiss him. This involved the setting up of a kind of tribunal to examine the state of affairs in Schoolhill. There were a number of grounds on which it was it was attempted to establish that the Rector was 'defective in his duty'. These were: unfair and capricious modes of punishment; failure to ensure attendance and obedience; indiscipline in class; indifference to the responsibility of the rectorship; and unsatisfactory teaching methods.

Carnie sat through the three days of interrogation and eventually published an account of the proceedings in 1859. Evans attended throughout, but took no part. Despite hearing evidence from twenty witnesses, only one of whom was sympathetic in his remarks to Evans, the authorities still decided that, on the evidence produced, dismissal would be too risky as it would have led to legal appeals, extra expenses and no certainty of legal victory.[10] So as Carnie put it, 'Mr. Evans, shortly after, moved from Aberdeen, bearing with him the respect due to a gentleman of his attainments. The Council, it was considered, dealt generously in the matter'. How generously? Five years salary at £300 per annum plus some back money owing – the equivalent of £117,000 when based on the retail price index of modern times or perhaps a more appropriate comparison £913,000 if one uses average earnings.[11] Evans was apparently still alive somewhere in the south late into the nineteenth century but in the eyes of the School he became a kind of 'non rector', never referred to except in the most dismissive terms. Years later one of the School's distinguished former pupils, Sir James Westland, on reflection felt that Evans never had a chance![12] Certainly the evidence of the tribunal indicated the hostility of Kelman and the continued opposition of Donaldson's supporters.

JAMES McLAUCHLIN: TEMPORARY RECTOR, 1859–1860

James McLauchlin (1834–1919) came from Boharm (near Keith) in Banffshire and attended Melvin's form V classes in 1847–8 and 1849–50. He gained his MA from Marischal in 1854 and took up the post of schoolmaster at Insch. (He was later to become parish minister of Inveravon and Rathven.) With Evans gone and McLauchlin holding the fort for eight months,[13] the task was to search again for a new Rector.

But there was another problem which had become quite pressing. It was recognised that the premises in Schoolhill had been allowed to deteriorate and that the accommodation there was too limited to allow for any improvement of facilities, so a new School was required. Again the first task was to secure a suitable site. The well-known pictorial map of Aberdeen drawn by the famous photographer, George Washington Wilson, in 1850, revealed a gap site on Union Street where Gilcomston South Church now stands at the corner of Summer Street. This was the chosen site for a new Grammar School. Specifications were drawn up for what was required and a competition was arranged for a suitable design to be considered. The winning entry came from an Edinburgh architect, George Smith. The plans were classical in design, not unlike the High School on Calton Hill in Edinburgh, but the scheme was abandoned and later generations must have been thankful that what would have been a congested site on an increasingly noisy street never materialised. However, it was not too long before a much more widespread search for a different site took place.

WILLIAM BARRACK: RECTOR, 1860–1868

In the meantime the choice as new Rector settled on William Barrack, who had attended the Grammar for Form V in 1847–8 and gained an MA from King's in 1852 and the Hutton Prize for the best Arts student. He had been appointed the headmaster of the GS of Old Aberdeen in 1857 and had made an immediate impact. In the 1858 Bursary Competition his pupils won sixteen of the twenty-seven bursaries at King's including 1st, 3rd, 4th, 5th, 6th and 8th place, and four of the sixteen bursaries at Marischal including 2nd place. So this time the choice of Grammar Rector was a teacher with a proven track record, with local connections and whose establishment in Old Aberdeen had benefited from the large number of pupils who had left during the time of Evans.

The appointment of Barrack in 1860 brought back to Schoolhill many of those who had previously voted with their feet and this helped not only to re-establish the numbers on the Grammar roll but also to revive the School's reputation in the Town. Barrack also brought with him a number of boys from the Old Aberdeen Grammar School. It had met in the ground floor of the Town House in the High Street of Old Aberdeen and had been controlled and financed by the Kirk Session of St Machar. Barrack thus saved the Grammar but left a hopeless legacy to his successor, Thomas Davidson, in Old Aberdeen.

The staff during Barrack's time were Rev. Alexander Beverly ('Dick'), who had been at the Grammar since 1844, and, with the departure of John Dun (1826–61) and John Brebner (1853–1861), Rev. James Wilson Legge and Rev. Charles Macdonald, whose background was similar to Barrack. Born in 1828, Macdonald had also studied at King's and won the Hutton Prize in 1850 for the most distinguished Arts graduate. He qualified in Divinity, becoming a Church of Scotland minister. He taught at the Grammar from 1861 until 1863, when he migrated to Canada to take up the chair of Mathematics at Dalhousie College, Nova Scotia.

With confidence restored in the School's educational future, attention turned once again to providing accommodation which would allow better facilities and a widening of the educational opportunities which the School could offer with new subjects and bigger staff. On this occasion the record of the search, for a suitable site and plans for a new building, can be found in great detail.

In general terms what was needed was a roomy site in a prominent position, easily accessible, at reasonable cost. Consideration was given as to how far any suggested site was from the centre of the town, deemed to be the junction between Union Street and Market Street. Sites were all measured in area to avoid landing up with the congested site situation of the Town's School in Little Belmont Street, though at that time little thought was given in Scottish schools for the desirability of much recreational space for school grounds. Costs involved in each site were carefully noted. The existing school roll of 272 boys was analysed to find the geographical distribution of the boys' homes east or west of the Denburn Valley. (It was found that 79 lived east and 88 west, the others being classified as 'country'.) Most important was the need to choose a site which would allow the erection of a building worthy of both the history and reputation of one of Scotland's oldest schools and in keeping with the pride and pretensions of a City which was rapidly expanding.

The outcome of this search was that eventually ten sites were selected for consideration. These were Schoolhill (redeveloping the old site); Belmont Street; Crown Terrace; Skene Terrace; Ferryhill; Justice Mill Lane; Rubislaw (centring on Albert Street and Lane); Westfield House (north of Whitehall Place); Gilcomston (the top of Skene Square); and the Westfield Model Gardens.

Writing nearly forty years after the event, William Carnie agreed that there were ten sites considered but his list differs slightly in detail from that previously noted. However, he recorded that the popular choice would have been Justice Mill Lane but the final choice was for Westfield Model Gardens. He also pointed out that the Gardens were in fact 'a number of paling-enclosed plots held at a small rent by members of the working class and cultivated by them in the evenings and on holidays'. The final meeting to choose the site took place in the Council Chambers and Westfield won out over Gilcomston by 60 votes to 28. It appears that the latter site was considered to be too close to Broadford Works whose mill girls were deemed to be too much of a moral danger to the Grammar boys.

James Matthews, a future Lord Provost, who had been runner-up in the contest for designing the Union Street site, was appointed as architect. A limit of £11,000 was put on the contract with the estimate for mason work making up about half of this total. As the Town Council itself had no funds to finance the undertaking it decided on 7 January 1861 that it would try to raise the money by public subscription. The scheme adopted was remarkably successful and within six weeks capital of £14,205 was raised, with the subscribers being rewarded with the right to enrol pupils in the School according to the size of their contribution to the fund.

The erection of the building was in the hands of the master-mason, Adam Mitchell, and the Scottish baronial style was accepted. On the outside of the building the names of three people most directly concerned with the project were commemorated by their initials: Sir Alexander Anderson, the Lord Provost (A.A.P) above the main door; William Barrack, the Rector (W.B.); and James Matthews, the architect (J.M.). The famous benefactor of the School, Patrick Dun, was also remembered on the clock-tower (P.D. 1631).

Matthews submitted his plans in October 1861 for consideration and, although there appears to have been some criticism, no alternatives were suggested and the plans were accepted. Unfortunately, following regionalisation in 1975 Matthews' plans were lost although an etching of the building and a photograph by Washington Wilson give a very clear picture of the original appearance. The only modifications at this time were to place the whole structure further away from the south boundary (Skene Street) and to ensure that it stood square with the north and east boundaries. Most of the land had been acquired from the trustees of Miss Janet Chalmers of Westfield (the family who controlled the *Aberdeen Journal*), but various extra pieces of land were acquired at the south and east sides of the site, following the decisions to allow easier access to the School and provide for a janitor's lodge.

Matthews received clear instructions as to what was to be provided inside the building. There was to be a Public School (School Hall) which would contain 550 scholars and accommodate 160 visitors, who were to be provided with a platform. The classrooms were to be designed to provide more room for writing instead of the cramped accommodation of Schoolhill days. They were also to have enough space for staff to be able to move about easily in them and they were to have sloping floors which allowed pupils to see and be seen.

The Rector's classroom was designed to take 160 boys, while four Latin classrooms, a Mathematics room, a Writing room and an English/Modern Languages room each housed 100 boys. There was also to be an extra room in case of overflow. Each classroom was to have a master's private room attached to it. A Committee Room was to be provided beside the Hall for the magistrates and examiners. Provision was also to be made for a room to be set aside for boys who were studying the higher grades of Mathematics, a combined room of 'good size' for a Library and Museum and an Observatory for teaching the use of astronomical instruments.

The Public School was to be heated by a hot water apparatus but the other rooms were to be heated by open fires. Outdoor accommodation in the shape of a covered arcade was to be provided as were sufficient and modern urinals and privies. Unfortunately the water for the building was to come from a three-inch main through a one-inch pipe. In 1986 what proved to be one of the main obstacles to containing the fire effectively was the lack of water!

The new building was opened by Lord Provost Anderson on 23 October 1863 with a large gathering of the local 'great and good' present. There was some criticism of the location of the building on the grounds that it was too far out of the town but Anderson pointed out that similar objections had been made about the old building in Schoolhill when it was opened in 1757. The date of the Opening was registered on the weather-vane above the centre of the building.[14]

STAFFING

Rector: James Dun, 1744–1791

(Dr) James Dun (*c.*1708–1798) graduated MA comparatively late in 1732 at Marischal. The same year he was appointed an under-master at the Grammar School and on the death of John Milne in 1744 he was elected Rector. In 1772 the university conferred on him an LLD given in recognition of a service of over forty years as a teacher of Latin. In 1791 Dun's advanced age led him to retire from active teaching, his place being taken by James Cromar Snr with the title joint-Rector.

1760 Apr. 23 – Alexander Fullerton, schoolmaster at Fetteresso, became an under-master (on the death of James Smith). He had graduated MA in 1757 and was allowed to continue after 1774 when he took up the ministry of Footdee. He died in 1787.

1760 Oct. 30 – John Dun, son of the Rector, became an under-master in place of James Beattie who had become a Regent at the University. He completed his MA in 1761.

1762 Charles Dun (who joined the staff in 1736, replacing Charles Kay (1717–36) produced 'A Compendious Grammar of the Latin Tongue: adapted to the Capacity of Youth'. He dedicated the work to the TC and was rewarded with payment of £5 5s Scots.

1770 June 15 – William Laing, tutor, became an under-master, replacing Charles Dun, who had died. He gained a Cumming bursary in 1762 and his MA in 1766. He was appointed an Episcopalian minister at Peterhead in 1771.

1771 May 11 – James Shirrefs became an under-master, taking Laing's place. He took his MA at Marischal in 1770. He demitted his post in 1778 when he took up his first ministerial charge in Aberdeen. He was awarded a DD from King's in 1795 and was Moderator of the General Assembly of the Church of Scotland in 1807. He died in 1830.

1778 Sept. 23 – James Cromar Snr became an under-master (in place of Shirrefs). He took his MA in 1770.

1787 Dec. 8 – Andrew Dun, assistant teacher in the School, was made under-master (following death of Fullerton). He had taken his MA in 1781.

Conjunct Rectors: James Dun and James Cromar Snr, 1791–1796

1791 Aug. 6 – Dr James Dun and James Cromar Snr were made conjunct rectors.

1796 Jan. 23 – James Cromar Snr was reported to have 'absconded' and John Dun, who 'has not attended or discharged any of the duties of his office for about twenty years past' was reported to have resigned.

1796 Jan. 23 – Alexander Leith, who for a good many years had been assistant to Dr James Dun, was made an under-master or usher (in place of Cromar).

1796 Jan. 27 – Dr James Dun and Andrew Dun were made conjunct Rectors.

Conjunct Rectors: James Dun and Andrew Dun, 1796–1798

1796 Jan. 27 – James Cromar Jnr, assistant in the school for three years, was appointed an under-master (in place of John Dun). He had taken his MA in 1788.

1796 Apr. 11 – William Duncan was made under-master (in place of Andrew Dun, now co-Rector). He had taken his MA in 1781 and was a Blackwell prize-winner in 1797.

Rector Interim: James Cromar Jnr, 1798–1803

1798 Mar. 5 – £10 was added to the salaries of Andrew Dun and the under-masters – Leith, Cromar and Duncan.

1799 Apr. 20 – Robert Forbes, schoolmaster at Inverurie, became an under-master in place of Leith, who had died.

1802 May 4 – Alex. Nicoll, master in Gordon's Hospital, became an under-master in place of Duncan who had died. He had taken his MA from King's in 1792.

Rector: James Cromar Jnr, 1803–1825

James Cromar Jnr (1765–1825) graduated MA in 1788 and joined the GS staff as a temporary assistant in 1793. He was paid only the emoluments of the class viz. £25 the first year; £22 the second year; and £20 the third. In January 1796 he was appointed one of the 'established ushers' and in March 1803 replaced Andrew Dun as Rector. According to the inscription on his memorial in St Nicholas churchyard, never before had the Grammar had a more skilful, more illustrious, or more successful Rector, nor one more beloved alike of pupils and citizens.

PUPILS

According to George MacDonald[15] it took three days for new entrants to get to know one another at King's. At Marischal, many of the bajans (first year students) already knew each other from their time in the Grammar. As a result nicknames and mock-Latin classroom slang were more prevalent there. The main division came between bursars and non-bursars. John Hill Burton recalled with distaste 'the healthy, smiling jackanapes, whose parents . . . have sent him to college to gain a bursary, that he may shew his talents, his wealth, and his contempt for his poorer competitors, by resigning it'. At King's the scorn was turned on private students who joined for a single session, entering and leaving without examination.

Entrants to King's owed much to a number of its alumni being parish schoolmasters who directed their pupils to the College; to the number of bursaries there to support them; to the rural setting and small size of Old Aberdeen and to prejudice in the counties against the utilitarian ethos of Marischal – 'the Broad Street Academy'. However, pragmatism prompted some choices: Alexander Bain, sought-after by both, chose Marischal because 'the walks to King's would have entailed an injurious amount of fatigue'.

The average age of entrants to King's in 1827 was fourteen, while at Marischal twelve was said to be the average age at entry. Those who entered earlier, according to one Marischal professor, were 'the students who have made the best figure, perhaps, in the Grammar School, and their parents, perhaps from vanity, wish to push them forward through the whole of their education, not knowing that they cannot make such a figure at College as they do while they are learning the Latin language'. These ages increased as the century went on, inflated by scholars who spent an extra year or more in attending the Grammar or other such institutions in order to gain a University bursary.

In the years up to 1863 Marischal recorded the fathers' occupations on matriculation and one would expect this to be mirrored by those attending the Grammar. The number of students from landed families continued to decline to 7.4%, while those in 'Commerce and Industry' (18.5%) and 'Working Class' (13.6%) categories were volatile. These probably reflected Britain's troubled urban economy or, in the case of the latter, a preference for the Mechanics' Institute. 'Agriculture' (19.8%), 'Professional' (27.1%) and 'Intermediate' – agents, craftsmen and tradesmen – (12.3%) remained stable.

At King's in 1826 there were 29 endowments providing 128 bursaries in arts, 60 of them competitive. At Marischal, 38 endowments supported 99 bursaries, 35 of them competitive. It probably took about £25 a year to pay all university fees and expenses but at Marischal 84 of the bursaries were for £10 or less. The Colleges accepted this situation believing something was better than nothing but overwork on a limited diet brought a toll of sickness and death.

The academic strength of the pupils attending the Grammar in its last years at Schoolhill is reflected in the following biographical profiles. Perhaps this can be best encapsulated by three of their number – George Slesser in 1858, James Stirling in 1860 and Thomas Barker in 1862 – going on to become Senior Wranglers at Cambridge (individuals who were first in Mathematics in their final-year exams at the university). In response, following his election as Rector of Aberdeen University, Earl Russell began his Address on 11th November 1864 with this opening sentence, 'I feel indebted to you for this honour on account of the fame and reputation of this University, on account of its ancient distinction – a distinction which has been enhanced of late years by Mathematical honours gained in an

English University – causing the name of your sons to be recorded in its honoured annals.' He could just as well have been talking about Aberdeen Grammar School.

PUPILS ATTENDING THE GRAMMAR BETWEEN 1758 AND 1863 (IN PROFESSIONS CHRONOLOGICALLY BY BIRTH)

Merchants (Businessmen) and Manufacturers (Industrialists)

James Hadden (1758–1845) attended the Grammar and Marischal before becoming a partner in textile companies. He served four terms as Lord Provost in 1801–2, 1809–10, 1813–4 and 1830–1. His major role in the development of Aberdeen in the early nineteenth century gave him the title of 'Father of the City'. He was involved in banking, insurance, canals and the Volunteer Movement during the Napoleonic Wars.[16]

Andrew Shirreffs (1762–1807) attended the Grammar and then graduated MA from Marischal in 1783. He began business in Aberdeen as a bookseller and bookbinder. He produced a number of dramatic and poetic works as well as being involved in early newspapers and magazines.[17]

Gavin Hadden (1770–1857) attended the Grammar between 1778 and 1783, being Dux in his last year.[18] He worked in the family textile business. He was Lord Provost in 1820–1, 1824–5, 1828–9 and 1832. He was assessor at Marischal, 1821–1833 and procurator at King's in 1833.

(Sir) Alexander Bannerman (1788–1864; Kt 1851) attended the Grammar between 1796 and 1801, entering Class I, and Marischal, before becoming a partner in textile and shipbuilding firms. He joined the Town Council in 1811 and played an important role during Aberdeen's financial problems in 1817–19. He was Liberal MP for Aberdeen from 1832 to 1847 then became successively Lt-Governor of Prince Edward Island, Governor of the Bahamas and Governor of Newfoundland. He was Rector of the University in 1834.[19]

George Auldjo (1790–1846) attended the Grammar between 1798 and 1803, entering Class I, going on to migrate to Canada to join his uncle there. He was agent for the Phoenix Assurance Co. of London but soon became involved in a leading export/import house in Montreal. He became a Director of the Bank of Montreal, 1822–5 and President of the Committee of Trade, 1825–33 and 1835–6. He was a leading financier in shipping and was responsible for a number of infrastructure improvements.

Robert Davidson (1804–1894) attended the Grammar in 1815–16, entering Class I, and Marischal on a year's scholarship. A Scottish inventor he made a model electric locomotive in 1837. He ran a successful business in Aberdeen and became a prosperous chemist and dyer. He invented a means of producing yeast on a large scale and manufactured perfumes, which allowed him to indulge in the collection of fine china, valuable pictures and a large collection of violins.

George Thomson Jnr (1804–1895), of Pitmedden, attended the Grammar between 1812 and 1815, before setting up his own business as a ship and insurance broker and developing shipowning interests. He established the Aberdeen White Star Line with South Africa and Australia and entered the Chinese tea trade. His clippers grew into a great British merchant navy line. He was Lord Provost of Aberdeen from 1847 to 1850 and Liberal MP for the Town between 1852 and 1857. He has been described as Aberdeen's most generous benefactor of the age.[20] A commemorative plaque to him can be found at 35 Marischal Street.

George Barclay (1820–1910) attended the Grammar between 1828 and 1833, entering Class I. He was a businessman in Leith from 1848 and was elected a member of the RSE in 1872.

(Dr) Charles Mitchell (1820–1895) attended the Grammar between 1828 and 1833, entering Class I, before studying Physics and Chemistry at Marischal. He then served an engineering apprenticeship with Simpson and Co. of Aberdeen before moving to Newcastle in 1842, where he worked in the shipyards. He became a leading Tyneside shipbuilder, many ships being built for the coal trade, while a major customer was Russia for warships and ice-breakers. He provided facilities for his workers and his philanthropy was well known. The Mitchell Tower of Marischal College was named after him.

Alexander Walker (1825–1903) attended the Grammar between 1835 and 1837, entering Class I, before joining the family firm of merchants. He served as Dean of Guild, 1872–80, and belonged to several educational trusts. He supported a number of charities all aimed at improving the lot of the poor or unfortunate in society.[21]

John Forbes White (1831–1904) attended the Grammar between 1839 and 1844, entering Class I, and becoming Dux in his final year. He entered Marischal as First Bursar in 1844 and was deemed the most brilliant student of his year when he graduated in 1848. He became an innovative flour miller and corn merchant. He was Scotland's foremost art critic and connoisseur, transforming the taste and teaching of art in the country.[22] He served on the

University Court, 1880–8, and was leader of the Liberal Unionists in Aberdeen in the 1880s. A commemorative plaque to him can be found at 60 Frederick Street.

James W. Barclay (1833–1907) attended the Grammar between 1845 and 1848, entering Class II, and then Marischal. He worked as a grain merchant before becoming a shipowner. An Aberdeen Town Councillor (1864–71), and MP for Forfarshire (1873–92), he was radical in his politics and supported tenants' rights and agricultural improvement. He purchased Glenbuchat estate in 1901. He was a strong supporter of the Aberdeen Agricultural College.

(Sir) Thomas Sutherland (1834–1922; KCMG 1891; GCMG 1897) attended the Grammar between 1844 and 1848, entering Class I, and then Marischal. He decided on a career in commerce and became a clerk in London in the Peninsular and Oriental (P & O) Navigation Company. He rose rapidly to become superintendent of its Hong Kong agency: in 1865 he established the Hongkong and Shanghai Banking Corporation, which was the founder member of the HSBC group. By 1881 he was chairman and managing director of the largest and most successful shipping company in the world. In 1884, Sutherland became Liberal (later Liberal Unionist) MP for Greenock, a seat he held until retirement in 1900. He stood highest among many clever shipowners at the peak of British maritime hegemony. He was proud to have been custodian of P & O, symbol of Britain's imperial strength over half the globe.[23]

John Maitland (1835–1917) attended the Grammar between 1847 and 1849, entering Class I. He worked with Florence Nightingale in the Crimea in the 1850s and spent his later career as a tea and coffee planter in Ceylon.

John Walker (1835–1916) attended the Grammar between 1846 and 1850, entering Class I. He worked abroad in Australia and South Africa, being involved in agriculture, mining (especially of gold), railways and politics. He obtained and lost a fortune twice. Back home he was responsible for the clearances for sheep in Shetland, and became a councillor in London and Aberdeen.

(Sir) William D. Gibbon (1837–1919; Kt 1912) attended the Grammar between 1848 and 1851, entering Class III, and Aberdeen University. He became chairman, Ceylon Planters Association in 1878. He was a JP, a member of Kandy Municipal Council and Fellow of the Royal Colonial Institute.

(Sir) George Stegmann Gibb (1850–1925; Kt 1904) attended the Grammar from 1860 to 1865, entering Class I, before joining Aberdeen University and then taking a Law degree from London University. He became general manager of the North Eastern Railway in 1891 and pursued innovative and vigorous practices. He was also successful when working as general manager of the London Underground. His readiness to learn from America was a factor in this.[24]

Churchmen

(Rev.) William Morgan (1752–88) was at the Grammar in 1762 and attended King's thereafter. He was Rector of Kingston, Jamaica, 1776–84 and gained a DD from King's in 1780. He was appointed Professor of Civil and Natural History in Marischal in 1788 but died before he took office.

(Prof.) Gilbert Gerard (1760–1815) was in attendance at the Grammar between 1771 and 1773. Following further education at Aberdeen and Edinburgh Universities he became minister of the Scots Church in Amsterdam. He was Professor of Greek at King's in 1791 and Professor of Divinity there in 1795. He was Moderator of the General Assembly of the Church of Scotland, 1803. He added to his professorship the ministry of Old Machar, 1811–15.[25]

(Rev. Dr) John Dick (1764–1833) attended the Grammar where he gained a scholarship to King's. He was ordained as a United Secession minister at Slateford, near Edinburgh, in 1785. He moved to Shuttle Street (Greyfriars) where he remained from 1801 to 1833. He gained a Divinity degree from Princeton, New Jersey. He gained a reputation as a theological writer, his most important works being his four volumes on Theology, which came to be used in American Presbyterian churches.[26]

John Strachan (1778–1867) attended the Grammar and entered King's on a bursary, graduating AM[27] in 1797. He worked as a schoolmaster while studying Divinity at St Andrews and migrated to Canada in 1799. Failing to obtain a Presbyterian charge he became a Rector in the Church of England. His ministering to the sick and wounded during the Anglo-American War of 1812 led to appointment to the Legislative Council of Upper Canada. He also became an Archdeacon. Although socially and politically conservative he promoted popular education. He became Bishop of Toronto in 1839 but his High Church Tory vision was not always popular.[28]

(Rev.) Alexander Black (1789–1864) attended the Grammar between 1798 and 1803, entering Class I, and then Marischal, where he studied Divinity. He became minister of Tarves in 1818 and Professor of Divinity at Marischal in 1831. A talented linguist, Black could converse in nineteen languages and correspond in twelve. At the Disruption in 1843 Black adhered to the Free Church and became Professor of Biblical Exegesis[29] in New College, Edinburgh.[30]

(Rev. Prof.) John Duncan (1796–1870) attended the Grammar between 1806 and 1810, entering Class I, and graduated MA from Marischal in 1814. He was ordained a minister in 1825 and served parishes in Perthshire and Glasgow. He was the first missionary to Jews from Scotland, spending three years in Hungary (1840–3). Following the Disruption he became Professor of Hebrew ('Rabbi Duncan') and Oriental Languages in New College, a post he held until his death.

(Rev.) Nathaniel Morren (1798–1847) attended the Grammar between 1806 and 1810, entering Class I, and then Marischal. He returned later to study Divinity and became a minister in Greenock in 1823. He combined intense scholarship with a devotion to the pastoral care of his congregation. After the Disruption he ministered in Brechin and was Evangelical in church politics.[31]

(Rev. Principal) David Brown (1803–1897) attended the Grammar between 1811 and 1817, entering Class I, and became Dux in his final year. He took his MA from Marischal in 1821 and was an assistant minister in London and Dumbarton. He was appointed a Professor in the Free Church College in Aberdeen in 1857 and was unanimously elected its Principal in 1876. He was Moderator of the General Assembly of the Free Church in 1885. He was one of the original Honorary Vice-Presidents of the FP Club in 1893.

John Longmuir (1803–1883) attended the Grammar between 1817 and 1821, entering Class I, and then Marischal, where he completed Divinity studies. He taught in schools and was ordained in Aberdeen in 1840. He and most of his congregation went over to the Free Church in 1843. He also lectured on Geology at King's. He published several books of verse and guidebooks and became a noted lexicographer. His revision of Jameson's *Scottish Dictionary* in four volumes was probably his most important work.[32]

John Cumming (1807–1881) attended the Grammar between 1816 and 1822, entering Class I, and then went on to study Divinity at University. He was ordained into the Presbyterian Church of England in 1832. He attracted large numbers to his services at the Crown Court Church, Covent Garden, in London, 1832–79, with preaching becoming the central feature of his ministry. He was elected a Fellow of the RSE in 1853. He proved exceptional in the breadth of his involvement in contemporary religious activities.[33]

Alexander D. Davidson (1807–1872) attended the Grammar between

1817 and 1821, entering Class I, and then Marischal, before being ordained into the ministry in Aberdeen in 1832. The transformation of religious opinion in Aberdeen from moderate to evangelical can be attributed largely to his influence. He led his own congregation into the Free Church and his lectures and sermons were published posthumously.[34]

(Dr) James Ogilvie (1811–71) attended the Grammar in 1828–9 and gained his MA from Marischal in 1833. He was Principal of the General Assembly's Institution in Calcutta, 1845–71. He is buried in the Scottish Cemetery, St Andrew's Church, Kolkata, India.

(Rev.) John Hay (1812–91) attended the Grammar in 1828–9, entering Class V, and took his MA at Marischal in 1833. In 1839 he joined the Madras Mission of the LMS. He wrote religious works and articles, and spent twenty years on the revision of the Telugu (an official language in India) translation of the Bible.

(Rev.) James Forbes (1813–1851) attended the Grammar briefly in 1818–19, entering Class I, and later went on to study Divinity at King's, 1826–9. He taught at Colchester Royal Grammar School before qualifying as a Presbyterian minister. In 1837 he migrated to Australia and was labelled 'Victoria's first educationist'. He founded Melbourne Academy, later Scotch College.

William C. Burns (1815–1868) attended the Grammar between 1827 and 1829, entering Class V, and then Marischal. He later studied Divinity at Glasgow. He was instrumental in the revival of religious life in various parts of the country. After joining the Free Church in 1843 his preaching made a great impression in Canada. He then went as a missionary to China and established an effective ministry there. He was exceptional in an age of exceptional missionaries and was one of the most remarkable figures in the nineteenth-century Scottish church.[35]

John M. Mitchell (1815–1904) attended the Grammar in 1828–29, entering Class V, and then Marischal, securing the second highest bursary with his Latin prose. He studied for the ministry at Aberdeen and Edinburgh. He then returned for a time to the GS as a teacher at the request of Rector Melvin. He went to Bombay as a missionary. In 1843 he joined the Free Church. He worked in India until the 1880s when he served the Scotch Church in Nice for ten years. He had the unusual distinction of serving his church at home, in the mission field and on the Continent.[36]

Islay Burns (1817–1872) attended the Grammar in 1830–1, entering Class V, and then Marischal, distinguishing himself in Classics and Mathematics before moving on to Glasgow to study Theology. He joined the Free Church, serving in Dundee. He became Professor of Theology at Glasgow in 1864.[37]

(Rev. Dr) George Philip (1819–1904) attended the Grammar between 1828 and 1833, entering Class I, and was First Bursar to Marischal in 1833. He became minister of the Stonehaven Free Church in 1843, the Free Union Church in Govan in 1851 and the St John's United Free Church in Edinburgh in 1866.

(Rev. Prof.) William G. Blaikie (1820–1899) attended the Grammar between 1828 and 1833, entering Class I, and became Dux in his final year. He then proceeded to Marischal, where he studied Divinity. His time at Pilrig in Edinburgh (1844–68) led to his involvement in improving social conditions for workers and their families. He was elected FRSE in 1862. He was appointed Professor of Apologetics and Pastoral Theology at New College, Edinburgh. He was Moderator of the Free Church General Assembly in 1892. He wrote extensively and produced a famous biography of David Livingstone in 1880.[38]

(Rev.) Hugh Martin (1822–1885) attended the Grammar between 1831 and 1836, entering Class I, and then Marischal, where he was awarded the Gray bursary, the highest Mathematical award. He went on to study Divinity at King's and in 1844 he became minister in the Free Church at Carnoustie before moving to Free Greyfriars, Edinburgh, in 1858. He wrote extensively on theological matters.[39]

(Rev.) Hugh Mitchell (1822–1894) attended the Grammar between 1835 and 1837, entering Class IV, and then Marischal where he gained an MA in 1841. He became respected as a geologist and palaeontologist. He was minister of the Free Church, Ferryden, 1848–94.

Charles Fraser (1823–1886) attended the Grammar between 1833 and 1838, entering Class I, and then Marischal, before studying Divinity. He helped establish a Presbyterian ministry in Christchurch, New Zealand. He founded schools and edited and published church magazines.[40]

(Rev.) Robert Hunter (1823–1897) attended the Grammar between 1833 and 1837, entering Class II, and was Dux in his final year. He was also First Bursar in 1837 (from seventy-nine competitors) and then went on to Marischal. He later studied Divinity at Edinburgh and joined the Free Church mission in central India in 1847. On his return he preached Presbyterianism and produced a seven-volume dictionary. He frequently contributed to religious periodicals. His interest in Geology and collection of fossils led to him becoming a Fellow of the Geological Society.[41]

(Rev. Dr) Walter C. Smith (1824–1908) attended the Grammar between 1833 and 1837, entering Class I, and then Marischal. He studied for the ministry of the Free Church at New College and was ordained in London in 1850. Other ministries followed. He represented a liberalising tendency but was still judged orthodox enough to be entrusted with the moderatorship of the Free Church's jubilee General Assembly of 1893. His poetry enabled him to deal with religious issues better avoided in the pulpit.[42]

(Rev.) John Chalmers (1825–1899) attended the Grammar in 1843–4, entering Class V. He became a Protestant Christian missionary with the LMS during the Qing period. He published a number of books on the origins of China and in 1866 produced an English-Cantonese dictionary. He was minister of the Union Church in Hong Kong in 1879.

(Rev.) Andrew Murray (1828–1917) attended the Grammar between 1838 and 1841, entering Class II. He took a degree in Arts from Marischal in 1845 and went to Utrecht to study Theology. He returned to South Africa, where his parents lived, and became a pastor in various churches. He became a leader of the Dutch Reformed Church.

(Prof.) William R. Clark (1829–1912) attended the Grammar, King's and Hertford, Oxford, entering the Church of England. He became Dean of Taunton and Prebendary of Wells Cathedral, 1859–80. He was Professor of Mental and Moral Philosophy, at Trinity College, Toronto, until 1908. He was President of the Royal Society of Canada, 1899–1900.

(Very Rev. Dr) William Mair (1830–1920) attended the Grammar in 1843–4, entering Class IV, and then, after gaining FCH at King's, went on to study at Marischal. He was ordained a minister in 1853 and served in various parts of the country. He wrote on Church Law and was Moderator of the General Assembly of the Church of Scotland in 1897.[43]

(Very Rev.) James Mitchell (1830–1911) attended the Grammar between 1844 and 1846, and then Marischal. He was minister at Peterhead and South Leith and Moderator of the General Assembly of the Church of Scotland in 1901.

(Rev.) Andrew B. Davidson (1831–1902) attended the Grammar in 1844–5, entering Class IV with a bursary, and then Marischal, before studying Divinity at Edinburgh. He was ordained as a minister in the Free Church in 1856 and elected Professor of Hebrew and Oriental Languages at New College in 1863.[44]

(Rt Rev. Dr) Andrew J. Milne (1831–1906), attended the Grammar between 1844 and 1846, entering Class V, and King's College. He became a minister in 1855 and Head of the Collegiate School in Jamaica. He took over the ministry in Fyvie in 1870 and was Moderator of the General Assembly of the Church of Scotland in 1905.

(Rev.) John Brebner (1833–1902) attended the Grammar between 1845 and 1848, entering Class IV, and went on to become First Bursar to Marischal. He won the Town Council Gold Medal in 1852 for being top graduate in his year. He joined the GS staff in 1853 but was disappointed not to be made Rector in 1856. He left in 1861 to become Rector of Albert Academy in Cape Colony, which he built up. Between 1874 and 1899 he held the post of Superintendent of Education in the Orange Free State.

(Rev.) George Grimm (1833–1897) attended the Grammar in 1855–6, entering Class V, and gained an MA from Edinburgh University in 1861. He migrated to New South Wales where he practised as a Free Church minister. He proved a gifted academic tutor in Theology and published extensively.

(Rev.) John Gibb (1835–1915) attended the Grammar between 1848 and 1853, entering Class I, and then studied at Marischal and Heidelberg. He was a minister in Malta and became Professor of Ecclesiastical History at the Theological College of the Presbyterian Church of England in 1877. He was President of Westminster College, Cambridge from 1899.

William Dower (1837–1919) attended the Grammar and won a bursary to Edinburgh, where he studied Divinity and was ordained in 1865. He went as a missionary to South Africa. He helped the Griqua become established in Griqualand East but then saw a proud community crumble in the face of colonial rule.[45]

Thomas Gentles (1838–1910) came from Falkirk and attended the Grammar between 1851 and 1853, entering Class V. He graduated MA in 1857 and became a schoolteacher. He was minister of Trinity Church, Edinburgh between 1872 and 1878 and took his DD in 1891. He transferred to the Abbey Church, Paisley, where he ministered from 1878 to 1905, during which time he effected the restoration of the church building at a cost reputedly of £1 million.

(Rev. Prof.) Stewart D.F. Salmond (1838–1905) attended the Grammar between 1850 and 1853, entering Class II, and then Aberdeen and Erlangen Universities. He was Professor of Systematic Theology in the United Free Church from 1876 and Principal of New College from 1898. He wrote numerous religious works, the most influential being *The Christian Doctrine of Immortality* (1895) and was editor of the Critical Review. He was a member of the University Court, the Aberdeen School Board and was one of the original Honorary Vice-Presidents of the FP Club in 1893.

(Father) William Humphrey (1839–1910) attended the Grammar between 1849 and 1853, graduating from Marischal and then in Law from Edinburgh University. He was an advocate until 1870 when he became a priest in the Episcopal Church. He joined the Society of Jesus in 1874 and became a noted preacher and controversialist in London. He wrote extensively.

(Rev.) William L. Low (1840–1929) attended the Grammar between 1856 and 1858, entering Class IV, and qualified in Divinity from Aberdeen University in 1862. An Episcopalian, he was Rector of St Columba's, Largs; Synod Clerk of Glasgow and Galloway, 1889–1914; Canon of Cumbrae Cathedral, from 1890 and Canon of St Mary's Cathedral, Glasgow, from 1908. He wrote biographies and novels.

(Rev.) William L. Baxter (1841–1937) attended the Grammar between 1850 and 1855 and was Dux and Gold Medallist at the School in 1855. He took Divinity after achieving a FCH in Classics at King's in 1859. He was a minister in Aberdeenshire, Perthshire and Fife.

(Rev.) David Reith (1842–1909) attended the Grammar in 1857–8, entering Class IV, and Aberdeen University. He was ordained into the Church of England in 1868. He became Vicar (1874) and Dean (1886). In 1891 he became Honorary Canon of Rochester.

(Rev.) George Reith (1842–1919) attended the Grammar between 1854 and 1857, entering Class IV. He studied at Aberdeen, New College Edinburgh, and Erlangen Universities. He was Moderator of the General Assembly of the Free Church of Scotland in 1909 and the father of John Reith of BBC fame.

(Rev.) John Smith (1844–1905) attended the Grammar and Aberdeen University. He was ordained in 1873 and held ministries in North-East and South-East Scotland, before becoming minister of Broughton Place Church of the United Free Church. He was active on missionary and social questions and published on religious topics.

John Hector (1845–1934) attended the Grammar between 1858 and 1862, winning the Dux prize. He gained his MA in 1860 and his DD in 1884. He attended the United Free Church College in Calcutta. He was appointed Principal of Duff College in Calcutta, 1887–1902.

(Rev.) William S. Bruce (1846–1933) attended the Grammar in 1862–64, entering Class V, and then Aberdeen, Edinburgh and Tubingen Universities. He was ordained at Banff in 1873 and spent over fifty years in the ministry. He wrote extensively.

(Rev. Dr) James Shepherd (1847–1926) attended the Grammar between 1859 and 1864, entering Class I. In his final year he won the Silver Medal for Science and went to Aberdeen University with a Trades' Bursary, graduating MA in 1868. He determined to become medical missionary so he returned to University and graduated in Medicine in 1871. Simultaneously he attended Theological College and was licensed as a United Presbyterian minister. He spent most of his life in Rajputana in India. In 1909 his Mission treated over 50,000 cases and he was awarded the Kaisar-i-Hind medal for his work.

(Prof.) William L. Davidson (1848–1929) attended the Grammar in 1859–64, entering Class I, and Aberdeen University, graduating with FCH in Philosophy in 1868. He was minister of Bourtie from 1873 to 1896. On his appointment as Professor of Logic and Metaphysics at Aberdeen in 1895, the GS was given a half-day holiday. He retired in 1926. He was President of the FP Club, 1908–10. He published extensively.

(Prof.) William G. Elmslie (1848–1889) attended the Grammar between 1861 and 1864, entering Class IV. He had a brilliant career at Aberdeen University and gained FCH in Mathematics in 1868, winning the Town Council Gold Medal as the best student of the year. He studied at Edinburgh, London, Berlin and Paris. He became Professor of Hebrew at the English Presbyterian College in 1883. He wrote weekly for the *Expositor* and the *British Weekly.*

(Rev. Dr) Peter T. Forsyth (1848–1921) attended the Grammar from 1859 to 1864, entering Class I, before gaining FCH in Classical Literature in 1869 from Aberdeen University. He was ordained a Congregational minister in 1876 and for twenty-five years held a series of appointments. In 1901 he was made Principal of Hackney Theological College and in 1905 chairman of the Congregational Union of England and Wales. He was the greatest Congregational theologian of his day.[46]

Venerable James B. Craven (1850–1924) attended the Grammar in 1862–3, entering Class II. He was ordained in 1875 and became Curate of St Andrew, Aberdeen. He was Rector of St Olaf, Kirkwall, 1875–1914, and Archdeacon of Orkney in the Scottish Episcopalian Church, 1913–24.

Military

Andrew Leith Hay (1758–1838) of Leith Hall was in attendance in the Grammar in 1771. He had been appointed a lieutenant immediately on birth, captain in 1768 and colonel in the army in 1794. He had reached the rank of full general just before his death in 1838. He was DL and JP for the county of Aberdeenshire.[47]

(Sir) James McGrigor (1771–1858; Baronet 1831) attended the Grammar, becoming Dux in 1784, and graduated MA from Marischal in 1788 before studying Medicine in Aberdeen and Edinburgh. He joined the army in 1793 and his career took him to Europe, West Indies, Ceylon and Egypt. In 1805 he became an Inspector-General of Hospitals working in northern and then southern England. In 1811 he was appointed Chief of the Medical Staff of the Peninsular Army under Wellington and it was there that he made his name as a medical director of the first rank. In 1815 McGrigor became Director-General of the Army Medical Department, a post he held until 1851, with the rank of Major-General. He carried through reforms of major significance which laid the foundation of the British Army Medical Corps. He was elected FRSE in 1805 and FRS in 1816, received the Freedom of Edinburgh and Aberdeen, and was elected Rector of Marischal in 1826, 1827 and 1841. A memorial obelisk to him was erected in Marischal quadrangle,[48] and is now to be found in Duthie Park.

(Capt.) William Gordon Cumming Skene of Pitlurg, Dyce and Parkhill (1784–1836) attended the Grammar between 1796 and 1798. Following in his father's footsteps he became a professional soldier and saw action in the Peninsular War and France.

(Capt.) James U.M. Leith (1785–1814) attended the Grammar between 1795 and 1798, going from Class IV to Marischal as First Bursar. He joined the 68th Foot Regiment as Ensign in 1804 and fought throughout the Peninsular War, reaching the rank of captain. He was killed towards the end of the War in France at the battle of Oergrequam.

(Admiral Sir) Arthur Farquhar (1815–1908; KCB 1886) attended the Grammar between 1825 and 1828, entering Class V, and joined the RN in 1829. He was promoted to lieutenant in 1840 and Admiral in 1866. He was Commander-in-Chief, Pacific Station in 1869, and C-in-C, Plymouth, in 1878.[49]

James A. Grant (1827–1892) attended the Grammar between 1838 and 1840, entering Class I, and then Marischal. He accepted a commission and served in the Second Anglo-Sikh War and the Indian Mutiny. He joined John Hanning Speke, a fellow Indian army officer, in the Royal Geographical Society expedition to find the source of the Nile. Grant's visual record of the journey can be found in the National Library of Scotland. He shared in the fame receiving the RGS Gold Medal in 1864. Grant continued his successful military career which confirmed him as a considerable figure.[50]

(Lt Col.) Francis Gellie (1834–1892) from King-Edward attended the Grammar between 1850 and 1852, entering Class V, and graduated MA in 1856. He joined the army and retired with the rank of Lieutenant Colonel in 1886. He saw active service during the Indian Mutiny (1857), the Bhutan campaign of 1865–6 and the Afghan War in 1879.

(Col.) Francis Duncan (1836–1888) attended the Grammar between 1849 and 1851, entering Class IV, and then Marischal. He was commissioned Lieutenant in the RA and served in British North America. In 1871 he was appointed Superintendent of regimental records at Woolwich and he wrote a number of works including a history of the artillery regiment. In 1881 he became a Lieutenant-Colonel and then, after action in Egypt, a Colonel in 1885. He was elected Conservative MP for the Holborn Division of Finsbury in 1885, holding the seat till his death.[51]

(Col. Sir) William Green (1836–1897; KCB 1884) attended the Grammar in 1851–2, joining Class V. He enlisted in the army in 1855 and saw action in the Crimean War, the Indian Mutiny, the Ashanti campaign, the Egyptian War of 1882 and the Sudan expedition of 1884. He retired in 1893. He was a DL and JP for the County of Banff.

(Brigade Surg.) William L. Center (1838–1900) attended the Grammar between 1850 and 1852, entering Class V. He graduated at King's with an MA in 1856 and a degree in Medicine in 1865. He joined the Indian Medical Service in Lahore, retiring in 1893.

(Surg.-Maj.) Peter Shepherd (1841–1879) attended the Grammar in 1857–8, entering Class III, before studying Medicine at Aberdeen University. He joined the RAMC in 1864 and served in South Africa, Ireland and India. Back home he joined with another GS former pupil, Colonel Francis Duncan, in developing the teaching of First Aid skills to civilians. His notes were later published by another GS former pupil, Lt General James Cantlie, and they became the manual for the recently formed St John Ambulance Service. He was killed at Isandlwana in the Zulu Wars while tending the wounded. A memorial was placed in the Leochel Cushnie Church (his birthplace) and a Shepherd Gold Medal is an annual surgical prize at Aberdeen University.

Andrew W. Baird (1842–1908) attended the Grammar between 1853 and 1857, entering Class I, and then Marischal. He took a commission in the Royal Engineers and served in India and Abyssinia. He was part of the survey of India and concentrated on tidal observations. His success led to an extended survey to cover the coast from Aden to Rangoon. The wave that followed the volcanic eruption of Krakatoa, Java, was traced in all his tidal diagrams and he was elected FRS. He was the author of many papers on tidal observations and surveying.[52]

(Lt Col. Sir) Alexander B. McHardy (1842–1917; KCB 1911) attended the

Grammar between 1853 and 1857, entering Class I. He was chair of the Prison Commission of Scotland, 1896–1909.

(Col. Sir) William S.S. Bisset (1843–1916; KCIE 1897) attended the Grammar in 1854–5, entering Class IV. He joined the RE in 1863 and was promoted to Colonel in 1895. He was decorated in the Afghan War. He was consulting engineer for railways mainly in central India till 1893. He was Secretary to the Government of India in Public Works, 1893–7 and Director of Indian Railways, 1897–1901.

Richard G. Brown (1845–1932) attended the Grammar between 1859 and 1861, entering Class IV, before graduating in Medicine at Aberdeen University in 1869. He joined the medical service of the RN (1871) and retired from the service with the rank of Deputy Inspector-General of Hospitals and Fleets in 1900.

(Maj. Gen. Sir) Alexander J.F. Reid (1846–1913; KCB 1900), attended the Grammar between 1859 and 1861, entering Class IV, and Aberdeen University. He joined the Indian Army and served in the Afghan War (1878–80). He also saw action on the North-West frontier of India and as part of the Chinese Expeditionary Force in 1900–1. He was DL for the County of the City of Aberdeen. Throughout his military service he continued to send cultural artefacts back to his brother, Robert Reid, Professor of Anatomy at Aberdeen University and founder of the Anthropological Museum. He was buried at the Old Kirk at Glenbuchat.

Medical

Alexander Gordon (1752–1799) probably attended the Grammar before going on to Marischal, graduating MA in 1775. He then studied Medicine at Aberdeen, Edinburgh and Leiden Universities. He joined the RN, becoming a Surgeon in 1782. He worked in London before returning to Aberdeen, which experienced an epidemic of puerperal fever, 1789–92. He found that the disease was contagious and could be carried from patient to patient by doctors and midwives. His *Treatise* of 1795 was only recognised as a masterpiece of epidemiology a century later.[53] A commemorative plaque can be found at 17 Belmont Street.

James Gregory (1753–1821) attended the Grammar and King's before studying Medicine at Edinburgh, Leiden and Paris. In 1776 he was elected Professor of the Institutes of Medicine in Edinburgh and was effectively head of the Medical Faculty. He produced a leading textbook in 1788, which was also the standard work for examination in medical Latin. He became

Professor of the Practice of Physic in 1790. He proved to be a superb lecturer. His name lived on well into the modern era with his powder which acted as an antacid, stomachic and cathartic. Gregory was a founding fellow of the RSE (1783), was appointed first physician to George III and George IV in Scotland, and was given a public funeral by the Corporation of Edinburgh.[54]

(Prof.) George French (1765–1833) attended the Grammar and Marischal between 1764 and 1768, graduating MA. He gained his MD in 1786. He practised as a Physician until his appointment as Professor of Chemistry at Marischal in 1793. He held this post for forty years.

Alexander F. Henderson (1779/80–1863) attended the Grammar between 1790 and 1794, where he was a prize-winner in Classics, and Marischal, before graduating MD from Edinburgh in 1803. His membership of the Royal College of Physicians in London led to him establishing his practice in Mayfair. He wrote on medicine and wines, and proved an improving landlord on his estate at Caskieburn in Aberdeenshire. He was also a local benefactor leaving money for housing for the labouring classes, endowing a chair in Medicine at Marischal and supporting industrial schools in Aberdeen. He left his library of over three thousand books and his collection of paintings, sculpture and antiquities to Aberdeen University.[55]

John Abercrombie (1780–1844) attended the Grammar and Marischal, before taking a medical degree at Edinburgh in 1803. He went into general practice giving up much time to the poor of Edinburgh. He also had published papers on pathological subjects. He became a Fellow of the RCP in 1824 and was appointed King's Physician for Scotland in 1828. He gradually established himself as the leading physician in the capital. He was elected Rector of Marischal in 1835 and was Vice-President of the RSE, 1835–44.

(Sir) John Forbes (1787–1861) attended Fordyce School before winning a Smith bursary to the Grammar which he attended in 1802–3, entering Class V. He then spent two years at Marischal, 1803–5. During the Napoleonic Wars he joined the Royal Navy and trained as a Surgeon, which he turned into an MD as a mature student when peace came. He began general practice first in Cornwall and then in Chichester, publishing on a wide range of medical issues, which led to his election as FRS. He edited a quarterly medical review, a new venture in medical journalism, and moved to Westminster in 1840. He was appointed Physician to Prince Albert and the royal household and became a Fellow of the RCP. He promoted a hospital for sick children at Great Ormond Street and left his library to Marischal.[56]

Neil Arnott (1788–1874) attended the Grammar between 1798 and 1801, entering Class I, and graduated from Marischal in 1805. His studies in Medicine led to the award of an MD from Marischal in 1814. He published the popular *Elements of Physics* in 1827, was a founder of London University, appointed Physician to Queen Victoria, and elected FRS in 1838. His most significant contribution was as 'part-shaper and highly effective disseminator of the Chadwickian or miasmatic theory of disease'. Neil Arnott prizes were later introduced by both Aberdeen and London Universities.[57]

(Dr) William Henderson (1792–1877) attended the Grammar between 1800 and 1805, graduating MA at Marischal in 1809 and in Medicine from Edinburgh in 1823. From 1818–48 he lectured in Materia Medica at Marischal, and in 1843 he was a member of the first General Assembly of the Free Church. He wrote the Second Statistical Account of Aberdeen and founded Henderson bursaries in Medicine at Aberdeen University.

Francis Adams (1796–1861) attended the Grammar and King's, graduating with an MA in Classics. He then studied Medicine and became a member of the Royal College of Surgeons, London. He spent most of his life practising in Banchory-Ternan and translating Greek texts on Medicine and Philology.

(Dr) William Leith (1802–1842) attended the Grammar between 1810 and 1815, entering Class I, before graduating MA from Marischal in 1819. He gained his diploma from the RCSE in 1823 and was the Evangelical minister of the South parish in Aberdeen from 1828, practising both professions concurrently.

(Prof.) Francis Ogston (1803–1887) attended the Grammar between 1813 and 1816, entering Class II, before proceeding to Marischal and completing his medical course at Edinburgh in 1824. In 1831 he was appointed city police surgeon and in 1839 the first lecturer in Medical Jurisprudence at Marischal. He became the first holder of the chair of Medical Jurisprudence and Medical Logic in 1857, which he held until retiring in 1883. He was appointed Aberdeen's first MOH in 1862, again retaining the post until retirement. Ogston was chosen Dean of the Faculty of Medicine.[58]

James Matthews Duncan (1826–1890) attended the Grammar between 1834 and 1839, entering Class I, and then Marischal. He studied Medicine and became James Young Simpson's assistant, taking part in the famous experiment which established the anaesthetic property of chloroform in 1847. He established a reputation as one of the leading obstetricians of his day. He was instrumental in founding the Edinburgh Sick Children's Hospital in 1860. He became a fellow of the RCPE, and the RSE in 1863. He accepted the posts of lecturer on Midwifery and Obstetric Physician to

St Bartholomew's Hospital in London. He became a fellow of the RCP and the RS. He contributed to medical journals and in 1866 produced the influential work on *Fecundity, Fertility and Sterility.*[59]

(Dr) Thomas Keith (1827–1895) attended the Grammar between 1840 and 1842, entering Class IV, and Marischal. He became medical apprentice to Sir James Young Simpson, being part of the team which pioneered the use of chloroform as an anaesthetic. He was also an early exponent of Joseph Lister's antiseptic procedures.

(Surg.-Gen. Sir) Colvin Colvin-Smith (1829–1913; KCB 1903) attended the Grammar and King's, qualifying in Medicine. He entered the Madras Army in 1851, serving in the Indian Mutiny. He was principal MO with the Indian contingent in the Egyptian campaign, 1882. He was Honorary Surgeon to Victoria and Edward VII.

(Surg.-Gen.) George Bidie (1830–1913) attended the Grammar between 1845 and 1847, entering Class V, and qualified in Medicine at Aberdeen. He became President of the Medical Faculty at Madras University, and Professor of Botany and Materia Medica there. He was Honorary Surgeon to the Viceroy of India (1887), Victoria (1898), Edward VII (1901) and George V (1910).

(Deputy Surg.-Gen.) William Walker (1832–93) attended the Grammar between 1844 and 1849, entering Class I. He graduated with an MA from Marischal in 1853 and an MD in 1855. He was an Assistant Surgeon in the Bengal Medical Service and saw service in the Indian Mutiny of 1857. He became Deputy-Surgeon General (= Colonel) in 1882. He was appointed Honorary Physician to Queen Victoria in 1890.

William Bruce (1835–1920) attended the Grammar between 1846 and 1851, and then graduated in Arts (1855) and Medicine (1858) at Aberdeen University. He practised at Crimond and founded the second cottage hospital in Scotland. He became MOH for Ross and Cromarty. He was the direct representative for Scotland in the General Medical Council, 1887–1907.

(Sir) James Mackie (1838–1898; KCMG) attended the Grammar between 1852 and 1854, entering Class IV, and then Marischal, where he studied Medicine. He was appointed Surgeon to HM's Consulate at Alexandria in 1868. He represented Britain at the Egyptian Quarantine Board. He was decorated after seeing action in Egypt in 1882 and was British representative at the International Sanitary Conference at Venice.

James A.S. Grant (1840–1895) attended the Grammar in 1856–7, entering Class V, and then studied Medicine at Aberdeen University. He migrated to Egypt to help fight a cholera epidemic. His success led to his title of 'Bey' (sort of knighthood) from the Khedive. He developed an interest in Egyptology and explored the Great Pyramid. He built up an extensive private collection of ancient Egyptian artefacts, many of which were donated to the Marischal Museum.

Thomas I. Rowell (1840–1932) attended the Grammar in 1854–5, entering Class V. First Bursar at King's he graduated in Medicine in 1863. Thereafter he was double Gold Medallist at Edinburgh Extramural Medical School, and continued his studies in Paris, Vienna, Berlin and Prague. In 1877 he was appointed principal civil MO of Singapore by the Colonial Office and in 1890 he became President of the Municipality of Singapore.

(Prof. Sir) David Ferrier (1843–1928; Kt 1911) attended the Grammar from 1854 to 1858, entering Class I, and then King's, where he gained FCH in Classics and Philosophy in 1863 and won the Ferguson Scholarship (Classical and Philosophical).[60] He studied Medicine at Edinburgh and began his long service with King's College, London, in 1871. He became Professor of Forensic Medicine the following year, retaining the post until 1889 when the chair of Neuropathology was specially created for him. His systematic brain research led to surgery to an extent not hitherto attempted and the claim that modern cerebral surgery was primarily due to Ferrier. He wrought a great change in cerebral diagnosis and treatment.[61] He was elected FRS in 1876 and FRSE in 1900. He was one of the original Honorary Vice-Presidents of the FP club in 1893.

(Dr) Duncan MacGregor (1843–1906) attended the Grammar in 1861–2, entering Class V, before winning Fullerton, Moir, Gray and Ferguson scholarships. He completed his MA at Aberdeen University and graduated in Medicine from Edinburgh University in 1870. He was then invited to fill the inaugural chair in Mental and Moral Philosophy at Otago University. In 1882 he became Inspector-General of Hospitals in New Zealand.

David Nicolson (1844–1932) attended the Grammar from 1856 to 1860, entering Class I, and Aberdeen University, completing a Medical degree. He worked as a Surgeon and MO in hospitals and asylums. He was the Lord Chancellor's Visitor in Lunacy, 1896–1921. He contributed numerous articles in medical journals on crime, criminals and criminal lunacy.

(Sir) Alexander Ogston (1844–1929; KCVO 1912) attended the Grammar 1855–8, entering Class I, and Marischal, where he graduated in Medicine, after spells in Prague, Vienna, Berlin and Paris. He was joint MOH for Aberdeen, 1868–72, and senior Surgeon at Aberdeen Royal Infirmary. He was Professor of Surgery at Aberdeen University, 1882–1909, and pioneered bacteriological research, discovering the staphylococcus aureus. He served in Egypt, the Boer War and the First World War and was influential in the establishment of the RAMC in 1898. He was Surgeon-in-Ordinary in Scotland to Victoria, Edward VII and George V.[62]

J.C. Ogilvie Will (1844–1922) attended the Grammar between 1856 and 1860, entering Class I. He qualified in Medicine from Aberdeen University in 1866 and was Assistant to Sir James Young Simpson in Edinburgh. He was Surgeon at the ARI and assistant professor and examiner in surgery at Aberdeen University. He produced numerous publications. He was one of the original Honorary Vice-Presidents of the FP Club in 1893.

John M. Bruce (1846–1929) attended the Grammar in 1861–2, entering Class V, and Aberdeen, London and Vienna Universities. He worked as a Surgeon in hospitals at home and abroad. He taught Physiology and Pathology, then Materia Medica and Medicine. He became Dean of School at Charing Cross Hospital and published extensively in medical journals.

(Surg.-Gen.) David Sinclair (1847–1919), attended the Grammar between 1859 and 1863, entering Class II. He went on to gain a Medical degree from Aberdeen University. He joined the Indian Medical Service as a Surgeon and was decorated for his service in Burma.

(Dr) Robert R. Alexander (1848–1914) attended the Grammar between 1858 and 1864, entering Class I. He qualified in Medicine from Aberdeen University in 1869 and worked in lunatic asylums in Aberdeen and Buckinghamshire. He was superintendent of the London County Lunatic Asylum, 1888–1905.

(Sir) James Cantlie [Cantley] (1851–1926; KBE 1919) attended the Grammar briefly in 1856–7, entering Class I. He took his first degree at King's in Medicine and by 1877 he was a Fellow of the Royal College of Surgeons. He was a Surgeon at Charing Cross Hospital, London, a pioneer in First Aid and influential in the study of Tropical Diseases. He was instrumental in the founding of the University of Hong Kong and the London School of Tropical Medicine.

Legal

John Burnett (1764–1810) attended the Grammar between 1775 and 1777 and was admitted Advocate in Edinburgh in 1785. He was appointed Advocate-Depute, 1792, Sheriff of East Lothian, 1803 and Judge-Admiral of Scotland, 1810. He was also sometime counsel for Aberdeen City. He produced *The Criminal Law of Scotland* (1811).

Hugh Lumsden (1783–1859) of Pitcaple attended the Grammar between 1791 and 1796 and was Dux in his final year. He joined the Faculty of Advocates in 1806 and was Sheriff of Sutherlandshire in 1827.

Andrew Skene (1784–1835) attended the Grammar and Marischal before studying Law at Edinburgh University. He became an Advocate in 1806. He succeeded Lord Cockburn in 1834 as Solicitor-General for Scotland, but held office only for a few days, when the Ministry resigned.

James Blaikie (1786–1836) attended the Grammar between 1795 and 1799, entering Class II, and Marischal, graduating MA in 1803. He became an Advocate and Lord Provost of Aberdeen, 1833–6, dying suddenly in the Town House in 1836.

(Sir) Alexander Anderson (1802–87) attended the Grammar in 1814–15, entering Class V, and Marischal, graduating MA in 1819. He was admitted to the Society of Advocates in 1827, and was involved in insurance and banking and promoting railways. As Lord Provost of Aberdeen, 1859–65, he developed new waterworks, inaugurated the new site for the GS and the new Town House. He promoted feuing of his lands at Rubislaw and Torry. 'He made the modern Aberdeen.'[63] A commemorative plaque can be found on the North Pier.[64]

Francis Edmond (1805–1892) attended the Grammar between 1814 and 1819, entering Class I, and became an Advocate in 1829. He was a founding partner of Edmond and McQueen, advocates, in 1850; the firm evolved into Ledingham Chalmers in 1991. He was legal adviser to his Alma Mater (Aberdeen University) for over half a century. He was instrumental in securing Melvin's book collection for Aberdeen and added to it in 1884. His gifts to the University and charities were reputed to have amounted to more than £100,000.

(Dr) John Hill Burton (1809–1881) attended the Grammar between 1819 and 1823, entering Class I, and then gained a bursary to Marischal, where he studied Law. He qualified for the Bar in Edinburgh. He wrote widely for journals especially on Philosophy, Political Economy and History. He was Secretary of the Scottish Prison Board, 1854–77 and Historiographer-Royal, 1867–81. He edited the first volumes of the *Register of the Privy Council*.[65]

John Webster of Edgehill (1810–1891) attended the Grammar and Marischal and joined the Society of Advocates in 1831. He was in partnership with his father and then his son. He proved a successful businessman with the Aberdeen Gas Company and the Aberdeen Music Hall Company. He was a strong supporter of the proposed merger of King's and Marischal. He became a Liberal MP in 1880, turning Liberal Unionist in 1881.

John D. Milne (1822–1889) attended the Grammar between 1831 and 1836, entering Class I, and qualified as a lawyer. Throughout his life he campaigned for women's rights. He served as City Assessor, Secretary of the Aberdeen Philosophical Society and was a member of the University Court.[66]

Middleton Rettie (1827–1910) attended the Grammar between 1839 and 1843, entering Class I, then Aberdeen and Edinburgh Universities. He was called to the Scottish Bar in 1855, and edited Law Reports of the Court of Session and House of Lords.

Henry Smith (1829–1910) attended the Grammar between 1837 and 1841, entering Class I, then graduating from Marischal in 1845 and becoming a WS in 1852. He was called to the Bar in 1857 and from 1874 and 1885 he was Sheriff-Substitute of Renfrewshire. He was Liberal MP for Falkirk Burghs, 1892–5.

Alexander Bruce (1836–1920) attended the Grammar in 1849–50, entering Class IV, and then Marischal. He was called to the Bar in Canada in 1861 and became a KC in 1885.

(Rt Hon. Sir) James Stirling (1836–1916; Kt 1886) attended the Grammar from 1846–7 and 1848–51, entering Class I, and becoming School Dux and Silver Medallist[67] in 1851. He went on to King's, where he showed marked ability in Mathematics. Proceeding to Trinity, Cambridge, he was Senior Wrangler and first Smith's prizeman in 1860. He was called to the Bar in 1862 and appointed a Judge in 1886. He was promoted to the Court of Appeal in 1900. In retirement his interest in Science led to his election as a Vice-President of the RS.[68] He was one of the original Honorary Vice-Presidents of the FP Club in 1893.

John Forbes (1838–1904) attended the Grammar from 1849 to 1854, entering Class I, and then Marischal. He was called to the English Bar in 1862. He became a QC in 1881 and was Recorder of Kingston-upon-Thames from 1887.

David Littlejohn (1841–1924) attended the Grammar between 1850 and 1854, entering Class I. He qualified as a lawyer from Aberdeen University and became an Advocate. He was Sheriff-Clerk in Aberdeenshire Sheriff Court, 1909–20. He edited the Records of the Aberdeenshire Sheriff Court in three volumes for the New Spalding Club, 1904–7.

(Sir) John Macdonell (1846–1921; Kt 1903; KCB 1914) attended the Grammar in 1860 1, entering Class V, before going to Aberdeen University after the Union of King's and Marischal, graduating with honours in Classics in 1865. He was an English master at the GS before being called to the English Bar in 1873. He wrote on Political Economy for leading newspapers. In 1889 he was made Master of the Supreme Court and held the chair of Comparative Law at University College, London from 1901 to 1920. He became first Dean of its Law Faculty. As a jurist, he was involved in government inquiries and commissions on Divorce, Shipping and First World War crimes. He was President of the Grotius Society and a Fellow of the British Academy. He frequently contributed to numerous periodicals.[69]

James Duguid (1849–1917) attended the Grammar between 1860 and 1863, entering Class III. Following a degree in Arts he qualified in Law and became an Advocate. He took a lectureship in Conveyancing at Aberdeen University in 1895 and the following year he became Sheriff-Substitute of Aberdeen, Kincardine and Banff.

Robert McK. Routledge (1851–1907) attended the Grammar between 1864 and 1869, entering Class I. He was called to the Bar in 1879. He was a colonial Judge in the Falklands, 1891–4 and Chief Judge of the West Indies, 1901–6.

Academic

Andrew Mackay (1758–1809) attended the Grammar but was self-taught thereafter. Nonetheless he was awarded degrees by Marischal and King's and was elected Fellow of the RSE in 1793. He corrected the latitude of Aberdeen, estimated its longitude and rated chronometers. He opened a naval academy in Aberdeen and was Superintendent of its Harbour and Keeper of Marischal's Observatory on Castle Hill. He taught in London and was the Examiner in Mathematics for the East India Company, Trinity House and Christ's Hospital. He published numerous works on Navigation, Astronomy and Mathematics.[70]

Alexander Crombie (1760–1840) attended the Grammar in 1774, when he became Second Bursar, and Marischal, where he graduated MA in 1778 and LLD in 1794. Although he qualified as a Presbyterian minister he became famous as a Schoolmaster. He ran a successful school in England and published extensively especially on language rules aimed at helping Classical scholars to produce a good Latin prose style.[71]

James H. Beattie (1768–1790) attended the Grammar from 1774/5 until 1781 and then Marischal, where his father was Professor of Moral Philosophy. After extensive canvassing by his father, Beattie was admitted assistant and successor to him in 1787. His early death, however, in 1790 and publication of his substantial collection of essays and poems led to him becoming more widely known.[72]

William Knight (1786–1844) attended the Grammar and Marischal, graduating MA in 1802. He was elected to the Professorship of Natural Philosophy at Belfast in 1816 and published his chief work on Geological subjects in 1818. He returned to Aberdeen when he was appointed Professor of Natural Philosophy at Marischal in 1822[73] and remained until his death. He published extensively.

(Dr) Alexander Nicoll (1793–1828) attended the Grammar in 1805 and Marischal, which he entered on a bursary. He was awarded the silver pen as the best Greek scholar in 1806. He moved to Balliol, Oxford on a Snell Exhibition and graduated BA in 1811. His linguistic ability led to his appointment as a Sub-Librarian in the Bodleian Library and he made his name by cataloguing its 30,000 oriental manuscripts. In 1822 he was appointed Professor of Hebrew at Oxford. It was said of him that he could travel to the Great Wall of China without the need for an interpreter.[74]

James Melvin (1795–1853; Rector 1826–53) was born of poor parents in the Gallowgate and attended the Grammar during Cromar's rectorship. He succeeded Cromar as Rector in 1826 as a result of competitive examination. He also became a lecturer in Humanity (Latin) at Marischal. His scholarship which inspired his pupils led to comparisons with Thomas Arnold in England. He produced a Latin Grammar and his *Latin Exercises* were published. In 1853 he was presented with a testimonial in the shape of £300 in a silver snuff-box. He is seen as probably the most accomplished Scottish Latinist of his day.[75] One of the modern School Houses is named after him.

William MacGillivray (1796–1852) attended the Grammar in 1811 and King's. He was a Curator of Natural History and published on the topic. He was influential on Ornithology in Britain and America. For a decade he was Conservator of the Museum of the Royal College of Surgeons in Edinburgh. In 1841 he became Professor of Natural History at Marischal and continued writing on birds, fish and mammals at an extraordinary pace.[76] A commemorative plaque can be found at 110 High Street, Old Aberdeen.

John Rae (1796–1872) attended the Grammar between 1807 and 1809, entering Class I and gained an MA from Marischal in 1815. He migrated to Canada in 1822. He produced a brilliant book on Political Economy in 1834, which initially was not well received but after the endorsement of John Stuart Mill it was accepted as a major contribution especially on the topic of the accumulation of capital. In the meantime he became a Headmaster of a grammar school in Hamilton.

(Prof.) Forbes Falconer (1805–1853) attended the Grammar between 1815 and 1820, entering Class I, and becoming Dux in his final year. He then proceeded to Marischal, where he obtained prizes in Classical Studies. He began studying Oriental Languages, continuing to do so in Paris for five years. He became Professor of Oriental Languages in University College, London and published a number of translations and critical studies.[77]

Hugh Falconer (1808–1865) attended the Grammar and studied Botany and Geology at Aberdeen and Edinburgh Universities. He worked in the Museum of the Asiatic Society of Bengal and as a Palaeontologist and Naturalist he was elected FRS in 1845. He became Professor of Botany at Calcutta Medical College and Superintendent of the Royal Botanic Garden, Calcutta. His home town of Forres commemorates Hugh and his brother, Alexander, in the Falconer Museum.[78]

John S. Blackie (1809–1895) attended the Grammar[79] and Marischal, where he studied Greek. He was admitted to the Faculty of Advocates in 1834, the year he published a translation of *Faust.* He was appointed to the chair of Humanity in Marischal in 1839, and then in 1852 became Professor of Greek at Edinburgh. He was elected a member of the RSE in 1853. He published a substantial translation and commentary on the *Iliad.* He raised the funds for the setting up of a chair of Celtic. He became fired with enthusiasm for Gaelic. He continued to publish widely on Greek, Scottish, religious, philosophical and political topics. On his death *The Scotsman* devoted nearly a whole page to his obituary.[80]

(Prof.) William Spalding (1809–1859) attended the Grammar between 1819 and 1823, entering Class I, and becoming Dux in his final year. He went on to Marischal and, in 1830, Edinburgh University. He was called to the Bar in 1833. He was Professor of Rhetoric at Edinburgh, 1840–5, and from 1845 until his death he was Professor of Logic at St Andrews. He published extensively in the *Edinburgh Review* and *Blackwood's Magazine.*

Andrew Findlater (1810–1885) attended the Grammar in 1827–8, entering Class V, and graduated from Marischal in 1828 as the most distinguished graduate of the year and won the Gray Mathematical bursary. He qualified in Divinity but remained a teacher at Merchiston Academy and became the Headmaster of Gordon's Hospital, a post he held from 1842 to 1849. In 1853 he began work with the publishing firm of Messrs Chambers of Edinburgh and as lexicographical editor he oversaw their encyclopedias and etymological dictionaries.[81]

Joseph Robertson (1810–1866) was born at No. 37 Woolmanhill and attended the Grammar in 1818-9, entering Class I, and then Marischal. He wrote articles in journals which evinced his Toryism and his topographical and antiquarian skills. He founded the Spalding Club, which published historical records relating to the north-east of Scotland. He was appointed Superintendent of the Literary and Antiquarian Department of Register House in Edinburgh in 1853. He became Vice-President of the Society of Antiquaries of Scotland.[82]

George Dickie (1812–1882) attended the Grammar between 1821 and 1826, entering Class I, and then Marischal, going on to study Medicine at Edinburgh. Although a local doctor his passion was Field Botany. He was appointed a lecturer in Botany in 1839 and the following year a lecturer in Materia Medica at King's. He was college Librarian and in 1849 became Professor of Natural History at Queens College, Belfast. He returned to Aberdeen as Professor of Botany in 1860 and was elected FRS in 1881.[83]

James Legge (1815–1897) attended the Grammar in 1829–30, entering Class V, and was First Bursar at King's, where he gained highest honours as the Hutton prizeman of 1835. He studied Divinity and learned Chinese to become a Missionary. As an accomplished missionary-scholar he translated twelve volumes of Chinese classics into English, the greatest single achievement of Western Sinological scholarship during the nineteenth century. He was appointed to the chair of Chinese at Oxford University in 1876. He published widely in his final years.[84]

Charles E. Wilson (1815–1888) attended the Grammar and then gained an MA from Aberdeen University. He was Classics master at Glasgow Academy, 1848–52. He joined HMI in 1852 and became a Chief Inspector in 1874. He was elected FRSE in 1877.

(Prof.) Alexander Bain (1818–1903), philosopher and educationist, attended the Grammar in 1835–6, entering Class V,[85] and Marischal, where he was educated in the Philosophy of Reid and Beattie. He proved a revolutionary figure in establishing education as a science and applying the scientific method to Psychology. From 1860 he was Professor of Logic at Aberdeen University, where he also held professorships in Moral Philosophy and English Literature. He produced several Grammar textbooks which were used extensively in Scottish schools. He was twice elected Rector of the University. He was one of the original Honorary Vice-Presidents of the FP Club in 1893.

(Prof.) George Ogilvie-Forbes of Boyndlie (1820–1886) attended the Grammar between 1831 and 1834, entering Class III, and becoming First Bursar in 1834. He became a lecturer on Physiology at Marischal and on the Fusion of the universities in 1860 he became Professor of Medicine at Aberdeen University until retirement in 1877.

David Grant (1823–1886) attended the Grammar and Marischal, where he took no degree. He taught in a number of Scottish schools before becoming a French teacher at Oundle, Northamptonshire. He later taught in private academies. He wrote on educational matters for newspapers and periodicals and published humorous tales written in the Scottish vernacular.[86]

George Ogilvie (1825–1914) attended the Grammar in 1843–4, entering Class V and then Marischal, where he gained a distinction in Mathematics. He taught at Dyce, Dunnottar and Turriff before his appointment as Head and House-Governor of Stewart's Hospital in 1856. He was the first Principal of the reformed George Watson's in 1870 which under his leadership became the model for all other secondary schools.

(Dr) James Macdonald (1826–1900) attended the Grammar in 1843–4, entering Class V. He was the First Bursar at King's in 1845. He was English master at Elgin Academy (1849) and then held the post of Rector in Ayr Academy (1862) and Kelvinside Academy (1883–95).

(Prof.) Andrew L. Adams (1827–1882) attended the Grammar in 1841–2, entering Class V. He became an army Surgeon, retiring in 1873. He was then appointed Professor of Zoology in Dublin and in 1878 became Professor of Natural History at Queen's, Cork. He was elected FRS in 1872. He published extensively.

John F. Watson (1827–1892) attended the Grammar in 1842–3, entering Class V, and graduated with an MA and MD from King's in 1847. He completed his education in London and Paris. He worked as an assistant surgeon in the Bengal Army Medical Service. He sought to encourage trade between Britain and India and he became an expert on India, producing an extensive ethnographic survey of India.[87]

Thomas F. Jamieson (1829–1913) attended the Grammar between 1838 and 1843, entering Class I. He then went on to Marischal. He corresponded with Sir Roderick Murchison and Charles Darwin. He was elected a Fellow of the Geological Society of London. His Geological studies provided evidence for the then fledgling theory of ice ages and his views only became fully acceptable in recent times.

(Sir) James Donaldson (1831–1915; Kt 1907) attended the Grammar between 1842 and 1846, entering Class I, and then Marischal. He became Assistant to the Professor of Greek at Edinburgh, Blackie. After two years (1854–56) as Rector of Stirling HS, he moved to Edinburgh High School where he was a Classics master for ten years and Rector from 1866 to 1882. During this period he made a major contribution to scholarship. He was elected FRSE in 1867. In 1882 he became Professor of Humanity at

Aberdeen University. In 1896 he became Principal of St Andrews University in which post he proved effective and forceful.[88]

Robert Machray (1831–1904) attended the Grammar in 1846–7, entering Class V and then King's from 1847 until 1851. He was Dean of Sidney Sussex College, Cambridge, 1859–65, and Archbishop of Rupert's Land in Canada. He founded the University of Manitoba, where he was Chancellor and became first Primate of the Church of England in Canada, 1893–1904.[89]

Joseph Ogilvie (1832–1914) attended the Grammar in 1851–2, entering Class V, before graduating in Classics at Marischal. He taught at Turriff and Methlick becoming Headmaster of Keith parish school. He was the first Rector of Aberdeen Training College in 1873 and the first lecturer in Education at Aberdeen University in 1893.

Robert Ogilvie (1833–1899) attended the Grammar in 1851–2, entering Class V, and Marischal. He was Rector of Milne's Institution between 1860 and 1868 (taking over from his brother, William). He was Senior Chief Inspector of Schools in Scotland, 1896–9.

(Prof.) George M. Slesser (1834–1862) attended the Grammar in 1848–9, entering Class V. In 1858 he was the Simpson Mathematical Prizeman and became Senior Wrangler while at Queens' College, Cambridge. He became Professor of Mathematics at Queen's, Belfast, 1860–2.

John Wilson (1834–1915) attended the Grammar between 1850 and 1853, entering Class III, and becoming First Bursar in 1853. He took an MA at Marischal in 1857 and became a schoolteacher in 1860. He was successor to Moir as Headmaster of Banff Academy in 1875, a post he held until retirement in 1900.

Alexander Dey (1836–1915) attended the Grammar in 1859–60, entering Class V. He took his MA and in 1885 was awarded an LLD by Aberdeen University. He was Rector of 'The Barn' – the Grammar School of Old Aberdeen – between 1870 and 1887. He was an Inspector of the Aberdeenshire parish schools set up under the Dick Bequest, a member of the School Board, 1891–4, and an Assessor on the University Court, 1889–1915.

Thomas Barker (1838–1907) attended the Grammar and King's, graduating in 1857 with great distinction in Mathematics. He entered Trinity, Cambridge, and became Senior Wrangler and first Smith's prizeman in 1862. He became a fellow of Trinity until appointed Professor of Pure Mathematics at Owen's College, Manchester, in 1865. He proved a successful teacher but only with the very talented mathematically: on these few he made a deep impression. He retired early in 1885 and became an authority on mosses.[90]

(Dr) David Duncan (1839–1923) attended the Grammar between 1850 and 1855, entering Class I, and the Universities of Aberdeen, Edinburgh and Berlin. He became Professor of Logic and Moral Philosophy in Madras; Registrar of Madras University, 1875–9 and 1881–6; Director of Public Instruction and Commissioner for Government exams; and Vice-Chancellor of Madras University, 1899.

(Rev.) James Robertson (1840–1920) attended the Grammar, King's, where he gained a FCH in Philosophy, and St Andrews. He did missionary work for the Church of Scotland in Turkey (1862–4) and Syria (1864–75). He was Professor of Hebrew and Semitic Languages, Glasgow University, 1877–1907. He produced religious publications.

(Prof.) George Croom Robertson (1842–1892) attended the Grammar between 1853 and 1857, entering Class I, and becoming First Bursar from Class IV. He graduated MA in 1861 from Marischal with the highest honours in Classics and Philosophy. He won a two-year Ferguson Scholarship (Classical and Philosophical) which took him to London, Heidelberg, Berlin, Göttingen and Paris. He was appointed Professor of Philosophy of Mind and Logic at University College, London, in 1866. He was the editor of *Mind* from its foundation in 1876 until 1891. He left little published but he followed Bain and John Stuart Mill.

(Rev. Prof.) George Pirie (1843–1904) attended the Grammar from 1854 to 1856, entering Class II, and Aberdeen University. He went on to Queens' College, Cambridge, where he was Fifth Wrangler in the mathematical tripos of 1866. He was a Fellow and mathematical lecturer at Queens and in 1878 was elected Professor of Mathematics at Aberdeen.

(Dr) Allan R. Andrew (1843–1921) attended the Grammar and Aberdeen University. He became Rector of Milne's Institution and in 1875 joined the HMI in Scotland. He became HMCI of Glasgow and Western Division in 1904.

(Sir) David Gill (1843–1914; KCB 1900) attended the Grammar between 1848 and 1851, entering Class I. He went on to Dollar Academy and spent two years at Aberdeen University where he was taught by James Clerk Maxwell. He was Astronomer-Royal for South Africa, 1879–1906. He was elected FRS in 1883 and was President of the Royal Astronomical Society, 1909–11.

William A. Hunter (1844–1898) attended the Grammar from 1855 to 1858 and 1859 to 1860, entering Class I, and gained a high place in the bursary competition to Aberdeen University. He graduated with highest honours in 1864 in Mental Philosophy and in Natural Science and in 1866 won the Murray, Ferguson (Philosophical) and Shaw Scholarships. He was called to the English Bar in 1867. He was appointed Professor of Roman Law at University College, London (1869) then Professor of Jurisprudence there in 1878. He became Radical MP for North Aberdeen (1885–96) and succeeded in 1890 in securing wholly free elementary education for Scotland, for which he received the Freedom of Aberdeen.

William Dewar (1846–1917) attended the Grammar between 1856 and 1858, entering Class II. He graduated in 1872 in Arts from Aberdeen University and became a Master at Cheltenham College, 1883–8. He was appointed Senior Modern Languages master at Rugby, 1888–1911. He was elected the chairman of Rugby District Council, a post he held between 1909 and 1912.

(Prof.) Alexander F. Murison (1847–1934) attended the Grammar between 1860 and 1863, entering Class III, and winning prizes for Latin and Greek, becoming the First Bursar to Aberdeen University from which he graduated with FCH. He returned to his old school (the GS) as Head English master (1869–77) and was reputed to have been an inspiring teacher. He was called to the English Bar and in 1883 he became Professor of Roman Law at University College, London. He went on to be Professor of Jurisprudence there in 1901. He became a KC in 1924. He gained an international reputation for scholarship.[91]

Financial

John Rae (1813–1900) attended the Grammar between 1823 and 1828, entering Class I and achieved his MA from Marischal in 1832 before migrating to Australia. He became Secretary and Accountant to the North British Australasian Loan and Investment Co. in 1839. He was the first full-time Clerk and Legal Officer to Sydney Town Council and Secretary to the Railway Commissioners.

George A. Esson (1815–1888) attended the Grammar between 1822 and 1827, entering Class II. He graduated in Arts from Aberdeen University in 1831 and studied Law at Edinburgh. He became an expert on insurance matters and was involved in founding the Faculty of Actuaries in Scotland.

George A. Jamieson (1828–1900) attended the Grammar between 1837 and 1842, entering Class I, and then Aberdeen University. He worked in Edinburgh and became a founder member of the Society of Accountants in 1854. He gained the reputation of being one of Scotland's most successful and influential CAs. He became a director of many companies and was President of the Society of Accountants between 1882 and 1888. He was elected FRSE.[92]

William Milne (1832–1906) attended the Grammar between 1844 and 1847. He trained as a lawyer in Aberdeen and as a CA in Edinburgh. By 1863 he had opened an accounting practice in Union Street. He became auditor of Robert Gordon's Hospital. He was President of the Society of Accountants in Aberdeen in 1881. He was involved with the Aberdeen Mechanics' Institute and the Aberdeen Philosophical Society.

(Sir) Robert G.C. Hamilton (1836–1895; KCB 1884) attended the Grammar in 1849–50, entering Class IV, and King's graduating in 1855. He entered the Civil Service as a clerk in the War Office, worked in the Office of Works and became an accountant in the education department. He was Accountant in the Board of Trade and Secretary to the Civil Service Inquiry Commission. He simplified the navy estimates and was made Permanent Secretary to the Admiralty, then Ireland. He was Governor of Tasmania (1887–92)[93] and helped to found the University of Tasmania. He was one of the original Honorary Vice-Presidents of the FP Club in 1893.

Harvey Hall (1841–1931) attended the Grammar between 1852 and 1856, entering Class II. He graduated MA in 1859 at Marischal and trained as a lawyer in Aberdeen and Edinburgh. He was admitted to the Faculty of Advocates in Aberdeen in 1866. Becoming a CA in 1871 he established a firm with accounting and legal services. He joined the Rifle Corps (founded in 1859). He was President of the Society of Accountants in Aberdeen in 1895.

(Hon. Sir) James Westland (1842–1903; KCSI 1895) attended the Grammar between 1852 and 1855, entering Class II, before going on to Marischal and Wimbledon. In 1861 he was first in the entry exam for the Royal Military Academy, Woolwich and later that year was first in the exam for the ICS. His mathematical aptitude resulted in posts in financial administration in Bengal. He was appointed Secretary to the Indian Government in the Department of Finance and Commerce and reorganised and simplified the accounting practices of the colonial administration. In 1899 he was appointed a member of the Council of India.[94]

Administrative (Politicians)

John Angus (1799–1878) attended the Grammar between 1807 and 1812, entering Class I, and Marischal, graduating MA in 1816. He was Town Clerk of Aberdeen, 1840–75.

(Sir) John Hay (1816–1892; KCMG, 1878) attended the Grammar in 1828–9, entering Class V, and graduating from King's in 1834. He then studied Law at Edinburgh before migrating to Sydney in 1838. He was elected to the first Legislative Assembly in New South Wales and for a brief period he formed a Coalition Ministry. In 1862 he was elected Speaker, and between 1873 and 1892 he was President of the Legislative Council.

Charles Robertson (1833–1898) attended the Grammar between 1844 and 1849, entering Class I, and was Dux and won the Silver Medal in his final year. He was also First Bursar in 1849 and took an MA with special Honours in 1853 from Marischal. He was fifth in the first open competition for the ICS. From 1877 to 1882 he was Secretary to the Government of Oudh. In retirement he was a leading supporter of the Hellenic Society. He founded and funded a fellowship at Aberdeen University in memory of his brother, George.[95]

(Sir) William M. Clark (1836–1917; Kt 1907) attended the Grammar between 1845 and 1847, entering Class I, and then Marischal and Edinburgh Universities. He became a WS and was called to the Bar in Toronto in 1861. He became a QC and was ninth Lieutenant-Governor of Ontario, from 1903 to 1908, supporting education and hospitals during his tenure.

Frederick Stewart (1836–1889) attended the Grammar between 1851 and 1854, entering Class IV, and then King's, where he headed the Honours list in 1859. For sixteen years he established, developed and managed both a school and a system in Hong Kong, learning and using spoken Cantonese and written Chinese in his work. He became the first Head of the Government Education Department in 1865. Stewart made an important impact on Hong Kong society and contributed to the modernisation of China.[96]

(Sir) George C. Strahan (1838–1887) attended the Grammar between 1846 and 1852, entering Class I, and the Royal Military Academy, Greenwich. He joined the British army in 1857 and held senior administrative posts in Malta, Bahamas, Nigeria, Gold Coast and Cape Colony. He was Governor of Tasmania, 1881–6 (the town of Strahan being named after him) and was appointed Governor of Hong Kong in 1887.

(Hon. Sir) William Bisset-Berry (1839–1922; Kt 1900) attended the Grammar between 1848 and 1853, entering Class I, then Marischal for an Arts degree. He graduated in Medicine in 1861 and was a ship's Surgeon in the Arctic before migrating to South Africa. As first Mayor of Queenstown he was responsible for major civic improvements. He became a Progressive member of the Cape Assembly in 1894 and held the position of Speaker, 1898–1908.

(Lt Col. Sir) George King (1840–1909; KCIE 1898) attended the

Grammar in 1849–50, entering Class I. He studied Medicine spending much time on Botany. He entered the IMS and held a series of military-medical positions in central India. He reached the rank of Lieutenant Colonel. In 1871 he became Superintendent of the Royal Botanic Garden, Calcutta, holding the post until 1898. He also was Professor of Botany in Calcutta and elected FRS in 1887. He was the author of over sixty botanical publications.[97] He has a memorial window dedicated to him in St Machar's Cathedral, Old Aberdeen.

James C. Geddes (1842–1880) attended the Grammar between 1852 and 1855, entering Class III. He was the younger brother of Principal Geddes. He joined the ICS in 1861 and became a magistrate in Bengal. He was deeply sympathetic to the natives following the great Orissa famine of 1866 in which about one and a half million died. He became a Positivist in 1870 and was highly critical of British rule. He became the first leader of the Calcutta Positivist Society.[98]

Robert Henderson (1842–1925) attended the Grammar from 1854 to 1856, entering Class II, and King's. He entered the service of HM Customs in 1862. He became Collector 1871; Secretary 1900 and Commissioner 1909.

Robert Walker (1842–1920) attended the Grammar between 1852 and 1857, entering Class I, and was an early graduate of the united University in 1861. He went on to Cambridge and was the fifteenth Wrangler in the Mathematics tripos of 1865. He was a Fellow of Clare, Cambridge, 1866–78. He was elected a FRSE in 1873. In 1878 he took on the roles of Aberdeen University Librarian (retained till 1893), Secretary to the University Court (retained till 1906) and Registrar, which he continued until 1920.

William Jenkyns (1847–1879) attended the Grammar in 1863–4, entering Class V. After graduating from Aberdeen University in 1868 he joined the ICS. He became the first Assistant Political Officer at the British Embassy in Kabul, Afghanistan, and was killed in its defence in September 1879.

(Sir) James Thomson (1848–1929; KCSI 1904) attended Grammar in 1863-4, entering Class V and went on to Aberdeen University. He was appointed to the ICS and served in Madras. He became a member of the Executive Council (1901-5), acting Governor in 1904 in the absence of the Viceroy, and member of the Council of India, 1908–15.

(Sir) George S. Forbes (1849–1940; KCSI 1909) attended the Grammar between 1860 and 1864 and then Aberdeen University where he gained an MA in 1871. He joined the ICS and held a series of important posts, culminating in becoming a member of the Executive Council of the Government of Madras from 1906 to 1909.

Writers (Poets, Journalists and Newspapermen)

James Perry [formerly Pirie] (1756–1821) was in attendance at the Grammar in 1769 and went on to Marischal, 1771–4. He moved to London in 1777 in order to break into the literary world. He did so with his reporting of the court-martial of Admiral Augustus Keppel over his conduct in the naval battle of Ushant. He became an admirer and supporter of Charles James Fox and he defended popular liberties in his editorship of the *Morning Chronicle*. He did much to make newspapers a force in the country and journalism a respectable profession.[99]

Alexander Chalmers (1759–1834) attended the Grammar between 1771 and 1774 before Marischal College, 1774–8. He moved to London and pursued a literary career. He became editor of three London newspapers – the *London Packet*, the *Morning Herald* and the *Public Ledger*. As an editor and biographer he made a considerable contribution to British literature. His 1798 *General Biographical Dictionary* remained standard for many years.

John Scott (1784–1821) attended the Grammar in 1795–6 gaining a scholarship to Marischal, leaving in 1799. After clerking jobs in Glasgow and London he became a journalist in the radical press. His impressions about a revisit to Paris in 1815 were well received. He edited the *London Magazine* which had a literary bias and in its political liberalism was an antidote to the rabid toryism of *Blackwood's Magazine*. However, venomous writing on both sides led to a duel, the wounds from which led to Scott's death.[100]

(Lord) George Gordon Noel Byron (1788–1824) attended the Grammar where he learned Latin for four years, leaving at the age of ten to move south when he inherited the title of sixth Baron Byron of Rochdale. There was a tradition that Byron had carved his name on a desk and in 1909 a letter from Dr Gordon Stables published in the School Magazine held that in his schooldays (1852–4) the desk was there 'in the fourth or fifth faction from the bottom'. In 1917 the City Librarian, G.M. Fraser, contributed an article on the Byron house which used to stand at Honeybrae, amid fields to the west of Morningfield Hospital. There Byron spent his summer holidays in 1798. Byron was well enough served by the GS in Latin, but the absence of Greek from its curriculum (it was not added until 1826) proved a handicap to him in the short-term.[101] His education was completed at Harrow and Trinity, Cambridge. Following an extraordinary life Byron achieved pre-eminent status within English and European Romanticism. He is seen as an iconic figure who gave his life in the cause of the liberation of the Greeks from Ottoman rule and was thus revered by the Greek people. 'No English writer except Shakespeare acquired greater fame or exercised more world influence.'[102] His statue dominates the new School frontage and one of the modern School houses was named after him.

John Ramsay (1799–1870) attended the Grammar between 1807 and 1813, entering Class I. He was Second Bursar to King's and graduated in 1817. He taught in RGH but gave up teaching to edit *The Aberdeen Journal* (till 1851). He was unsuccessful as a candidate for the Professorship of Mathematics at King's.

James Moir Ferres (1813–1870) attended the Grammar between 1822 and 1827, entering Class I. He migrated to Montreal in 1833 and founded a weekly newspaper which voiced vehement Toryism. In 1839 he became editor of the *Montreal Herald* and from 1848 till 1854 he was editor and chief proprietor of the *Montreal Gazette*.

(Prof.) David M. Masson (1822–1907) attended the Grammar between 1831 and 1835, entering Class I, and then gained the First Bursary (of seventy-six candidates) at the age of twelve to Marischal, where he completed an Arts degree and stayed to study Divinity. He contributed articles to the magazines of the period. He was appointed Professor of English Language and Literature at University College, London, in 1852. He launched *Macmillan's Magazine*, as editor, in 1859. He became Professor of Rhetoric and Literature at Edinburgh in 1865 and was elected FRSE the following year. His literary output was prolific: his biography of Milton was thorough and detailed: he also was editor for twelve volumes of the Privy Council Register of Scotland. He was made Historiographer-Royal for Scotland in 1893. In his retirement he wrote about Melvin, his legendary teacher. He himself left an indelible mark on numerous students.[103] He was one of the original Honorary Vice-Presidents of the FP Club in 1893.

(Dr) Peter Bayne (1830–1896) attended the Grammar between 1844 and 1846, entering Class V, and graduated from Aberdeen in 1850. He became a journalist and wrote mainly for magazines. He was the leader writer of the *Christian World*, an influential paper, for two decades and wrote books on historical and literary topics.[104]

James Innes (1833–1903) attended the Grammar in 1846–7, entering Class V. He migrated to Canada and worked as a reporter on newspapers in Toronto and Hamilton. As a reform candidate he was elected MP for Wellington South, 1882–96. He was chair of the Local Board of Education in Guelph and became noted for his philanthropy.

(Dr) W. Gordon Stables (1840–1910) attended the Grammar in 1852–4, entering Class IV, and then Aberdeen University, where he studied

Medicine. He became a naval Surgeon. Ill-health resulted in him writing boys' adventure stories. He became an authority on dogs, cats and rabbits, and wrote a number of books on such animals.[105]

William Wallace (1843–1921) was educated at the Grammar and Aberdeen, before qualifying in Law at St Andrews. He was a Barrister and teacher before turning to journalism, working as such in Dumfries, London and Glasgow. He was editor of the *Glasgow Herald* (1906–9). He produced a number of publications and articles for magazines.

Alexander Allardyce (1846–1896) attended the Grammar in 1862–3, entering Class V, and then Aberdeen University. In 1868 he became a journalist in India and became editor of the *Ceylon Times*. He worked in Berlin, London and Edinburgh, contributing to periodicals. He wrote on historical topics and novels on Indian and Scottish themes.[106]

James Fowler K. Johnstone (1846–1928) attended the Grammar between 1857 and 1859, entering Class II. He qualified as an Accountant and worked in Aberdeen, Liverpool and London. However, he then devoted his life to research becoming one of the foremost authorities on the bibliography of Aberdeen and the North-East. His lifetime research culminated in the compilation, with Alexander W. Robertson (GS 1856–62, entering Class I), of *Bibliographia Aberdoniensis* (2 vols, Aberdeen, Third Spalding Club, 1929–30). He helped acquire important book and manuscript collections for the University of Aberdeen and made generous personal gifts to the University Library.

Arts

John Smith (1781–1852) was educated at the Grammar and apprenticed as a stone-mason to his father before studying architectural design for four years. He established himself in business in 1805 and became the first City Architect and Superintendent of Public Works. He designed the model village at Footdee, Balmoral Castle, several churches and the west wing of King's College quadrangle, Trinity Hall and the Advocates' Hall.[107] He designed the colonnade at St Nicholas' Kirk frontage, Union Street, where a commemorative plaque can be found.

Archibald Simpson (1790–1847) attended the Grammar between 1799 and 1803, entering Class I, and thereafter, for a brief period, Marischal. He received initial training in Architecture in Aberdeen before moving to London. On his return to Aberdeen in 1813 he emerged as the leading architect of the City, which he stocked with a fine series of buildings. He also dominated architecture in the North-East.[108] A commemorative plaque can be found in Bon Accord Square.

James Logan (1794–1872), writer on Scottish Gaelic culture, attended the Grammar between 1807 and 1810, entering Class I, before matriculation at Marischal. His most significant work, *The Scottish Gael*, appeared in 1831 and it contained a commentary on Highland mores and traditional lore. He contributed to other publications and served as secretary of the Highland Society of London.[109]

John Imlah (1799–1846) attended the Grammar between 1809 and 1814, entering Class I, and was apprenticed as a piano-tuner. Ultimately he joined the London firm of Broadwood. He composed from boyhood and had poem and song collections published in 1827 and 1841.[110]

John Bruce (1802–1869) attended the Grammar between 1812 and 1816, entering Class I. He trained as a lawyer but instead followed historical and antiquarian pursuits. He published extensively in historical books and periodicals. He was for some time Treasurer and Vice-Chairman of the Society of Antiquaries.[111]

William Dyce (1806–1864) attended the Grammar between 1814 and 1819, entering Class I, and then Marischal, where he took up Theology. Early talent in painting was confirmed by Sir Thomas Lawrence, President of the Royal Academy, so he took up painting professionally. He was elected as a Fellow of the RSE in 1832 and three years later became an associate of the RA. He did not gain full membership until 1848 for, as a genuine polymath, his breadth of interests reduced his output as a painter. He was Superintendent of the Government School of Design. The Church was very important for him and he became an authority on Church Music. Much of his later days were overshadowed by the decoration of the new Palace of Westminster. His paintings are enduring masterpieces of Victorian art.[112] A commemorative plaque can be found at 48 Marischal Street.

William Smith (1817–1891) attended the Grammar between 1828 and 1832, entering Class I, and Marischal where he graduated MA. He studied sketching and watercolour under James Giles. Working with his father he worked on the construction of Balmoral Castle for the Prince Consort in 1853–59. By then he had succeeded his father, John, as Superintendent of the Town's Works. Although he was involved in many local structures his reticence lost him the commission for Aberdeen's Municipal Buildings, which was a major disappointment for him.

John Forbes-Robertson (1822–1903) was educated at the Grammar and won a bursary to Marischal. He later attended University College, London.

He wrote extensively on art, his major work being *The Great Painters of Christendom*, and was art critic for a number of journals.[113]

William Keith (1838–1911) attended the Grammar between 1845 and 1850, entering Class I. Talented artistically he left School to become an apprentice to a wood carver. In 1852 he migrated with his mother and sisters to America, living in New York then San Francisco. He began to exhibit his landscape watercolours professionally in 1864 and for some decades his work dominated Californian painting. He exhibited at Chicago's World Fair in 1893. Unfortunately the San Francisco earthquake of 1906 destroyed much of his work.

(Sir) George Reid (1841–1913; Kt 1891) attended the Grammar, leaving in 1854 when his father was declared bankrupt. He established himself as a portrait painter, and became a member of the Royal Scottish Academy in 1877. He became its President between 1891 and 1902. A commemorative plaque can be found at the Gordon Highlanders' Museum, Viewfield Road, previously known as St Lukes, his home.

Archibald D. Reid (1844–1908) was transferred to Gordon's Hospital in 1854 when his father went bankrupt. He went on to a distinguished career as a painter.

Sport

George H. Mackenzie (1837–1891) was educated at the Grammar between 1852 and 1854, entering Class IV. He went on to Marischal, Rouen and Stettin Universities. He was placed third in the world chess rankings and won various international tournaments. He was inducted into the American Hall of Fame in 1992.

SIX Recollections of the School at Schoolhill

This chapter gives a selection of recollections and reminiscences, usually from former pupils looking back at their schooldays. The extracts give a comprehensive view of the Grammar School in the century before its move to its modern site.

THE GRAMMAR SCHOOL IN 1764

The following extract comes from *Recollections* written by Alexander Jaffray of Kingswells, a descendant of Alexander Jaffray who was Provost of Aberdeen in 1635–36, and of his better known son, also Alexander Jaffray, who was Provost of Aberdeen in 1649. Jaffray wrote his *Recollections* in 1826 and remembers attending Paterson's seminary, a Reading and Writing School, for about a year in preparation for the GS, which he entered in 1764:

> [The Grammar School] is a large public seminary for the Latin language established under the patronage of the City of Aberdeen: it has four masters elected with the greatest care by the Magistrates and Council of the City, and paid yearly salaries by the municipality. The masters are also paid half a crown by the quarter from the pupils of their several classes. The number of scholars are generally from two hundred and fifty to three hundred; they are put through a thorough and regular course of the Latin language, to prepare them for the University. The masters at that time were the Rev. James Dun, the Rector or Principal Master for the First Class; the celebrated Dr. Beattie, known to the literary world as the author of *The Minstrel* and other poems, for the Second Class; the Rev. Alexander Fullerton for the Third Class; and John Dun (the son of the Rector) for the Fourth Class.

In the junior class – each Class had a separate School room – it was my fate to fall under, not the care, but the tyranny, of John Dun, the junior master. He was unfortunately, for the boys in his class, of a most irritable and bilious habit, which the merest trifle provoked to ire, and excited to the exercise of punishment, in which seemed to consist his principal delight as a means of venting his fury. His instrument of correction was a leather thong cut at the end into a number of strips, which he appeared to take particular pleasure in applying with all his force on the breeches of the scholars, hoisted up for that purpose on the back of the school servant or porter. The boys often remarked that in the winter season, he took the opportunity while warming himself at the fire, of preparing a warmer application of the thong to the skins of the pupils by hardening the ends in the fire.

Some time later, the violent temper of poor John Dun, my late master, terminated in settled insanity, and next vacation he went to London in one of the regular traders, with the avowed intention of assassinating the celebrated John Wilkes, in revenge of the abuse which he had heaped on Scotland and on Scotchmen in his noted publication of the paper No. 45 against the administration of Lord Bute. Dun's design was prevented by the timely interference of friends who had him secured.

I do not recollect my deserving correction, while I remained at that School, for wanting attention to the business of the class, or for the imperfection in repetition of the lessons of the day, but merely for trifling faults which had little, if any, connection with the discipline or duties of the School.

The boys of the junior class had as a matter of course, and according to the long established laws of School practice, to support all the gibes and scoffs, and pass the ordeal of all the practical jokes which the domineering spirit, and the fertile invention, of the more established members of the school chose to exercise upon our patience."

Such issues as drastic corporal punishment and widespread and institutionalised bullying in the Grammar School led young Jaffray to complain constantly to his parents and relatives about his sufferings. Fortunately for him his pleas were listened to and he was sent to Banff Academy for the rest of his schooling.

BYRON ON HIS SCHOOLDAYS IN ABERDEEN IN THE 1790S

Between May and October 1821 Lord Byron recollected his days at the Grammar School in the 1790s. These were reproduced by Thomas More in his *Works of Lord Byron* (London 1835) vol. 1 and revisited by R.E. Prothero in *Letters and Journals* (London 1898–1904) vol. V:

> For several years of my earliest childhood I was in that City [Aberdeen], but have never revisited it since I was ten years old. I was sent at five years old, or earlier, to a school kept by a Mr. Bowers,[1] who was called 'Bodsy Bowers' by reason of his dapperness. It was a school for both sexes. I learned little more there, except to repeat by rote the first lesson of monosyllables – 'God made man, let us love him' – by hearing it often repeated, without acquiring a letter. Whenever proof was made of my progress at home I repeated these words with the most rapid fluency; but on turning over a new leaf, I continued to repeat them, so that the narrow boundaries of my first year's accomplishments were detected, my ears boxed (which they did not deserve, seeing that it was by *ear* only that I had acquired my letters), and my intellects consigned to a new preceptor. He was a very decent, clever little clergyman, named Ross,[2] afterwards minister of one of the Kirks (East I think). Under him I made an astonishing progress, and I recollect to this day his mild manners and good-natured painstaking.
>
> The moment I could read, my grand passion was *history;* and why, I know not, but I was particularly taken with the battle near the Lake Regillus in Roman History . . .
>
> Four years ago, when standing on the heights of Tusculum, and looking down upon the little round lake, that was once Regillus, and which dots the immense expanse below, I remembered my young enthusiasm and my old instructor.
>
> Afterwards I had a very serious, saturnine, but kind young man, named Paterson,[3] for a tutor: he was the son of my shoemaker, but a good scholar, as is common with the Scotch. He was a rigid Presbyterian also. With him I began Latin in Ruddiman's *Grammar,* and continued till I went to the Grammar School, where I threaded all the Classes to the Fourth, when I was recalled to England (where

I had been hatched) by the demise of my uncle.

I acquired this hand-writing, which I can hardly read myself, under the fair copies of Mr. Duncan[4] of the same city. I don't think that he would plume himself upon my progress. However, I wrote much better then than I have ever done since. Haste and agitation of one kind or another have quite spoilt as pretty a scrawl as ever scratched over a frank.

The Grammar School might consist of over a hundred and fifty of all ages. It was divided into five classes, taught by four masters, the chief teaching the Fifth and Fourth himself, as in England the fifth, sixth forms, and monitors are heard by the Headmasters.

THE SCHOOL IN BYRON'S DAYS

In his Book published in 1906 Morland Simpson gives his account of what the Grammar School was like in the 1790s:

> When Byron entered the Grammar School, probably in January 1795, the building erected, or opened, in 1757, consisted of a low, one storeyed structure, standing in Schoolhill . . . In shape it was like the letter H, the front bay, railed off from the street, forming a small, roughly paved yard. The front wings to right and left had separate entrances, and were occupied by two classes. The centre of the building, or 'Public School', extending across to the outer walls, was reached up two or three steps by a door in the middle, above which was the humble belfry, along with Ferguson's bell. Facing the door inside stood 'the desk' on a broad, low platform, sufficient to accommodate the 'Visitors' at the annual Visitations; and on both sides of this the rows of scholars' desks or factions faced each other, with a passage down the centre. From the Public School doors opened into the wings to back and front, occupied by the classes I., II., III., and IV. with V., the Public School being occupied only for prayers at assembly, on public occasions, and when the room for IV. and V. proved too small for the numbers. Mean as the building was in appearance and accommodation, even for Byron's days, when the City must have numbered some 26,000 inhabitants, it had to do duty for nearly seventy years longer, and was still, in 1853, held sufficient to accommodate as many as 436 boys, the largest number

attained under Dr. Melvin. Of these 102 were in Class V., and 69 in IV., together 171, in charge of the Rector. But in Byron's days the total numbers never exceeded 160.

At that time, and for many years before and since, the custom was for the three Under-Masters or 'Ushers' to take the first three classes in rotation, being promoted, so to speak, along with their class, till they passed the boys over to the Rector in IV. The numbers in the First or 'Elementarian' class vary considerably throughout the whole period during which this custom prevailed, and afford some insight into the popularity, and success as teachers, of the three masters. Parents were not slow to make their arrangements accordingly, either by early entry, or by keeping their sons back for a year or so with their preparatory schools or tutors, in order to enrol the boy with a favourite teacher. Possibly some such consideration may have induced Byron's mother to enrol her boy, precocious though he was, at the tender age of seven, when he must have been some three years younger than most of his class-fellows. At a time when it was quite usual for schoolboys of fair average ability to complete the course in Class V. at the age of fourteen and proceed to the University, Byron, who in 1798 left the School, in Class IV., at the age of ten and a half years, would have attained the University entrance standard, such as it was, before he was twelve years at age. Nay it was no uncommon thing for boys to leave from the Fourth, at least five of Byron's class-fellows doing so in 1798.

This fact is to be borne in mind when we consider his quarterly class places, determined, no doubt, solely by such proficiency in Latin Rudiments and 'Version' writing as could be drilled into boys, who spent their weary days in the exclusive study of Latin, and that on the narrowest basis ever devised by educational pedantry. Byron was 23rd, 16th, 6th and 22nd in Class II (1796); 13th, 18th, 21st and 22nd in Class III (1797) and 22nd, 5th and 17th in Class IV (1798), the numbers in his Class varying from 28th at lowest and 38th at highest.

In the Visitation Book it is recorded that in 1824 James Watt was in charge of Class I., James Melvin of Class II., and Robert Forbes of Class III. Working backwards through the succession of teachers, it appears that Byron's teacher was Alexander Leith, who had taught in the School since about 1777, first as assistant in place of John Dun, the invalid son of the Rector, and, since 1791, as full

Under-Master, on the appointment of James Cromar, Senior, to be Conjunct-Rector.

VISITATIONS

John Ramsay attended the School between 1807 and 1813. He wrote an article on 'The Visitation' which was published in the *Aberdeen Journal* on 1 March 1842.

In our day the Visitation of the Grammar School was an occasion marked by a solemnity bordering on the awful. Its advent was looked forward to with much anxious forecast of its eventualities, for at least three months previous to its actual arrival. As it approached, the anxiety felt by youthful aspirants to scholastic distinction increased to rather painful intensity. In the two junior classes, what keen competition to secure a seat within the honoured bounds of the first four 'factions', before the places were stopped – when fixed the fate of all remained! In the higher classes, what hoarding of 'phrases'! what collation of 'idioms'! what rivalship in daily 'trial versions'! The day before the Visitation was a half-holiday, but most falsely so called, for its afternoon was one of painful preparation, and no trifling perturbation of spirit. No use *now* to count the hours to the great day – it came with tomorrow's sun! In vain, the endeavour to beguile the moments of aching suspense by the ruling of version paper, the mending of pens, and the revisal of neglected lessons. All this brushing up of arms only served to keep up the anxiety connected with the approaching contest. Then there was such rigorous ablution of the person – that of Saturday was nothing to it! No wonder; had we not to pass muster before 'authorities' – civic, clerical, and academic! At length the appointed hour of meeting approached. How many smartly arrayed, rosy little fellows, did that morning behold trudging rather pensively from all quarters towards Schoolhill, bending under load unwonted of dictionaries, and grammars, and phrase books, that nothing might be wanting in such munitions of scholastic war. Manifold their conjecturing as to 'the version' – serious the speculation as to the chances of individual failure or success. Some, with a modesty which became their idleness as much as their youth, would declare that they did not expect 'a book'. Others, whose experience had sought consolation under disappointment by reference to cases of neglected desert, ventured an opinion that they ought to get prizes; but they had their doubts about getting fair play. They had no friends – not they – in the Council.

But the actual hour of meeting disperses the little groups of such speculators; each takes his seat in the 'public school'; the catalogue is called amid silence as universal as unwonted, and all is tiptoe expectation for the arrival of the visitors. The whole school has undergone a lustration which carries something solemn with it, from its very rarity. The floors have actually been dusted over with clean sand, which gives additional impressiveness to the authoritative tread of the 'Masters', as they pace to and fro. And is not the Rector, arrayed in his gown, so grand? – just like a professor! – an indication of pomp and circumstance to be seen on such occasions only – a demonstration which impresses the 'Elementarians' with ideas of the dignity of 'the seminary' which have ne'er before entered their little craniums, although, with the upper classes, it is rather the butt of daring witticism. But bold indeed are they who would hazard even a suppressed titter, whatever the provocation, at such a crisis, for the hour is come, and the men! It is heralded by the measured tread of the town sergeants, glimpses of whose red coats are caught through the windows, like flashes of lightning.

What solemn courtesy in the greetings between masters and visitors, the former positively appearing bareheaded, which shows us boys that there are greater men in the world even than they, albeit that may avail us not in subferulary hour!

Then the Rector delivers a speech – a Latin one! It sounds like a trial version. The great 'version' is then given out. It is something about the Romans, or the Greeks, or the Carthaginians; Epaminondas; Turnus, king of the Rutuli; or at least Hamilcar – all familiar acquaintances of ours. Perhaps it is a plaguy passage from modern history – a thing by no means agreeable to our classical tastes; or it may smack somewhat of the marvellously philosophical, beginning with – 'A certain author relates', followed by the qualification, 'but I know not whether it be true', which is merely a trap for young grammarians; for it is of no earthly consequence whether the relation be true or not. Ah! The careful pen-scraping distinctly audible in the hush of that awful hour! Is it not the commencement of a struggle on which is hung the chance, not of a 'book' merely, but, tentatively, of a 'buss'? The dictation ended, the competitors are left to their fate. Unassisted, they must fight it out. Some get through the business rather rapidly. On the painful labours of others, the shadows of that shortish day rather ominously fall – and the latest at length leave the School. Each has done his best.

In our day the prize-books were given on the night of the day on which they were won. During the whole evening the Schoolhill was in an uproar. It swarmed with groups of scholars comparing notes about their versions. Here and there might be seen a 'colleginer' laying down the law grammatical to a 'buroch' of eager, inquiring juniors; squibs and crackers flew about in all directions; bells and knockers were compelled to vigorous exercise of their calling; shutters were exposed to wanton assault and battery. Old folks wondered what things would come to; that finishers of the law would have more work was quite clear!

The row at length was extinguished on the appearance, about ten o'clock, of the municipal authorities, in darkling procession, guided by the leading lights of the sergeants, two and two abreast each bearing a lantern radiant with a couple of candles. Again the place is crowded with the honourable, the reverend, the learned. The well-powdered head of the Town Clerk towers amid the full blaze and he unrolls the scroll of fate. The names of the successful competitors are announced by him rather with the voice of one having authority than of a mere scribe. Each fortunate rogue bustles up in front, and receives from the Provost's own hand the much-prized book – the honour acknowledged by a bow, bespeaking more gratefulness than gracefulness. Many, of course, are disappointed, but they soon forget their sorrow in the pastimes of the holiday week.

From October 1765 there is a record in the Minutes of the Town Council of the Annual Visitation, without intermission, until 1856, when it stops.

The Records detail the Annual Visitation of the Grammar in 1824: the Rector dictated an English theme to be translated into Latin by the third, fourth and fifth classes; the visitors then attended, for nearly two hours, the examination of the first and second classes, in both of which the scholars acquitted themselves with great ease and correctness, in translating Latin into English, and English sentences into Latin, as well as answering questions connected with the syntax and grammar of the latter language. In the afternoon, the visitors again met to examine the Latin versions written by the three higher classes and determine their order of merit. The performance of the versions was exceedingly creditable, not a few of them being free from errors and many of them evincing a skill in the choice of words and an acquaintance with the Latin idiom, which would not have been acquired without care and diligence on the part of the teachers.

The effect of Visitations cannot be over-estimated in stimulating staff and scholars and in establishing confidence in the School. In burgh schools it was common to have an annual exhibition of work and scholars sitting public examinations and schools receiving government grants were inspected by HMI. Independent examiners were praised and supported in the 1868 Report into Burgh Schools and the 1872 Education Act.

ASSESSMENT OF DR MELVIN

Dr John Hill Burton (1809–1891) attended the Grammar School between 1819 and 1823 and in his final years at the School was taught by Melvin. Here is his assessment of his teacher:

> I believe there is a considerable number of men now in middle life, who, if they were to recall their earliest impulse towards the emulation and intellectual enthusiasm which has brought them to eminence, would carry it back to the teaching of Melvin.
>
> But Melvin's scholarship arose neither from ambition to rise by it, nor from a peculiar call to the dry analysis of a dead language. He was a man of bright active intellect and fine taste, and that he should have come to use, as the tool of his intellectual activity, the language of Rome instead of that of his own country, was probably incidental; possibly it may have been from a remnant of the shyness of competing in the language of England with Englishmen, which lingered long in Scotland, especially with those whose opportunities of mingling with the world happened to be limited. However it was, Melvin, like the great master he revered, made for himself an intellectual home in the language of Rome, and became as familiar with everything written by Roman writers, or about them, as the old frequenter of a town is with the houses and the stones he passes daily. His editions of 'Horace for every Day in the Year'[5] were

merely a variety of the conditions under which he kept up constant companionship with an old ever-welcome friend.

THE GRAMMAR SCHOOL IN THE EARLY 1840S

John Forbes White attended the GS between 1839 and 1844, entering Class I, aged eight years of age, in October 1839. He had previously attended James Ledingham's Academy in Correction Wynd, where the curriculum had been mainly Reading and Writing with a little English Grammar.

> By good fortune I entered the GS under the master-ship of Mr James Ogilvie, a young man who ten years before had been First Bursar at Marischal College and who, in 1837, was appointed interim master of the GS in place of Mr. Forbes. A tall, gaunt man, sallow and saturnine, with prominent nose and black beady eyes, lethargic and slow to move, was 'Poker' Ogilvie. But he taught Latin well . . . He was too lazy to use the tawse or cane except under great provocation, or rather from loss of temper.
>
> To prepare us for Melvin he used many of the Doctor's old Versions . . . He carried this to such a fine point that, at the end of the third year, he was so confident as to results that he requested that two of us should try the Bursary Competition at Marischal College . . . One of us succeeded in gaining the seventh bursary of that year under the age of twelve, but was wisely kept at School for another two years, when the First Bursary fell to him.
>
> Strange to say, Ogilvie never attained the position of Rector in the School. Even in 1843 he was appointed only an Under-Master, in place of Mr. Watt, deceased.[6]
>
> Melvin was the splendid example of an old grammarian laying the foundations for wider and fuller scholarship in later years. The education was absurdly one-sided, and the methods ludicrously imperfect, but these were the faults of the time . . .

SCHOOL LIFE UNDER MELVIN IN HIS LATER YEARS

Alexander Forbes joined the First Class of the GS in October 1845 from the Town's Schools and had Rev. Alexander Beverly as his teacher. He lived in trepidation because of the treatment meted out to his friend, James Bremner, by the younger Dun. Bremner had entered the School the previous year. According to Forbes, looking back in June and October 1910:

> Beverly was a severe man and not a very successful teacher. He had little knowledge of boys' nature, and acted as if he believed that the only way to impart knowledge was by a constant use of the strap. [However] in the Second and Third Classes Beverly was not nearly as severe as in the First, and made use of the strap much less frequently, but he never, so far as I could judge, was a persona grata with the pupils. He had no magnetism to draw out their affection towards himself, which is not desirable in an instructor of youth.

Forbes entered the Fourth Class of Melvin in October 1848: 'Many more lads left his class equipped to take distinguished positions in life than, I believe, any other teacher of his generation could lay claim to'.

John Walker entered the First Class in 1846 and remained four years at the Grammar. He left an account, 'Memories of over sixty years ago', written about 1905, of his time at the School:

> Providence has endowed me with more than average abilities, which I am now ashamed to say I did not do full justice to when a scholar. Still, the only teaching which has stuck to me through life was that imparted by 'Grim'.
>
> Other masters would attempt to thrash lessons into you; but Melvin, with no greater manifestation than a well-planted punch from his thumb on the 'funny bone' of your arm, would make a lasting impression. Beyond this, all the Doctor ever hinted at by way of punishment was the threat to bring out the strap, which he told us had lain unused for so many years in the library, or placing you for a time upon what he called his 'stool of repentance'.
>
> I am still puzzled to account for the quiet power which ruled his teaching. No sooner had he opened the door, holding up his right hand, with the thumb and forefinger grasping a pinch of the snuff he loved so well, than all was perfect silence.

EDUCATION AT THE GRAMMAR SCHOOL, 1846–1851

Sir James Stirling entered the Aberdeen Grammar School in October 1846, and left it in October 1851.

The Rector at that time was Dr. James Melvin. There were three masters. Mr. John Dun, Mr. James Dun, and Rev. Alexander Beverly: Mr. James Dun died in 1848, and was succeeded by Mr. William Duguid Geddes, who afterwards succeeded Dr. Melvin as Rector and became Professor of Greek, and ultimately Sir William Duguid Geddes and Principal of the University of Aberdeen.

The School was divided into five classes, of which the Fourth and Fifth were taught by the Rector, and the others by one of the masters; the arrangement being that the master under whom a pupil entered the School remained his master during three years, until the pupil reached the Fourth class, when he passed into the charge of the Rector.

The main subject of instruction at that time was the Latin language; but the histories of Scotland, England and Rome were taught in the first three classes, as also modern Geography; and Greek in the Fourth and Fifth classes. The introduction of Greek into the curriculum was largely due, as I believe, to the pressure of John Stuart Blackie, then Professor of Humanity at Marischal College, who maintained that *Humanity* (Literae Humaniores) included *both* Greek and Latin. However this may be, both King's College and Marischal College began, about 1846, to require knowledge of Greek in the Bursary Competitions, and it became imperative that the language should be taught at the Grammar School.[7]

The master whose pupil I became was Mr. John Dun. My earlier education had been entirely conducted at home, and I watched the proceedings at School with much interest. On the first day Mr. Dun confined himself to getting the names of his new pupils, and instructing us as to the books required. On an early day afterwards we found, on assembling on the morning, that on the blackboard at the head of the classroom there had been written *Fee 13s.*, ; and before commencing lessons, the master explained that the school fee for the quarter, October to December, was immediately payable, and amounted to 13s., made up of 10s.6d for tuition and

2s.6d. for coals: the latter being exacted for that quarter only. For some days subsequently a short portion of the morning was devoted to the collection of these fees . . .

Mr. Dun had a well-founded reputation as a strict upholder of discipline, which he enforced by a liberal (but not harsh) use of the *tawse.* This instrument was kept in a drawer in the master's desk, which was kept carefully locked . . .

The elementary Latin Grammar then in use at the School was Ruddiman's *Rudiments of Latin Grammar*, edited by John Hunter, Principal of the University of St Andrews, an excellent book which had a great vogue in Scotland in the first half of the nineteenth century; and in it we were most thoroughly drilled. When sufficiently advanced we were introduced to a book which bore the title, *Maturini Corderii Colloquiorum Centuria Selecta*, commonly known as Cordery's *Colloquies.* This was a selection from a larger work of a celebrated teacher of Latin, Maturin Cordier, the tutor of Calvin when a student at the Sorbonne. It was admirably adapted for the acquisition of conversational Latin, and Mr. Dun used it with great skill, in such a way that his pupils acquired some facility in speaking Latin.

In the second year Cornelius Nepos was read, and Ferguson's *Grammatical Exercises* were used. We were also introduced to Melvin's *Latin Grammar*, a book which embraced only etymology and prosody, but did not extend to syntax. It was a wonderful storehouse of minute learning on the subjects with which it dealt.

In the third year Caesar's *Gallic War* and Ovid's *Metamorphoses* were read, and we began to write *Versions*, pieces of English dictated by the master in the School to be translated (usually there and then) into Latin, with the assistance of the Latin dictionary. This practice formed the most prominent feature of the teaching in the higher classes.

Excellent as was the teaching of Mr. Dun, entry into the Fourth class disclosed a higher standard. Dr. Melvin taught the Fourth and Fifth classes together. He devoted a few days at the beginning to what was termed a revision of the grammar, beginning with some instruction as to the vowel sounds . . . Another subject of minute learning was the division of Latin words into syllables, as to which he laid down rules which were expected to be observed in all written work submitted to him.

When the revision was concluded we began to read a portion of Caesar's *Civil War*, and continued to do so until the end of the first quarter. In the second quarter (January–March) portions of Vergil were read, usually the first and second books of the *Aeneid* (one book in the fourth year, the other in the fifth), some of the *Eclogues*, and the latter part of the fourth *Georgic* (*Pastor Aristaeus*). In the third quarter the Odes of Horace were read, usually two books in the fourth year, and two other books in the fifth. In the fourth quarter a portion of Livy was the subject. In dealing with all these portions of Latin literature Melvin was careful to give an accurate literal translation, but besides this he called the attention of his scholars to everything which required elucidation, displaying an easy mastery over etymology, syntax and prosody. Not infrequently he commented on the defects and mistakes in the school editions of the classics then in use . . .

Yet with all the pains bestowed on this part of tuition, it could not but be felt by his pupils that everything was subordinate to the version. On it turned the places held by them in the classroom; on it turned the places in the prize list at the end of the year; for these purposes no weight was given either to translation from Latin into English or any other mark of scholarship.

In the Fourth and Fifth classes the usual practice was that two Versions were written in the classroom in each week, generally on a Tuesday and Friday. Once a fortnight there was given out what was called a *trial* Version, and by it the places in the classes for the next fortnight were determined. Generally the trial Version was written on Friday morning, and the result was announced on the following Monday. In the interval Melvin had gone through all the versions and carefully marked and estimated the errors in them. On Monday morning he brought them into the classroom arranged in due order. The seats, beginning with the first in the fifth class, were emptied one by one – Melvin began, *Sine errore A.B.;* thereupon A.B. took his place at the head of the class; and so on down to the last. If more than one of the versions was *Sine errore*, they were arranged according to his view of their merits, special regard being had to elegance of expression. On rare occasions he would pronounce a version *Sine errore, elegantissime.* Errors were divided into three classes, minimi, medii and maximi: a minimus counted as one, a medius as two, and a maximus as four. The non-trial versions were read and marked, and were publicly commented on, but the errors were not estimated numerically. Finally, Melvin dictated his own translation of the English he had given out, which was always composed by himself, with the special object of testing the Latinity of the pupils: I never knew him to use an extract from an English author for the purpose . . .

The School broke up for the summer holiday in the last week of June, and the vacation lasted for a little more than a month . . . The last quarter (August to October) was marked by a great influx into the Fifth class of new scholars from country schools, who desired to take advantage of Melvin's instruction in order to prepare themselves for the Bursary Competitions at the two Colleges in the last week of October. Many of these were older than the scholars of the three preceding quarters, and by the help of the trial versions not a few of them rose to high places in the class.

No direct religious instruction was given in the School, but before the commencement of the morning lesson a short prayer was said. Where, in the ordinary course of teaching, a fitting opportunity occurred, Melvin never hesitated to quote the Bible. A favourite passage was Proverbs XXX., 8–9, "Give me neither poverty nor riches; feed me with food convenient for me: lest I be full, and deny God, and say who is the Lord? Or lest I be poor, and steal, and take the name of my God in vain." There was a custom of prescribing what was called a 'sacred lesson' on Saturday for the following Monday. It began in the first class, where the Lord's Prayer, the Ten Commandments, and the Apostles' Creed in Latin (all found in Ruddiman's *Rudiments*) had to be learnt by heart . . .

Melvin had but little difficulty in maintaining discipline. His stern features, disfigured by the ravages of small-pox, gave rise to the name of 'Grim', frequently applied to him. In most cases a look from him was enough to deter a pupil from indulging in any liberty; and the utterance of a few scathing words inflicted a deeper sting than any physical punishment. Only on a few occasions did he lay his hand on a pupil.

Melvin was a great personality in the School, and was recognised as such by the citizens of Aberdeen. He was an excellent and successful teacher, and all that he taught was sound and good. For myself, I gratefully acknowledge the benefit I received from his training.

'REMEMBERING THE DAYS OF OLD'

John Johnston, Vice-President of the Marine National Bank of Milwaukee, attended the GS between 1847 and 1851, entering Class II. This choice was made in the belief that its bursary winning record was better than that of the Gymnasium. Aged twelve, he was taken by his mother to be interviewed by Dr Melvin in his Library at his home in Belmont Street. Having ascertained that Johnston had mastered his Latin rudiments and had tackled the work of Cornelius Nepos, Melvin decided that he should join the Second Class, taught by the veteran, John Dun ('Dunnie').

> He was far from brilliant, but he was wise and safe. While he was not a strict disciplinarian he always maintained good order in his Class, because the boys liked him. He would frequently joke with us, and occasionally he would get off what he considered a good pun. He was accustomed to wear a blue dress-coat with brass buttons . . .
>
> A prize was given annually to the best-behaved boy in the Class, and it was decided by a vote of the scholars. The most popular boy was apt to get it, if he was not too unruly.

According to Johnston, Melvin had his favourites; not the sons of the rich but more usually the able sons of the leading citizens of Aberdeen. However, his real criticism was aimed at the intensity of the work-load imposed on the pupils by Melvin and his staff, the result of their dedication to ensure success in the Bursary Competition examination. 'Three of the best scholars of our Class died young from the effects of too much hard study and too little recreation.'

'WHEN WE WERE BOYS'

The Hon. Sir James Westland attended the School in 1852–5:

> Of Mr Beverly I remember very little, except his kindly manner, which interfered not one whit with his capacity for keeping order in his class. He was lame, and unable to move even in his classroom without the aid of a thick stick . . .
>
> I think it must be admitted that Mr Evans never had a fair

> chance . . . [He] came from Ireland, and we took it as an insult to us that any Irishman should be thought capable of teaching us. He pronounced Latin and Greek after the English fashion, which we, of course, considered unscholarly. He offended the sense of the School by showing that he was capable of questioning their dicta; and in this way he stirred the prejudices of his pupils. He was, unfortunately, short-sighted, and this gave these prejudices the opportunity of breaking out in violent breaches of discipline. In short, his failure arose less from incapacity in respect of scholarship than from want of knowledge of the Aberdeen schoolboy.

'MY GRAMMAR SCHOOL EXPERIENCES, 1858–1860'

Extracts from the articles written by James Fowler Kellas Johnstone, were reproduced in the School magazines of October 1911 and February 1912:

> [In the first half of the nineteenth century] the full curriculum required an attendance of five consecutive years . . . Entrants at the beginning of the first year had equal prospects, outstanding genius and other causes excepted, but it was to be expected that care would be taken that boys joining the class in its subsequent years possessed the qualifications requisite to begin its work at the point of progress already reached by the earlier students. Unhappily there was no preliminary examination, and as admission to a class was absolutely within the control of its master, who pocketed all the fees paid by his pupils, instances of abuse and injustice were not only liable to occur, but were not infrequent. The school was mainly Classical, the subjects taught being much Latin, less Greek, still less of Geography and History, with a minimum of advanced English. For writing, arithmetic, mathematics, modern languages, elementary science and art the boys must attend elsewhere. There was no library or museum, no printed school magazine, no drill, while athletic exercises, swimming, or sports of any kind were not encouraged. Holidays were as few as possible: statutory days, the half-yearly feasts of the Kirk, May Day, a week at New Year, the summer vacation of five weeks, which comprehended the whole month of July, and two or three days in late October or early November following the annual examination, when advanced scholars of the

Rector's classes passed forward to the universities, of which at that time Aberdeen [still] had two.[8]

In 1858 the School was reopened after the summer holidays on Monday, 2nd August, and one afternoon of the same week Mr. Robert Sim, for many years the proprietor of a successful elementary school in the city, led his two best scholars to the door of the second class room, where he introduced them to the master, with whom he had a slight personal acquaintance. After a brief conversation, the master undertaking to do his best for them when he had ascertained their fitness, the little lads were left in his charge. When five o'clock came, the class was dismissed, but the newcomers remained.

John Brebner, the master, great, broad-shouldered, fair blonde, ruddy and rustic-looking from holiday sunshine, approached to interview them. He was the son of the village blacksmith of Fordoun, had attended the rector's classes in the school ten years before, was the First Bursar of Marischal College in 1848, and M.A. there in 1852. Questioning them upon their attainments, particularly their knowledge of Latin, he was made aware that they had studied Ruddiman's *Rudiments* as far as the verb, and the short exercises in the primer of Alexander Adam, the once famous Rector of Edinburgh High School, but they had never seen a Latin grammar or classic, did not know what a Version was, and did not possess a Latin dictionary. He told them to procure Melvin's *Latin Grammar, Cornelius Nepos,* Milton's *Paradise Lost,* Stewart's *Geography,* and a Latin dictionary, that the hours of attendance were 9 to 11am and 3 to 5pm., and that the fee of 10s.6d. was payable in advance. Thus were the writer and his school friend, George Masson, admitted to the Grammar School class of 1856–61 in the fourth term of its second year . . .

I was pleased to be of the Grammar School, for I had lived close to it for years; my mind was full of its minor traditions, the names of famous students were familiar to me, I had witnessed . . . many a battle between the boys of the School and those of Gordon's Hospital, and five years before had watched . . . the long and mournful procession which followed the bier of its most celebrated Rector [Melvin].

I was at the bottom of the class, and the main test of position was the bi-weekly Latin version. Progress was small and slow and I never reached a middle position. Latin lessons occupied all my time and were imperfectly learned because I was floundering in dark ignorance of the first principles of Latin syntax . . . Other lessons were sufficiently studied to pass muster, but could never counterbalance defective Latinity.

Only one poor boy held a presentation bursary as in those days such gifts were under the control of private patronage, which was tapped by influence, so that they were usually held by the sons of citizens who could not only well afford to pay for education, but ought to have been ashamed to seek the aid that belonged by right to indigent scholars. So abominable was their administration that the editor of *The Scotsman*[9] then denounced it in the strongest terms, declaring that the State ought to take charge of funds left for the public purpose of education, and if one should leave a bursary limited to the inhabitants of Dunse, with a preference to red-haired youths of the name of Noodle, our public functionaries should not be obliged to carry out such absurd directions, but should award it to the best and most aspiring scholar, the strongest intellectual athlete in public competition . . .

It was no great rarity to find full-grown men in all the classes, and in the Fourth and Fifth there were always a dozen or more . . . but in 1858 most of the boys were quite young, from eleven to fourteen years of age, the great majority of them conscientiously doing their best to perform the class work. The Dux was John Scott . . . In Latin he was never beaten at School, being the first prizeman every year of the five and Medallist when the class completed its course in 1861.

Late in October [1858] came the examination by which not only was the prize list determined but also which pupils were fit to go forward to the Third Class with the master. This, however, was very largely a foregone conclusion for, as the master took all the class fees, he also took great care to leave behind as little as possible for his successor. The writer was declared to have passed . . . I doubt whether a single 10s.6d. was left behind.

There followed the Annual Visitation by the Lord Provost, Magistrates and Council, and several of the more prominent clergymen, attended by the city officers in scarlet livery, bearing ancient halberds. The Rector, an erudite but unpopular little Irishman named Evans, and nicknamed *Paddy,* made a Latin speech, followed by English speeches by the Lord Provost [John Webster] and others to the whole school assembled in the large public room. The prizes, most of which were for proficiency in Latin, were distributed to the successful competitors, and we were dismissed for two or three days' holiday . . .

The work of the Third Class required some new books: *Caesar de bello Gallico,* Virgil's *Georgics,* with more Melvin rules for scanning the lines of Latin verse, Geddes' *Greek Grammar,* and White's *History of Rome* . . . There were very few new faces to note but among the newcomers was a tall, handsome young Boer named Fehrsen, who boarded with the master, whereby, possibly, began the connection with South Africa which led to John Brebner becoming, some years later, Minister of Education in the Orange Free State at Bloemfontein.

An even more remarkable accession was Robert Macdonald Conley,[10] a handsome youth of seventeen, with dark eyes, curly brown hair, and healthy-looking, intelligent features, who spoke English well. As he pronounced Latin words after the English method, his class performances greatly amused us, and were roundly denounced by the master, who tried to cure the defect by calling on him more frequently than the others. The boy explained that he had been trained at the Grammar School of Newcastle-upon-Tyne, but the master insisted he must acquire the Scottish and only correct method, everywhere followed except in England . . . Robert Conley did not remain long in the class, for its work was really below his attainment, and I believe he went to Old Aberdeen Grammar School, for, upon the appointment of its Rector, Mr. William Barrack, to our School, he reappears on the roll of the fifth class for three months. He gained the Third Bursary in 1860, severely defeating our Dux, John Scott, and, after taking his degree, became a Classical tutor in England. I may add here that corporal punishment was not very frequent in the class, and was never unfair, for the best scholar was as liable to receive it as the worst for any infringement of discipline. Nor should I call it severe . . .

Entered the classroom two minutes late upon a sunshiny afternoon, and shuffled as quietly as possible to his place, the writer, his face and hands and little handkerchief besmeared with blood, which still trickled slowly from one of his nostrils. 'Have you been fighting, Johnstone?' said the master, interrogatively. 'Yes, sir; but he was a Sillerton [Robert Gordon's Hospital] boy, replied I, communicatively and extenuatively. No further question was asked. Isolated conflicts of this kind were not uncommon, but the pitched battles of school versus school, in which crowds of boys engaged with sticks and missiles of various kinds, had become rare. Happier are the present days of school rivalries in the pleasures of legitimate sports with their rewards of glory and honour . . .

Then came the vacation, followed by another quarter's diligent study: an eventful time filled with rumours that Rector Evans, whose two classes numbered only a dozen scholars, was to be dismissed by the Town Council if they had the power, which some doubted: a time of crisis in our educational annals, for greater than the ruin in our School was the overwhelming calamity, as it was then considered, of the new Act of Parliament uniting the two Universities, directing the Faculties of Arts and Theology to be taught only at King's College, and leaving to Marischal merely scientific instruction. The city was overcast with a general gloom, through which the swiftly increasing importance of Science was invisible and unsuspected, and the approaching glories of Marischal undreamed.

My fifteen months under John Brebner were sadly misspent, although not entirely wasted: the system was more at fault than the teacher, then very inadequately remunerated for his arduous work . . . I now passed forward to the Rector's class. Before assembling in the Fourth classroom I believe we all knew that Paddy Evans was leaving Aberdeen with £1,500 of Town Council compensation money in his pocket, and that we were to have a new Rector. In perfect silence and with feelings of inexpressible curiosity, we now saw the very tall, spare, slightly-stooping figure, ashy-pale close-shaven visage, and stony eyes of James McLauchlin as he strode solemnly into the classroom for the first time with a faint ghost of a smile directed towards us.

Nine years before he had been First Bursar at King's College, and he was schoolmaster of Insch, but had accepted the appointment of pro-Rector until the position could be filled by the man to whom popular opinion had assigned it. He was dressed in solemn black, even to the neck-tie and shirt-studs, as for a funeral, and in a most unmistakable although well-fitting tie-wig of a deep brown colour, which contrasted awfully with his ghastly complexion. His voice was clear, even, and pleasant, his manner firm yet sympathetic, and for the first time we heard ourselves addressed as 'gentlemen'. He gave immediate evidence that he knew well how to teach, and that he was a good Classic. As a teacher, from the very first hour, the class did not dislike him: rather the reverse: but, he was novel, his appearance was at least peculiar, and very soon that spirit of mischief which abideth for ever in Aberdeen boys began to manifest itself, for one afternoon, when he took his seat at the high desk from which he conducted the work of the class, he became painfully aware that the upholstery of his chair had been effectively fortified against such aggression by the insertion of sharp tacks and bent pins with their business ends pointed in the most promising directions. His pallid face flushed slightly as he hastily assumed an erect position, pushed the chair into a corner, stood to the desk, and began the lesson with an admirable show of complete indifference which was rather discomfiting to the mischief makers, who had hoped to create a disturbance.

But they were comforted and amused next morning when snuffy old John Gray, the janitor, told of the busy half-hour he had spent with the Rector extracting the thistles. Immediately they set to work anew, and when the rector sought to open his desk to bring out the muster roll, he found its keyhole so tightly packed with small pieces of paper that it took him quite fifteen minutes to pick them out with his pocket knife. He remonstrated quietly in denunciatory language, well-chosen and appropriate, but, strange to say, still calling us 'gentlemen'.

A day or two afterwards, when he entered the classroom he found its atmosphere rather peppery from the fumes of capsicum powder well circulated by a heated fire-shovel, and joined vigorously in the chorus of sneezing which prevailed until they subsided. The fumes of gum asafoetida similarly produced were less effective upon another occasion, for he made no remark.

Then came the climax, for next afternoon, on reaching the classroom door, I found it surrounded by a small but rapidly increasing crowd of boys unable to find admission. We were joined in a minute or two by the rector, who vainly tried the door and shouted to those within. Everything short of actually breaking the panels was tried, but the oak was as obdurate as the now besieged rebels. The classroom windows, which overlooked an enclosed grass plot and faced those of the third classroom, were tried and found impossible. Finally, after an hour's unavailing effort and remonstrance, the rector took a note of our names and dismissed us. I ran home at once with my mouth full of the news, and know nothing of the subsequent emergence of the self-besieged: nor did I ever learn, as far as I remember, by what means the barring-out was contrived and performed so effectively.

During the next day or two the class was unwontedly quiet and subdued, for we felt that something very serious was impending of which the Rector gave no hint whatever, and our boyish intercourse became stifled and curtailed. Then came a morning when all the classes assembled in the public school before the Rector, masters and a deputation of the Council, and seventeen members of the Fourth Class were called out and stood together in a long row. A speech was delivered from which we gathered that it had been decided to punish the gross insubordination by the expulsion of those seventeen gentlemen 'unless they each made a personal apology to the Rector, who was willing to accept it rather than allow them to be so heavily disgraced'. All apologised . . . and were humbled and contrite for the Rector was an excellent teacher, his temper well controlled, his conduct at a difficult juncture unexceptionable, he proved in wisdom a Triton among the minnows. Henceforth the work proceeded with perfect smoothness during his nine months administration, and I feel sure that the respect I shall always cherish for him is shared by every survivor of the class. He afterwards became minister of Inveravon.

The Fifth Class was small, but the Fourth was very large and included some newcomers, mostly from the country. Our new books were Cicero, Ovid, and Xenophon's *Anabasis* . . . When the vacation arrived we bade farewell to pro-Rector McLauchlin, and I to the School as well, for before the class resumed its duties in August I had begun to learn how to earn my own living. In the nine months under McLauchlin I had made more satisfactory progress than in the preceding fifteen months, but as it was doubtful whether I could gain a place in the University Bursary list, it was decided that I should accept an opportunity which offered of learning a profession. I have always regretted the unfinished fourth but my love of books enabled me to educate myself, almost all my leisure being spent in reading – a wretched training for one who has to make his way in the world, for books cannot teach how to fight the battles of commercial and social life.

AT THE SCHOOL IN THE SIXTIES (1861–1864)

Extracts taken from *Memoirs of 88 Years,* an autobiography written in 1935 by Alexander Falconer Murison:

On the cruelly cold morning of Saturday, 19th January, 1861 . . . we hurried off to the New Market in the Green, and upstairs to the commanding book-shop of John Adam. My father, I suppose, had got from my future master a list of the books I should require; and we carried away Andrews' *Latin Dictionary,* Riddle's *English-Latin Dictionary, Selections from Ovid* (Chambers), White's *History of Rome,* and two or three other small volumes, at the total cost of £3.5s. A trifling literary outfit, you will say; and so it was: but proud as I was of my new possessions, my heart was wrung to think how long and how hard my father had had to work to save even that petty sum . . .

On Monday morning, 21st January 1861, I shouldered my parcel of new books, and set out to discover the Grammar School . . . up Crown Street, to the right over Union Bridge, to the left along Belmont Street, into School Hill . . . Now I joined the stream of pupils and passed through the small stone-paved court, and up the entrance steps, when I came right in the face of the Masters, standing under the clock till it should strike nine, and disperse them to their several class-rooms. My class was the Third; and I passed to the third class-room by the left. The master – the Rev. James Wilson Legge, M.A. – followed immediately.

The room was spacious enough, but bare of ornament, and scarcely inviting. A passage ran up the middle, and forms – 'factions' they were called – extended on both sides from the passage to the walls, the master's raised seat overlooking directly the left group of forms, at the inner end of the room. There might have been 60 to 70 pupils. I took my seat at the bottom, of course; that is, at the end of the last occupied form on the right side from the entrance – on the left side from the master. As the lesson went on, I now and again ventured to ask my neighbour – a charming boy, son of a banker –

what this or that meant. The uniform answer, perfectly indifferent, was: 'Don't know'. Presently a question was put to a boy in the first faction on my side: he failed to answer, and the master's finger moved steadily down faction after faction till it rested on me. I rose and answered correctly. Accordingly, I had to go up and take my place above the pupil that had failed; the fact of a new boy's sudden rise, and, perhaps, no less his astonishing *impedimenta* of books, creating somewhat of a sensation. But this was only a beginning. Hardly had I settled down in the first faction on the left side (from the master) when a boy in the first faction just under the master failed to answer, and the moving finger again rested on me. Again I answered correctly. And there I was already in the first faction of the class, and only two pupils above me . . . Thereafter I was seldom dislodged from the first faction.

Mr. Legge was a man of about thirty, slightly built, with firm, not to say severe, features, which readily opened in sunny kindliness, even tenderness. He loved us all, and we all loved him, and respected him profoundly: he never had to raise a finger to check disorder; he very seldom had to speak a word of remonstrance. He was a good scholar, and he was a constant student. He was also a good Conservative, and stood on the ancient ways stoutly, in education as in politics. I do not know whether he had been a pupil, or even a colleague, of the celebrated Dr. Melvin, a recent Rector of the School, whose fame as a Latinist was great and widely recognised; but to him Melvin's name was sacred.

Our great subject was, of course, the *Version* – that is, the translation of a passage of English into Latin. Once a week a passage was read to us, and we took it down, and turned it into Latin. In two or three days Mr. Legge read out the results, and according to them we took our places afresh. The papers without error were marked *sine errore*: the blunders were marked 1, 2, 3, 4, according to their heinousness, 4 being styled a *maxie* (*maximus error*) – e.g. a misconjugation of a verb, or a wrong gender, etc. We did not read much Latin but what we did read was very thoroughly analysed, not only in all grammatical bearings, but also with an eye to utilisation in the *Version*. Of course we were thoroughly drilled in Latin grammar. I forget whose *Grammar*, I think Ruddiman's? Also we had a single terror of a book, so portentous a book that it is strange that I should forget its author's name: was it Ruddiman? Or was it Melvin himself?

– a book wherein the genders of nouns, the longs and shorts of vowels, and heaven knows what, were set forth in groups with strings of exceptions, in exhaustive detail, in hexameter verses: and these verses, in their hundreds, we had to commit to memory! . . .

We no doubt read some prose, but I remember only that we sampled those *Selections from Ovid*, and did not find them too easy. History, Geography, etc.: all these I forget, for everything else was overshadowed by Latin. White's little sketch of Roman History was mainly, if at all, read at home. Our programme might have been considerably varied with great advantage, but what we learnt we learnt.

We had no playground. We had no library. We had no hostel. How different from the ample provisions of the present day! But we did have a sort of debating society, at any rate in the last quarter of stay in the Third Class.

In October, 1861, I passed on to the Fourth Class. The Fourth and Fifth Classes were under the charge of the Rector. They were seated on opposite sides of the passage running up the middle of a huge room, the fourth on the left (as you enter), the fifth on the right, with the Rector's desk at the top. In my fourth Class there were 62 pupils; the fifth had somewhere about as many, but it was usually much increased in the quarter before the *Competition* by an influx of pupils seeking a final polish for the contest.

The Rector, the Rev. William Barrack, M.A. (later LL.D.), was about forty, fully middle-size, vigorous, with fresh, open, genial countenance, and hearty bearing; and he was greatly liked by all of us, in spite of a somewhat trenchant manner. He was a good scholar, and a skilful and energetic teacher. What he might have done in complete freedom can only be surmised: his business there and then was to prepare his pupils directly for the *Competition*; and that he did with might and main, and with great success. A dozen years later he became head master of a new secondary school of high aspirations in Glasgow, but he soon died, prematurely.[11]

Versions were written twice every week, on Tuesday and Friday afternoon in School; and usually three Exercises viz., a Translation, a Greek Exercise, and Latin Sentences, were written at home weekly. The Tuesday's Version was always a Trial Version i.e. the errors were counted, and the place of the pupil in the class was assigned accordingly. The Translation was read, examined, and criticised in school, and the Greek Exercises and Latin sentences were carefully examined, corrected, and returned to the pupils. Frequently on a Monday afternoon, a Translation, or a Greek Exercise, or a Version was written in School without the use of Notes or Dictionaries, and afterwards examined and corrected.

Obviously the office of Rector was no sinecure! The marking followed the same plan as in the Third Class. I have hardly any recollection of the Latin authors we read: I have but a vague notion of Livy, and of Cicero *pro Milone*; nor of anything in verse. I think we must have begun Greek in the Fourth Class: though it is not easy to see how beginners in the fourth could work with the fifth who had been working at it for a year. We mastered Geddes's Greek Grammar, and we read Xenophon's *Anabasis* – two books at least. History and Geography were *Ancient,* not modern; and we read them up at home. And we had a taste of English: we read *Julius Caesar* and *The Merchant of Venice* in class, with a minimum of comment; but we were in no way prepared to meet the sort of English papers set at the *Competition.* Even the energy of the Rector had a limit.

We had no Mathematics, or Writing. For these pupils had to go to the Town's Schools in Little Belmont Street; fee 5s. a quarter for one hour daily. I did not go: it was all I could do to afford the Classical fee at the school. I got to know some Euclid and only Book I was required for the *Competition.* I believe French and German classes were offered in the School at 15s. per quarter 'if a class of at least eight could be formed'. I do not recollect the formation of a class.

In 1863 the Visitation was held, not in the time-honoured building in Schoolhill, but in the spacious new building in Skene Street West, this being the opening ceremony. I did very well . . . From the fourth I had gained the 32nd Bursary (£12) at the *Competition;* but I resigned it, partly in view of its smallness, more, perhaps, because I thought it wiser to be better prepared before entering the University. I was generally regarded as sure to come out pretty near the top but I had no official tutor and having no plan I read whatever came into my hands . . .

Murison was First Bursar in 1863 and returned to the School as a member of the English staff in 1869.

THE CLOSING YEARS OF THE GRAMMAR AT SCHOOLHILL

James Valentine attended the Grammar between 1858 and 1862, entering Class II. He left an account of his time at the School:

> In the dying years of the School in Schoolhill the accommodation cannot be described otherwise than as mean and shabby. The exterior of the structure was weather-beaten and the interior decrepit . . . The only playground was the small, roughly-paved courtyard in front of the School. The well at the rear was an inaccessible wilderness. The 'kits' or latrines would have disgraced the precincts of the residence of an unspeakable Turk.
>
> Legge was the youngest of the teachers. He was very popular with guardians and well liked by his pupils. He thus usually had a larger class than the others. One of the masters had the misfortune to be permanently lamed while a child [Beverly]. Rector Evans lacked the power of maintaining discipline and was a failure as a teacher under the Scotch system. His senior classes did pretty much as they liked. William Barrack, however, was the prince of teachers. He had a magnetic power over the young fellows and was gifted with a fine voice. He had a happy knack of giving short mnemonics for the better understanding of the sequence of tenses and other niceties of Latin idiom. He hardly ever required to have recourse to the tawse.
>
> We started a debating society, which gave a soiree, said to be the first in the history of the School, which was a decided hit. Cricket clubs were also revived. The Aulton Links was our practice and match ground. In times of snow, the tricky fellows, entrenched behind the dwarf wall and iron railing along Schoolhill, proved a great annoyance to the female passers-by, whom they ungallantly bombarded with snowballs.
>
> Most of the Schoolhill Grammarians looked down on the Gordon's Hospital boys, their uniform of corduroy trousers, brass-buttoned serge vest and jacket, and Glengarry bonnet to match, being regarded as the livery of a charity school. Besides, the Hospital lads were known all over the city by a vulgar epithet, which is explained by a well-known local antiquary as due to the kailyard food of the inmates being insufficiently boiled in the kailpot.

SEVEN Years of Inquiry, 1863–1880

This chapter has three main sections. The first pertains to the inquiries into educational provision and the resulting detailed information on the state of the Grammar School in its new surroundings. The second main theme on the staff concentrates on the Rectorships of Barrack, Stewart and Martin and the curriculum and resulting staffing changes in this period. Finally, the chapter ends with a selection of the pupils who go on to achieve success in their different walks of life, practically always after completing a successful time at Aberdeen University, following the Fusion of King's and Marischal in 1860.

EARLY INQUIRIES INTO THE STATE OF THE GRAMMAR SCHOOL

In Scotland's burgh schools the town councils had an obligation to see that standards were being maintained and this was carried out by the annual Visitation when local dignitaries assembled to hear pupils being put through their paces. Whilst most of the proceedings were concerned with the teaching of Latin and were preceded by an address of welcome in Latin to these visitors, it was a matter of amused conjecture among the pupils of how much was actually understood by at least some of the visitors.

Periodically it was felt that standards were requiring review and improvement but on most occasions these inspections were more in the nature of a social call than a time for appraisal of educational performance. However, in the period of general reform which the 1830s brought to Britain, one significant change was the decision by the Westminster Government to make some money available to education. By today's standards the sums of money involved were tiny but the Government soon showed that the idea of "accountability" was not a modern idea because it recognised that if it was to spend money on education it had to try to make sure that this money was spent on desirable projects and that this could only be done by having Government agents to gather information and to ensure that instructions were carried out. Hence the creation of the School Inspectorate to undertake what was a vast job. At first there was only one inspector appointed for the whole of Scotland.

The burgh schools were not the main targets for the early inspectors and the first major inspection of the Grammar came in the 1860s. It is true that there had been a major inquiry in Aberdeen into the state of the Town's Schools in the mid-1830s but it concentrated on the sorry state of the school in Drum's Lane. It was as a result of that inquiry that the decision was made to build the new Town's Schools in Little Belmont Street. Proposals that it might be possible to put a second storey on the Grammar in Schoolhill came to nothing.

Shortly after this local inquiry there was a national inquiry into education in Scotland which covered parish and non-parish schools. This was conducted in the typical Victorian way in 1839: questionnaires were completed by headteachers and a picture of the education provided was gathered. Melvin's answers gave the roll of the Grammar as 190 boys in 1836 and 170 in 1837. It was a day school attended by boys between nine and fifteen years of age, who usually stayed for four years but could stay on to complete a full course over five years. Melvin referred to four staff (including himself) who taught English, History and Geography (as well as Latin and some Greek) and a permanent teacher of Arithmetic as well as separate teachers for 'other branches'. The hours of attendance were 9–12 noon and 3–5 p.m. with Arithmetic classes at 12–1 p.m. and 1–2 p.m. The holidays were the first three days of May, four weeks in July and eight days at Christmas. Prize books were awarded and bursaries given as 'rewards'. The mode of punishment was defined as 'reproof, disgrace, extra employment and corporal punishment'.

Melvin's answers were predictable in a 'Classical seminary' based on 'the principles of the Church of Scotland' but his description of what the teachers taught suggested a wider curriculum. The teaching of Arithmetic was the result at that time of the poor state of the Town's Schools in Drum's Lane and the practice was abandoned when the new premises in Little Belmont Street became available in 1841.

THE FEARON INQUIRY

The first major inquiry into the Grammar was made by an eminent English educationist, D.R. Fearon. He was appointed by the Taunton Commission to examine the state of the provision of secondary schools in England other than the great public schools. These schools were termed 'endowed' schools because they were funded by the income from some gift or bequest. The inspection of these schools in England revealed many kinds of situations and led to efforts to regulate these organisations into some kind of uniform system. Some schools had been blessed with income much greater than the uses to which they were put justified, while others had not flourished at all.

To try to obtain fair standards of comparison and assessment the inspectors came across the border to Scotland to look at some similar schools – Hamilton Academy, The High School of Glasgow and Aberdeen GS. The Grammar's visitation was justified on the grounds of 'its antiquity, its reputation, its endowments and its close connection with the University of Aberdeen' and it was noted as 'one of the most important in Scotland'. Fearon also remarked that the School more nearly resembled an English grammar school than any of the other burgh schools which he visited (Ayr Academy, Edinburgh Royal HS, Inverness Academy, Stirling HS and the Academies of Perth and Dumfries).

The two sources of income with which the Grammar was endowed with were the Dun bequest and the grants of money from the Town Council of Aberdeen. Sadly, the enormous potential value of the Dun bequest had been frittered away by the Council over the years. Its value to the school by 1866 only reached just over £166, which was small indeed given the industrial, commercial and domestic developments which had taken place on Ferryhill land. The Council itself had had to pay for the costs arising from a new building and increased staff which had totalled £1,180.

The other source of funds interested Fearon considerably viz. the 'bursaries' which enabled pupils to study at the School. Fearon found six such bursaries: three established in the seventeenth century and three in the eighteenth. By 1866 there had been widespread discussion in the Town on their purpose and the methods of awarding them. Fearon's investigations certainly seemed to confirm that they were 'presentation' awards – to those who were 'well-connected' and the recipients performed very poorly in the tests which were carried out. No examinations were conducted by the School either to establish that a bursary boy was fit to start the course or to ensure that, once started, his progress was satisfactory. How to remedy this situation was a matter of dispute. Was competition healthy among pupils? Was competition even fair because boys from more prosperous homes would almost certainly be better prepared than those from more modest backgrounds?

For five days in June 1866, Fearon delved into the inner workings of the School and produced, as a result, his revealing report on the finances of the School, the methods of teaching, the qualifications of the staff, the social composition of the pupils, the attainments of the pupils in their different subjects, the state of the buildings, the organisation of the School and its curriculum and the discipline and tone of the School.

Of course it was impossible to isolate each topic because the practice in one area almost inevitably had ramifications in others. For example, pupils had to pay fees for their education, not an all-embracing fee but payment for each class which they took. This meant that there were times when the boys were out of class and completely without supervision. The fees were paid to the staff who derived a large part of their income from them. A boy entering the School had the same Classics master for his first four years and so it was in the master's interest to keep the class together whatever their limitations in achievement or attitude. This meant that there was no attempt to impose any restriction on a boy going on from year to year, falling further and further behind the best scholars and facing the master with an element who were both incapable and unwilling to make any serious effort. Unless the master was a very strict upholder of order the class could, and sometimes did, have serious disciplinary problems. This particularly applied in Classics but the fee-paying also meant that teachers were not keen to try to enforce order because of the fear that the pupils might vote with their feet and leave the class – lost fees!

The Report tried to analyse the social composition of the School according to the occupation of the parents and came up with the result that of the 308 boys enrolled that year 'the Aberdeen school is patronised in almost equal numbers by the professional men, the wholesale tradesmen, and the labourers or workmen'. Fearon drew a contrast with Glasgow High where one class of parent predominated – 'the tradesman or large shopkeeper', adding the observation that there was said to be not one representative there of labourers or workmen. The surprisingly large portion of working class pupils at the Grammar, Fearon reckoned, was due to various factors: the high quality of education in the parochial schools round about; the presentation bursaries given to the 'lad o' pairts' and the great enthusiasm to obtain a Classical education which opened the door to the

University and the social status of the ministry. A large number of boys from the parochial schools came into the Grammar at the later stages 'to receive a final polish before going to College' and stayed only a short time.

In Classics the standards reached by the pupils were reckoned on the whole to be better than a comparable English school but individually they were inferior to the best English schools. Latin was still the main subject in the School, Greek was taught, but only from the Third year, so it was perhaps not surprising that the performances were quite poor.

Since the opening of the new School in 1863, other subjects had been introduced but were obviously not fully accepted as equal in status to Classics. For one thing, they were not compulsory, as was Latin, so the numbers taking the classes were very low and the attendance was poor and irregular. The day the Mathematics class was visited, out of a roll of twenty-seven, only fourteen attended. While the teaching was done by an able enough master, his control of the class was poor and the standards were correspondingly low. Geometry was taught quite well but Algebra was hardly taught at all. Here the influence of the University Bursary Competition could be seen because in it only Book One of Euclid's Geometry was tested, so effort elsewhere was a waste of time. Not surprisingly, Fearon estimated the standard of Mathematics performance was lower than any of the other burgh schools.

The foreign language teaching was done by Mr Muller. He taught French and German but only seven boys took French and none took German. One factor in the small number was the timing of this voluntary class which was scheduled over the lunch-time break when the noise from the rest of the School made teaching extremely difficult. Despite these drawbacks, the pupils who did take French were commended for their progress even though the non-appearance of French in the Bursary Competition was a major discouragement.

Drawing was run by Mr Cleland who had only fifteen pupils altogether. Though he was well trained and anxious to pursue progressive methods he found that the course which was suggested was so hard and unpopular that he abandoned the pure doctrine in case he drove away all his pupils. In this dispiriting atmosphere, Cleland could console himself by reflecting on the fact that, according to Fearon, the situation was no better almost everywhere in Scotland where 'Art is at a decided discount'. The English class was also poorly attended, with only fourteen boys in the senior class out of sixty who did Classics with the Rector. The work that was done appears to have been dreary and anything but stimulating.

On the whole, Fearon was impressed with the qualifications and training of teachers who were either university graduates or trained in some other recognised institution. What also impressed him greatly was the friendliness and courtesy with which he was received by the staff and also the pupils. In particular, he was very pleased and even surprised by the willingness of the teachers to teach their classes in his presence because he had, he records, found a very great reluctance to do this among teachers in England.

At the end of his inquiry Fearon made a number of critical observations about the Grammar. The building itself he admired but found the rooms were so high that they made teaching difficult because of the echo. The toilets were well-constructed but spoiled by the poor flow of water to cleanse them. Despite having ample grounds in area, he remarked on the lack of sports facilities and commented on the School rule which ordered pupils to clear out as soon as School was over and the general Scottish reluctance to encourage pupils to play together after schools ended for the day.

One problem which was to remain for at least another generation was the very poor level of attainment which pupils had reached when they entered the School about the age of twelve from elementary school. When he tested the First Class Fearon found that, despite having an able teacher and effective disciplinarian, a few of the fifty-two boys showed an inability to write grammatically or spell accurately. When tested, the boys had been in the School for eight months so he reckoned no blame could be placed on the teacher but remarked that "the boys of twelve years of age come to this School very moderately prepared in the elements of English. In this respect, however, this School is certainly in no worse a position than most of our English middle schools".

When turning to the tone and discipline of the School Fearon noted how the provisions of Dun, that the Rector should be in general control of the School, were by then ignored and every teacher was left to his own devices. Probably the best way to sum up Fearon's general impression, is simply to quote at length his own words.

> I have already spoken of the want of order in some of the classes. There might also, I think, be some improvement in the order of the boys when out of class, in the corridors and passages of the School buildings. The want of a responsible governing Head or else of an efficient janitor seems to me to be decidedly felt; and I am sure there is no English middle school of the first grade in London in which

> so much noise and disorder would be allowed to be made on the premises as are here made by the boys out of class. I remember this especially when engaged in inspecting the French master's class. Number three of the Rules and Regulations, approved by the Lord Provost and Town Council, says 'Playing, running about, shouting, or making any needless noise within any part of the building is strictly forbidden'. This rule is evidently a dead letter as regards 'shouting and making needless noises'.
>
> In other respects I did not remark any want of good tone and behaviour among the pupils. The Fifth Class was in remarkably good order; and I am much indebted to the young men and boys for the good nature and courtesy with which they received a rather troublesome visitor and for the pains they took to answer my questions. They appeared, as a rule, to be hard workers and to enjoy working with their able and judicious Rector.

THE SEQUELS TO FEARON'S VISIT

The Council was seriously disturbed by the implications of Fearon's comments. It decided to approach Fearon to make an official report on the state of the School. Lord Provost Anderson visited London, met Fearon and pursued the possibility of a further inquiry. Fearon declined, suggesting a Scottish educationist, who turned out to be unavailable. The Council turned to Principal Campbell of Aberdeen University and HMI John Black, later Professor of Humanity at Aberdeen and a member of Aberdeen's first School Board in 1873, to produce a report.

In November 1866 Campbell and Black duly reported on the state of the School to the Council. Their method was to submit the Classes from II to V to an examination in a variety of topics and then classify the pupils in general bands of attainment – Very good (VG); Good (G); Middling (M); and Bad (B). The results confirmed much of what Fearon had found. There were a small number of 'very good' pupils in most subjects, more who were 'good' but more than half fell into the two lower categories of 'middling' to 'bad'.

In the Rector's Class V, which had been commended on the whole by Fearon, the average figures were: in Latin – VG 6; G 9; M 20; B 21 (the Greek results were somewhat better).

In Class IV: Latin – VG 5; G 7; M 10; B 17 (again the Greek results were somewhat better).

In Class III: Latin – VG 9; G 18; M 15; B 16.

In Class II: Latin – VG 4; G 4; M 20; B 18.

Class I was not tested in the same way but the general verdict saw it as a well organised class with a gentlemanly atmosphere and a highly satisfactory morale. It was especially commended because there was no copying and this was contrasted to this common malpractice in other classes.

These statistics for Classics did not make very good reading and some general observations were made as well of a critical nature. For example, the practice of concentrating effort only on the best boys was condemned. Campbell and Black pointed out that all the classes fell into 'a few very well-taught boys, a large number inferior and a considerable number who do little or nothing'. They also noted the very poor quality of some of the pupils suggesting they were hardly literate. Fearon had been surprised by the fact that he found there was no effort made to make pupils memorise things in Scottish schools and this was confirmed and commented on by Campbell and Black. It was suggested that a more vigorous approach to teaching would secure the attention of the whole class. The lack of a stringent examination to test the capacity of pupils to proceed from one class to the next again struck a familiar note. On the question of records or incentives they said at one time there were too many prizes but now there were none. It was suggested that there was a need for tougher inspection by two examiners to ensure adequate standards.

In the other section of the School there was also a repeat of this sorry state of affairs. Mathematics had only twenty-six boys who studied only one book of Euclid in Geometry and little more. The attendance was voluntary and so the classes were small and the attendance irregular. English with twenty-four boys in Class V and fifteen in Class IV had the same problems where the needs of the Bursary Competition at the University dictated a very narrow, dreary curriculum, of parsing, analysis and derivations, which was not very attractive. In Writing, Drawing and French the same story was told of voluntary attendance and small numbers.

Perhaps the most surprising part of Campbell and Black's report was their general verdict given their detailed critical appraisal: 'Notwithstanding some deficiencies, the Grammar merits the support and confidence of the public.' This suggested a lower level of expectation in educational standards than one might consider likely at this time particularly from an inspector who daily inspected Scottish schools and a University Principal who had a wide knowledge of the standards of attainment of students leaving School and embarking on their university courses.

THE ARGYLL COMMISSION OF 1867–1868

While the Taunton Commission was busy in England gathering information about the state of education there, a similar type of investigation was carried out in Scotland by a Commission under the Presidency of the Duke of Argyll. Having looked at the condition of elementary education in its earlier work, the Commission turned its attention in 1867–68 to producing a *Report on the State of Education in the Burgh and Middle Class Schools of Scotland – Public Schools.* Middle-Class schools were defined as those where pupils left school at the age of sixteen. Two Assistant Commissioners, Messrs Harvey and Sellar, toured round Scotland and in April 1867 they spent two days at Aberdeen GS.

Following so closely on from the work of Fearon, Campbell and Black, one would not expect a very different final report from their predecessors. Nevertheless the two visitors diligently gathered information about the School, starting with a brief outline of its 'history, constitution, and management'. They took a great interest in the buildings, a topic they pursued wherever they went. With regard to the Grammar they were found to be 'very handsome' and were as good as those of any school in Scotland. They noted the size of the rooms and commented that the only ornament in the Hall with its gallery for visitors was a portrait by Jameson of the school's seventeenth-century benefactor, Dr Patrick Dun (this was destroyed in the fire of 1986). The Library had few books. The gravel playground was an acre in extent but the School rules required pupils not to use it after school hours. The corridors in the School were used for hanging the boys' coats and caps and for shelter during wet weather. They were not intended for play, but referring to the School rules they noted sarcastically that 'A rule more absolutely ignored by the youths attending the Grammar could not easily be imagined'. The capacity of the school was estimated at 755 boys on the ground floor and 460 boys on the first floor but the actual roll was a mere 272!

The next aspect of the School which took up their attention was finance. As usual they identified where the money for running the school came from and what salaries and expenses these funds were expected to cover. However, what fascinated them – as it had Fearon – was the subject of the bursaries which were available in the School. These they carefully listed, noting their names, dates of funding, the amount, number and length of time they were tenable for, and who presented them. But what was particularly interesting to them was that hardly any were presented as a result of competition. Most of them were presented in accordance with the wishes of the Council and 'the effect of this is that some of the very worst scholars in the School were bursars'. To prove their case they quoted the places in class held by the twenty-four bursars who were in school during their visit.

The seven bursaries presented by the Town were worth £5 or £7 and their average position in class was 40th (the average class size being 55). The ten bursaries presented by masters under the direction of the Council were all worth £3 each and their average position in class was 24th (the average class size being 60). There were seven other bursaries presented by private patrons worth various values from just under £7 to £16 and their average position in class was 29th (the average class size being 54).

The bursaries were deemed fairly generous and the two commissioners were convinced that some radical review of how they were awarded was necessary. They quoted the view of a long-established master that in his experience the poor performance of bursars had always existed. However, the visitors also recognised that there was a case for those who held the belief that a change to competitive awards would penalise poor boys whose education was unlikely to allow competition on equal terms. Nonetheless, the terms of the original endowments, it was argued, allowed for a more careful and rigorous scrutiny of the bursary holders.

The cost of educating a boy was estimated to be 'extremely moderate' ranging from £7 1s in years I and II to £10 17s in years IV and V, but it was pointed out that, because pupils were allowed a free hand in choosing which classes they were to attend, they could reduce these sums by abandoning some of the subjects. Moreover, money could also be saved as about some 10% were bursars and yet the Town also paid for the books for a number of poor scholars.

The salaries of the teaching staff were examined. They were derived from three sources: Dr Patrick Dun's foundation; the Council; and fees from pupils. The Rector received £82 from source 1; £82 from source 2 and £176 from source 3: in total £340 per annum. The three Classical masters received £27 6s 8d each from source 1; £22 13s 4d from 2; and £150 from source 3: in total £200 pa. The Mathematics master received £20 from the Town and collected £231 in fees but had to pay two assistants from his salary. The other masters – English, Modern Languages and Drawing – depended completely on the fees from their poorly attended classes and so earned £70, £12 and £16 respectively. In these circumstances it is understandable why Sellar and Harvey noted that these last three masters had made little impact on the Classical nature of the School.

The Rector and the first three Classical masters were appointed by written examinations but all the others were appointed by testimonials. For the first three years of the course the Classics masters taught not only Classics but English grammar and modern Geography and History. In Classes IV and V the subjects of ancient Geography and History were taught. It was noted that the Prospectus at the time offered a sixth class but that it had never existed. It was suggested that 'the Aberdeen system was apparently to do little, but to do it accurately'.

Of the 272 boys on the roll some 260 attended during the inspection. Class size usually ranged from 40 to 63. In Classes I to IV most pupils came from the town or nearby but in the Rector's class there were more 'country' than 'town' boys. This was explained by the presence of many 'extranei' who attended the School only for the last year to prepare for the university, particularly the Bursary Competition. The ages in the Rector's class ranged from thirteen to twenty and the parental occupations included among the forty-three boys, quite a few professional people, three labourers, eleven farmers and five clergymen. (As some 74 (of 220) boys in 1873–4 came from outside the town, from as far away as Caithness, some twenty-four of them lodged in Aberdeen.)

In the first three years all boys had to attend the Latin classes but the other subjects were optional. In Classes IV and V all classes were optional. The usual practice was for boys to attend until Class IV and then many left to go into business or to university. The Commissioners noted later that some of the boys left after Class IV to avoid the examinations in the Rector's Class V because the classes at University were easier than at School. To a great extent the Bursary Competition dictated what was studied in School because, to the individual pupil, success in it gave a certain amount of local prestige or even the means to study for the professions, while collectively the School's success was for a long time, almost up to our own times, judged by the performance of the pupils in the Competition.

The main topic in the 'Comp.' was the 'Version' which meant translating an English passage into Latin and 400 marks were awarded. For Latin into English only 150 marks were awarded, for Greek into English 175 marks, English grammar and composition 175, Arithmetic (including fractions and proportion) 100 and Euclid book 1 some 200 marks. The targets of both masters and pupils were set by these topics and the marks attached to them, and this had the consequence that the aims were narrow and the practice very repetitive. Setting themselves these limited targets the School performed very well and still produced pupils who did very well later academically and even won appointments in the East Indian Civil Service and filled important posts in all walks of life at home and abroad.

The classes were all inspected in Classics and the performances were highly commended but 'the one great blemish running through all the classes more or less was the difference between the top and the bottom and the lengthened tail in most of them'. While the teaching was going on, Sellar and Harvey made notes on the methods employed and pinpointed the practice of promoting the whole class by 'years' which was of 'doubtful propriety' with the lower half being 'sacrificed to the upper' for the sake of the Bursary Competition. Teaching to the top half meant the neglect of the bottom half which was generally left undisturbed in its indolence. Only in one class was there a different approach. Nonetheless, despite the great spread of ability and attainment in the classes the Commissioners believed that 'Classical learning was still appreciated in Aberdeen more than anywhere else in Scotland and at least as well taught; and that the material given the boys to work on was first rate.'

If this verdict on the Classical side of the School was sympathetic and reasonably favourable a very different view was expressed on the behaviour of the boys, which had been found to be 'rude and boorish'. Generally but not always the boys behaved in class 'but as soon as the work was finished, before they had left their rooms and more notably still in the corridors and passages, the noise and turbulence were quite remarkable. Of their rudeness to strangers we heard of an instance that had happened shortly before our visit. A German, we were told, had lately come to do some repairs in the classrooms. As soon as the boys knew he was not only a stranger, but a foreigner, he was hooted at and insulted during his stay; and he remarked that in all the schools he had visited he had never been subjected to such treatment. Our experience coincided with his.'

Making due allowance for the boys becoming somewhat wearied of inspections and visits, Fearon had already made similar remarks about the rowdiness and Sellar and Harvey added a footnote to the effect that records of the turbulence and unruliness of the boys were nothing new, being referred to in the early nineteenth-century history of Aberdeen, Kennedy's *Annals of Aberdeen* and later recorded by Morland Simpson in his book *Bon Record*.

These adverse comments on behaviour were then followed by a report on the non-Classical side of the School. This was strongly critical of the way in which all non-Classical subjects were given inferior status in the School. All the masters of English, Modern Languages and Mathematics complained bitterly about their weak position vis-à-vis Classics.

A visit to the IVth year English Class had found thirteen boys stuck in a corner of a room which could have held a hundred. The boys were uncooperative and the control of the class was poor; the work they did was dull, dreary grammatical exercises in preparation for the 'Comp.'. Despite this concentration on basics, the boys' performance in a piece of dictation from a newspaper was condemned as 'without exception the worst piece of dictation we have had throughout the Inquiry'. In Class V only twelve took English and only five turned up on the day they were visited. They did worse than boys from other schools taking the same examination, although their dictation was better than Class IV.

The French Class had seven boys taking the subject and no boy was taking German. As French was taught between 1 and 2 p.m. – the dinner hour – boys participating had to give up their play or dinner hour and the class was constantly interrupted by the noise and rowdiness of the rest of the school. Only after the Rector had intervened and the janitor was posted 'like a sentry' in the corridor was it possible to get some work done. However, clearly any subject which had no direct bearing on the 'Comp.' was discouraged and penalised by unsympathetic construction of the timetable. The performance of the boys who did take the Class was highly commended.

The results of the Mathematics department were poor. Class IV, of whom only nineteen were present, sat an Arithmetic paper and the average was only 33 out of 200, and 'eleven out of nineteen were unable to do simple Arithmetic'. However, when the boys were tested on Euclid book 1 – included in the 'Comp.' – they shone with marks of 160–170 out of 200.

In sum, the main criticisms of the School were the bursaries, which should be thrown open, so doing away with the long tails of unfit scholars; the need to integrate the Modern side of the School though this would be difficult given the Bursary regulations; the need for a Rector to control the working of the School more thoroughly, as it seemed his authority was inadequate and unsatisfactory, and for him to deal in particular with the noise and turbulence of the boys.

The Argyll Commission Report did not make good reading but similar criticisms were levelled at most of the Scottish schools like the Grammar. Moreover, the Report held that only six schools in the country provided a genuine secondary education for their pupils. These were Glenalmond College, Edinburgh Academy, the Royal High School, the Gymnasium in Old Aberdeen, the Old Aberdeen GS and the New Aberdeen GS. One can hardly resist the temptation to point out that three of these establishments were to be found in Aberdeen.

As an Appendix to the Report, Sellar and Harvey detailed the papers they had set in the various subjects at various standards in the schools they had visited. The standards expected were very high and the passages they set were, to modern eyes at least, very difficult. In Latin the junior groups were faced with the task of translating into that language: 'The fervency of thy studies did require that I should not for a long time recall thee from that philosophical rest thou now enjoyest, if the confidence reposed in our friends and ancient confederates had not at this present disappointed the assurances of my old age . . .' The seniors had to tackle 'They who have presumed to dogmatise on nature as on some well-investigated subject, either from self-conceit or arrogance, and in the professional style, have inflicted the greatest injury on philosophy and learning . . .' In French, the juniors were expected to give the plurals of some words and the feminine form of others and to write out 'the compound preterite indefinite of the verb *se lever*' and the present subjunctive of *s'asseoir*. To complete their assignment they then had to translate a fourteen-line passage of French on the appeal of Maria Theresa to her Hungarian subjects. Similarly in each subject examined the demands on a pupil's knowledge appear to have been very testing, so perhaps 50 out of 200 may not have been as bad as it appears at first glance.

In the School Magazine of December 1959, Dr A.A. Cormack noted his thanks to a former pupil, Harry Slater, who had brought to his attention yet another report on the School in the 1860s. This was to be found in a survey of British education by two French academics, Demogeot and Montucci, entitled '*De L'enseignement secondaire en Angleterre et en Ecosse*' (1868). Details of their Report are recorded in the Magazine article. They covered much the same ground as the other visitors but their conclusion is worth adding to the others: 'We left Aberdeen GS fully convinced of the excellence of its instruction, but likewise desirous of seeing its circle of regular subjects enlarged after the manner of Edinburgh's High School.'

WHEN THE VISITS WERE OVER

One person who was closely involved in these visits was the Rector, William Barrack. His classes had been inspected and highly commended but in his other role, as the Rector rather than teacher, he was obviously unhappy or uneasy about what was happening. In March 1867 Barrack was reported in the *Aberdeen Herald* as complaining about the testing of pupils and staff where the onus was on the staff and pointing out that this led to bad relationships between the pupils and staff and to poor discipline. And yet, Barrack recognised the need for weeding out careless and lazy pupils and suggested that quarterly examinations might be the answer to the problem.

However, Barrack also identified the problem of what the purpose of the Grammar was to be. Was it to be essentially an establishment providing instruction which prepared pupils for the university or was it to be what he called a 'liberal institution'? Barrack criticised the educationists of the time who, he claimed, were confusing the issues and he quite bluntly declared that he wanted 'a Classical school not a Modern school'.

In the light of these views it is probably not surprising that Barrack decided to leave the Grammar and to accept a post as the Head of Dollar Academy. Local opinion was not very happy about what it must have seen as desertion and in one paper the editorial scathingly referred to his departure to a 'rural seminary'.

(DR) THOMAS A. STEWART: INTERIM RECTOR, 1868–1869

On Barrack's departure an interim of a year was filled by Thomas A. Stewart (1847–1904). He had attended the GS between 1861 and 1863, entering Class V, and had been Dux in his final year. At Aberdeen University he won the Town Council Gold Medal, the Simpson Greek Prize, the Ferguson (Classical) Scholarship and Fullerton Prize in Classics and Mental Philosophy. He gained a FCH in Classics and had begun to lecture at the University when the call came from the Grammar. When he had completed his year he went back to lecturing until 1874 when he was appointed an inspector of schools. In 1888 he was made Chief Inspector and this promotion was unprecedented as he succeeded over nine senior colleagues. He continued his rise to the top by becoming Senior Chief Inspector in 1899 and held this office until his early death.

ALEXANDER MARTIN: RECTOR, 1869–1881

Alexander Martin (1825–1907) attended the Grammar between 1834 and 1840, entering Class I, and gained his MA from Marischal in 1844. He was Principal Classics master in the Gymnasium School, Old Aberdeen and when Beverly left the Grammar in 1863 Martin joined the staff. The Council must have been pleased with his performance and also the completion of his book *The School Latin Grammar* in December 1868. In its preface he spelled out his ambitious aim to replace Ruddiman's *Rudiments* and Melvin's *Latin Grammar* which he deemed 'defective in several important respects'. He contended that previous works contained 'a great deal of matter never turned to any use'. His belief was that if Classical Languages were to be taught then it would be necessary to jettison Latin rules. Such thinking and his reputation for being the sternest of disciplinarians helped secure him the vacancy left by Barrack in 1869.

However, not only did Martin have to cope with the various points criticised by the visitors but in 1873 he also had to cope with the transference of control of the School from the Town Council to the Aberdeen School Board. Here again, a man whose teaching skills were never in question was faced with problems which were administrative in nature, involving the need for a stricter control over both staff and pupils.

In the report of 1868, the two French academics had been aware of the need for sanctions of some sort to maintain acceptable standards of behaviour. They had reported that 'once a week the teachers met in the Hall to discuss, in the presence of pupils, any questions of discipline and suitable reprimands and punishments'. For punishment, pupils were detained after 4 p.m. or on a Saturday. It was stated that the tawse was seldom used and expulsion was the ultimate sanction.

No one else mentioned these weekly meetings and the ineffectiveness of the sanctions was what made the biggest impression on most visitors. The new Board after 1873 continued to be concerned about the discipline in the School and in 1875 tried to introduce a more rigorous regime.

With a form of educational anarchy developing under Martin, who claimed it was neither his right nor duty to interfere with individual teachers' conduct of their classes, the maintaining of discipline in the School was put into the hands of a Board of Masters, consisting of the Rector, the Classics masters, the English and the Mathematics masters. In addition, this Board was responsible for the school-timetable and the yearly programme and had the power of expulsion from Class or School. The staff in general could temporarily exclude from a Class and were required to keep a log book of all punishments. This log was to be inspected by the Board of Masters so that it could be fully informed about what was going on in the School. Moreover, the Board was responsible for drawing up rules for discipline in the playground and ensuring they were observed.

When matters arose which concerned members of staff not members of the Board, they were to be allowed to attend meetings but not to vote on any proposals. Other important functions of the body were to act as the channel through which Aberdeen School Board could make its decisions known and also through which suggested amendments to School regulations could be made by the School.

The log books kept by the staff under this scheme still exist but they show signs of what so often happens to those plans, the initial impetus is lost and apathy sets in. What they do record is that the most common form of punishment was writing out impositions, while there are also references to 'pandies' being administered. This peculiar term was derived from the Latin order 'Pande manum' (Hold out your hand), the signal for the traditional Scottish method of advancing education and good manners.

THE DONALDSON-FULLER REPORT 1880

The School Board was unhappy about the lack of progress towards an efficient and well-administered establishment under Martin. Again they were facing the situation that a well-liked and very able teacher was apparently failing to give the leadership which the Board considered necessary in a modern school. So in 1880 yet another inquiry into the School's operations took place.

As always the value and credibility of such an enterprise depended largely on the competence and standing of those who were selected to carry it out. The two selected were Frederick Fuller, the recently retired Professor of Mathematics at Aberdeen University and James Donaldson, the Rector of the Royal High School in Edinburgh.

Fuller had been appointed to his professorship at King's, Old Aberdeen, in 1851 and at the fusion of King's and Marischal in 1860 became the first Professor of Mathematics in the newly created University of Aberdeen. He was highly respected as a teacher of his subject and also as an administrator in the University and was very suitable to carry out the inspection of the aspects of the organisation and curriculum assigned to him in the School.

To inspect the teaching of Classics and Modern Languages, Dr James Donaldson was equally well-qualified. He was a former pupil of the Grammar who had, as Rector of Stirling HS, unsuccessfully competed for the post of Rector of the School in the controversial contest of 1855 when "Paddy" Evans was unexpectedly chosen. His scholarship had been recognised but his religious connections to the Congregational Church in

Blackfriars' Street made him unacceptable to the majority of the interview panel which made the recommendation. Though unsuccessful then, he had moved to the Royal HS in Edinburgh, first as a Classics master, then Rector and was to reappear in Aberdeen in 1881 as the Professor of Humanity before taking up his final appointment as Principal of St Andrews University in 1886 and receiving a knighthood in 1895.

Although his appointment as Principal was largely political as he was well-known in Liberal circles, Donaldson had already by 1880 played an important part in the school reform of long-established endowed schools and hospitals. He had been involved in the reorganisation of Bell-Baxter School in Cupar, Madras Academy in St Andrews, Kelvinside Academy in Glasgow and, most ominously, Robert Gordon's Hospital in Aberdeen, which in its day-school transformation became a rival and an additional threat to the Grammar as Gordon's College.

So, in June 1880, an inspection was carried out which was to lead to fundamental changes in the way the Grammar was organised. Donaldson's general impression is worthy of recording. 'On the whole I consider the Grammar is doing good work in the departments which I have examined . . . The organisation of the School is bad. Boys are in classes for which they are utterly unfit, the average merit of the class is thus lowered and a tendency to general depression is apt to prevail.' However, drawing on his wide experience Donaldson drew a more flattering picture of the pupils in the School. 'I formed a very favourable opinion of the boys of the School' he reported. 'Their behaviour during the whole examination was gentlemanly. The order in all the classes was good. The conduct in the classes for foreign languages was perhaps a little free and easy – in all others the boys were obedient, attentive and respectful.' He went on: 'If I compare the results attained in the subject (Latin) in Aberdeen GS with those attained in other schools I have examined, I do not think that the Aberdeen School is behind any of them.'

So while Donaldson found plenty of scope for criticising the methods of teaching and performance in almost every Class he examined on the language side of the School curriculum, again his general observations were not particularly critical when using other schools of the time as a comparison. He also made the point how in the days of Melvin, pupils concentrated their efforts on a very narrow field of study whereas by the 1880s they had less time to study particular subjects and a greater diversity of subjects to deal with in the School week.

Professor Fuller examined the School in Mathematics, Arithmetic,

Geography and History, along with some English grammar in the lower classes. Like his fellow examiner, Fuller found much to criticise in detail. He found, for example, that classes were arranged according to their ability in Classics rather than Mathematics so that the Fourth class could score better than the Fifth. One also detects a note of frustration at the very limited progress the senior pupils had made and the accurate but slow and laborious methods used to solve problems in Arithmetic. The limited progress in Algebra and Geometry Fuller blamed on the 'Comp.' which still required only a very restricted curriculum.

This state of affairs Fuller criticised strongly because he pointed out that pupils at the School who had no intention of going to university were not allowed to enjoy instruction in a wider and more advanced range of mathematical skills because success in the 'Comp.' still remained the prime consideration. In the lower classes also the limited scope of the work and the laborious methods employed were criticised. While the teaching of Geography was highly commended, in History it was suggested that for young pupils 'it would appear better to lay stress on the broad facts rather than committing to memory the lengths of reigns and the duration of dynasties'. On the whole, Fuller felt that there was a lack of enterprise and effort in the teaching but what was taught was done satisfactorily.

One strange omission to which Fuller referred was the fact that the School Prospectus mentioned Natural Sciences but they were not taught at all. He suggested that some elementary Chemistry, Physics and Biology could be introduced 'without any detriment to the teaching of Classics and Mathematics'.

The two examiners could not agree on how best to produce an immediate improvement in the School. Fuller suggested that more imaginative timetabling could solve some of the problems he had identified, but Donaldson disagreed and he referred to current German educational practice which insisted on setting standards to be reached by pupils at various stages before they could advance to the next level. What they did agree on was that to face the challenges of new reformed educational establishments like Gordon's, Aberdeen GS would have to undergo fundamental reorganisation.

Much of their consideration was directed towards financial matters. The existing system of paying masters by fixed salaries and fees or by fees alone was condemned as causing division and making staff reluctant to try any new methods in case it affected their income. The salaries of the staff were compared unfavourably to those prevailing elsewhere in Scotland in similar schools and even in large primary schools. It was suggested that the Rector should have at least £500 per annum and the principal masters between £300 and £400.

As far as fees were concerned they were reckoned to be very low in the School. Various ways of dealing with the reassessment of fees were considered giving particular attention to the problem of making the School accessible to pupils from poorer families. After due consideration, they recommended that a 'slump fee' should be charged. Instead of fixing a separate fee for each subject, they suggested that a pupil paid a fee which would cover the cost of a whole course of study. Such a charge would have the additional benefit of removing the undesirable effect of differing values being put on subjects. 'Boys cannot fail to undervalue those subjects for which a smaller fee is charged.'

Fuller and Donaldson did not offer much in the way of detailed programmes of study because this they felt was the responsibility of the Rector but they did emphasise that a prescribed course should be taken by all pupils and that classes should be limited in numbers and arranged according to ability and progress; though as previously noted the two examiners disagreed about how such arrangements should be made to grade pupils.

One of their main recommendations was that 'to make and carry out the arrangements necessary in a properly organised school, it is essential that there should be a real Rector'. It is somctimes tempting to think that writing out detailed 'job descriptions' is one of the requirements of modern personnel management and bureaucracy but here in 1880 one can find Donaldson and Fuller producing just such a job description for a 'real Rector'.

The 'real Rector' should be responsible for the efficient working of the whole School. To establish their efficiency he would have to inspect the classes regularly and be prepared to correct any defects in the teaching. Moreover, he would have to check on the books used in the School and prohibit the use of any of which he disapproved. As far as the pupils were concerned, the Rector should superintend the general discipline of the School. As far as the staff, parents and School Board were concerned he was to act as the 'medium of communication' between any of these groups.

Up till that point in time, it had always been the accepted belief that the Rector was primarily a teacher of the senior classes in School, but now it was stated that to carry out the above duties effectively the Rector could no longer be tied to the classroom but should be free to carry out the multifarious duties and tasks which appear as routine or emergencies in such a job. However, although administrative and disciplinary commitments would be a primary consideration in the Rector's duties, Donaldson and Fuller stopped short of him giving up all teaching because they recognised that contact in the classroom was a useful way of keeping a finger on the pulse of the school.

One of the other issues they considered was the power the Rector should have over the appointment and dismissal of staff. On the one hand, they recognised the logic of the argument, that if the Rector is solely responsible for the whole School, he should also have the power of 'hiring and firing' staff. However, the examiners suggested that to concentrate so much in the hands of one man would create problems. For example in appointments they felt that a wider choice of candidates would apply if the final decision was made by the School Board with the proviso that the Rector should have the power of veto when there was the possibility of unsuitable or unacceptable candidates being chosen by the Board.

They felt that the Rector should have greater power to dismiss teachers, but again drew back from allowing absolute powers and suggested various checks and balances to try to ensure fairness and justice to anyone on whom the wrath of the Rector fell. They saw that staff discipline would be much easier to enforce if the Rector had this power of dismissal but still felt the Board should be involved.

Their final considerations were directed towards the so-called 'Modern side' of the School, i.e. those pupils who generally had no desire to proceed to higher education at University. Recent experience, they claimed, had not been encouraging. 'Too frequently' they wrote, 'the Modern classes have been composed of boys who have failed in Classics and in nearly everything else'. Boys had not been allowed to choose 'Modern' subjects until they had already tried and failed the earlier stages of the Classical course. It was also noted that finding teachers who were equipped to teach 'Science, Modern Languages and other Modern branches' in such a way as to make them interesting was very difficult. Because of having to teach those who were essentially 'educational rejects' the staff concerned were regarded as of less value than the other masters.

The solution to the 'Modern' problem, Donaldson and Fuller suggested, was the drawing up a programme of study which boys could choose at the beginning of their school careers. The programme they suggested should concentrate on basics, the three Rs, with the gentle introduction of more Science and more advanced Mathematics in the latter stages. Despite the 'Modern' label they still insisted that Latin, albeit in a modified form, should be part of the course rather than Modern Languages because apart from its own educational merits it had the advantage of allowing easy transfer to the Classical side of the School if at a later stage a pupil wished to prepare for one of the learned professions, e.g. Medicine or Law.

THE AFTERMATH OF THE 1880 REPORT

Faced with this Report recommending fundamental restructuring of the whole School, the School Board started its discussions by noting the complaint of one of its members, Major Ross, that details of the Report had been leaked to a local paper. Such was the interest in the inquiry and its findings. The Board, however, accepted most of the points made by Donaldson and Fuller. While insisting that the Grammar should remain primarily a Classical School with the provision of Modern subjects for those who wanted them, it recognised that the main task was to define clearly what the Rector's authority should be. It was agreed that he should have the right to supervise closely class-work and to control staff and pupils. To allow this new regime to operate successfully it was agreed that a new Rector 'wholly unidentified with the old system' would have to be appointed.

In carrying out this plan one major obstacle was foreseen. Rector Martin had been appointed for life – 'ad vitam aut culpam'. Fortunately, he agreed to retire provided he was granted a pension of £200 per annum. With the way now open the Board moved to appoint James Moir, Head of Classics at Glasgow Academy, as the new Rector.

The suggestion of having a 'slump fee' to cover a whole course of study instead of separate fees for each subject was put into effect. The staff were no longer to depend on this source of income and were awarded moderate increases in their salaries. These changes cost money and to cover the anticipated shortfall in income it was reluctantly agreed that the additional costs should be borne by the school rates – the local tax raised for educational provisions. This additional charge on the rates led to great opposition, as hitherto the rates had been used for elementary education only. This discontent was not silenced by the decision that the fees charged in the School would be increased also, on the grounds that 'there is nothing to warrant the belief that the social position of the great majority of those whose sons attend the Grammar renders them unable to pay higher fees'.

This proposal was bitterly attacked by critics of the School Board.

The Board summed up its general attitude to the changes by stating that 'It was not keen to spend on the Grammar but it was an absolute necessity of giving the School a fair prospect of regaining the support of the public to an extent worthy of its past history and of the expenditure of the City in the erection of the present building. The committee are of the opinion that the Grammar has been conducted under conditions of so inelastic a nature as to render its adaptation to modern requirements a matter of the greatest difficulty, and extra expenditure must be accepted.' It also claimed that in time the improved organisation and facilities in the School would attract more pupils and the School would then become self-supporting and no longer a charge on the rates.

Public reaction to these proposals was very strong. In the local press both in editorials and in letters to the editor, criticism poured onto the Board and the School. Much of the comment was so hostile and bitter that the modern tabloid press would have been hard pressed to equal, far less surpass it. There was generally and understandably indignation about the proposal of increasing rates to support the Grammar. There was equal indignation that raising fees would exclude working-class children from the School. It was widely believed that a large proportion of the pupils were 'country' boys who used the improved railway facilities as well as local lodgings to attend the School. Why, it was asked, should the town ratepayers be asked to subsidise the country incomers?

The lack of educational success in the Grammar was commented on again and again. 'Why should what the Gymnasium and the Old Aberdeen GS do every year be impossible to the Aberdeen GS any year?' The local weekly paper *Bon Accord* attacked the School Board in March 1881, condemning it for 'total disregard of economy' and its domination by 'one or two ecclesiastical cliques'. As far as the School was concerned the *Bon Accord* claimed 'this institution has been for years running to seed owing, as the most superficial observer could not fail to see, to the feebleness and inefficiency of the Rector and his teaching staff. Yet it has taken the Board several years to ascertain this fact and great expense has been incurred in making examinations and obtaining reports on the School.' The paper went on to emphasise the upper-class image and nature of the School and to lament the sentimental effort to restore the School at public expense. 'On the working classes will fall the chief burden and they will derive no benefit.'

The People's Journal, at the same time, attacked the payment of the Rector's salary on the grounds that it was ten times that of a working man.

William Barrack, Rector, 1860–68, was the last Rector at Schoolhill and the first at Skene Street.

Alexander Martin, Rector, 1869–81, was promoted to Rector from the staff.

ames Moir, Rector, 1881–93, and Co-Rector 1893, was a popular, distinguished scholar whose career nded in disappointment.

Henry F. Morland Simpson, Rector, 1893–1920, laid the basis of the modern Grammar School.

J. Mackay Thomson, Rector, 1920–1, left for a successful career as an HMI and became Secretary of the Scottish Education Department.

Douglas G. Miller, Rector, 1921–24, witnessed the War Memorial, Byron Statue and Rubislaw Pavilion.

David M. Andrew, Rector, 1924–42, led the School carefully through the inter-war problems and the early stages of WWII.

Sir James J. Robertson, Rector, 1942–59, was knighted for his services to education at home and abroad.

John Vass Skinner, Rector, 1959–72, faced the introduction of comprehensive education.

Robert D. Gill, Rector, 1972–87, saw the introduction of co-education and the devastation of the 1986 fire.

The old pavilion at the rear of the School in the 1880s.

The Melvin Window in King's College commemorates Scotland's great Latinists – Buchanan, Johnston, Ruddiman and Melvin. (University of Aberdeen)

ABOVE. Chalmers School was established by the Chalmers family of Westfield.

LEFT. Plaque on Chalmers School for 'the Poor Girls of Gilcomstoun'.

Westfield School, 1900, was the site of the first gymnasium and technical departments.

The original Hall was the centre of School life but underwent many modifications.

Samuel Pope conducted Art and Writing Classes in the School from 1867 till 1912.

The first school gymnasium with a 'Drill' class in progress about 1903.

A picture of the Lower School with young hopefuls in the early 1900s.

The School pre-1914 with no Byron Statue, and no Shanghai Clock.

The *Bon Accord* continued its attack by claiming that 'practical and economical representatives were needed rather than a few parsons, priests, professors and 'professional men' but not working class men'! Later in May it accepted that its campaign had achieved little but fired two parting shots, on the one hand condemning 'the process of muddle and addle so long and successfully carried on in the School under the pseudonym of education' and on the other hand producing a poetic jibe – 'A Nut for the School Board':

> Is it right to retrieve our scholastic disgrace
> By taxing the working-man and grinding his face
> While the doors of the School only open to gold
> And the working man's family stands out in the cold?

Amid this torrent of criticism and abuse there were some who did not accept the common views. One correspondent in the *Daily Free Press* in April 1881 had the courage to challenge them by suggesting that the claims that the School was so inefficient were greatly exaggerated. He pointed out that success in the 'Comp.' could be gained only by special training. Was this preparation good for the pupils in the long run? He justified his point of view by reminding people of the success that former pupils of the School had at the University in all the faculties, graduating with honours and winning class prizes. Again the writer asked whether such success could have been achieved if the 'previous education had been so deplorably inefficient'? He ended by commenting that after reorganisation the School might be better 'but even if it were no worse I don't think it will have cause to feel ashamed'.

The Board could hardly be expected to remain silent when under such bitter criticism, and it sought to justify the steps it proposed to take. It admitted that its handling of the affair could have been done more effectively if it had explained its case better to the public. For example the Board said that it had two real objectives in dealing with the Grammar: to resuscitate the School and to do so at as little cost as possible. To reach these objectives, it had two options: either to make the School a select school for the wealthy or to have an open school with low fees and a temporary charge on the rates. The Board rejected the first option and promised to safeguard the entry of poorer boys by providing bursaries and reduced fees and free books. While still clinging to the hope that the School would soon be self-supporting, the Board proceeded to suggest that the increase on the rates would be very small and was after all divided between the occupier and the owner. Sympathetic to the suggestion of lower fees and higher rates, the Board pointed out that most of the burden of the rates actually fell on the upper and middle classes. In Edinburgh, these classes paid eight-ninths of the total rates, while in Aberdeen it was estimated these classes would pay three-quarters of the total rates. The Board posed the question of why should the working-class pay for secondary education and answered it by pointing out that the upper classes paid the biggest share of the costs of elementary education in which they did not participate.

The storm around the School gradually abated though as late as the end of June, the *Bon Accord* was still sniping away at the Board, rejoicing that its term of office was over and the paper and its readers had 'witnessed the death struggles of an educational system that was visibly and with parasitical persistency dragging this once famous seat of learning into lamentable disrepute'. So with the pious hope that only by the introduction of new and vigorous measures could the new Board expect to 'recreate the fallen prestige of this Temple of the Tawse', the *Bon Accord* closed its campaign of opposition and criticism and awaited the arrival of the new regime.

STAFFING BETWEEN 1863 AND 1880

When William Barrack took over the new building of 1863 he took with him the Classics teachers who had worked at Schoolhill. All including the Rector were licensed to preach as well as teach and so the Reverends Still, Beverly, Macdonald[1] and Legge joined Barrack in Skene Street West. However, with the purpose of having all the teaching there, teachers of English and Mathematics were added to the staff and an additional Classics master was also enlisted. The new Classics teacher was Alex Martin who subsequently became Rector from 1869 to 1881. The youthful James Legge, who graduated from King's in 1850, was first appointed as a temporary replacement then to a permanent post in 1861 and remained on the staff until 1890. He had been a pupil of Dr Melvin and throughout his long career stuck closely to the methods of his revered teacher much to the growing annoyance of Dr Moir at the end of the century. As one whose gentlemanly ways and eccentric practices endeared him to his pupils, when he died in 1894 a glowing tribute was contributed in the Magazine. This precedent was to be followed for many members of staff.

Making successful appointments to the new posts was not easy as experience proved that distinguished academic achievements were not the only requirement for successful teaching performance. Rev. George McArthur was probably an able mathematician but he was apparently quite incapable of maintaining order in his classroom. The general tone of the school was rough and this perhaps explains why many of the teachers in subjects other than Classics found the going hard and did not stay for very long. For example one who took on the English post, A.F. Murison, a former pupil and recent graduate, lasted only a brief period before moving south to London where he became a Professor of Law in London University and actually held two chairs at one time.

Perhaps the problem was lack of experience to deal with a new situation in some cases but the appointment of Charles Sleigh to the post in Mathematics and Arithmetic changed the atmosphere in that department. He took his MA in 1850 and the Simpson Memorial prize. He was Mathematical Master at the Grammar from 1861 till 1893, dying the following year from peritonitis. He was very strict and gruff in the classroom but a very successful teacher. He was to be the first in a long line of masters to establish the Grammar Mathematics department as one of the strongest in the North-East.

Another who joined the staff in the early years at Skene Street was Samuel Pope (born 1839). The Prospectus for 1867–8 announced that Writing would be taught by Mr S. Pope. At that time it was clear that serious attention had to be given to instruction in penmanship because communication depended on the written word in every walk of life. When he retired in 1911 he could look back to having served five Rectors from Barrack to Simpson and seen nine English masters come and go. In his forty-five years at the School he witnessed many changes, not least in his own remit, as the importance of Handwriting declined and that of Drawing took over. He took a great interest in all aspects of School life and this was demonstrated by the tributes and gifts with which he was presented by pupils, staff and Former Pupils. Modern requirements and regulation had caught up with him when a new provision for superannuation required his reluctant retirement.

The Prospectuses of the 1860s and 1870s list a variety of options which were available for pupils including Gymnastics, Phonography (Shorthand), Elocution, Natural Science and Fencing, though these were taught only if a pupil selected them and paid the appropriate fees. A succession of foreign gentlemen, Messrs Muller, Krueger, Klem and Hein, struggled to teach Modern Languages in an atmosphere of hostility and prejudice emphasised by unsympathetic time allocation.

While it was one thing to present a fine building and another to offer a more generous range of subjects in the curriculum, what was essential to win and retain the confidence and support of the public was a competent and harmonious staff producing a steady output of well-disciplined, able and well-educated pupils. After 1863 did the Town Council and then the School Boards after 1873 succeed in these objectives in the Grammar?

Sadly, the local press and the public were not impressed by the School's performance in the second half of the nineteenth century. There was strong criticism of the School in the press, often making adverse comparisons to local rivals, the Old Aberdeen GS and the Gymnasium, the Chanonry House School. The public was very critical of the behaviour of the pupils and what was felt to be a lack of discipline in the Grammar.

The staff did begin to have a more settled appearance but the old attitude, of leaving every teacher to do his own thing, took a long time to disappear. The drastic appraisal of the School in 1880 and the reforms which were brought in then did not overcome the lack of strict organisation. When Moir took over from Martin in 1881 it was expected that a real Rector would then produce the more orderly atmosphere which was required. But the public was not convinced of much improvement and continued to complain to the School Board. Moir, a great scholar with progressive ideas for a wider curriculum, was no man-manager. Personally very popular with the pupils he incurred the hostility of his colleagues for what they considered was a lack of support in disciplinary situations.

One bright note, however, was James Brebner, French master, who taught gratuitously in the School for two years. He undertook the office to give the Board time to obtain a properly qualified master, and was succeeded by Maxwell Mackie. Brebner was an enthusiast in French, and conducted classes in the Mechanics' Institute, with conspicuous success for many years using his own excellent grammar. He resigned his seat on the Board, came to the School and in 1887 gifted his salary for prizes in French and German.[2]

PUPILS ATTENDING THE 'NEW' GRAMMAR SCHOOL BETWEEN 1863 AND 1880[3]

By 1866 the roll had reached 308, of whom over one-third were the sons of merchants, traders, farmers and shop-keepers, and nearly one-third came from professional families. Of the remainder, nine were from the landowning class, forty-seven from families with small businesses, farms or shops, and fifty-one from the labouring class. Clearly the Grammar at this time had little to offer the majority of local children.

A decade later it remained a simple matter to discover the background of most School parents as most were to be found in the *Aberdeen Directory* suggesting that they were reasonably prosperous. This lack of broad social representation was confirmed from two sources. The School Board expressed unhappiness about this state of affairs and said it was anxious to open the School to boys from all social classes and during the controversy about the School in the early 1880s there were numerous complaints about the socially exclusive nature of the School then, caused by the rising cost of education. According to the *Bon Accord* 'the number of "poor parents" who send their sons to the Grammar is almost nil and the Grammar scholars are, with one or two exceptions, exclusively composed of those whose parents are in good circumstances and well able to pay handsome fees'. Although the Board was blamed for this the evidence from the School registers suggests that they inherited rather than created this situation.

The following profiles highlight certain educational practices at the Grammar: a significant number of boys joined the School for a final year to prepare for University; many boys left School without completing the five-year course; 'total education' allowed pupils of very mature years to enrol in the School; and 'family grouping' was practised by having brothers of varying ages sitting in the same class.

Another feature of former pupils in the mid-Victorian period was their contribution to the shaping of the British Empire. They served in the armed forces, colonial administrations, medical services and in building the infrastructure of the Empire as engineers, cartographers, botanists, geologists and linguists and the like. A number became prominent and celebrated personalities especially as colonial officials, explorers and missionaries and their high profile further strengthened the widely held view that the School was playing its full part in producing well-educated individuals.

Merchants and Manufacturers

(Sir) James C. Inglis (1851–1911; Kt 1911) attended the Grammar between 1863 and 1867, entering Class I, and Aberdeen University. He became consulting engineer (1892), and general manager (1903), of the Great Western Railway. He was President of the Institution of Civil Engineers.

James C. Glegg (1852–1921) attended the Grammar between 1863 and

1867, entering Class I. He went on to become an apprentice in Messrs Glegg and Thomson, iron merchants, and later a partner in the firm. He was President of the FP Club in 1919–20.

Alexander S. Macdonald (1855–1927) attended the Grammar between 1871 and 1873, entering Class III. He joined his father's import merchant and herring factors business [David Macdonald and Sons]. He was President of the FP Club in 1911–2.

Robert G. Nicol (1858–1934) attended the Grammar between 1871 and 1873, entering Class I. He was apprenticed in engineering and in 1895 became the Aberdeen Harbour Engineer. He convened the Engineering Committee of the Robert Gordon Technical Colleges and was a founder of the Aberdeen Mechanical Society. He was President of the FP Club in 1912–13.

William S. Benton (1859–1914) attended the Grammar between 1871 and 1872, entering Class III. He migrated to Texas and was involved in gold and silver mining before becoming a ranch owner in Mexico. He was killed near Jaurez on the orders of General Villa.

George B. Esslemont (1860–1917) attended the Grammar between 1871 and 1876, entering Class I. He became senior partner in Esslemont and Macintosh and in 1905–6 was Chief Magistrate of Aberdeen. From 1907 to 1917 he was Liberal MP for South Aberdeen.

George Watson (1862–1952) attended the Grammar between 1873 and 1877, entering Class I. He entered business as a junior clerk with the Glasgow Bank and thereafter was in India with a firm of merchants. He was Chair and Managing Director of Lidgerwood Ltd, export merchants and engineers, and held many company directorships. When the Boarding House Company was formed in 1928, he became the Company's largest individual shareholder. He was President of the FP Club, 1934–5. He left £15,000 on his death to provide scholarships for boys destined for commercial life to enable them to live abroad for a year to become proficient in a foreign language.

James Esslemont (1863–1914) attended the Grammar between 1875 and 1880, entering Class I. He was apprenticed to Messrs Esslemont and Macintosh, warehousemen, and became a partner. He was President of the FP Club in 1913–14.

David McD. Kilgour (1867–1927) attended the Grammar between 1876 and 1882, entering Prep III and leaving School to take up an engineering apprenticeship. On the death of his father in 1896 he became sole managing director and senior partner of his family's textile business. He was a

Governor of RGC and the North of Scotland College of Agriculture. He was Convener of the Incorporated Trades of Aberdeen and, in 1926–7, Dean of Guild. He was a founder of the Bach Choir in Aberdeen.

Churchmen

Alexander M. Mackay (1849–1890) attended the Grammar between 1863 and 1866, entering Class V, and then took a degree in Engineering at Edinburgh. After working in Germany he decided to take up the challenge issued by the explorer, H.M. Stanley, for Christians to go to Uganda. He did so in 1876 and his practical skills proved of great use to the Church Missionary Society and the Kings of Buganda. He died of malaria in 1890 and is remembered in Uganda as one of the most successful missionaries of the later nineteenth century.[4]

(Rev.) George Ferries (1852–1938) attended the Grammar between 1865 and 1867, entering Class IV. He took FCH in Classics in his MA of 1871 at Aberdeen University. He taught at Stirling HS and was assistant Professor in Latin at Aberdeen University before he took his BD in 1878 studying further in Berlin and Leipzig. He was minister of Cluny, Aberdeenshire, from 1885 until 1921.

(Rev.) James Hastings (1852–1922) attended the Grammar between 1864 and 1871, before graduating at Aberdeen University. He then studied Divinity and was ordained as a Free Church minister in 1884, working in the North-East until retirement in 1911. He promoted knowledge of the Bible and wrote works of reference to make it more accessible.[5]

(Rev. Canon) Charles T. Wakeham (1852–1931) attended the Grammar between 1865 and 1870, entering Class I, then Aberdeen University and Theological College in Edinburgh. He was ordained in 1876, becoming Rector of St Kiaran, Campbeltown from 1885 to 1923. He was Canon of Cumbrae from 1900 to 1923 and Synod Clerk of the Diocese of Argyll and the Isles from 1905 till 1922.

George Cockburn (1853–1898) attended the Grammar between 1865 and 1870, entering Class I. He took his MA at Aberdeen in 1874 and was a Church of Scotland missionary to China, 1877–93. A tablet to him was erected in the King's College chapel by his classmates, 1901.

James Henderson (1855–1906) attended the Grammar between 1866 and 1870, entering Class II. He took his MA at Aberdeen University in 1874 and became a Free Church minister at Insch, and Queen's Park and Broomhill (both Glasgow). He was missionary to the Jews in Constantinople, 1885–92.

Alexander King (1858–1919) attended the Grammar between 1863 and 1867, entering Class II. A journalist, he studied for the ministry and became a missionary for the LMS in 1880. He was engaged in missionary work in Tientsin until 1917.

(Very Rev.) James W. Harper (1859–1938) attended the Grammar between 1873 and 1877, entering Class II. He graduated from King's, Aberdeen and went on to Theological College in Edinburgh. In the Scottish Episcopalian Church he was created a Curate (1884), Rector (1890), and Canon (1909), before becoming Dean of St Andrews in 1927. He made a significant contribution to the School Magazine.

(Rev.) James Harvey (1859–1950) attended the Grammar between 1870 and 1875, entering Class I. He went on to Aberdeen University, the Free Church College, Göttingen, and Strasbourg. He was for sixty years minister of the North Church, Edinburgh. He became Moderator of the General Assembly of the United Free Church[6] in 1925. He was Principal Clerk to the General Assembly of the new Church of Scotland, 1929–39.

(Right Rev.) James N. Ogilvie (1860–1926) attended the Grammar between 1872 and 1876, entering Class II. He went on to Aberdeen, Edinburgh and Leipzig Universities. He was a chaplain in India for twenty years; minister of New Greyfriars' Church, Edinburgh, 1905–19 and Moderator of the General Assembly of the Church of Scotland in 1918.

(Rev. Dr) Alexander M.F. Macinnes (1866–1934) attended the Grammar in 1885–6, entering Upper School Classical II aged nineteen. He took Divinity at Aberdeen and Edinburgh and graduated with distinction. He became minister at the United Free Church, Kirkliston in 1918, and was the author of *The Kingdom of God in the Apostolic Writings* which brought him into prominence.

Military

(Major-General Sir) James R.L. Macdonald (1862–1927; KCIE 1904) attended the Grammar between 1873 and 1876, entering Class II. He proceeded to Military Academy, Woolwich, where he gained many prizes. He then took a two-year course in Engineering at Chatham. He was involved with railway construction in India, Afghanistan and Uganda. He was Acting Commissioner for the Uganda Protectorate, saw action in the Boer War, was director of railways for the China Expeditionary Force in 1901 and commanded troops in Tibet, India and Mauritius. He reached the rank of General in 1909.[7]

(Col.) Harry J. Kinghorn (1867–1947) attended the Grammar between 1876 and 1880, entering Prep. IV. He enlisted in the Volunteer Battalion of the Gordon Highlanders in 1885; was commissioned in 1894, and commanded as a Major in 1910. He was severely wounded on the Western Front in 1915. He became a Lt Col. in 1916 and chair of the Aberdeen TAA, 1927–31. He was DL for the County and City of Aberdeen. He was FP Club President, 1935–6.

Medical

(Prof. Sir) William J. Sinclair (1846–1912; Kt 1904) attended the Grammar briefly in 1864–5, entering Class V, gaining a bursary to Aberdeen where he graduated in Medicine with the highest honours. After further study in Vienna he worked in Manchester and in 1888 took the chair of Obstetrics and Gynaecology at Owen's College. He was a pioneer in his speciality and was prominent in the campaign for the registration of midwives.[8]

(Sir) James Reid (1849–1923; KCB 1895; 1st Baronet 1887) attended the Grammar between 1862 and 1865, entering Class III, and becoming Dux and Gold Medallist in 1865. He took his MA at Aberdeen in 1869 graduating with honours in Natural Science and winning the Town Council Gold Medal. He qualified in Medicine in 1872. He studied further in Vienna. He was resident Physician to Queen Victoria, 1881–1901, then Physician to Edward VII and George V. He was a Fellow of the Royal Society of Medicine.

(Prof. Sir) (William) Watson Cheyne (1852–1932; 1st baronet 1908; KCMG 1916) attended the Grammar between 1863 and 1865, entering Class I, and at Aberdeen and Edinburgh Universities. He studied Medicine, excelling academically especially in Chemistry. After further study in Vienna and Strasbourg he returned to Edinburgh to work with Joseph Lister, accompanying him to King's College Hospital in 1877. He became FRCS. He was appointed Professor of the Principles of Surgery at King's in 1891, then Professor of Clinical Surgery in 1902. He was instrumental in establishing the science of Bacteriology in Britain and was elected FRS. In 1924 he was awarded the first Lister medal in recognition of his contributions to Surgical Science.[9] He was MP for the Universities of Edinburgh and St Andrews in 1917; and the Scottish Universities, 1918–22.

George Henry (1854–1893) attended the Grammar between 1867 and 1872, entering Class I, and becoming Gold medallist and Second Bursar in 1872. He took degrees in Arts (1885) and Medicine (1887) and became a medical missionary at the mission at Lake Nyasa in Central Africa, where he died young.

(Prof.) James G. Smith (1854–1897) attended the Grammar between 1864 and 1870, entering Class I. He qualified in Arts (1873) and then Medicine (1876) at Aberdeen University. He became Professor of Surgery at University College, Bristol, and Surgeon at Bristol Royal Infirmary. He was elected FRSE in 1883.

(Dr) Arthur A. Morrison (1858–1934) attended the Grammar between 1870 and 1873, entering Class III, and becoming Gold medallist in his final year. He completed a Medical degree at Aberdeen University. He was British delegate on the International Quarantine Board of Egypt from 1897. He became consulting surgeon, Anglo-Swiss Hospital in Alexandria. He gave up private practice to treat the wounded from Gallopoli in 1915 and had a street in Alexandria named after him (Dr Morrison Street).

(Sir) (Robert) John Collie (1860–1935; Kt 1912; CMG 1918) attended the Grammar between 1873 and 1876, entering Class I. He qualified in Medicine in 1882 and worked for thirty years in medical practice, latterly specialising in medico-legal work. During the First World War he rose to the rank of Lt Col. and worked on Neurasthenia and Psychotherapeutics. He became MP for Partick, Glasgow, in 1922.

(Sir) John Baker (1861–1939; Kt 1919) attended the Grammar between 1875 and 1879, entering Class II. He went on to qualify in Medicine from the University of Aberdeen in 1883. He became the Home Office expert on Lunacy and for a number of years was the Medical Superintendent at the State Asylum at Broadmoor.

(Dr Col.) John S. Riddell (1864–1929; CBE 1917) attended the Grammar between 1876 and 1879, entering Class III and graduated from King's and Marischal. He lectured in Surgery at Aberdeen, 1888–95, and was consulting Surgeon at Aberdeen Royal Infirmary, where he became chair of the Board of Directors. He became a Col. in the TA and DL of the County and City of Aberdeen. He followed Morland Simpson as the second President of the FP Club, 1902–8.

(Prof.) David A. Shirres (1864–1945) attended the Grammar in 1879–80, entering Class II, and qualified in Medicine at Aberdeen University in 1886, heading his year. He went to Canada on the staff of the Governor-General, the Earl of Aberdeen, in 1893. He became a lecturer on Neuropathology at McGill and Professor of Nervous Diseases at Vermont State University. He was a pioneer in his field.

(Dr) David Rennet (1866–1941) attended the Grammar between 1877 and 1883, entering Class I. Following a degree in Medicine at Aberdeen University (1889) he took a DPH. He was MOH in Chester, 1911–32.

(Dr) Lindley M. Scott (1866–1939) attended the Grammar between 1877 and 1882, entering Class I. He qualified in Arts (1886) and Medicine (1889) from Aberdeen University before becoming a medical practitioner and eminent Surgeon based in London. He was a Captain in the RAMC in 1917–18. He was a collector of furniture, fine porcelain and works of art.

(Dr) William Findlay (1867–1904) attended the Grammar between 1879 and 1884, entering Class I. He took his MA in 1888 before qualifying in Medicine in 1891, both at Aberdeen University. He was in medical practice in Aberdeen. He was the original Secretary of the FP Club, 1893–1904.

Legal

John Adam (1849–1914) attended the Grammar between 1862 and 1864, entering Class IV. He was the most distinguished Mathematician of his year at Aberdeen in 1868 and won the Ferguson (Mathematical) Scholarship. He was 23rd Wrangler at Cambridge in 1872. He was Special Correspondent of the *Glasgow Herald* during the Franco-Prussian War and Principal of a College in Madras before being called to the Bar of the Middle Temple in 1895 and becoming an Advocate in Madras. He was Crown and Public Prosecutor in Madras, 1900–13.

Logan Shirres (1852–1920) attended the Grammar between 1864 and 1866, entering Class V. He was Dux and Gold Medallist in 1866. He took his BA at Oxford in 1875 and became a barrister at Lincoln's Inn, London, in 1879.

(Sir) John Duthie (1858–1922; KBE 1918) attended the Grammar between 1871 and 1873, entering Class I. He was called to the Bar, Lincoln's Inn, in 1880. He represented the London CC on the Board of the London Port Authority. During WWI he was Assistant Director-General of Voluntary Organisations.

Robert M. Williamson (1867–1955) attended the Grammar in 1882–3, entering Classical II, and graduated in Law at Edinburgh University in 1891. He was admitted an Advocate in Aberdeen. He became a partner in the firm of Paull and Williamsons and between 1908 and 1933 lectured in Constitutional Law and History to University students. He was President of the Chamber of Commerce, 1932–3, and chair of the Boards of both the Aberdeen Savings Bank and the Royal Mental Hospital.

William Brown (1868–1901) attended the Grammar in 1884, entering

Classical III, and graduated from Aberdeen University with a FCH in Philosophy in 1888, having won the Bain Gold Medal. He gained a Law degree from Edinburgh University in 1892 and became an Advocate that same year. He was lecturing in Criminal and Civil Law at Edinburgh when he died early.

Charles E. Lippe (1868–1919) attended the Grammar between 1879 and 1881, entering Class II. He took a degree in Arts (1888) and then Law (1895). He was admitted to the Society of Advocates in Edinburgh in 1903 and became advocate depute in 1917 and a KC the same year.

Academic

Alexander Green (1845–1915) attended the Grammar between 1864 and 1866, entering Class V. He opened a proprietary school in Academy Street in 1871 and after five years he was asked to initiate a Prep. department at the Grammar by transferring his pupils there. He remained Head of the Lower School until 1888. He was later Headmaster of Causewayend and Skene Square schools.

Andrew Craik (1847–1874) attended the Grammar between 1864 and 1866, entering Class V. He was a top student at Aberdeen where he took his MA in 1870 and read Mathematics at Emmanuel College, Cambridge, where he was Fourth Wrangler in 1874. He was a fellow and tutor at the College when he died early.

Henry Stephen (1847–1927) attended the Grammar in 1865–6, entering Class V. He took his MA in 1870 at Aberdeen with FCH in Classics and was the Classical master at Dollar Institution. He became a missionary to India and was Professor of English Literature at Calcutta.

John Cook (1848–1915) attended the Grammar between 1863 and 1865, entering Class V and becoming First Bursar in 1865. Having completed his MA he became Assistant Professor of Natural Philosophy at Aberdeen University, 1870–3, Mathematical and Science master at Arbroath HS, 1873–7 and the Principal of Colleges in Madras and then Bangalore in India, 1877–1908.

Alexander L.H. Dawson (1849–1913) attended the Grammar between 1863 and 1867, entering Class III. He took his MA at Aberdeen in 1871 and was editor of the *Leeds Daily News,* 1872–7. He was Rector of Timaru HS in New Zealand, 1880–9 and Professor at Otago University before qualifying in Law and being called to the bar in Melbourne, 1892. He was a director of mining companies and breeder of stock.

(Prof.) George Chrystal (1851–1911) attended the Grammar from 1863 to 1867, entering Class I, winning several prizes and gaining the Williamson scholarship to Aberdeen University, where he graduated with FCH winning the Ferguson (Mathematical) Scholarship. He was a polymath and won an open scholarship to Peterhouse, Cambridge, in Mathematics, and became Second Wrangler (second in Mathematics) and Smith's Prizeman in 1875. He studied Experimental Physics under Professor James Clerk Maxwell. In 1877 he became Professor of Mathematics at St Andrews and in 1879 gained the same chair at Edinburgh, occupying it with distinction for thirty-two years. He became Dean of the Faculty of Arts in 1891 and was involved with the training of teachers and secondary education. He was elected FRSE in 1880 and became its Vice-President and Secretary. He continued his research which brought him awards from the RSE and the Royal Society.[10]

(Dr) Henry O. Forbes (1851–1932) attended the Grammar between 1863 and 1867, entering Class IV, then going on to Aberdeen and Edinburgh Universities. His exploration of Indonesian and Pacific Islands resulted in important biological, geological and geographical collections. He became Reader in Ethnography at Liverpool University from 1905 and was Director of Museums in Liverpool. He published a number of books on Natural History.

(Dr) William L. Mollison (1851–1929; LLD 1897) attended the Grammar between 1864 and 1868, entering Class I. He went on to Aberdeen University and to Clare College, Cambridge on the Ferguson (Mathematical) Scholarship in 1872. He was Second Wrangler and Smith's Prizeman in 1876 and became a Mathematical lecturer at Jesus, Cambridge. He was Master of Clare College from 1915.

(Rev. Prof.) James A. Paterson (1851–1915) attended the Grammar between 1864 and 1867, entering Class IV and becoming School Dux and Gold Medallist. He won Honours in Classics and Philosophy at Aberdeen University, becoming Fullerton, Moir and Gray Fellow. He gained further prizes at Pembroke, Oxford. He became Professor of Hebrew and the Old Testament in New College, Edinburgh, in 1876. He published extensively.

(Prof.) Robert W. Reid (1851–1939) attended the Grammar in 1865–6, entering Class V. He qualified in Medicine at Aberdeen University in 1872 and became a lecturer at St Thomas' in London from 1872 till 1889. He was appointed Professor of Anatomy at Aberdeen University, a post he held between 1889 and 1925. He discovered Reid's Base Line[11] and created the University's Anthropological Museum.

(Prof. Sir) George Watt (1851–1930; Kt 1903) attended the Grammar between 1867 and 1869, entering Class III. He completed a Medical degree at Glasgow. He joined the Indian Service as a scientific and medical officer. He was Professor of Botany at Calcutta University, 1873–84. He won the Gold Medal of the Pharmaceutical Society. He wrote a number of scientific publications.

Robert A. Neil (1852–1901) attended the Grammar in 1865–6, entering Class V, going on to become Simpson and Fullerton prizeman at Aberdeen. He studied further at Peterhouse, Cambridge, taking FCH in Classics and becoming a Fellow, Tutor and Principal Classical Lecturer. He also lectured in Sanskrit. He was one of the original Honorary Vice-Presidents of the FP Club in 1893.

Alexander Mackie (1855–1915) attended the Macduff Free Church Institution and then the Grammar between 1870 and 1872, entering Class IV. He gained the sixth Bursary to King's and graduated MA in 1876 winning the Seafield Gold Medal in English. He began teaching in 1880 and from 1886 till 1915 he was proprietor and Principal of Albyn Place School, a private school for girls. Under his leadership it became renowned as an intellectual seminary and successful cramming school for girls aiming at University entry.

William Keith Leask (1857–1925) attended the Grammar between 1868 and 1873, entering Class I. After taking his MA at Aberdeen University, he was a scholar at Worcester College, Oxford, between 1878 and 1881. He was Assistant Professor of Greek at Aberdeen, 1881–6. In 1907 he became an Editor of the School Magazine and was a frequent and erudite contributor.

(Rev. Prof.) George Pittendrigh (1857–1930) attended the Grammar between 1872 and 1876, entering Class II. He became Dux and Gold Medallist before going on to Aberdeen University. He was Professor of English Literature in Madras Christian College, 1885–1920, and member for Madras University in the Legislative Council, 1914–19. He was President of the FP Club, 1921–2.

(Rev. Prof.) John Macnaughton (1858–1943) attended the Grammar in 1874–5, entering Class III. He studied at Aberdeen and Cambridge before completing his Divinity studies at Edinburgh, Heidelberg and Berlin. He became Professor of Classics at McGill University and Professor of Latin in Toronto University.

William S. Littlejohn (1859–1933), attended the Grammar between 1872 and 1875, entering Class III, and Aberdeen University, graduating in 1879. He was Principal of Nelson College, New Zealand (1899–1904) and then from 1904 Principal of Scots College, Melbourne until his death in 1933. He modernised and expanded the School which grew from 240 in 1904 to 1,200 by 1923.

(Prof.) Eugene de Faye (1860–1929) attended the Grammar between 1873 and 1876, entering Class III, and graduated with an MA from Aberdeen University in 1881 with FCH in Classics. He studied further in Paris, Göttingen and Berlin. He became Pastor of the Reformed Church at Roubaix, 1886–90, when he became a Professor at the Sorbonne. He served as a Chaplain with the French army during WWI and in the 1920s became a strong supporter of the League of Nations, lecturing all over France. He had four brothers at the Grammar: one of them – Alexander – was Dux (prizeman in Latin) in 1879.

(Prof.) Robert J. Harvey-Gibson (1860–1929; CBE) attended the Grammar between 1872 and 1876, entering Class II. He completed his education at Aberdeen, Edinburgh and Strasbourg Universities. He was Professor of Botany at the University of Liverpool, 1894–1921. He was elected FRSE in 1885. He published a number of academic works.

(Prof.) William R. Cassie (1861–1908) attended the Grammar between 1871 and 1876, entering Class I. He graduated from Aberdeen University and was Fifth Wrangler at Cambridge in 1884. He lectured at Cambridge before becoming Professor of Physics at London University in 1893.[12]

(Prof.) John Nicol Farquhar (1861–1929) attended the Grammar for fifteen months in 1882–3, entering Classical II at the age of twenty-one and becoming First Bursar. After another two years at Aberdeen University he won an Exhibition to Christ Church, Oxford, where he gained a FCH in Classical Moderations and Literae Humaniores in 1887 and 1889 respectively. In 1891 he began ten years' teaching in Calcutta for the LMS. He then served the YMCA in India and Ceylon. His work was significant in interpreting Indian religion for the West. In 1923 he was appointed Professor of Comparative Religion at Manchester University. He was in the first rank of Indologists.[13]

(Prof.) Thomas W. Griffith (1861–1946) attended the Grammar between 1871 and 1876, entering Class I, before going on to Aberdeen University. He was Professor of Anatomy at Leeds University, 1887–1910, and Professor of Medicine there between 1910 and 1925. He was a member of the GMC, 1918–27.

Alexander Thomson (1861–1941) attended the Grammar between 1872 and 1877, entering Class II. He was Gold Medallist of the Grammar aged fifteen. Following an Arts degree at Aberdeen University in 1881 he became

Professor of Mathematics at the Scottish Churches College in Calcutta, retiring in 1913.

John Minto (1863–1935) attended the Grammar between 1878 and 1880, entering Class IV before going on to Aberdeen University. He worked in Librarian posts in King's, Aberdeen, 1885–96; Perth, 1896–1902; Brighton, 1902–6, and then became Librarian of the Signet Library in Edinburgh, 1906–35. He published numerous works.

James Allan (1864–1943) attended the Grammar in 1880–1, entering Class V, and graduated MA from Aberdeen University in 1886. He taught in Aberystwyth and was appointed Classical master in Watson's College in 1888 and was latterly head of the department. He retired in 1928 after forty years' service.

(Prof.) Edward Fiddes (1864–1942) attended the Grammar from 1876 to 1881, entering Class I, and winning the Gold Medal in his final year. After graduating from Aberdeen University he also did so from Peterhouse, Cambridge. He became Professor of History at Manchester University, 1903–20 and senior Pro-Vice Chancellor, 1920–6. He wrote an unfinished autobiography in which he detailed his recollections of the Grammar.

(Prof.) John Wight Duff (1866–1944) attended the Grammar between 1877 and 1882, entering Class I. In his final year he was Dux and Gold Medallist and went on to became Simpson Greek Prizeman at Aberdeen University. He gained FCH at Pembroke, Oxford and studied also in Leipzig. He was Professor of Classics at Newcastle, 1898–1933, and Acting Principal there in 1918–19. He was prolific in his publications.

(Prof.) William Bulloch (1868–1941) attended the Grammar between 1877 and 1880, entering Prep. IV. He studied Medicine at Aberdeen graduating with highest honours in 1890 and 1894 before further study in Leipzig, Vienna, Paris and Copenhagen. He lectured in Bacteriology and Pathology and was appointed to a London University chair in 1919. He was elected FRS in 1913. His publications numbered over a hundred.

Administrative (*Politicians*)

(Sir) William MacGregor (1846–1919; KCMG 1889; GCMG 1907) attended the Grammar between 1865 and 1867, joining in Class IV, becoming Second Bursar and going on to complete a Medical degree at Aberdeen in 1872. He worked overseas gaining administrative experience and in 1888 was appointed First Administrator of British New Guinea. In 1898 he became Governor of Lagos then in 1904 of Newfoundland and in 1909 of Queensland. In 1910 he became the first Chancellor of the University of Queensland. He is regarded as one of the most able of Britain's colonial administrators, aided by his knowledge of Languages, Botany, Ethnology and Medicine.[14]

William D. Spence (1848–90) attended the Grammar in 1863–4, entering Class V. He gained his MA from Aberdeen University in 1868 and became an interpreter in China. He was acting consul at Taiwan, 1884–6 and helped develop Chinese railways. He became a barrister in the Inner Temple in 1883.

James Scott (1850–1920) attended the Grammar between 1864 and 1867, entering Class V. He completed his MA in 1871 at Aberdeen University and became an interpreter in the British Consular Service, China. He published a Korean grammar and a Korean dictionary – the first English books on the Korean language. He was Vice-Consul of Shanghai and Consul of Canton.

James L. Chalmers (1854–1914) attended the Grammar between 1867 and 1869, entering Class I. He studied Chinese in Canton before joining the Chinese customs service under Sir Robert Hart. He became Statistical Secretary of the Inspectorate General in Shanghai.

(Lt Col. Sir) David Prain (1857–1944; Kt 1912) attended the Grammar for the session 1872–3, entering Class IV, and went on, with a bursary, to graduate from Aberdeen University in Natural Science. He qualified in Medicine in 1883 with the highest honours. He joined the IMS and by 1898 he had become Director of the Botanic Garden, Calcutta. He was elected FRSE in 1888 and FRS in 1905, the year he became Director at Kew Gardens.[15]

(Sir) Francis G. Ogilvie (1858–1930; Kt 1920) attended the Grammar between 1872 and 1874, entering Class V. He graduated from Aberdeen and Edinburgh Universities. He was Science master at Gordon's, 1882–6; Principal of Heriot-Watt College, Edinburgh, 1886–1900; Secretary to the Board of Education, 1910–20; Director of the Science Museum, 1911–20 and chair of the Geological Survey Board, 1920–30.

Arthur M. Chalmers (1862–1949; CMG 1917) attended the Grammar in 1881–2, entering Classical III aged nineteen. After School he entered the Japanese Consular Service. He became a Consul in 1903; Consul-General of Korea, 1912–14 and Consul-General for Yokohama, 1914–20.

(Dr Sir) (William) Leslie Mackenzie (1862–1935; Kt 1919) attended the Grammar between 1876 and 1878. He graduated from Aberdeen University in Philosophy and Classics winning prizes and scholarships in 1883, and then achieved honours in Medicine in 1888. He turned to public health and in 1894 he became MO for Leith, dealing with smallpox, tuberculosis and diphtheria. He served on a number of government and medical commissions. The plans he laid down for medical services were followed by the governments of Canada, America and South Africa. He wrote widely in medical journals.[16]

Charles W. Sleigh (1863–1949; CBE) attended the Grammar between 1874 and 1879, entering Class I and in his final year won the Gold Medal. He gained a FCH in Science from Aberdeen University. He worked as an estate factor in Lanarkshire and Aberdeenshire. He was first chair of the Education Committee for Aberdeenshire CC, 1919–42, and Convener of the Council from 1942–5. In 1945 his unique record of public service involved membership of 81 committees and sub-committees.

(Sir) P. Chalmers Mitchell (1864–1945; Kt 1929) attended the Grammar in 1879–80, entering Class IV, and King's, Aberdeen, before winning an Exhibition to Christ Church, Oxford, where he obtained FCH in Comparative Anatomy in 1888. Having lectured in medical schools in London he was elected as Secretary of London Zoo in 1903 and introduced well-ventilated animal accommodation and confinement by moats rather than bars. He opened an aquarium and new reptile house. He was responsible for the development of Whipsnade, opened in 1931. He became FRS in 1906 and by the time of his retirement in 1935 he had tripled visitor attendances to London Zoo. He wrote an autobiography, *My Fill of Days* (1937).[17]

(Sir) James S. Meston (1865–1943) (1st Baron Meston of Agra and Dunnottar cr. 1919) attended the Grammar between 1876 and 1880, entering Class II, and became Dux and Gold Medallist in 1880. He went on to Aberdeen University, passed the ICS exam and went to Balliol, Oxford. He was Financial Secretary to the Indian Government, 1906–12, and Lt Governor of Agra and Oudh from 1912. He influenced the substantial constitutional reforms of 1919 and achieved remarkable success in the financial arrangements of the League of Nations. He was President of the Liberal Party Organisation after 1936. He was President of the FP Club, 1929–30. He was Chancellor of Aberdeen University from 1928 until his death. He became a Freeman of the City of Aberdeen in 1935.[18]

(Sir) George Carmichael (1866–1936; KCSI 1919; LLD 1921) attended the Grammar between 1876 and 1881, entering Class II, and winning the Dux medal in his final year. He went on to Aberdeen University and Balliol, Oxford. He joined the ICS in 1886 and was Collector for Bombay, 1894–1909. He was Chief Secretary to the Government of Bombay, 1910–11 and 1912–15, and member of the Bombay Executive, 1915–20.

Writers

(Sir) William Robertson Nicoll (1851–1923; Kt 1909) attended the Grammar in 1865–6, entering Class V, and then Aberdeen University. He went on to train as a Free Church minister and was ordained at Dufftown in 1874 and Kelso three years later. His ill-health ended his promising preaching career and he turned to journalism. Gladstone's Midlothian campaign won him over to the Liberal cause and he wrote for the large Nonconformist constituency. He became editor of the *British Weekly*; founded a successful literary monthly and in 1893 *Woman at Home*. He was prolific in his journalistic output and is regarded as the 'intellectual leader of Noncomformity'.[19]

(Dr) John Malcolm Bulloch (1867–1938) attended the Grammar between 1877 and 1880, entering Prep. IV, and going on to Aberdeen University. He was a journalist and editor of *The Free Press* and *The Graphic*. He was literary critic of Allied Newspapers from 1924. He wrote many articles and books and was the genealogist of the House of Gordon. He was a dynamic member of the FP's London Centre and was FP Club President, 1927–8.

Arts

Arthur Clyne (1853–1924) attended the Grammar between 1863 and 1868, entering Class I. He was apprenticed to James Matthews and set up architectural business with John Pirie. His strong Episcopalian connections helped the business but it was unsuccessful in a number of building competitions. He designed churches in an original Gothic style. He retired in 1914.

Samuel Reid (1854–1919) attended the Grammar between 1868 and 1871, entering Class I. He exhibited at the Royal Academy and the Royal Scottish Academy. He won the Gold Medal at Crystal Palace in 1899. He contributed numerous illustrations in a variety of publications.

James Cadenhead (1858–1927) attended the Grammar between 1870 and 1874, entering Class II, before going on to Aberdeen University. He was National Gold Medallist (1879) and exhibited landscapes and portraits at the RSA, becoming a full member in 1921.

John W. Beattie (1859–1930) attended the Grammar between 1871 and 1873, entering Class I, before migrating to Tasmania in 1878. He became the colony's official photographer in 1896 and was well known for promoting Tasmania and the tourist trade. He was an antiquarian, conservationist and museum administrator.

James Cromar Watt (1862–1940) attended the Grammar between 1875 and 1878, entering Class I. He went on to the Royal Academy, the London Architectural School, in 1888, and was a competition prize-winner. He turned to decorative art work especially enamelling. He was much involved with the restoration of the Elphinstone tomb at King's. A commemorative plaque can be found for him at 71 Dee Street.

EIGHT Recollections of The 'New' School in the 1870s

An anonymous writer penned this retrospect about the Grammar School of 1870:

While other voices, strange to us, resound
Above thy doors, thy face of granite grey,
Thy rising towers remain the same as when,
That crisp October morn, we entered first
Thy echoing corridors, and joined our names
To those of centuries past, and scanned with awe
The volume of *alumni,* flowing through
The years from darker times to brighter, like
A stream that glides for ever to its home –
The seething, fathomless, insatiate sea.
　　Our first friend was the kindly, genial *Legge,*
With thin, cold face, and slow, deliberate ways,
The type of nature's truest gentleman,
Whose mild, paternal glance lives with us still.
Led by his hand, we groped our faltering way
Through Livy's[1] childish myths of Romulus
And Remus, and the she-wolf's wondrous care;
Or struggled hard to find fit words and terse
To construe Tully's[2] brilliant thoughts on Friends;
Thermopylae and Salamis, besides
Feared Marathon filled us with glowing fire;
Through Virgil's[3] polished page in Aeneid[4] Sixth
Down to Avernus[5] grim, descent we made,
Shuddering at Cerberus'[6] bark and Charon's[7] boat.
Alas! Blind Atropos,[8] before his time,
Cut short his thread of life, and left us poor.

Next *Martin,* more severe, stricter in rule,
But sympathetic too, revered by all –
A devotee to powdered nicotine
And handkerchiefs of colour bright – explored
The depths – or what seemed depths – of Greek;
With interest clothing grammar, syntax dry,
And weary Xenophon's[9] dull parasangs;
Anacreon's[10] odes of love we read, too young
To feel the flame, but felt the music sweet.
Then *Murison* – who, from erect, stiff back
Had been re-christened by another name;
Our English master he; now versed in Law,
Professor, author, critic, editor;
Aspiring, too, towards Parliament, and once
With the Rectorial scarlet all but decked.
O'er niceties grammatical of Bain
He sharpened keen our wits, and introduced
Us to 'Sir Roger' – quaint and humorous Knight –
The friend of Addison's 'Spectator' bland.
The hard-grained Mathematics were the care
Of one *McArthur,* blind, unfit to rule,
Whose class became a bye-word and disgrace;
Red herrings, mice alive, and eggs not fresh,
And other missiles drove him from his post:
Albeit he was a man of parts, and skilled
In various learning, provided in wider fields.
To him succeeded *Sleigh,* with gruffer voice,
And better knowledge how to quell misrule.
Good work he did, until he crossed the bourne.
Forget not also *Beverly,* called 'Dick'.
In truth, kind providence had not been kind
To him; for lame he was, and somewhat cross
In temper; so 'twas said, but we who saw
Him only at examination times
Could not presume to judge; his versions well
We conned, and varying profit thence derived.
Attainments scientific he could boast,
For which he earned – Doctorate of Laws.
And one, thou hast him yet, the final link

That thirty years have left unsnapped and sound,
Old *Pope;* like soldier still, with hearty ways
And gen'rous sympathy for youthful pranks.
A manly soul; long may he live to write
That fair, clear hand, the marvel of his time!
Our forty classmates also! Where are they?
The gods loved some, who died, alas! Too young;
And others, grown to manhood, left their dust
On alien shores, in lands that love the sun,
Or in that Greater Britain o'er the seas.
The rest are scattered wide, and hard to trace;
Some few are rooted in their native soil;
Their sons now ranging round thy grassy lawns,
And treading paths their fathers trod before.
But thine amenities, kind Nurse, have changed!
Thy terraced 'slopes' are levelled to a plain,
Flat and insipid, fitter, true, for game
Of bat and ball, though wanting in romance
And picturesque suggestion; while the burn
That wimpled in our sight – a crystal thread
In summer, and a tawny, tearing flood
When dark November's rains had filled its banks –
Is now, like Arethusa,[11] a hidden stream.
Thy wide demesne, once fringed by gardens fair,
Is now engulfed by rows of sombre streets –
Dull mass of populous tenements, though one
Is styled an avenue, a Provost's scheme
That keeps his name in mem'ry for all time.
Thy dwindling acres would have stayed an impious Board
From planting as they ground another school,
Of kind called primary, not wanted there.
Thy little commonwealth is quite transformed;
We had but classes five – a simple scheme,
Without thy complex Lower, Middle, Higher.
No infantile department in our time,
Nor teachers fair of other sex than ours.
Changed, too, the guiding hands that rule thy flock.
The arenas of the south thy Rector formed,
And made him stately form; the foe of sneaks

And all unmanly deeds; but votary, too,
Of outdoor sports and corporal sanity;
A worshipper of Byron's fame, who will not rest
Till justice crown that bard's achievements high,
And signalise thy greatest son's career
With sculpture due, after a hundred years.
    Nor pass we by his colleague, worthy *Moir*,
A loyal adjutant, whose claims unique
In modern letters and in classic lore
Our Alma Mater twice has recognised;
A man of warm heart, beloved and straight,
Though not without a dash of Celtic fire.
    And many more there are, did time permit:
McLeod and *Murison*, and *Mackie*, *Ward*
And *Brownie*, *Philip*, *Davidson* a pair
Each toiling hard to keep thy fame secure
Against thy wealthy rival of Schoolhill,
Which pious Gordon never meant to drain
Thy strength, as nurse of academic youth.

William K. Leask attended the GS between 1868 and 1873. In February 1910 he looked back on his schooldays:

> About half of the First Class wore the kilt, myself included; one had black velveteens and red stockings; breeks and knickerbockers claimed the other half . . .
>
> [My teacher] was Rev. Alexander Beverly, who had been Dux of the GS in 1840, and First Bursar at Marischal College . . . He died in 1887, in the sixty-fourth year of his age, and is buried in the entrance pathway of St Machar's . . . His lameness cost him the Rector-ship in 1853, when the late Principal Sir William Geddes was elected. I have rarely seen a more competent man than 'Dick' . . .
>
> James Wilson Legge stood, boy and man, for the GS, and was a class-fellow of (Sir) James Stirling. I question if Legge has lost the affection all through life of a single boy. He had one idol in life – Melvin. 'Leggie' was the only Conservative on the staff, the rest being Liberals and Free Church men.
>
> Thomas Still took the Second Class on the election of Martin as Rector, and carried us through the Third and Fourth Year. Still's

memory I hold in high regard: he knew his work, taught the Version well, and was strong in the Melvin tradition. English became an integral part of the course in 1869 when Murison, First Bursar from the School in 1863, and now Professor of Roman Law, University College, London, was appointed. Bain's *Grammar* then became a recognised feature in the School . . .

To think of Mr. Pope is to feel young . . . To me since 1869, when I entered his class, he had been 'Sammy' . . .

Mathematics I have never affected, and the work of the Rev. George McArthur and Mr. Charles Sleigh lives simply in memory as physical torture. The first was not supported in his discipline as he ought to have been, and his class was chaos. But he was the best man all-round of his year in King's College, graduating in 1850 . . .

Martin was Rector. He is in my heart of hearts, for he discharged the duties of the office to perfection. The world thought him cold, and he certainly never affected the popular role. The School . . . under the Town Council, was under-staffed, under-paid and under-encouraged. There was no co-operation, no recognition of its work, and little appreciation or knowledge of its great traditions. But Martin did his work admirably, teaching the Fourth Class in Greek, as well as the Fifth or Rector's Class. His discipline was perfect.

Born in 1863 John Crombie was sent to the Grammar School in 1874, following his older brother, William, who had joined the First class the previous year. They had only a short walk to School from their home at 30 Albert Terrace. Both boys left together in 1878 and entered their father's business. In February 1912 John wrote an article for the School Magazine on his schooldays, 1874–8:

When I joined the School in 1874 'Sandy' Martin was at the head of affairs but I saw very little of him, not even being distinguished enough to be taken in front of him for corporal punishment. A former master, 'Dick' Beverly, used to visit periodically, and some of us by no means looked forward to those days of inspection, as our work was of the nature better appreciated by kindly home people than by the sterner critics as represented by Beverly.

The first class I attended was that taught by Mr. Still, and I can yet remember his warm welcome. I am afraid he did not then realise the herculean task in front of him trying to impart knowledge of the ancient language he was there to teach. Although he was wonderfully patient, I feel sure I experienced a good share of the particular punishment which earned for him his sobriquet, 'Boxer', but I retain nothing but the kindliest memories of him . . .

The English class during the first period of my attendance was under the charge of Mr. A.F. Murison who has long occupied a position of eminence in London. I think Bain's *Grammar* at that time only half its present size – had been recently introduced, and 'Poker', so called from his erect bearing, was full of its praises: but we boys did not agree as to the excellence of the work although we may have altered our views since. There were stiff times ahead, and, considering the amount of brain power which had to be expended by the master in trying to instil the principles into our craniums, one is surprised that our good friend's mental abilities have for so long maintained such a high standard. The 'tawse' he used was not kept in the classroom, but had to be sent for when occasion required, and it is hardly possible to conceive the time taken by the youths – usually impetuous – who were commissioned to bring the instrument of correction. There were to be noted on the face of the master certain signs by which we judged how far it was safe to go in the matter of wrongdoing, and by these we decided whether discretion were the better part of valour. Sometimes, alas, we did not accept the warning, and consequently suffered. Later, Mr. James Macdonell, a member of a family long distinguished for erudition, took charge of the English class. I remember him as a cultured gentleman with perhaps too keen sensibilities for the exacting duties pertaining to the training of youths such as we were.

The Arithmetic hour was somewhat of a terror, and the presiding genius got full scope for his biting sarcasms, but I fear these, and later on, 'Davie' Rennet's withering remarks, were lost upon me. The use of the 'tawse' was not very frequent in the Arithmetic classroom, and I was an eye-witness of it only twice and a hand-witness once, and the sight and feel of it were awesome in the extreme.

At the date I am dealing with, the ground to the east of the front gate was not made up as at present, but there were high walls, over which we peered into gardens far below the street level, and it is a wonder to this day that many a neck was not broken by the

> reckless youths who climbed the giddy heights. One of the gardens belonged to the genial and delightful teacher of writing [= Samuel Pope], still happily on the staff, who seems to have the blessing of perennial youth. All his spare hours were spent in the garden referred to, and doubtless his love for it enabled him to forget the distractions of the day . . .
>
> Customs have changed in many ways, and one remembers how we boys used to visit the harbour when a ship with locust beans arrived. The word soon passed and a raid being made, we returned with pockets bulging out . . .
>
> Then there was the day, long looked forward to, when our writing books were finished and we hied to the New Market to exchange them for pieces of candy . . .
>
> Spelling Bees were then in full swing, and I recall that two Grammar boys, Thomson and Leslie, won great distinction in these competitions. If one may judge from one's own experience of youths fresh from school, it would not be a bad idea to have these tests revived.

Both John and William Crombie became partners in the firm of Messrs James Crombie and Sons, wholesale produce merchants and shipping agents.

Joseph D. Carnegie was born in 1866 and lived at 33 York Street. He joined the First class of the Grammar School in 1877, leaving in 1880. In the School magazines of February and October 1913 he wrote articles about his schooldays:

> My first recollections associated with the School are not of the rector, or the masters, or the boys, but of my father. With a small income and large family, what self-denial was his in taking me away from St. Clement's Board School, with its small fees, to send me to the Grammar. How little I then realised what it all meant when my father told me that I, his eldest son, was to join the First class and that, if I applied myself, I might have the five consecutive years preparatory to entering King's College, and the new suit of clothes to fit the new school standing – the pledge of much more to follow, all given without a grudge!
>
> I well remember the morning when led by my father, I made my first pilgrimage from the remote east end of the city – our street

joined the Fisher's Square – to the palatial School of the Far West. (No other boy of my day came from so extreme a point of Footdee, although Alfred Greig, in the class ahead of me, a close companion, who died on the eve of graduation at King's, started from a home only two hundred yards nearer the School) [Alfred Greig born 1864 attended the GS between 1876 and 1882 and lived at Seaview Cottage, Links. He attended the University as an Arts student and died in April 1884.] . . . Passing the janitor's lodge, I trembled up to the west wing of the School, tottered in by the door and round the corner, where, by arrangement, I was to be introduced to the Rev. James Legge and his class. Nor can I forget the benign influence which encompassed me the moment I saw the master, to whom I became ardently devoted during my School life and with whom, after leaving School and Aberdeen, I was privileged to keep in intimate touch.

I met the Rector, Mr. Martin, immediately after the opening prayer in Mr. Legge's classroom in book form, that is, in the pages of his *School Latin Grammar*. At once I felt in awe of him. How often afterwards my awe deepened as I wrote out page after page, penalties for being late. And yet, to see the Rector himself and to be in his Greek class, my happy lot later, was to have nothing but that reverent fear which is akin to love. Once I did quake on being summoned to his sanctum, but I left without the dread 'application', which, by the way, marvellous to relate, I never received from his strap. His big red handkerchief, with its fragrant Rectorial snuff, I did 'feel' more than once; yea, with dreamy delight I sniff it now . . .

In now running upstairs and walking most soberly into the classroom of Mr. Sleigh, I am conscious of awesome contrast. And, indeed, what monotony if there were but one type of master, sameness of face, voice, method and everything else! The dulcet, classic tones downstairs were the best preparation for listening to the complementary, if sterner notes of the counting room above.

We took our seats at our desks, fortified by a great central calm. Not always, at the time, did we realise the reasonableness of the austere air of our master in Arithmetic and Mathematics. Some of us lost our calm as Mr. Sleigh moved from his desk in front and came passing up and down at the back of our seats. The very slates before us seemed to quake at his approach. And then, O then, as he bent over us with his long, index finger pointing at the folly of our figures, and with a pinch of his snuff falling on our slate, mingled were our feelings. To mention nothing else, we thought that our master had lost more than his snuff. Now that we know how obtuse and slow was the thing we called our mind, we do not say that there was a loss of temper, but only the needful, quickening expression of righteous indignation. Our point of view has changed!

From Mr. Sleigh to our English master, Mr. Macdonell! Who that recalls both will wonder at the exclamation mark? At the same time, each was after his own order. And all the masters, with all their characteristics, were there for our good. Many-sided was our education through their respective personalities. In the daily 'quick-change' from master to master, we boys were receiving probably more unconsciously than otherwise – not the least formative part of our education. Although Scotch in name and by birth, Mr. Macdonell was surely English by training. With us he was English in his accent and manner no less than in his subject! . . . Little did we then know of the larger meaning of culture, but somehow we felt that culture was what Mr. Macdonell embodied. And our brusqueness was something which he never 'suffered gladly'. This, more than anything else, made those searching eyes of his flash on the offender . . . Was there ever a greater master of withering rebuke? The Doric avalanche of Mr. Sleigh left us far less injured. And yet, when Mr. Macdonell left us to go to the Bar in London, we were not without an under sense that he had served us well. It had been a hard task to teach grammar at the Grammar School – harder, no doubt, than to practise it in the Courts.

Our next English master Mr. Beaumont – who came from Shetland – was suavity itself. His facial expressions were a daily entertainment . . . [He] was genuinely a man of feeling. He read in class really melting passages . . . After Mr. Beaumont became headmaster of Commerce Street Board School, I met him more than once in a social circle, and it did not surprise me to find that he was 'the life of the party'. He bubbled over with almost boyish spirits.

I forget whether the teacher of History and Geography was assistant to the English master. At any rate these subjects were taught . . .

The years in the Writing class were of unqualified pleasure.

> And, if you could see my handwriting, how dare you say, without marked profit! It is safe to say that never in all the centuries of its history has our School had a more genial and human master than Mr. Samuel Pope – the ineffable, the incomparable, the immortal Pope. I say that even with my eye, as I write, on my knuckles! What boy ever resented the spiral descent of our master's ruler? It was done so smilingly, so often with rhyme, and always with reason . . . And the extreme penalty of the papal law, the writing out of the 119th Psalm, who did not pay it with cheerful submission? . . .
>
> In the Magazine I read with wonder touched by envy of the School sports of present pupils. What variety, facilities, and not least vestments compared with the lot of last generation! As to our vestments, we wore nothing to distinguish us from ourselves as we were when hard at work in the classroom – not even a fancy cap . . . Whatever our rig, and however imperfect the organisation of our games, we had real sport and were not one whit behind the real sportsmen of to-day. Gone are the sloping 'Kits', absorbed by Esslemont Avenue, where, even more than in the spacious field behind the school, we had many a game contrary perhaps to rule and system but certainly in harmony with the spontaneity and resourcefulness of boys 'let out' of school. For instance, there was that extemporaneous wrestling, now no more . . . Gone, too, is the Gilcomston dam which in those frosty winters used to be a skating annexe of the School. Glowing memories, however, remain.

After leaving the Grammar in 1880 at the age of fourteen Joseph Carnegie spent four years working in a local advocate's office. He then did attend King's and completed preparation for the Congregational ministry at Nottingham and London. As a chaplain he played his part in the First World War in France and with the British Army of the Rhine.

NINE Years of Expansion and Change, 1881–1920

This chapter discusses the failure of the 'new regime' and its replacement by Morland Simpson, whose changes successfully won over many critics of the Grammar and laid the basis of the modern School. Accommodation and staffing changes are particularly examined and the chapter ends with biographical details of many Former Pupils who go on to success in their careers.

JAMES MOIR: RECTOR, 1881–1890; CO-RECTOR 1890–1899

James Moir (d. 1902) was a native of Kildrummy and received his early education at Keith parish school, where he was a pupil-teacher from 1860 until 1865. He entered Aberdeen University as Seventh Bursar and graduated with a FCH in Classics in 1869. He gained teaching experience as a substitute in Keith for his former teacher, as Rector in Peterhead Academy and as Classics master in the Chanonry School. He spent 1870–1 as assistant to Professor Geddes, Professor of Greek at Aberdeen University. He was a founder of the Aberdeen University Literary Society and was its first Secretary. He spent two years as head Classical Master at Stewart's College in Edinburgh, 1871–3, and then two years as Rector of Banff Academy, 1873–5, before being Head Classical Master at Glasgow Academy for five years. His manual of *Continuous Latin Prose* was well regarded by Latinists as a textbook of considerable value. He was one of the founders of the New Spalding Club and produced for it a translation of Boece's *Lives of the Bishops.* He was awarded the degree of LLD from the University of Aberdeen in 1891 and then received the first award of DLitt. in 1898 given out by the same body. He received the latter for his edition of Blind Harry's presentation on Sir William Wallace. He was President of the Aberdeen Philosophical Society in 1890. An ardent believer in all forms of outdoor recreation, he was a very keen golfer. His wife predeceased him but his two sons both graduated from Aberdeen University.

THE NEW REGIME (1881–1883)

James Moir took up his post in 1881 and put into operation the changes which the School Board had sanctioned. By the time he arrived most of the dust had settled on the squabbles of the previous few months and the way seemed clear for the re-establishment of the School's reputation at the forefront of Scottish schools. But the educational scene had changed in a way which brought new pressure to bear on the School. There had been a major review of the many charitable foundations in Scotland and in order to modernise them, the decision was made to convert them from 'hospitals' into secondary day schools.

For Aberdeen Grammar, this meant that, although its rivals in Old Aberdeen – the Gymnasium in the Chanonry (opened by Rev. Alexander Anderson in 1848 but hit badly by the opening of Fettes College in Edinburgh in 1870 and an attack of scarlet fever in 1877) and the Grammar School (opened in 1758 as the parish school of Old Machar) – were in decline, it now had a new and powerful rival in RGC which was competing for the favour and support of the parents of the boys of Aberdeen. As a residential establishment offering a practical education for a limited number of boys, Gordon's Hospital had offered no threat to the Grammar but now in 1881 it emerged as a serious competitor.

One of the major considerations was the ability of the two schools to finance the radical changes which both faced. It had been asserted from time to time during the previous wrangles over the future of the Grammar that the School was well-endowed, that is to say that it had its own considerable financial resources on which to draw. In fact, there is no doubt that of the two schools the financial position of Gordon's was much the stronger.

However, reforms were introduced into the Grammar, new subjects were introduced, the Primary Department strengthened to provide a steady stream of well-prepared pupils for the secondary school and it seemed that the School was thriving under an able and popular Rector.

Yet, within ten years, the School once again found itself plunged into a furious controversy leading to that same James Moir only just escaping dismissal and having to accept the indignity of being reduced to co-Rector and senior Classics master with control of the School being taken out of his hands and being placed in those of a new Rector, Morland Simpson.

There seemed something of a mystery about why Moir was ousted from the Rectorship because there was no doubt that he was very well-liked by the pupils and had considerable support among the influential citizens of Aberdeen who rallied to his cause in the 1890s. When questioned about the affair, James Walker, a former pupil and former Principal Teacher of History, smiled and said 'He was too popular'. This response raised the possibility of all kinds of conjecture. When Morland Simpson's grandson, Morland Craig, was asked why his grandfather had come to Aberdeen he denied any detailed knowledge but said his understanding was that the School was in a 'bit of a mess'.

The reasons for the Moir controversy remain obscure until the School Board minutes are examined. There one reads of another 'state of the School Inquiry' in 1890. Its report was the outcome of parental complaints the previous year which in itself casts doubt on the oft-expressed view that only in our own time have parents come to interfere in educational matters. In response to the complaints the Board undertook to investigate the situation in the School by conferring with the Rector and the masters about the 'tone and discipline of the School generally'. What the Board was to consider in particular was the 'desirableness of strengthening the hands of the Rector and masters in all points relating to the efficiency of the School'.

Throughout the second half of 1889 inquiries were made and early in 1890 a Report was issued. The Rector had been called before the Board to answer various charges and there then ensued a procession of members of the School staff who were also questioned by the Board. The result was a fascinating 'no holds barred' account of relations between the Rector and his staff and insights into the working of the School.

When the Rector first appeared there emerged the grounds for complaint by parents about the state of the School. The allegations all have a surprisingly modern ring about them. The School was beset by truancy, pupils leaving School during school hours, general rowdiness of pupils, swearing, smoking, insubordination in classrooms and obscenities written in the toilets. As a result, it was claimed, pupils were leaving to go to Gordon's College.

While the Board issued its conclusions about the state of the School after its meeting in March 1890 what is even more revealing is its decision to record, in an Appendix to its Report, all the evidence it had gathered in its interviews with the Rector and his colleagues in October 1889, along with written statements made by various parties to enlarge on or to clarify their views. In the twenty-five pages of the Appendix one finds a much more intimate picture of what was happening in the School than in any of the previous reports.

The picture which emerges is of a School where there was great rowdiness and noise in the corridors where the pupils were largely left to their own devices. The Rector and his staff were in nearly open conflict amid claims of lack of support for masters from the Rector when cases of insubordination were reported to him. Almost all of the masters complained about the unruliness and insubordination of the pupils in class but blamed this on the manners of the time and lack of parental training. Moir was, on the other hand, inclined to blame much of the trouble on the shortcomings of the staff as teachers and disciplinarians.

In our time 'staff appraisal' has become one of the key terms in modern school management but here more than a century ago was this concept in practice. Moir, in defending his running of the school, pointed to defects in his staff and Messrs Pope, Legge and Campbell were all openly criticised for their conducting of their classes. These teachers then retaliated by criticising, with equal candour, how the School was being run. Samuel Pope, the Art master, came in for some of the most bitter of attacks, even condemned as not being able to 'belt' pupils efficiently when they caused disruption. His reply was to ask how one could keep order when one had to deal with a hundred pupils at a time, of different ages and covering three different subjects – Writing, Drawing and Book-keeping. Mr James Legge, a Classics master of thirty-four years' experience, was branded by the Rector as being out of date in his methods and too old to learn modern ideas. What was just as bad, the Rector claimed, was that Legge sat in his room with the windows open, draped in an overcoat and scarf while his pupils sat in their overcoats and caps. Parents complained about colds and chills. Legge defended vigorously both his methods and his 'open window' policy – the result of large classes, small rooms, poor ventilation and unhealthy atmosphere. English master Campbell was also attacked for his inability to keep order, his inclination to lecture rather than teach and generally his tendency in the face of trouble just to let matters 'slide' in his own phrase.

In addition to the main accusations about the School's shortcomings there emerge other issues like the failure of School reports to reach home or get there only after pupils had altered them. Copying in examinations was also a major problem. Most of the staff believed that football and cricket took too much of the pupils' attention and the necessity of playing against teams of adults, because there was no school opposition, led to undesirable influences.

Moir defended himself against the complaints in terms which had a very modern ring about them. For example he pointed out that the pupils who were seen out of school during school hours could have been members of the cricket team out to get a team photograph or, seeing the complaint was made about events which had happened in June 1889, they could have been boys who were not taking subjects in the Leaving Certificate which were being sat on that day. (Pupils had to pay for sitting the Leaving Certificate so they could not be forced to take it if they objected to paying.) Truancy was accounted for by the large number of boys who lived in 'digs' and who could persuade their land-ladies to provide them with notes.

So accusations and counter-accusations flew about. The Rector made charges of incompetence and the masters replied with charges of lack of organisation, lack of support, and lack of tact in the presence of pupils.

Despite the hopes expressed in 1881 about the reorganisation of the School it seems that Moir had failed to provide a timetable which allowed the teaching of reasonable-sized groups of well-graded ability. He certainly gave his staff the impression that in cases of dispute he favoured the pupils. All in all, the School was in a shambles though Moir claimed that no complaints had been made to him directly by parents. The decline in numbers, which was occurring as pupils drifted off to Gordon's, Moir claimed, was really due to parents wanting to take advantage of the cheaper education it offered.

By and large the Board accepted that the School was not functioning satisfactorily and rejected Moir's claim 'That on the whole there is no more roughness, truancy and insubordination in the School than in any school of the same size and nothing to justify an investigation like the present, or the Board's interference'. The Board blamed the trouble on Moir's reluctance to order the staff to take a more active role in maintaining order throughout the School. This reluctance was based on Moir's belief that to give such an instruction was 'outside their agreement on appointment'. So the Board declared 'Devising of ways and means for securing the aid of his staff, the efficiency, good order and firm contol of the School as a whole is the duty of the Rector' and 'within the classrooms the masters are responsible for the discipline and work of their several classes and are in possession of powers of discipline consistent with such responsibility – subject always to the Rector's right of supervision'.

Having once again stated the need for a 'real Rector' the Board then stressed the need for careful organisation and tactful staff relations and support. On a practical level the Board emphasised the need for strict control of the pupils and the need to have thorough, accurate and regular checks of their attendance and performance every quarter. It accepted the Rector's modification of his condemnation of Legge and Pope but reprimanded Campbell for his failure 'to exert himself sufficiently as a teacher or a disciplinarian'. The Report ended with the pious hope that 'by a united and harmonious effort on the part of the Rector and the staff generally it may be unnecessary for the Board to take any further action in the matter'.

Sadly the Board's desire for peace and progress was not realised. By March 1892 the Board faced reports of continuing strife within the School. Relations between the Rector and Campbell had led to rows between them in front of an English class. It was reported that the School faced a crisis severely damaging to its reputation given the Rector's lack of judgment and self-control. The Higher School Committee of the Board entertained the gravest doubts whether it could accept Moir's assurances that there would be no repetition of such undignified conduct on his part. Campbell was reprimanded for his part in the affair and, soon after, voluntarily left teaching to study and practise Law.

Moir's future as Rector of the Grammar was clearly in jeopardy and the Board moved toward a reorganisation of the School. Moir defended his position, helped by the lack of complaints from parents following the Campbell affair. Indeed the School roll had begun to rise and in the Bursary Competition Grammar pupils secured twenty-nine of the sixty places.

Moir never seemed to realise how precarious his position was. The Board asked him to submit a scheme for reorganisation and hinted that he should consider reverting to a teaching role as Classics master. A motion asking for the Rector's resignation was put forward but defeated in October.

In November, Moir submitted his scheme for reorganisation, proposing that he should be given greater power over the staff and that there should be meetings with the staff to secure better control in the classrooms and corridors. These proposals exasperated the Board which viewed with horror the idea of the Rector having even more power and it pointed out that if meetings with staff were so necessary why had none been held after eleven years in office. Insult was added to injury by Moir publicising his plans for reorganisation without consulting the Board and before they were submitted for approval by the Board.

In the circumstances, it is not surprising that while the Board emphasised the need for reorganisation immediately it expressed the opinion reluctantly that such a difficult and delicate task was beyond Moir and so long as he remains in office 'it will be hopeless to attempt to put the Grammar in a position fully to regain the confidence of the public, which during the past few years, it has in large measure forfeited'. So the Board rejected Moir's reorganisation plans.

Town opinion on the matter was divided. Many of the notables of the day supported Moir – including Bain, Ogilvie and Minto and his senior pupils, all of whom bombarded the Board with 'Memorials'. Moir's former pupils presented him with £300 as a mark of their respect and gratitude. But all this proved in vain as the Board's growing sense of frustration with the conduct of Moir convinced them the School needed a new Rector. In March 1893 it presented Moir with an outline of its proposals. Moir was to resign his position in July 1893 and become senior Classical master and Co-Rector (at a salary of £350 per annum), confining himself to teaching his classes and leaving the management and administration of the School to the new Rector who would have full charge of the School and control of the teachers. Moir would also be expected to give loyal support to the new Rector.

A sub-committee of the Board visited leading secondary schools in Dundee, Edinburgh, Glasgow and Ayr to find out what talent was available. There was no advertising of the vacancy, although word of the search soon got round because one gentleman contacted the School saying that he heard there was to be a vacancy and asking for information. Moir, needless to say, was not amused to receive the letter which he forwarded to the Board. Thomas Hector, Secretary to the Board, was not amused either at this unexpected disclosure of the Board's plan.

The selected candidates were interviewed. Two of them withdrew from the possibility of receiving a 'poisoned chalice'. The final choice was between a Mathematics/Science teacher and a distinguished teacher of Classics with linguistic attainments in Modern Languages and a high degree of literary culture. The winner was the latter, Henry Fife Morland Simpson, the gentleman whose inopportune inquiry had annoyed both Moir and Hector. In selecting him the Board seemed to be repeating the experience with Evans, for Morland Simpson was also a non-Scot with no experience or knowledge of Scottish educational practice or tradition. However, after the initial 'faux pas' of his premature inquiries, it did not take the new Rector long to make an impact.

Henry (Harry) Fife Morland Simpson (1859–1920) was born in Newcastle in 1859 and was partly of Scots descent. Although many of his forebears were English he thought of himself as a Scot[1] and one of his great-great grandfathers was the Rev. William Graham, a dissenting Presbyterian who came from Edinburgh to take over a congregation in Newcastle in 1770.

His own father was described as an accountant on his birth certificate but with eleven children he struggled to bring up his family. However, Harry had an aunt Annie, a childless widow who ran a dame school in Kirkby Lonsdale in north England. Her husband, a Rev. Kirkpatrick, caught cold on their wedding day and died of pneumonia a fortnight later. Mrs Kirkpatrick, having presumably identified Harry as a bright child, offered to take responsibility for him, promising to make sure he received a good education.

Harry was probably not consulted on the matter. His aunt was something of a dragon and as a young boy he was frightened of her. Nevertheless he got the promised education. Harry won a scholarship to Oundle and from there another to Pembroke College, Cambridge. He rowed for the latter. His first teaching post was as an assistant master at Marlborough College and then he moved to Fettes[2] in 1883, being promoted to Housemaster of School House there in 1887. As a single man he lived with the boys in his House, a bedroom with adjoining study and full board being provided. The salary was accordingly small and ruled out marriage. In the summer holidays a single master could earn a little extra by acting as tutor to a boy and as Simpson had studied German he did this, going to Eutin near Kiel. Neighbours of his host family, including their seventeen-year-old daughter, Jenny, were invited to meet the 'English' guest and after correspondence and further visits Simpson and she became engaged in 1886. It was, however, another seven years before they could afford to get married, when he left Fettes for the Rectorship of the Grammar. During that long wait Jenny's family pressed her to give up on the 'tall Englishman' and find someone else. Nonetheless, they were married in Germany and travelled from Hamburg to Aberdeen by steamer, in the days when there was a regular service.

Morland Simpson had a successful career at Fettes. According to its records he 'quickly won esteem in spite of peculiarities to which boys are cruel'. His complexion earned him instantly the nickname, 'Pleuky John'. He was very tall, gaunt, and awkward; his voice had a sing-song tone in it. But 'his true kindliness, his wide toleration of trifling offences, above all, his humour, made him a favourite'. He came to be called 'Simonides' and his good performances on the rugby field also endeared him to the boys.[3] In the final verse of the Viva-La sung on Founder's Day 1893 he was merited with:

Now weep woeful shepherds, the tear's in the eye;
Mr Simpson, alas, will soon bid us good-bye;
And we wish him prosperity, wealth and renown

In his new northern home of the Old Granite Town.

Simpson's new wife was terribly seasick the whole journey. She had clearly been working on her English and she became completely fluent but to begin with she had difficulty with the Doric tongue. They lived at first at 80 Hamilton Place, where all four of their family were born: the boys (Harry) Graham and (William) Douglas and the girls, Muriel and Margaret. Both boys attended the Grammar – Graham between 1899 and 1912 and Douglas between 1901 and 1913 – and this cannot always have been an easy situation for them, their father and the staff. When they moved to Foresterhill House they took in up to six boarders – boys whose parents had sent them home to attend the GS from India or Africa and who lacked Aberdeen relatives to live with. So the Rector's children grew up in a sort of extended family, most of the boys being there all year round. Three servants were employed. It may be that the outbreak of the First World War prevented the arrival of new boarders. Certainly at some point later on the family moved to what became the Amatola Hotel (at the corner of Anderson Drive and Great Western Road).

In the years leading up to the War and of course during it anti-German feeling intensified and perhaps this explains why the children were not brought up to be bilingual. The Simpsons left the congregation of St Andrew's Cathedral because of the virulently anti-German sermons being preached there. Once the War had started someone complained to the police that the German woman living in Foresterhill House was signalling out to sea with a lantern – in fact, the lantern belonged to a neighbour going out to see his hens after dark. All this and Graham's decision to enlist in the Gordon Highlanders – he had been working as a railway engineer since leaving School – caused the family much worry and stress. Douglas tried to follow suit and enlist but was rejected as unfit. However, he obtained a job organising Scouts to act as relief coastguards but had to resign when a complaint was made that having a German mother made him unfit for the role. Graham survived until 1918 to be killed near Reims in the last German offensive of the War.

ACCOMMODATION

Since taking over control of public education from the Town Council in 1872–3 the School Board had been faced with a massive shortage of adequate schools. It offered two solutions – one, the building of new schools and two, the more economic use of existing accommodation. In the latter capacity, the Grammar was an obvious target and it was claimed that the Board had at its disposal a building capable of holding more than a thousand pupils which, in fact, held only about half that number. Suggestions were made that here was a chance to save money by using the surplus space as an elementary school. These proposals were not pursued because the Board of Education in Edinburgh ruled that they were illegal within the terms of the 1872 Education Act. Instead the Aberdeen School Board undertook a building programme which saw the erection of a school in Skene Street (1878) and others in Commerce Street (1876), Middle (1877), Causewayend (1877) and in Ferryhill (1877). It is worth remembering that when Esslemont Avenue was planned to connect the west end of Union Street via Rose Street, the Council approached the Board for a piece of ground on the east side of the School grounds. The Board rejected the request, fortunately, as otherwise the Westfield School of 1900 and the additional wings of 1914 could not have been built.

When there was concern expressed about the academic performance in the Grammar it was felt that an improvement could be made and secured by introducing an elementary stage for the school. To allow this the first extension northwards of the school was carried out in 1882. The fire of 1986 revealed how an early north wing had been demolished to make way for this extension.

The Board recognised the need for increased and improved accommodation for the widening choice of subjects and shortly after Simpson's arrival in 1894–95 a large-scale redevelopment of the interior of the School took place. Large rooms were divided and, most spectacularly, the roof of the original hall was lowered to allow the creation of three rooms above it which the Art Department eventually took possession of completely. The Hall had then been used for Gymnastics for several years; this was accommodated in Skene Street Congregational Church at the corner of Esslemont Avenue and Skene Street. Better provision was made for the Kindergarten and Lower School pupils and accommodation for the Museum and the old Library and Reading room was established.

As the School was coming to terms with these changes a new crisis hit the headlines in Aberdeen. With the opening up of Esslemont Avenue, new tenement buildings were put up which greatly increased both the adult and juvenile population of the area. A reminder of this expansion is found in the Foresters' Buildings (1895) which stand at the corner of Leadside Road and

Esslemont Avenue. This Friendly Society (the Foresters) had decided to invest its resources in these buildings. (Another large block of tenements, the Victoria Buildings, had already been erected in 1887 along Whitehall Place, called Leadside Road at that time.)

When the Board decided that another school was required in the district it proposed that a suitable site existed in the ground between the Grammar and Chalmers School. This proposal was met with a storm of protest from many quarters and a large public meeting in Rosemount School which condemned this 'intrusion'. The Council stepped in to add to the opposition and challenged the legal right of the Board to carry out its scheme. One of the most active opponents of the proposal was Rector Simpson, who felt so strongly about the subject that he publicly attacked it in the local newspaper, the *Free Press*, and was later reprimanded for daring to challenge openly the Board's decision.

The controversy about the building of Westfield School and the open hostility of Morland Simpson to the scheme strained relations between him and the Board. This was illustrated by the fact that a request for a salary increase for the Rector and two of his colleagues had resulted in the granting of an increase only to the colleagues but not the Rector. In a letter to a member of the Board, Simpson compared his lot unfavourably to similar positions in Scotland and England and threatened to leave.

However, he remained and was soon involved in negotiations between the Board and the Governors of Gordon's College. The idea had been put forward that it would be advantageous if an attempt was made to avoid duplication of educational effort by concentrating Classical studies at the Grammar and Science at the College. This suggestion never materialised and the schools continued their separate ways.

Meantime, the Board began to plan the erection of the new building. One of Aberdeen's most notable architects, Marshall McKenzie, whose most famous work was the frontage of Marischal College in 1906, was employed to design the new school, Westfield. Preliminary work had to be stopped while a legal opinion from the Court of Session ruled on the School Board's right to build on the new site. Despite protests that three elementary schools, Rosemount, Skene Street and Westfield would be too close together, the Court ruled in favour of the Board and the building which was first Westfield School, then the Lower School of the Grammar and now the Language Block, was opened in 1900.

The Grammar had been for some time agitating for a new Gymnasium, Swimming Pond and Workshop and its plea was dealt with in the new

Westfield School. The project for a swimming pond was abandoned on the grounds that there were greater needs than a place for pupils to bathe. But the building was designed to offer extra accommodation for the Grammar as well as the Elementary School. The southern half of the ground floor, nearest Skene Street, was allocated to the GS and the first Gymnasium was established at the east end of the building and a Manual Instruction or Technical Workshop at the west end. There were originally two separate entrance doors, but one was later closed up and left the building with its slightly off-centre entrance.

In 1905, the north wing for the Lower School was further extended which also allowed for more provision for the secondary school, notably the Library which occupied a large part of the upper storey of the wing.

With the school roll increasing – it reached 611 by 1911 – and a much more varied curriculum requiring even more accommodation, the last major addition was undertaken in 1913–14 when the two wings to the original building were added. These additions gave contemporaries the impression of the lowering of the whole building by extending the frontage. At the same time these extensions provided the accommodation which was needed to house the School during the First World War, while Westfield School was used at various times to house wounded soldiers and the residents of Oldmill Poorhouse (Woodend), whose building, like others, was taken over as a hospital and the pupils (male and female) of the Central School shared accommodation on a part-time basis as they did in the Second World War.

THE IMPACT OF MORLAND SIMPSON (1893–1920)

During his twenty-seven years as Rector of the School, Simpson's views on education proved to be shrewd and far-sighted and he, in essence, created the modern Grammar. He was very much an advocate of the *mens sana in corpore sano* (a healthy mind in a healthy body) approach to education although this was at first viewed with suspicion and opposition. Many years later, during the First World War, he pointed out how ironic it was to have parents complaining about the lack of physical education. The views he held on any subject he held very strongly and he had no hesitation in crossing swords with any opponents, even the School Board itself, corresponding in the nearly illegible handwriting he used.

In 1897, Simpson was in correspondence with the Rev. J. Gordon Murray, who was chairman of the Higher School Committee of the Board and minister of Greyfriars' Church. He was writing about the need for an increase in his salary. In order to strengthen his claim for an improvement Simpson felt it was appropriate to describe the state of the Grammar School he inherited in 1893. He described a disorganised, depleted and discredited School, with a roll of only 241 boys (in all 268 former boys eventually returned), notorious for 'its truancy, ill-conduct and rowdyism'. Each member of staff more or less worked for himself and individuals were at loggerheads with each other, several of them influenced by mutual recriminations and scarcely on speaking terms. It included two men who had failed as Headmasters, including his embittered predecessor.

Simpson's savage description was basically fair according to the details of the Board's inquiry into the state of the School in 1889–90, found in the long Appendix to the minutes of the Board at that time. The lack of organisation had resulted from Rectors being appointed for their qualities as teachers rather than administrators and with the increasing complexity of schools this proved disastrous. As for its reputation in the Town, the local press took great interest in critical observations on the state of the School. As for Dr Moir, he retained his popularity and respect among the pupils but cut a sad and lonely figure as he wandered round the grounds at morning intervals reluctant to join his colleagues in the staff room and an exile from the Rector's room.

By 1897 the School's reputation had been re-established. A Former Pupils' Club had been begun which became an enormous support for the School in all its various ventures. Further a School Magazine had been established which was used as a means of fostering relations with Former Pupils and through its articles giving information about what was going on in the School and what Former Pupils were engaged in at home and abroad. For anyone interested in the history of the School, the Magazine is an unrivalled source of information from 1893 up to the present day. (Moir had made an early modest effort to produce a school Magazine but perhaps a better memorial to him was the establishment of a Literary and Debating Society which continues to flourish.)

One of Simpson's ambitions was to have a suitable memorial of the School's most famous former pupil, Lord Byron. The Gordon family quickly rallied to support the project but despite this initial enthusiasm it did not produce the splendid statue until 1923, some three years after Simpson's death, largely as a result of being unable to raise the necessary money. Two major wars elapsed before the statue was in place and the inflation which resulted left the sculptor, Pittendrigh Macgillivray, very unhappy given the failure to adjust his fee for the work to take this into account.

There was a great effort made to widen pupils' appreciation of the past and the wider world. A Museum was built up by encouraging people to donate all kinds of material from home and abroad. The School Hall of the original building was changed to play an important active part in School life. It became the scene of morning assemblies, a portrait gallery of distinguished Former Pupils to remind pupils of the School's contributions to many walks of life, the venue for the dramatic performances which flourished over the years and not least the place where celebrations were held to recognise occasions of local or national importance. Eventually it was there that the War Memorial was placed to identify the great number of Former Pupils who gave their lives in two World Wars.

Another useful insight into these developments is found in the School Prospectuses which were the means for providing information about the textbooks to be used, timetables, prize lists and a record of past prize-winners and distinctions gained at University and elsewhere by Former Pupils. For the history of the School, as important as any part of the Prospectus was the Rector's report for each session. This was taken as an opportunity to indicate changes which were to be introduced and also to emphasise the size of the School roll and appeal to parents to cooperate in reducing absenteeism.

Although the Boer War had made little direct impact on School life between 1899 and 1902 one of its sequels had. Baden-Powell, one of the personalities who had emerged during that conflict, started a youth movement – the Boy Scouts (1908) – which fitted in perfectly with Simpson's ideas of broadening the perspectives and experiences of the young. So it is not surprising that the 1st Aberdeen troop was based in the School. The movement proved so successful that eventually there were four troops associated with the School offering boys a wide variety of interests and activities. In the First World War in particular they made a substantial contribution to the war effort by serving at the coastguard stations, military hospitals, YMCA and fire stations.

In another direction, always anxious to further the welfare of the pupils, Simpson decided that it would be interesting and useful to carry out a programme of measuring their physiques and health. This was done before the state eventually began to take an interest in the health of the young after the poor physical condition of those volunteering for service in the Boer War became obvious. In the Prospectus of 1904–5 it was reported by the

Rector that 'a special Report on the Physical Registration of our boys is printed with the Board's sanction, a considerable percentage of boys with defective sight and hearing require medical attention'.

In 1906 the University of Aberdeen celebrated the opening of the new frontage of Marischal College with a visit from King Edward VII to carry out the official ceremony. The whole Town was decorated to welcome the monarch. Not surprisingly, Simpson seized the opportunity to remind everyone that the School was celebrating its 650th Anniversary with a night of social celebrations coinciding with those at Marischal.[4] An evening of music and dancing, amid a School transformed for the occasion, saw the return of prominent FPs and visits from the Archbishop of Canterbury and Lord Strathcona among others. The resources of the Town were enlisted to carry out all the work involved but for the pupils probably the best thing was that they were given an extra week's holiday. It was also an opportune time for Simpson to publish his book about the School *Bon Record*.

In 1907 an agreement was reached with the Former Pupils' Club that the financial responsibility for the publication of the School Magazine should be assumed by the FPs thus removing the considerable burden that the School had hitherto borne. The section devoted to the FP element was considerably extended and for many years three editions per year were published until the financial constraints in the post-war era saw this number reduced to two and finally to one issue per year. Apart from cementing the bonds between the School and its Former Pupils it provided through the advertisements included in its pages an interesting list of the commercial enterprises in the town at various periods.

In 1911, to the great delight of staff and pupils, Simpson was honoured by the University of Aberdeen. Like his predecessor, Moir, he was granted the degree of LLD. This was recognition of the status of the School in the community as well as the contribution to the School and the community that Simpson had made personally. In accepting from staff and pupils the presentation of academic robes he emphasised that the honour was as much to the School as to himself.

During the First World War the School continued to operate within its own premises, unlike the High School which had to operate in private houses rented by the School Board. However, it had drastically to rearrange its organisation as it had to share its facilities with the pupils of the Central School, an arrangement which was repeated in the Second World War. The new School hours were based on a day starting at 8 a.m. and finishing at 1.30 p.m., Monday to Saturday. The Rector pointed out that this gave the pupils the chance for outdoor recreation every day though the gymnasium was lost in school hours by the commandeering of all of Westfield School. The playing-field behind the School was used for military training of recruits and at first all organised games had to be abandoned but were eventually restarted to face mostly adult teams like the officers and men of the Gordon Highlanders. The only local school opposition came from Gordon's College. Gradually the Bleachfield site was made ready for Games though problems emerged with the demolition of remnants of the old Bleachfield buildings and the need to deal with the small burn which ran through the area.

One of the important contributions to the School community was the continued publication of the School Magazine. On the one hand, three times a year it recorded what was going on in the School and also the list of distinctions awarded to individuals. But it also carried out the sad task of recording the heavy losses sustained among the ranks of the Former Pupils. Members of staff were called up to serve in the Forces and one of the first was George Dawson, who was killed in 1916. There are also reports on the experiences of various individuals in the many theatres in which they served. As the War progressed the staff was further depleted by the calling up of Messrs J.B. Summers, J.C. Knox and W.N. Hendry and this put an extra load on the rest of the staff which the Rector praised for its willingness to shoulder the burden.

One piece of excitement for the pupils was the arrival of ten Serbian refugees. Some had briefly gone to Gordon's but it was decided that all should attend the GS where they stayed until the end of the War.

In 1916 the official opening of the Games Field took place. It was quite a grand occasion with the ceremonial cutting of the ribbon conducted by the wife of Mr A.T. Cruickshank who, along with Mr James Esslemont, had been largely instrumental in acquiring the field. Alongside the many dignitaries of the time were wounded servicemen brought from the various hospitals by cars supplied by an FP, Harry Holmes. One of the strange parts to the story is that the event was filmed, giving great interest and amusement to the younger pupils in particular. Unfortunately, who did the filming was not identified. However, one morning many years later the actual film was left in the PE department. Its fragile form was treated and the silent film was given a sound track with the commentary provided by Freddy Edwards, a great character in the School, who had actually been present at the occasion and who was able to identify the main participants.

In 1917 the Board was informed by the Lord Lyon King of Arms that the School was using a coat of arms to which it was not entitled. It was pointed out that continued use of this unregistered coat of arms could result in a heavy fine. After due deliberation, it was decided that the wise course would be to have the arms registered for a fee of £45 (slightly less than the Rector's secretary's annual salary!). However, when the approved design was submitted Simpson took the opportunity of suggesting that the original motto '*Ratio Confirmatioque Doctrinae*' should be replaced by the neater '*Bon Record*'. This proposal was accepted.

After celebrating twenty-five years in office and still subject to criticism, by parents, of the conduct of the School's affairs Simpson was still ready to defend his achievements and so he submitted to the Board a long detailed account of what had been achieved since he came. He poured scorn on the member of a prominent Aberdeen family who dared to suggest that with the end of the war in sight, he should be replaced.

However, there were signs that his health was beginning to deteriorate and the death of his older son at the front in May 1918 affected him deeply. He attended the FP Dinner in 1919 but his health broke down and he was absent from School until 1920 when, with his cancer spreading, he tendered his resignation to the Board. He was saved from a possible lingering death by a heart attack in May 1920. With no occupational pension for teachers at that time his death left the family in financial straits. Although Muriel had completed a degree in German and trained as a teacher she had had to give up work when she married. Douglas was left responsible for supporting his mother and to some extent his sister, Margaret, who worked as a secretary and lived at home until marriage. He had to turn down the offer of a PhD scholarship to Cambridge and accepted the offer (having completed his history degree) of a junior lectureship in Aberdeen.

In a generation Simpson had created the modern Grammar School, leading it away from the narrow curriculum of earlier times to a much broader view of what a school should seek to achieve for its pupils. Not everything he tried succeeded. Pupils and parents did not support his effort to encourage the wearing of the kilt. Though swimming was always popular in the School, efforts to have a Pool had to wait for many years. As early as 1913 hopes had been expressed that the statue of Byron would soon be placed in the School grounds but Simpson did not live to see this happen. Nonetheless, tributes, from many quarters, recognised his contribution to education in Aberdeen. In his tribute in the School Prospectus of 1920–1 Dr Charles McLeod summed him up by writing: 'He was honest, fearless, honourable and ever dignified.' He joined the list of the most distinguished headmasters of the Grammar – Cargill, Wedderburn, Melvin and Simpson.

When reviewing the curriculum in the School late on in his career Simpson emphasised the need for someone to look after and organise the Games in the School. In this he stressed that the qualities he sought in such a man were not those of a Gymnastics teacher, admirable and desirable though these were, but someone who could command the respect of all his academic colleagues – he had to be an officer and gentleman. The choice fell after interview on Duncan McGregor from Glasgow, an ex-officer. In retrospect, he proved an admirable choice and Simpson would have felt vindicated in choosing someone who became one of the most influential and respected members of staff in the inter-war years, raising the status of the School particularly on the rugby field but also in most other fields of athletic activities.

STAFFING: 1881–1920

In present-day education there is great emphasis on the need for a review of teaching staff performance and the effectiveness of the organisational structures. This took place in the Grammar in the 1890s. Faced with the constant criticism from parents and public, the School Board called Moir before it to answer the public's complaints about the poor image the School offered to the outside world. In the course of his defence Moir criticised his colleagues for their competence as he saw it. All the main characters on the staff were summoned to answer the criticisms. Sleigh, Pope, Campbell (the English teacher), Legge and Clarke from Classics all appeared. Sleigh, as one would have expected, said he had no problems. Clarke, who had been a headmaster, also claimed he had no particular problem though he soon left the Grammar for a lectureship in Education at the University.[5] Campbell admitted that he had given up reporting misdemeanours like smoking, even drunkenness, to the Rector and he withdrew shortly after the inquiry to become a member of the legal profession. Moir bluntly said at first that both Legge and Pope should be dismissed because for different reasons they were incorrigible and their lack of control over their pupils contributed largely to the restlessness and unruliness in the corridors and classrooms of other teachers. To be fair, Moir later retracted these opinions and Pope continued for another twenty years while Legge retired shortly after the inquiry.

Other lesser lights were called and offered their own woes, contributing to the picture of an unhappy staff. Bentley Philip, later a respected senior teacher in charge of Geography, complained he had had a difficult early spell because of lack of support and guidance from the Rector. A.V. Lothian, a noted footballer and sportsman and a popular member of staff coming from a wider experience, offered the opinion that 'the boys were no worse behaved than boys in other schools'. Mackie, who also became an influential figure in later years, taught French with no discipline difficulties though he too referred to unruliness in the corridors. Like others he was not happy about grading the pupils to appropriate classes.

By the time that Morland Simpson was appointed in 1893, it is interesting to compare the staff lists of 1890 and that of 1893. James Legge had retired and been replaced by William Brownie, a strict and effective member of staff who unfortunately died aged only forty-three. Charles Sleigh had retired and been replaced by Charles McLeod. The Mathematics/Science department had been supplemented by the arrival of Henry F. Menzies[6] to replace A.V. Lothian. This was a case of one noted sportsman replacing another as Menzies was a Scottish rugby internationalist. Campbell had left teaching to follow a legal career and in his place had come William Murison, a noted scholar, who was to fill the English post for many years. Samuel Pope's remit had been changed to Drawing alone.

The calibre of these new appointments was high and formed the backbone of the staff of the late 1890s and early 1900s. Eventually, when George Middleton arrived in 1899 to head the Classics department the notable quartet of the 'four Ms' was complete and McLeod, Mackie,[7] Murison[8] and Middleton[9] were to prove a great asset to the teaching force for a number of years. McLeod was awarded a doctorate in Science and Middleton, already a graduate of both Aberdeen and Cambridge, was awarded an LLD by Aberdeen University.

Probably one of their major contributions was to provide a stable force during the First World War when several of the staff were called to serve in the forces and temporary or inexperienced teachers helped a depleted staff to cope with the wartime circumstances. Sadly, George Dawson,[10] who had been a Mathematics and Science teacher, was killed in the War but Messrs Summers, Knox and Hendry survived to rejoin the staff after 1918. One very satisfying outcome of the War was how the staff responded so willingly to the extra demands which were made upon them. Their efforts were not everywhere appreciated and Simpson faced considerable criticism which he robustly answered.[11]

For nearly a century a part of the School which endeared itself to those who had enjoyed its offering was the Lower School. Its origins can be traced back to the awareness of the wide variations not so much in ability, as in preparedness among the young boys who entered the Grammar School. To set standards for those who were to enter the early stages of education the Lower School emerged in the 1870s. It catered for boys aged from four years to those ready to enter secondary education. For fairly modest fees boys entered the Initiatory department aged four and progressed to the Lower School from age seven to ten and then entered the Middle School from ten to thirteen years. Parents were encouraged to enrol their sons in the earliest classes and to continue through the whole course, which many did.

The first master in charge was Alexander Green, who attended the Grammar as a pupil between 1862 and 1864. He had opened a Proprietary School in Academy Street in 1871 and his success led the Town Council to invite him to open a Preparatory (or Lower) School for the Grammar. He did this in 1876 and remained in charge until 1888. He was assisted by a number of ladies, many of whom were accorded the distinction of LLA (Lady Licentiate in Arts) because they were not allowed to win a full University degree. One of the features of its history was the great loyalty and service of its staff; Miss Ledingham, Miss Gracie and Miss Ethel Mary Stewart, all served for more than forty years, while Miss Mackie served thirty-two years and Mrs Angus for twenty-three. The first two stages of Preparatory and Lower School were very much the preserve of lady teachers but for the older boys in the Middle School they became the responsibility of the junior members of the male secondary staff.

The Preparatory School was originally made up of a Junior Division of Classes I and II, and a Senior Division of Classes III, IV, V and VI. In 1881 the structure was changed to an Initiatory Department, divided into Junior and Senior, of three Classes (I, II and III) which led to the Lower School (of Classes I, II and III) and then to a Middle School (of Classes I, II and III). In 1893 Initiatory was changed to Preparatory and two classes were introduced (Classes I and II) and the division into Junior and Senior was abandoned. By 1913 the Junior and Senior Infant classes had been reintroduced and the Lower School was made up of five classes (I, II, III, IV and V) with no longer mention of Middle School. Regarding class sizes they varied in this period from twenty to thirty-five.

An interesting side-light on the status of lady teachers was the appointment of Miss Bow to take Gymnastics in the School Hall and to organise the School Sports. She was already on the staff teaching in the Lower School. As a result of her ill-health she was replaced by a Miss Moffat. Faced with a vacancy on the School teaching staff Simpson informed the Board that he would have no objection to the appointment in the secondary School of a suitably qualified woman.

In the post-war period the 'old guard' had all gathered many years of service and first Maxwell Mackie retired in 1923 after forty-three years, latterly in charge of the French department, and was succeeded by Henry Paterson. Soon after, Dr McLeod retired from his post in charge of the Mathematics and Science departments after thirty-four years and it was decided by the Educational Authority that he would be replaced by appointing separate heads of department in the two subjects. Peter Edward, who was a long-serving master under McLeod, became Head of Science and John Robertson was recruited from the Central School to take over in the Mathematics department. The latter, invariably known as 'Jock', subsequently returned to the Central to become its famous Headmaster.

Other notable figures appeared, often Former Pupils. James Walker joined the English and History department after a brief spell in Fraserburgh and later became Principal History master before retiring in 1961. Archie Hyslop, a multi-talented Classical scholar, who provided the Aberdeen comedian Harry Gordon with much of his repertoire of music and song, was persuaded to move to Manchester GS but later returned to Scotland to become a school inspector in charge of the areas of Kincardine and the Northern Isles but also having his great musical accomplishment used by the inspectorate in a specialist capacity.

PUPILS

Class of Sixth Form (Classical) in 1894–1895

This class was made up of thirty boys, although a number of them were moustached. The oldest, John Cameron (GS 1894–5) was born in 1865. Two of them – Malcolm Macarthur (GS 1893–5) from Lewis and Murdo Morrison (GS 1894–6) from Stornoway, who became Director of Education for Inverness-shire in 1919 – were twenty-three years of age. Finlay Smith (GS 1893–6) was twenty-one and William Fraser (GS 1893–6) from Rogart was twenty. The youngest boys were George B.T. Michie (GS 1887–97), who was fifteen, H.F.L. Grant (GS 1888–95), James G. Slessor (GS 1891–6), Edward A. Strachan (GS 1892–5) and George R. Watt (GS 1885–95 and 1897) (who later became a professor of English and Philosophy in South Africa), were sixteen.

Of the class, twenty-two graduated MA at Aberdeen University: of these, six took a second degree – three a BL; two a BSc and one an MB ChB.

Two graduated BA at Cambridge – James Strachan (GS 1885–95) being Seventh Wrangler – and one BA at Oxford.

Fourteen went into Education, four to Law, three to Divinity, two to the Army and one to Medicine, while two became managing directors of family businesses. Accountancy, Engineering and Journalism were other single occupations.

Honours were won by George A. Combe (GS 1889–95), later a Consular Civil Servant in China, who gained a CBE; Arthur Dymock (GS 1887–95), who joined the Army and won an OBE; James W. Garden (GS 1886–95), who became an Advocate, and H.F. Lyall Grant (GS 1888–95), who joined the Army – both won the DSO. Minto Gillanders (GS 1881–95), who taught Science at Elgin Academy, gained the MC.

John Badenoch (GS 1894–5) died in WWI in Basra in 1917, while George Mackay (GS 1894–7) from Bettyhill emigrated to Canada and fought with the Canadian forces.

PUPILS ATTENDING THE GRAMMAR SCHOOL BETWEEN 1881 AND 1920

According to Rev. Dr W. Walker[12] there remained in this period a marked difference between the students of Marischal and those of King's. A large proportion of Marischal men continued to come from New Aberdeen, while the King's men came mostly from the country districts including a number from the Highlands. Students at King's were still the older of the two: 'they were also generally more diligent plodders, steadily burning the midnight oil, and seldom indulging in recreation of any sort. Doubtless, mainly for these reasons, the Marischal students did not, as far as I can judge, attain to the same standard of scholarship as the King's men, especially in Mathematics and Physics.'

Be that as it may, in March 1899 the *School World* monthly educational magazine analysed the schools which the leading scientists of the country had attended. The Grammar School with seven 'distinguished living men' was a close third behind Edinburgh High School (with ten) and Edinburgh Academy (with nine). Others mentioned were Glasgow High School with three and Glasgow Academy with two.

Although the professions dominated the careers of FPs in this period the Edwardian era (1901–10) marked the high point of the social power and influence of the Presbyterian bourgeoisie.[13] The gradual erosion of the religious factor increased with the growth of the State and the reorganisation of local government and the abolition of the old parish councils in 1929. As church membership declined fewer FPs trained for the ministry and this trend is reflected in the following profiles.

Merchants and Manufacturers

Alexander W. Christie (1871–1955) attended the Grammar between 1878 and 1887, entering Prep. I. He became a businessman in Aberdeen and London. He was the original Treasurer of the FP Club in 1893. He managed a manufacturing business in Huntly, 1903–22 and founded the Gordon Cleaning Company. He was Provost of Huntly, 1920–35.

(Lt Col.) Thomas Ogilvie (1871–1944) attended the Grammar between 1884 and 1887, entering Middle III (juniors). He joined his father's woollen merchant business. During WWI he served on the Western Front, 1914–19. He was a hat manufacturer who brought the top hat to Aberdeen. He retained the architect William Kelly to build his stately wool warehouse on the corner of Dee Street and Dee Place. He was President of the FP Club, 1920–1.

Alexander G. Nicol Smith (1872–1959) attended the Grammar between 1880 and 1888, entering Prep. II. He joined the family firm of Messrs A. & J. Smith (founded in 1867 by his father and uncle), prolific jewellers who specialised in Highland and Scottish jewellery. He became senior partner. He served as a Lt Col. in France, 1915–19. He was President of the FP Club, 1926–7.

John M. Fyfe (1875–1948) attended the Grammar between 1882 and 1887, entering Initiatory. He joined the family firm of Messrs John Fyfe Ltd, leading granite quarry owners and merchants. He owned Pitfodels House during WWII. He was President of the FP Club in 1925–6.

(Brig. Gen.) Magnus Mowat (1875–1953) attended the Grammar between 1882 and 1884, entering Initiatory. He completed a degree at Aberdeen before taking up an Engineering apprenticeship in Glasgow railways. He worked as an Engineer at home and abroad and contributed significantly to the RE during WWI. He was Secretary to the Institution for Mechanical Engineers, 1920–38. He was elected FRSE in 1934.

Robert G. Combe (1880–1917) attended the Grammar between 1894 and 1897, entering Middle III. He served his apprenticeship as a chemist in Aberdeen. He migrated and in 1907 started business on his own in Saskatchewan. He served in WWI on the Western Front as a Lieutenant in the Manitoban Regiment of the Canadian infantry. He was killed in action on 3 May 1917 and on 27 June 1917 was awarded posthumously the Victoria Cross for 'most conspicuous bravery and example'.

Maitland Mackie (1884–1975) attended the Grammar between 1897 and 1902, entering Middle I. He became a prominent farmer in the North-East, farming at North Ythsie, Tarves, from 1904. He was known as an innovator who pioneered progressive methods in agriculture especially in poultry and pig-rearing. He was President of the Scottish National Farmers' Union. His three sons, all FPs, distinguished themselves in public life: John (at GS 1924–6) became Labour MP for Enfield East, 1959–74; Maitland (at GS 1926–8) became Lord Lieutenant of Aberdeenshire and Convener of Aberdeen CC until local government reorganisation and George (at GS 1933–5) became a Liberal MP and Chairman of the Scottish Liberal Party.

Wilfrid P. Barron (1888–1979) attended the Grammar between 1896 and 1903, entering Lower II. He served an Engineering apprenticeship with the Aberdeen Harbour engineer. During the Great War he served with the RE. He was Chief Engineer to the Chittagong Port Commissioners in Bengal in 1921, returning as Chief Engineer with the Port of London Authority until his retirement in 1953.

George G. Nicol (1888–1967) attended the Grammar between 1894 and 1903, entering Prep. After an apprenticeship in Civil Engineering he was in business on his own account. He designed the Churchill Barrier at Scapa Flow. He was Vice-President of the FP Club and chair of its Executive, 1928–30.

George A. Ledingham (1890–1978) attended the Grammar between 1894 and 1905, entering Prep. After an apprenticeship to Civil Engineers in Aberdeen, 1906–8, he studied at the Royal Technical College, Glasgow, 1908–11. He played rugby at School and for Glasgow University and, as a wing three-quarter, was the first FP selected to play for Scotland (against France in 1913). He served in WWI, was wounded in 1915 in France, reaching the rank of Major and gaining the MC. He continued working as a consulting Engineer.

Francis S. Anderson (1897–1966) attended the Grammar between 1909 and 1912, entering Classical I. He served in British and Indian armies, 1914–17, and joined his father's granite business. He unsuccessfully contested West Renfrewshire as a Liberal in 1929. An Aberdeen Town Councillor, 1935–40, he was Director of the British Sugar Corporation Ltd, 1960; chairman of the Bacon Market Council, 1964, and appointed chair of the RGC Governors also in 1964.

J. Lennox Riddell (1899–1982) attended the Grammar between 1907 and 1916, entering Lower II. He worked in the family business of oil and lubricant manufacture. He founded the FP cricket club in 1917 and was its first Secretary. He served the Club Executive, 1925–47 and together with Theodore Watt kept the Club going during WWII. He was President of the FP Club, 1958–9.

Harold Esslemont (1901–1992) attended the Grammar between 1915 and 1918, entering Classical IB. A former Director of Esslemont and Macintosh Ltd he spent his whole working life with the firm that his grandfather had founded. He joined in 1918 as an apprentice but was away during WWII. He resumed his career after the War and rose to be Managing Director and Chairman of the company. He stepped down as chairman in 1982 and from the Board in 1990.

Ian G. McPherson (1903–2000) attended the Grammar between 1910 and 1917, entering Senior Infants, and followed his father into the family bakery business. He joined the Incorporated Trades in 1934 and held the two principal posts – Master of Trades Hospital, 1954–6, and Deacon Convener, 1956–8. He was a member of Aberdeen's Town Council for sixteen years, for five of which he was Convener of the Links & Parks Committee. He was President of the FP Club in 1965–6.

Robert J. Maitland (1905–1987) attended the Grammar between 1912 and 1918, entering Senior Infants. He started his own successful business in Glasgow as a builders' merchant. He was chair of VSA in its centenary year (1970); he chaired the Aberdeen Lads' Club and the Victoria Hostel.

Churchmen

John Cameron (1865–1943) attended the Grammar in 1894-5, entering the highest class – Classical VI – at the age of twenty-eight. He graduated in Philosophy from Aberdeen University in 1898 and became a minister in the United Free Church, retiring in 1936.

(Very Rev.) Joseph B. Jobberns (1868–1936), attended the Grammar from 1880 to 1886, entering Prep. V. He went on to Aberdeen University and became a Curate in the Scottish Episcopal Church, 1894. He was Rector of The Holy Rude, Carnoustie, 1898–1922, Canon of St Paul's Cathedral, Dundee, 1918–31, and Dean of Brechin Cathedral from 1931.

(Bishop) Anthony Mitchell (1868–1917) attended the Grammar between 1882 and 1886, entering Middle II and becoming Dux and Gold Medallist in his final year. He won prizes and medals before graduating from King's,

Aberdeen, with FCH and then BD honours. He studied further at Caius, Cambridge and Edinburgh University. He was ordained in 1892 and became Curate, Rector and Canon before his time as Bishop of Aberdeen and Orkney, 1912–17.

(Rev. Prof.) Adam F. Findlay (1869–1962; DD, LLD) attended the Grammar between 1879 and 1885, entering Prep.VI and being Gold Medallist in 1885. He studied at Aberdeen University where he gained a FCH in Classics, and Athens and Berlin. He held ministerial posts in Whithorn, Arbroath, Edinburgh and Linlithgow. He became Professor of Church History and Practical Theology at Aberdeen University in 1935 and Master of Christ's College in 1937 (retiring from both posts in 1947). He played in the first rugby match at Old King's playing field. He was an original member of the FP Club.

(Very Rev.) John E. Macrae (1870–1947) attended the Grammar between 1883 and 1887, when he pioneered rugby, continuing his studies at St Andrews University. He was Deacon, Priest, Curate and Rector of the Episcopal Church in Scotland. He was editor of *The Scottish Chronicle*, 1925–8 and *The Scottish Guardian*, 1929–35. He was Dean of Brechin from 1936.

(Rev.) John S. Macdonald (1871–1956) attended the Grammar in 1886–7, entering Classical III, and gained a FCH in Philosophy at Aberdeen University. He was ordained at Stornoway, 1897, and held ministries in Nairn, Wemyss Bay, Dalkeith, Liverpool, and, between 1931 and 1939, the First Presbyterian Church in Syracuse, New York.

(Rev. Prof.) William Meston (1871–1933) attended the Grammar between 1881 and 1886, entering Lower II. He completed his studies at Aberdeen, Edinburgh and St John's, Cambridge. He was a Missionary of the Free Church in Madras, becoming Professor of English at the Christian College there in 1893. He was ordained in 1895 and was a member of Madras Legislative Council, 1921–3, 1927 and 1928.

(Ven.) Frederick H. Petrie (1875–1948) attended the Grammar in 1890–1, entering Classical II. He continued his education at Aberdeen University and Edinburgh Theological College. He was a Deacon, Priest and Rector; a Missionary in Melanesia; a Vicar in New Zealand, 1909–46; and an Archdeacon before being appointed Vicar-General, 1944 and Archbishop, 1946.

(Rt Rev. Dr) (Ernest) D. Logie Danson (1880–1946; DD) attended the Grammar between 1892 and 1894, entering Classical I. He was one of five brothers who attended the School. He was ordained a Priest in 1907, became

Bishop of Labaun and Sarawak, 1917–31 and Bishop of Edinburgh, 1939–46. He was Primus of the Episcopal Church of Scotland, 1943–6. He was President of the FP Club, 1932–3.

(Rev.) George S. Russell (1883–1957) attended the Grammar between 1894 and 1901, and then Aberdeen University. His ministerial charges were mainly in England, his final post being Grafton Square Congregational in London. In 1929 he moved to Deer Park United Church in Toronto. He published a number of works including his autobiography *The Road behind Me* in 1937. He was first schoolboy editor of the School Magazine.

(Rt Rev. Mgr) William R. Clapperton (1886–1969) attended the Grammar between 1899 and 1901, joining Classical IV. He was educated further at Durham and Scots College, Rome. He was ordained a Priest in 1913, and became Private Chamberlain to the Pope (Monsignor). He was appointed Rector of Scots College, Rome, in 1922 and remained there, other than the War years, until his death. In 1955 he was created a Protonatory Apostolic, the highest position for a priest, short of bishop.

William E. Adam (1897–1963) attended the Grammar between 1902 and 1909, entering Prep. He served in WWI in France and Flanders. He was Rector of St Magnus Episcopal Church in Lerwick, 1930, and Rector of St Kentigern's, Ballater, 1945. He was Provost of Ballater, 1947–52. He was Canon of St Andrew's Cathedral, Aberdeen, 1948.

(Rev. Prof.) David Cairns (1904–92) attended the Grammar between 1912 and 1916, entering Lower II. He went on to Merchiston Castle School; Aberdeen University; Balliol, Oxford, where he gained FCH; Christ's, Aberdeen; and Zurich. He was inducted to Bridge of Allan and served during the War in the Royal Army Chaplain's Department. In 1947, he was appointed Professor of Practical Theology at Christ's College, a post he held until retirement. He wrote a number of books.[14] A commemorative plaque can be found at the former Christ's College, Alford Place.

Military

James S. Barron (1867–1911) attended the Grammar in 1880–1, entering Class I. After 1885 he prospected for gold in South Africa. He served under Colonel Plumer in the Matabele War and in the South African War, 1899–1902, being present at the relief of Mafeking.

(Maj.-Gen.) Patrick B. Sangster (1872–1951; CB, CMG) attended the Grammar between 1884 and 1888, entering Middle II Senior. He was commissioned into the Indian army, 1894. He was active in France, 1914–15, and Palestine, 1916–20. He served in India, Burma and China in the 1920s.

R. Bruce M. Cameron (1873–1926) attended the Grammar between 1886 and 1889, entering Classical I. He entered the RA in 1894 and retired as a Captain in 1910, taking up residence in British Columbia. He joined a Canadian battalion in 1915 and was severely wounded on the Western Front in 1917. He was a significant contributor to the School Magazine.

(Gen. Sir) Andrew Skeen (1873–1935; KCIE 1921; KCB 1925) attended the Grammar between 1880 and 1886, entering Prep. IV. He joined the army in 1891 and was commissioned into the Indian army in 1893. He served on the North-West frontier, China, and East Africa. He was active on the Western Front, 1914–17. He was appointed Chief of the General Staff of the Indian army from 1924 to 1928.

(Lt Col.) Ernest A. Ewart (1876–1943) (pseudo. Boyd Cable) attended the Grammar in 1882–3. He had a number of careers including professional soldier and author. He was editor of *The Trident – Magazine of Sea and Travel.* He was a prolific author in his own name and as Boyd Cable.

(Col.) Archer Irvine-Fortesque (1880–1959), attended the Grammar between 1892 and 1897, entering Middle I. He went on to qualify in Medicine from Aberdeen University and joined the RAMC in 1907. He saw active service in Persia, Iraq and India, becoming a Colonel in 1935 and retiring in 1937. He was called up during WWII. He specialised in foreign languages, becoming proficient in at least nine. He was DL for Kincardineshire. He was President of the FP Club, 1939–46.

(Maj. Gen.) Alexander D. Fraser (1884–1960) attended the Grammar between 1898 and 1900, entering Classical IV. He qualified in Medicine in 1906 from Aberdeen University and joined the RAMC the following year. He worked in the Colonial Office before serving in France, Russia, Mesopotamia, Palestine, Sierra Leone, India and Egypt. He later commanded the RAMC Depot and Training Establishment at Aldershot, retiring in 1941.

(Surgeon Vice-Adm.) C. Edward Greeson (1888–1979) attended the Grammar between 1902 and 1905, entering Modern III. He graduated in 1910 in Medicine at Aberdeen University. He was a Surgeon in the RN in WWI and during WWII was Mediterranean Fleet Medical Officer (1939–42). He was Medical Director-General of the RN, 1948–52 and Honorary Surgeon to George VI.

(Maj. Sir) John F. Ferguson (1891–1975; Kt 1953) attended the Grammar between 1904 and 1909, entering Classical III. He studied at Aberdeen University and Sandhurst. He was a professional soldier from 1912 to 1933, and saw active service in WWI in India, Mesopotamia and Palestine. In a second career he was Chief Constable of Sussex, Assistant Commissioner of the Metropolitan Police and Chief Constable of Kent.

(Maj. Gen.) Kenneth A.M. Tomory (1891–1968) attended the Grammar between 1899 and 1908, entering Lower II. He qualified in Medicine from Edinburgh in 1914. He joined the army, serving in the Great War in India, Mesopotamia and Persia. Post-war he saw active service in Hong Kong and India. He became a specialist in Anaesthetics. In WWII he served in France and West Africa and later in Egypt.

(Lt Col.) Robert Scarth (1894–1966) attended the Grammar between 1910 and 1912, entering Modern IV. He went on to Aberdeen University before becoming a professional soldier. He saw active service in the two World Wars. He was a Sheriff Substitute and Lord Lieutenant for the County of Orkney from 1959.

John M. McBain (1895–1916) attended the Grammar between 1903 and 1913, entering Lower II, and was Dux in his final year. At Edinburgh University he joined the OTC and served in France in 1915–16 before being killed on the Somme.

(Wing Commander) Robert D. Bruce (1904–1994) attended the Grammar between 1913 and 1922, entering Lower II. He graduated in Medicine from Aberdeen University in 1928. He received a permanent commission in the RAF in 1938. During WWII he served for some time in the Middle East and was a Wing Commander by 1944. He then commanded the RAF Hospital in Changi, Malaya. In 1958–9 he was senior Medical Officer on Christmas Island when the atomic tests were being carried out. From 1963 until retirement he was a Medical Officer with the Ministry of Defence in London.

Medical

(Dr) Francis Kelly (1868–1939; CBE) attended the Grammar between 1879 and 1885, entering Class I, and then Aberdeen University. He became a Surgeon in Aberdeen Royal Infirmary and served in the RAMC in WWI. He was a Deputy Commissioner in the Ministry of Pensions, 1919–29.

(Sir) Alexander Hendry (1869–1932; KCVO 1931) attended the Grammar between 1883 and 1886, entering Middle II. He went on to qualify in Medicine at Edinburgh University in 1892. He set up a medical practice at Ballater and was appointed Medical Attendant at Balmoral in 1904. He was the Provost of Ballater in 1931.

(Dr) Joseph Ellis Milne (1869–1917) attended the Grammar between 1882 and 1884, joining Classical II and then graduated with an MA (1888) and MD (1894) from Aberdeen University. He worked in general practice in Aberdeen, 1895–1915 until being attached to the RAMC during WWI, winning the DSO in 1916. He reached the rank of Captain before being killed in action in France.

(Dr) John F. Christie (1870–1931) attended the Grammar between 1878 and 1887, entering Prep. III. He graduated in Arts and Medicine (1895) at Aberdeen University. He specialised in skin and venereal diseases. He was a Major in the RAMC in WWI. He captained Aberdeenshire CC, 1907–9. He was President of the FP Club in 1922–3.

(Dr) Robert Bruce (1872–1949) attended the Grammar between 1886 and 1889, entering Classical II, and qualified in Medicine at Aberdeen University. He was a general practitioner in Cults, 1898–1946. He was a Lt Col. of the 7th Battalion, Gordon Highlanders, in WWI and was later active in the TA. He became DL for the County of Aberdeen.

William Rudolf Center (1872–1916) attended the Grammar between 1883 and 1885, entering Middle II (Senior). He qualified in Medicine at Edinburgh University, 1893, and Surgery at London University in 1896. He joined the RN as a surgeon in 1896 and was promoted to Fleet Surgeon in 1912. He was killed while on active service in the Mediterranean in 1916.

(Dr) Thomas W. Lumsden (1874–1953) attended the Grammar between 1883 and 1887 and 1889 to 1891, entering Lower II. He went on to Aberdeen University where he won a number of prizes in Anatomy and Surgery while qualifying in Medicine with honours. He worked in private practice in London for twenty-five years and then as a cancer researcher, becoming Director of Cancer Research at London Hospital from 1930 to 1942.

(Dr) Alexander B. Walker (1875–1907) attended the Grammar between 1883 and 1889, entering Lower I. He was Captain of the FP Rugby Club in its foundation year of 1893–4. He qualified in Medicine from Aberdeen University in 1898 and practised in Peterhead and Glasgow.

(Dr) W. Clark Souter (1880–1959) attended the Grammar between 1893 and 1898, entering Middle III. He graduated from Aberdeen University in Medicine in 1903. He gained the Polar Star for his work as surgeon on *Terra Nova,* the Antarctic relief ship, in 1903–4. He served with the RAMC during WWI. He specialised in Ophthalmic Surgery in his career in Aberdeen which ended with retirement in 1946. He was President of the FP Club, 1949–50.

Robert A. Salmond (1883–1953) attended the Grammar between 1891 and 1899, entering Initiatory, and then studied Medicine at Marischal and Cambridge. He was consultant Radiologist to the British armies in France and the University College Hospital in London.

(Dr) Naughton Dunn (1884–1939) attended the Grammar between 1891 and 1899 and in 1902, entering Initiatory. He further studied at Aberdeen becoming a surgical officer and demonstrator. He was a Major in the RAMC. He was a lecturer in Orthopaedic Surgery at Birmingham, and a Surgeon in Warwickshire and Derbyshire. As an assistant to Sir Robert Jones he gained an international reputation for Orthopaedic Surgery and made a significant contribution to the literature on the subject.

John D. Fiddes (1884–1966) attended the Grammar between 1896 and 1902, entering Middle II. He took degrees in Arts, Science and Medicine all with distinction. He was a brilliant student at Edinburgh University and won many academic prizes. He was a Lt Col. in the RAMC in wartime. He remained a GP in Essex despite his Gold Medal in Surgery.

(Prof. Sir) (William) Wilson Jameson (1885–1962; Kt 1939; KCB 1943) attended the Grammar between 1892 and 1902, entering Lower I. He graduated in Arts from King's in 1905 and in Medicine, with distinction, from Marischal in 1909. He was a noted athlete at School, but played only golf thereafter. He was President of the SRC in 1907. His earliest medical years were involved with the treatment of Pulmonary Tuberculosis and he became a member of the RCP in 1913. His work in Public Health in London led to his appointment as lecturer at Guy's Hospital. In 1929, he became the first Professor of Public Health at London University and in 1940 he became the country's Chief Medical Officer, a post he held for a decade. He gave special attention to the nutrition of children and expectant mothers and introduced a nationwide scheme for immunisation against diphtheria. He was elected FRCP in 1930. He received the Buchanan Medal of the Royal Society in 1942. He played a prominent part in preparing the legislation behind the NHS.[15]

Harry J. Rae (1886–1955) attended the Grammar between 1898 and 1904, entering Middle II. He qualified in Medicine at Aberdeen University in 1911 and won an MC during his WWI service with the RAMC. He was appointed MOH for Aberdeenshire, 1925–8; and MOH for Aberdeen and Head of the Public Health Department of Aberdeen University, 1928–52. He was Honorary Physician to George VI and Elizabeth II.

Andrew J. Shinnie (1886–1963) attended the Grammar between 1897 and 1903, entering Middle I. He studied further at Aberdeen and University College, London. He joined the Public Health Service in 1913 and was

MOH for the City of Westminster from 1924 until 1953. He wrote a number of articles on public health issues in medical and technical journals.

(Dr) Alexander M. Brown (1887–1959) attended the Grammar between 1894 and 1904. He graduated MA in 1907 and in Medicine in 1911, both from Aberdeen University before specialising in Public Health. After working as assistant MOH in Doncaster and Chester he became MOH for Hereford in 1921. By 1957 he was chair of the BMA's Private Practice Committee.

Robert Richards (1887–1965) attended the Grammar between 1899 and 1904, entering Middle III. He graduated from Aberdeen in Arts (1907) and Medicine (1910). He reached the rank of Captain in the RAMC in wartime. He became a member of FRCSE in 1920 and Head of the Department of Forensic Medicine in Aberdeen University in 1933. He was chair of the Mental Hospitals' Board (1954) and Police Surgeon for Aberdeen.

(Brig.) Douglas G. Cheyne (1889–1966) attended the Grammar between 1901 and 1905, entering Middle II. He qualified in Medicine from Marischal in 1910. He served in the RAMC from 1914 until 1948 and saw active service in France, Belgium and Italy in WWI. Post-war he served in Shanghai and India. He then was Director of Public Health in Sicily, Greece and Germany and worked in the Ministry of Defence until final retirement.

Kenneth P. McKenzie (1889–1968) attended the Grammar between 1901 and 1907, entering Middle II. He qualified in Arts (1910) and Medicine (1914) at Aberdeen University. He joined the RAMC and gained a commission in the Indian military. He was captured in World War II by the Japanese and wrote a best-selling book – *Operation Rangoon Trail* – on his experiences in Burma. He served on Inverness Town and County Councils.

(Sir) (Arthur) Landsborough Thomson (1890–1977; Kt 1959) attended the Grammar between 1899 and 1908, entering Lower III. He studied further at Aberdeen, Heidelberg and Vienna. He served the entire war in France being promoted to Lt Col. He joined the new Medical Research Council in 1919 as Assistant Secretary and remained there until retirement in 1957. His work on bacteriological research was subsumed into the NHS to fight everyday infections. He was also influential in Ornithology through a number of publications. He was elected FRSE in 1938. He was President of the FP Club, 1954–5.[16]

Robert Forgan (1891–1976) attended the Grammar between 1898 and 1908, entering Initiatory. He graduated from Aberdeen University in Arts (1911) and Medicine (1915) and went on to Cambridge. He served as a Captain in France with the RAMC until 1920. He specialised in the treatment of Venereal Diseases in Lanarkshire in the 1920s. He was elected as Labour MP for West Renfrewshire in 1929 but transferred to the New Party of Sir Oswald Mosley. He became Deputy Leader of the British Union of Fascists but resigned when it began to campaign against Jews. He worked for a pharmaceutical manufacturing firm and gained a hockey cap for Scotland in 1921.

(Dr) Robin D. Lawrence (1892–1968) attended the Grammar between 1900 and 1909, entering Lower II. He went on to Aberdeen University, where he gained a number of awards, graduating in Medicine with honours in 1916. Unfortunate to contract diabetes, he was fortunate that insulin saved his life. He learned how to manage diabetes and acquired a large practice in the specialism, publishing *The Diabetic Life* in 1925. He was appointed Physician in charge of the Diabetic Department at King's College Hospital in 1939. He dominated the diabetic scene in Britain to a unique extent for thirty years.[17] A commemorative plaque can be found at 10 Ferryhill Place.

(Maj. Gen.) Thomas Menzies (1893–1969) attended the Grammar between 1905 and 1910, entering Classical IV. He qualified in Medicine at Aberdeen University in 1914 and joined the RAMC. He saw active service on the Western Front and in India and Mesopotamia. He continued his military career in the inter-war period and again served in the 1939–45 War, in France, North Africa and Italy. He retired in 1953 and was Provost of Kirriemuir, 1958–64.

(Dr) Redvers N. Ironside (1899–1968) attended the Grammar between 1907 and 1917, entering Lower I. He served in the RA in 1917–18 before graduating with FCH and the Gold Medal in Medicine from Aberdeen University in 1922. He became Registrar in the Neurological Department of Guy's Hospital, 1927–32; consultant Neurologist to the RAF, becoming an Air-Commodore in 1944, and to Charing Cross Hospital and Maida Vale Hospital for Nervous Diseases.

Legal

Alexander T. Cruickshank (1869–1947) attended the Grammar between 1882 and 1887, entering Middle II (seniors). He took an MA at Aberdeen University and became an Advocate in Aberdeen in 1897. During WWI he was chair of the Aberdeen Central War Savings Committee. He was an original member of the FP Club and played a major role in the scheme for opening Rubislaw Field (as Convener of the Secondary Schools Committee of the School Board). He had a role in the unveiling of the Byron statue and proposed the opening of the Boarding House. He was President of the FP Club, 1923–5.

John E. Rae (1870–1953) attended the Grammar between 1885 and 1887, entering Classical II. He qualified at Aberdeen University in Law and was admitted to the Society of Advocates in 1896 (he became President in 1940–2). He was clerk of both the JP and Juvenile Courts in Aberdeen.

James Hay (1871–1953) attended the Grammar between 1883 and 1887, entering Middle III. He qualified in Law at Aberdeen University in 1896. He was on the Town Council, 1928–45 and developed the city's sporting facilities. He was DL for the City of Aberdeen, and President of Aberdeen Society of Advocates, 1936–8. He was Secretary of Royal Aberdeen Golf Club (and President of the Scottish Golf Union). He chaired the Board of ARI and was a member of Aberdeen University Court for eighteen years.

Alfred W. Edwards (1873–1929) attended the Grammar between 1881 and 1888, entering Lower II. He qualified as a Law Agent, 1894 and became a Notary Public in 1895. He was Clerk of the Peace for the County of the City of Aberdeen, 1904. He was Secretary of the FP Club, 1896–1906.

(Sir) Robert (William) Lyall Grant (1875–1955; Kt 1934) attended the Grammar from 1884 till 1891, entering Lower III. He went on to Aberdeen and Edinburgh Universities before he was called to the Scottish Bar in 1903. He was Attorney-General of Nyasaland, 1909, then Kenya, 1920, and became Chief Justice of Jamaica, 1932–6. He was an original member of the FP Club.

Charles J. Davidson (1875–1941) attended the Grammar between 1886 and 1891, entering Middle II. He took an Arts degree at Aberdeen University, 1895, and qualified in Law in 1897 with distinction in Forensic Medicine. He became an advocate and a very committed FP Club member.

Alexander M. Mackay (Hon. Lord Mackay – senator 1924) (1875–1955) attended the Grammar from 1882 until 1891, entering Initiatory. He gained a FCH in Philosophy and Classics at Aberdeen, winning the Ferguson (Philosophical) Scholarship, going on to Trinity, Cambridge and Edinburgh. He was Scottish Singles Lawn Tennis champion, 1905–7, and President of the Scottish LTA, 1919–24. He was called to the Scottish Bar in 1902 and was one of the Senators of the College of Justice in Scotland, 1928–54. A mountaineer of repute, able golfer, curler, cricketer and rugby player, as well as a violinist of distinction, he was said to have been 'the best all-round pupil the School ever had' (according to Rector D.M. Andrew in 1928). He was FP Club President, 1931–2.

Arthur R. Brown (1876–1955) attended the Grammar between 1884 and

1890. He qualified at Aberdeen University in 1896 and was called to the Scottish Bar in 1903. He became Junior Counsel for the Treasury in 1919 and a KC in 1925. He was Sheriff-Substitute of Lanarkshire, 1927–46.

Charles B. Milne (1880–1960) attended the Grammar between 1893 and 1896, entering Middle III. He gained an MA LLB from Edinburgh University and joined the Bar in 1904. Between 1925 and 1928 he was Junior Counsel to the Secretary of State for Scotland. He lectured in Scots Law at Edinburgh (1930) and took Silk in 1932. He was Conservative MP for West Fife from 1931 to 1935, and from 1939 to 1960 he was the Sheriff of Dumfries and Galloway.

James Hay (1881–1954) attended the Grammar between 1893 and 1895, entering Class I. He qualified as a Law Agent and was admitted to the Society of Advocates in 1919. He was a member of the Town Council, 1937–46 and was a leading figure in the fishing industry.

John A. Lillie (1884–1983) attended the Grammar between 1893 and 1903, entering Lower II. He took an MA in 1906 at Aberdeen and a Law degree in 1910 at Edinburgh. He became an advocate in 1912 and took silk in 1931. From 1928 to 1947 he was a lecturer in Mercantile Law at Edinburgh, and between 1941 and 1971 he was Sheriff Principal of Fife and Kinross. He was President of the FP Club in 1952–3.

John R.W. Burnet (1886–1941) attended the Grammar between 1899 and 1901, entering Middle I, before studying at Aberdeen and Cambridge Universities. He joined the Faculty of Advocates in 1912, becoming its Clerk from 1927 to 1934, when he took Silk. He was Junior Counsel to the Admiralty in Scotland and Sheriff of Fife and Kinross from 1937.

(Sir) Patrick Ashley Cooper (1887–1961; Kt 1944) attended the Grammar between 1896 and 1901 (entering Lower III) and completed his schooling at Fettes. He went on to Trinity, Cambridge and Aberdeen, where he graduated in Law in 1912. He served on the Western Front and in the Ministry of Munitions in WWI. He became Governor of the Hudson's Bay Company, 1931–52; a member of the Court of the Bank of England; High Sheriff for the County of London in 1944 and 1957; and was given the Freedom of London in 1947. He was President of the FP Club in 1937–8.

(Lt Col.) Charles D. Peterkin (1887–1962) attended the Grammar between 1893 and 1905, entering Initiatory. He took his degree at Aberdeen and became an advocate in Aberdeen in 1914. He served in WWI in France and Flanders and was with the British Army of the Rhine. He was President of the Society of Advocates in Aberdeen, 1952–4.

James C. Duffus (1891–1962) attended the Grammar between 1897 and

1904 before moving to Fettes and going on to Aberdeen University where he graduated in Arts (1912) and Law (1914). A Major in WWI he joined the Society of Advocates in 1919. During WWII he was Controller of Civil Defence for Aberdeen. He chaired the first Aberdeen Council Hospitals' Board of Management. He was President of the FP Club in 1951–2 (the first son of a former president to attain that distinction, his father, Alex Duffus, being President in 1910–11).

(Sir) David Edwards (1892–1966; Kt 1951) attended the Grammar between 1903 and 1909, entering Middle II. He graduated from Aberdeen in 1921 and joined the Colonial Office. He held legal posts in Kenya and Palestine where he was a Judge of the Supreme Court (1941–7). He was Chief Justice in Uganda, 1947–52 and acted as Senior Judge of the Special Court in Cyprus, 1959–60.

Robert M. Ledingham (1893–1969) attended the Grammar between 1897 and 1909, entering Prep. He took his MA in 1913 and LLB in 1920. He became a partner in a law firm. Before WWII he served the FP Rugby Club and after the war he was on the SRU Committee. Thirty years' involvement in North District Rugby resulted in his election as the first President of the SRU from the FP Club and from Aberdeen, 1961–2.

(Hon.) Dougall Meston (1894–1984) attended the Grammar in 1901–2, entering Prep. He went on to Charterhouse and the Royal Military Academy. He was in the RA during WWI and afterwards on the North-West frontier of India. He became a barrister in 1924. He was a defeated Liberal candidate in 1927 and 1929 but after succeeding to a title in 1943 he became an active Liberal in the House of Lords. He wrote a number of publications.

(Sir) George A. Williamson (1898–1975; Kt 1953) attended the Grammar between 1904 and 1912, entering Prep. He was commissioned in the Indian army in 1916 before completing a Law degree at Aberdeen in 1926. He entered the family firm of Paull and Williamsons, advocates, becoming a partner in 1928 (until 1969). He was elected to the Town Council, 1934–7, and was Convener of Planning. He was President of the Scottish Unionist Association, 1951–2. He was associated with Aberdeen Savings Bank and was its chair from 1953.

R. Bertram Williamson (1901–1976) attended the Grammar between 1906 and 1918, entering Prep. He graduated with distinction in Law at Aberdeen University in 1922 and with his brother, George, developed the legal firm of Paull and Williamsons. He served in WWII in the 51st Highland Signals and was a POW from 1940 to 1945. He was Secretary of the Aberdeen Granite Association, Secretary of Albyn School for Girls and

Vice-Convener of the Business Committee of the General Council of the University. He was President of the FP Club, 1960–1.

Alexander Gray (1904–1981) attended the Grammar between 1910 and 1922, entering Senior Infants. He took a Law degree and was senior partner in a legal firm from 1930. He was President of the Society of Advocates, Treasurer of the Franco-Scottish Society and President of the FP Club, 1962–3.

J. Lindsay Duncan (1905–1954) attended the Grammar between 1911 and 1924, entering the Junior Infants Class. He completed his education at Aberdeen (winning the Edmond and Cruickshank prizes) and Edinburgh Universities. He was called to the Scottish Bar in 1931. He was Sheriff-Substitute of Ross, Cromarty and Sutherland, 1940–2; of Ayrshire, 1942–51, and of the Lothians and Peebles, 1951–4. He contributed extensively to Scottish legal literature.

Academic

(Prof.) Alexander Low (1868–1950) attended the Grammar between 1883 and 1886, entering Classical II. He went on to further study at Aberdeen, Freiburg, Vienna and Zurich. He became Professor of Anatomy at Aberdeen University, 1925–38, and was a recognised authority on anthropology.

Donald C. McIntosh (1868–1957) attended Tomintoul, Keith and the Grammar before gaining an MA (1890) and BSc (1906) from Aberdeen University. He was a Mathematics teacher at George Watson's between 1890 and 1899; head of the Mathematics department at Edinburgh Ladies' College from 1899 to 1918 and Director of Education for Moray and Nairn, 1918–33. He was elected FRSE in 1903.

James C. Murdoch (1868–1921) attended the Grammar aged twenty in 1888 (until 1890), joining Classical III. He gained his MA at Aberdeen in 1894 and became Classical master in Dundee HS and first master at Alloa Higher Grade School. He went on to the Headship of Alva Academy and finally between 1907 and 1921 that of Musselburgh GS.

James Georgeson (1869–1960) attended the Grammar between 1883 and 1886, entering Middle III and becoming Third Bursar. He gained a FCH in Classics at Aberdeen University, and studied at Pembroke, Oxford. He lectured at Aberdeen, 1896–8, and he was head of Classics at the High School for Girls in Aberdeen from 1898 until retirement in 1932.

Andrew Munro (1869–1935) attended the Grammar in 1885, entering Classical III. He graduated MA from Aberdeen in 1889 winning the

Ferguson (Mathematical) Scholarship. He was Fourth Wrangler in 1892 at Cambridge. He became Fellow, Bursar, Proctor and Mathematical Lecturer at Queens', Cambridge, 1893–1935.

Charles Davidson (1870–1959) (known as C.D.) attended the Grammar between 1882 and 1886, entering Middle III. He graduated from Aberdeen with an MA in 1890 and three years later he returned to the School to teach English and Classics, staying for twenty-seven years. He left to teach Spanish at the University in 1920 (until 1939). He was one of the original editors of the School Magazine and he was the source of the 'Notes about Old Boys'. He was President of the FP Club, 1947–8.

Christian H.M. Milne (1870–1945) attended the Grammar between 1881 and 1887, entering Middle I, and gained a FCH in Philosophy at Aberdeen University. He taught in Watson's College, 1892–1900, was Rector of Arbroath High School, 1900–11 and Headmaster of Stewart's College, 1911–35. He became FRSE in 1905.

(Rev. Prof.) Alexander R. Gordon (1872–1930) attended the Grammar between 1884 and 1888, entering Middle III (Seniors) and becoming Dux and shared Gold Medallist in 1888. He entered Aberdeen University as First Bursar and graduated with FCH in both Classical Literature and Mental Philosophy, winning the Simpson Greek prize, the Hutton prize, the Bain and Town Council Gold Medals and later became the Fullerton scholar. He studied further at New College, Edinburgh and at Freiburg, Göttingen and Berlin. He was Professor in Presbyterian College, Montreal from 1907, Professor of Hebrew at McGill, 1914–30 and appointed Professor of Hebrew and Oriental Languages at St Andrews University shortly before his death in late 1930. He wrote numerous publications.

George Andrew (1873–1956; CBE 1937) attended the Grammar in 1885–6 and completed his MA (1894) at Aberdeen and his BA (1899) at Oxford. He was a Classics master at Hillhead HS, before joining the school inspectorate in 1901. He became FRSE in 1905; HM Chief Inspector, 1931–5, and finally HM Senior Chief Inspector, 1935–8.

Murdo Morrison (1873–1975) attended the Grammar between 1894 and 1896, entering Classical VI at the age of twenty-one. He gained fifth place in the Bursary Competition of 1896 and graduated with honours in Mental Philosophy at Aberdeen University. He joined the HMI in 1903 and was Director of Education for Inverness-shire from 1919 to 1937.

(Prof.) James C. Philip (1873–1941) attended the Grammar between 1886 and 1889, entering Classical I, and gained the Gold Medal in his final year. He studied further at Aberdeen and Göttingen. He was Professor of Physical

Chemistry at Imperial College, London, 1913–38. He was awarded FRS in 1921. He produced a number of publications. He was President of the FP Club, 1938–9.

Alexander Findlay (1874–1966) attended the Grammar between 1882 and 1891, entering Lower I. He continued his studies at Aberdeen and Leipzig Universities. He was Professor of Chemistry at the University College of Wales, 1911–19, and Professor of Chemistry at Aberdeen University from 1919–43. He was President of the Royal Institute of Chemistry, 1943–6. He produced a number of publications.

Francis W. Michie (1874–1962) attended the Grammar between 1885 and 1890 and in 1891, entering Middle II. He graduated in Arts at Aberdeen in 1894 but taught Science at Dundee HS. He was appointed to the HMI in 1901 and became HMCI in Highland from 1932 and then in the North (centred in Aberdeen) in 1935. He retired in 1938.

(Sir) Robert S. Rait (1874–1936; Kt 1933) was educated at the Grammar and King's, graduating MA in 1894. He won an Exhibition to New College, Oxford and took FCH in 1899 in History. After a Fellowship at Oxford he became Professor of History at Glasgow University in 1913 and published extensively. From 1929 to 1936 he was Principal and Vice-Chancellor of Glasgow. He was appointed President of the Scottish History Society in 1933 and the expansion of Scottish historical studies at this time owed much to him.[18]

George Stewart (1874–1953) attended the Grammar between 1889 and 1892 being Gold Medallist in his final year. He graduated from Aberdeen with an MA (1897) and BSc (1901). He became a Mathematics and Science teacher at the Grammar 1897–1900 and 1940–4. He also taught at Campbeltown GS, Cambuslang and was Rector of Strathaven Academy, 1920–39.

(Prof.) Robert Scott Troup (1874–1939) attended the Grammar between 1889 and 1891, entering Middle II. He continued his studies at Aberdeen University and engineering college in Surrey where he trained for the Indian Forest Service. By 1906 he was a Forest Economist and then became a leading authority on the silviculture of Indian trees. He published three volumes on his systematic research. In 1920 he was elected Professor of Forestry at Oxford and became an FRS in 1926.[19] He was Director of the Imperial Forestry Institute, 1924–35.

George L. Barrie (1876–1938) attended the Grammar in 1893–4, entering Classical III. He took his MA in 1898 at Aberdeen University. He taught Modern Languages at Dumfries and Ardrossan Academies before joining

Glasgow Academy in 1903 and was Head of Department of his subject there from 1918 to 1936. He was a cousin of Sir James Barrie.

(Prof.) John J.R. Macleod (1876–1935) attended the Grammar from 1884 until 1893, entering Initiatory. He took his studies further at Marischal, Leipzig, Berlin and London. He held the post of Professor of Physiology at Cleveland (Ohio), 1903–18; Toronto, 1918–28; and Aberdeen, 1928–35. In 1923 he shared the Nobel Prize for Medicine for his work on the discovery of insulin. He published some two hundred medical papers. He was elected FRS in 1923 and FRSE in 1932. He was President of the FP Club, 1930–1.[20] A commemorative plaque can be found at 32 Cairn Road, Cults.

George R. Watt (1879–1908) attended the Grammar between 1885 and 1895 and in 1897, entering Initiatory. He was Dux and Gold Medallist in 1895 and was First Bursar in 1897. He graduated from Aberdeen and Cambridge and lectured in Greek at the former. In 1908 he was appointed Professor of English and Philosophy in Calcutta but died before taking up the post.

Henry J. Watt (1879–1925) attended the Grammar between 1891 and 1896, entering Middle II. He was Dux and Gold Medallist of the School. He graduated FCH in Philosophy at Aberdeen University in 1900 and studied Psychology at Berlin, Würzburg and Leipzig. From 1907 he lectured at Liverpool then Glasgow. He was interned by Germany during the first part of WWI, which permanently damaged his health. He published several books.

(Prof.) R.L. Graeme Ritchie (1880–1954) attended the Grammar between 1894 and 1899, entering Middle III. He studied at Aberdeen University gaining a FCH in both Classics and Modern Languages. A Carnegie scholarship allowed him to study modern languages further at Strasbourg and Paris. He was Professor of French Language and Literature at Birmingham, 1919–46, and Professor of French at Exeter, 1946–52. He produced numerous publications.

Basil G. McLellan (1881–1971) attended the Grammar between 1887 and 1889, entering Initiatory. He went on to Gordon's and took a Science degree at Glasgow Technical College. He was Chief Chemist with Rowntree & Co. Ltd, in York, from 1922 to 1944. He became Director of the Scottish Seaweed Research Association, 1944–5. He was elected FRSE in 1953.

(Prof.) William P. Milne (1881–1967) studied at the Grammar between 1897 and 1899, entering Classical VII, and was Dux in his final year. He gained a FCH in Mathematics and Natural Philosophy at Aberdeen University, where he accumulated a number of prizes. He was Fourth Wrangler at Cambridge in 1906. He was Professor of Mathematics at Leeds,

1919–46, and Pro-Vice Chancellor there from 1943 to 1945. He published a number of works and paid a handsome tribute to Rector Simpson (under whom he studied at the School) in the *Transactions* of the Buchan Club, which was reprinted in the School Magazine.

James Strachan (1881–1962) attended the Grammar between 1885 and 1895, entering Initiatory. He gained FCH in Mathematics and Natural Philosophy in 1899 at Aberdeen University and then gained a BSc with distinction in Botany. He gained a scholarship to Cambridge, where he was Seventh Wrangler in 1901 and President of the Union in 1903. He was chief Mathematics master at Merchant Taylor's School, London, before in 1919 joining the English school inspectorate, being a HMCI from 1928.

Robert S. Clark (1882–1950) attended the Grammar between 1894 and 1901, entering Middle I. Having taken an MA and BSc he became Zoologist to the Scottish Oceanographical Lab in Edinburgh. He was the scientific member of Shackleton's 1914–17 expedition to Antarctica, being one of the twenty-two men marooned on Elephant Island during 1916. He served on minesweepers in WWI. In 1925 he became Director of the Fisheries Research Lab at Torry. He became a member of the RSE in 1935. He played cricket for Scotland.

(Prof.) James M. Hector (1882–1955) attended the Grammar between 1889 and 1900, entering Initiatory. He gained a BSc in 1904 and lectured at the Northern Agricultural College. In 1917 he was appointed Professor of Agricultural Botany at the University of Pretoria.

(Prof.) John A. Stewart (1882–1948) studied at the Grammar between 1897 and 1899, entering Classical VI. He studied at Aberdeen, gaining FCH in Classics in 1903, and Christ Church, Oxford, joining the ICS in 1904. During the war he served in Burma, Mesopotamia and the North-West frontier. He became Professor of Burmese at the School of Oriental and African Studies in London.

James M. Milne (1883–1959) attended the Grammar between 1895 and 1902, entering Middle I. He studied further at Aberdeen and Rennes Universities. He taught in schools – Campbeltown, North Kelvinside, HSOG and Bell-Baxter, before becoming Rector of Nairn Academy, 1920–47. He produced some publications.

John Minto Robertson (1883–1951) attended the Grammar between 1894 and 1901, entering Middle I, and leaving as Classical Dux. He took his MA from Aberdeen University in 1905 and after a number of teaching posts in the North-East he became headmaster of Kemnay Secondary School in 1923. He was a prolific writer and contributed significantly to the School Magazine.

William S. Catto (1885–1956) attended the Grammar between 1895 and 1902, entering Middle I. He was Modern Dux of the School in 1901 and graduated with honours in Mathematics and Natural Philosophy at Aberdeen University. He taught at Dumfries Academy and Kirkwall. He joined George Watson's in 1913, becoming head of Mathematics there in 1926 and retiring in 1949 as Deputy Head of the College.

(Prof.) William S. Mackie (1886–1980) attended the Grammar between 1895 and 1901, entering Middle I. After an MA (1906) and further study at Oxford (1909) he became a lecturer at Southampton University. He held the post of Professor of English Language at Cape Town University, 1921–51.

(Prof.) John Laird (1887–1946) attended the Grammar between 1901 and 1903, entering Classical IV. He gained a FCH in philosophy from Edinburgh in 1907 and won the much-coveted Shaw Prize. He took a FCH in both tripos in Moral Sciences at Trinity College, Cambridge. He was Professor at Dalhousie University, Nova Scotia, before in 1913 becoming Professor of Logic and Metaphysics at Queen's, Belfast. In 1924, he became Professor of Moral Philosophy at Aberdeen, a post he held until 1946. In 1933 he was elected a Fellow of the British Academy. He published extensively. His realist position directly opposed the idealism of his contemporaries, Bradley and Joachim.[21]

Herbert J.M. Milne (1888–1965) attended the Grammar between 1900 and 1905, entering Middle III. He was Classical Dux of the School and achieved a FCH at Aberdeen University in Classics in 1909. He went on to Caius, Cambridge, 1909–12. He was an assistant in the Department of Manuscripts in the British Museum, 1912–53. He was an expert linguist and an authority on Greek Palaeography, and Papyrology. He contributed to many volumes of the catalogue of additions to the manuscripts of the Museum.

John W. Robertson (1888–1957) attended the Grammar between 1903 and 1905, entering Classical VI. He gained FCH at Aberdeen in Mathematics and Natural Philosophy, and the following year in 1910 a distinction in his BSc. He taught at Gordon's and became Head of the Mathematics department at the Grammar, 1925. He took over the Headship of the Central Secondary School in 1926.

(Prof.) James O. Thomson (1889–1971) attended the Grammar in 1899–1900, entering Middle I. He went on to Gordon's, took an MA at Aberdeen University, and at Trinity, Cambridge. He was regarded as the 'most distinguished Latinist of his day' gaining a number of scholarships including the Ferguson and Fullerton prizes. He served in WWI as infantryman on the Western Front and intelligence officer. He was Professor of Latin at Birmingham University, 1919–55 and published extensively.

(Prof. Sir) Hubert D. Henderson (1890–1952; Kt 1942) attended the Grammar between 1901 and 1904, entering Middle III. Following attendance at Rugby he went up to Emmanuel, Cambridge, in 1909, with a Mathematical Exhibition, but changed to Economics and gained FCH. In 1912 he was President of the Union. He was rejected on physical grounds for military service and joined the Statistical Section of the Board of Trade. He accepted a Fellowship at Clare and a Cambridge lectureship. As a Liberal friend and colleague of John Maynard Keynes, he was persuaded, in 1923, to become editor of the weekly *Nation and Athenaeum*. He was influential on economic affairs but stood unsuccessfully as a Liberal in the election of 1929. However, he became Joint-Secretary of the Economic Advisory Council of the Labour government in 1930–1. Throughout the 1930s he continued to advise Whitehall and in June 1939 was one of the 'three wise men' called on to advise on the economic plans for the War. In 1945, he became Professor of Political Economy at Oxford and a Fellow of the British Academy in 1948.[22]

Andrew Milne (1890–1972) attended the Grammar between 1903 and 1909, entering Middle II. He became School Classical Dux and Gold Medallist in his final year and was Second Bursar. He went on to gain a FCH in Classics from Aberdeen University in 1913. He was Senior Classics Master at Montrose Academy (1923–26) and the Grammar (1929–55) before lecturing in Classics at Rhodes University, Grahamstown, SA.

Adam A. Ritchie (1890–1974) attended the Grammar between 1903 and 1908, entering Classical III. He took his MA (1912) and BSc (1914) at Aberdeen, becoming a science teacher at Aitchison College, Lahore. He was the first FP hockey cap, playing for Scotland three times in 1914.

(Prof.) John Macmurray (1891–1976) attended the Grammar between 1902 and 1904, entering Middle II. After a spell at Gordon's he went to Glasgow University and in 1913 secured a Snell Exhibition to Balliol, Oxford. He took this up after war service (and the award of a MC) and graduated in 1919. He held posts teaching Philosophy at Manchester, Witwatersrand and Balliol before his appointment to the chair of Philosophy of the Mind and Logic at London University, which he held from 1928 until 1944. He then took the chair of Moral Philosophy at Edinburgh until retirement in 1958. He became a popular and controversial BBC radio broadcaster; he was a successful teacher and in later life became a member of the Society of Friends.[23]

(Prof.) Louis A. Reid (1895–1986) attended the Grammar between 1904 and 1909, entering Lower III. After studying Engineering at Edinburgh

University he was a member of the RE in 1914–15. He then took a FCH and prizes in Mental Philosophy in 1919. After lecturing in Philosophy at Aberystwyth and Liverpool he was Professor at Newcastle, 1932–47 and then Professor of the Philosophy of Education at London University, 1947–52. He produced a number of publications.

William Douglas Simpson (1896–1968), the younger son of Rector, Morland Simpson, attended the Grammar between 1901 and 1913, entering Prep. He was discharged from the army for medical reasons but graduated with FCH in History from Aberdeen University and lectured there until 1926 when he was appointed Librarian, Registrar and Clerk to the General Council, posts he held until 1966. He was chair of the Ancient Monuments Board for Scotland. He directed excavations at a number of castles and published a series of works, a number aimed at the general reader. He proved a pioneer in Scottish history and he was an immensely successful and popular lecturer. He was President of the FP Club in 1953–4 and 1963–4.[24]

Lawrence Ogilvie (1898–1980) attended the Grammar between 1907 and 1916, entering Lower III. He graduated with a BSc and MA from Aberdeen University in 1921 and studied Botany at Emmanuel, Cambridge in 1922. He became Bermuda's first Plant Pathologist and identified the virus which had devastated the island's lily-bulb crop, 1923–8. He worked at Long Ashton Research Station (near Bristol) and became the UK expert on diseases of cereal crops and vegetables. His advice was crucial for Britain during WWII and in the post-war period.

Murray R. Henderson (1899–1982) attended the Grammar between 1914 and 1917, entering Classical IVA. He qualified in Botany from Aberdeen University and did most of his botanical work in the Straits Settlements and South Africa. He was elected a Fellow of the Linnean Society in 1922. He became Herbarium of the Singapore Botanical Gardens in 1924 and Director in 1946. He wrote extensively.

Charles B. Bisset (1900–1966; CBE) attended the Grammar between 1909 and 1918, entering Lower II. He served in the forces in the last months of WWI, taking his BSc from Aberdeen University in 1923. He was the Geologist with the British Arctic expedition of 1925 and wrote a report for the School Magazine. He joined the Colonial Geological Survey Service and worked in Nyasaland, Uganda and Tanganyika. After 1945 he was engaged in advising African governments on water supplies.

(Sir) James R. Sutherland (1900–1996; Kt 1992) attended the Grammar between 1907 and 1917, entering Lower II. He graduated with FCH in English at Aberdeen University in 1921 and went on to Oxford. He lectured at Saskatchewan, Southampton and Glasgow. He gained a chair in English Literature at Birkbeck, London, in 1936, and became Professor of English Language and Literature at Queen Mary College, London. He delivered the Wharton Lectures in English Poetry to the British Academy and was visiting Professor at Harvard in 1947 and Indiana University, 1950–1. He was a prolific writer.

(Prof.) David Landsborough Thomson (1901–1964) attended the Grammar between 1911 and 1918, entering Lower IV. He studied at Aberdeen, Grenoble, Graz and Gonville and Caius, Cambridge. He was Professor of Biochemistry at McGill University, 1937–60. He was also Dean of the Faculty of Graduate Studies and Research, 1942–63 and Vice-Principal from 1955. He produced a number of publications.

James W.S. Marr (1902–1965) attended the Grammar between 1913 and 1919, entering Lower VA, and then Aberdeen University. Chosen from a field of several thousand scouts he gained experience with Shackleton in 1921 on his final Antarctic expedition as cabin-boy on *The Quest*, and in 1925 was Zoologist to the British Arctic Expedition in Iceland. His work with whales led him to three further Antarctic trips. He returned to the area as a plankton specialist and worked as a Principal Scientific Officer in the Royal Navy Scientific Service. He produced a number of publications.[25]

(Prof.) Edward J. Wood (1902–1993) attended the Grammar between 1908 and 1921, entering Prep. He achieved FCH degrees at Aberdeen and Trinity, Cambridge. After academic posts at Manchester and Aberystwyth, where he was appointed chair of Latin in 1932, he became Professor of Latin at Leeds University, 1938–67, and Pro-Vice Chancellor, 1957–9. He was President of the FP Club, 1966–7.

Financial

Charles Williamson (1869–1960) attended the Grammar between 1883 and 1885, entering Classical I. He graduated from Aberdeen University in 1889 and then qualified as an Accountant in 1894. He was the first to pass the exam to be called 'chartered' in Scotland and spent his career working as a CA. He was an original member of the FP Club.

John Rae (1870–1932) attended the Grammar between 1882 and 1885, entering Middle II. He took up Banking in 1885 and rose to the position of Treasurer of the Bank of Scotland in 1917–21. He became Chief General Manager of the amalgamated Westminster and Parr's banks and a Director of the Bank of Scotland.

John Brown (1871–1943) attended the Grammar in 1886–7, entering Classical I, and spent his career in Banking and Life Assurance in Aberdeen, London and Dundee, retiring in 1935. He was a nephew of Queen Victoria's attendant of the same name and she took a special interest in his welfare.

James F. Taylor (1873–1960) attended the Grammar between 1886 and 1888, entering Classical I, and by 1891 was an apprentice clerk in Aberdeen. He worked in India and England gaining experience and promotion. He worked successfully in Canada and set up in Montreal as an independent Financial Agent. He was then called in by the Bank of England to reorganise a major engineering business in difficulty. He went on to play a key role in Britain's industrial reorganisation in the inter-war years.[26]

William Mackintosh (1879–1931) attended the Grammar between 1893 and 1896, entering Class III. He was successful in the financial world becoming Secretary of the Royal Insurance Co. in Aberdeen and then New York. He was a successful cricketer for Aberdeenshire between 1908 and 1912, before he migrated.

James G. Kyd (1882–1968) attended the Grammar between 1891 and 1898, entering Lower I. From 1919 to 1921 he acted as Ireland's Actuary Officer before five years as Chief of HM Government's Actuary and Treasury Department. He was Registrar-General of Scotland, 1937–48, President of the Faculty of Actuaries, 1944–6, and he was responsible for suggesting the completion of a Third Statistical Account for Scotland. He was elected FRSE in 1940. He was President of the FP Club, 1950–1.

(Col.) E. Birnie Reid (1896–1980) attended the Grammar between 1902 and 1913, entering Prep. He studied at Aberdeen and Clare, Cambridge and became a CA in 1922. He was the senior partner in Meston & Co. and President of the Institute of Chartered Accountants in Scotland. He was the Rector's Assessor to the Aberdeen University Court. He was Hon. Col. of 51st Divisional Signals and President of the Cairngorm Club.

Alan McBain (1897–1954) attended the Grammar between 1903 and 1914, entering Prep. He became Dux in 1914 and the winner of the first All-Round Trophy. He took his MA at Aberdeen University in 1920 and then qualified as a CA. He was a fine cricketer for the School and the FPs.

Douglas P. Cochran (1898–1985) attended the Grammar between 1906 and 1915, entering Prep. He joined the Northern Assurance Co. in 1915, moving on in 1921 to Royal Exchange Insurance from which he retired in 1960. He was President of the FP Club, 1957–8.

J. Patrick Jeffrey (1902–1962) attended the Grammar between 1906 and 1918, entering Prep. He studied Civil Engineering at Glasgow and qualified as a CA in 1929. He was the first chairman of Aberdeen Progressive Association and represented Rosemount Ward, 1951–4. He was President of the Chamber of Commerce. He was Vice-President of the FP Club and chair of its Executive, 1936–9.

Eric Ros Birkett (1905–1998) attended the Grammar between 1920 and 1922 (following a spell at Gordon's) and became a CA. He was Secretary of John Menzies & Co. Ltd from 1930 until his retirement in 1969. He was President of the FP Club, 1968–9.

Administrative (*Politicians*)

(Rt Hon.) Robert Munro (1868–1955) (1st Baron Alness cr. 1934) attended the Grammar in 1884–5, entering Classical II, and graduated MA from Edinburgh in 1889 and LLB in 1892. He was called to the Scottish Bar the following year and became a KC in 1910. He won the seat of Wick Burghs for the Liberals and was Lord Advocate between 1913 and 1916, when he became Secretary of State for Scotland, a post he held until 1922. He was appointed Lord Justice Clerk until 1933. He introduced the Education Act (1918) into Scotland; and a reform of Scotland's Divorce Law, enacted in 1938. He was DL for Edinburgh as well as being a Freeman of the City.[27] He is associated with securing the Rubislaw Playing Fields for the School (1913–16); he unveiled the School War Memorials in 1923 and 1950, and was FP Club President, 1928–9.

Hugh Gunn (1870–1931) attended the Grammar in 1888–9, when he entered Classical III and became Dux in 1889. He went on to Aberdeen and Edinburgh Universities and taught at Brora. He acted as an HM Sub-Inspector between 1898 and 1902. He was Director of Education and a member of the Legislative Council in Orange River Colony, 1902–10. He organised the University of Western Australia, which was being set up in 1912–13. As an educationist his last plea (in 1931) was for the creation of a bilingual University for the Scottish Highlands.

(Dr) William A. Mackenzie (1870–1942) attended the Grammar in 1886–7 entering Classical II and studied Medicine at Marischal. He was Secretary-General of Save the Children International Union, Geneva, 1920–40. He published poems, novels and serials.

Claud A. Barron (1871–1948) attended the Grammar between 1880 and 1887, entering Prep. III. He studied further at Aberdeen and Clare, Cambridge, joining the ICS in 1892. He was Chief Secretary, Punjab, 1912–16; Chief Commissioner, Delhi, 1918–24; member of the Council of State of

India, 1921–4; and Financial Commissioner, Punjab, 1924–7.

Alexander R. Cumming (1871–1955) attended the Grammar between 1880 and 1887, entering Prep. IV. He was Dux and Gold Medallist at School (1887) and First Bursar to Aberdeen University. He joined the ICS, becoming collector and magistrate for Madras.

James Moir (1875–1929), elder son of Rector Moir, attended the Grammar between 1881 and 1893, entering Initiatory. He was an outstanding pupil at the School winning prizes in practically all his subjects. He was Third Bursar (Arts) in 1893. He combined his MA and BSc and graduated in 1897, with FCH in Chemistry, Mathematics and Physics. He did research in London but his bronchial condition led him to migrate to South Africa where he worked as an analytical chemist. He was elected a Fellow of the Royal Society of South Africa.

George A. Combe (1877–1933) attended the Grammar from 1889 until 1895, entering Middle II. After Aberdeen University he became an interpreter in China, 1901. He was appointed Consul in 1919 and was the Commissioner on the Nanking Commission, 1928–30. He was Consul-General from 1929 to 1932.

Arthur J. Milne (1879–1940) attended the Grammar between 1884 and 1896, entering Initiatory. He qualified in Medicine at Aberdeen University and served as a Surgeon in the South African War. He took his DPH in 1903 and joined the Colonial Medical Service in 1904. He became the MOH for Johannesburg, 1918.

(Commander Sir) Jameson B. Adams (1880–1962; KCVO 1948) attended the Grammar in 1893–4, entering Modern IV. He was second in command of Shackleton's British Imperial Antarctic Expedition in 1907–9 which progressed to within a hundred miles of the South Pole. He became a civil servant and was General Manager of Employment Exchanges in London and became Controllor of Exchanges in north-east England.

(Lt Col.) Henry J. Butchart (1882–1971) attended the Grammar between 1890 and 1899, entering Initiatory. He went on to Aberdeen and Edinburgh Universities, qualifying as a Law Agent in 1906. He was admitted advocate in Aberdeen in 1908 and was appointed Secretary and Factor of Aberdeen University, posts he held from 1920 until 1952. His contribution was particularly valuable in developing the University's sporting facilities. He was a DL for the County of Aberdeen and President of the FP Club in 1955–6.

Theodore G. Gray (1884–1964) attended the Grammar between 1895 and 1901, entering Middle I. He qualified in Medicine at Aberdeen University. He moved to New Zealand where he was Director-General of Mental

Hospitals from 1927 until 1947. He produced a number of publications.

Alexander J. Findlay (1886–1976; CMG) attended the Grammar between 1898 and 1904, entering Middle II. He went on to study at Aberdeen University and the College of Agriculture. He served in the Nigerian Department of Agriculture (1912–31) and that of Zanzibar (1931–7).

(Sir) W. Arthur C. Lothian (1887–1962; KCIE 1941) attended the Grammar between 1892 and 1894 and between 1898 and 1904 (entering Initiatory). He gained a FCH in Arts at Aberdeen University in 1908 and a BSc with special distinction in 1909. He went on to Christ's, Oxford before joining the ICS. He reached the top echelons in India, being appointed in 1942 to be the Premier Resident at Hyderabad. He was President of the FP Club in 1948–9.

(Prof.) Robert N. Gilchrist (1888–1972) attended the Grammar between 1901 and 1905, entering Classical IV, and went on to gain a triple honours in Economics, History and Philosophy at Aberdeen University. He was appointed to the Indian Educational Service in 1910 and was Principal and Professor of Political Economy and Political Philosophy at Krishnager College, Bengal, from 1916 until 1921. He was Labour Intelligence Officer and Labour Commissioner of the province from 1922 to 1934; Joint-Secretary to Bengal's Government, 1934–41 and Principal of the India Office, 1940–8. He produced a number of publications.

(Sir) William Peters (1889–1964; Kt 1947) attended the Grammar between 1900 and 1906, entering Middle II. He went on to Aberdeen University and gained a FCH in Mathematics and Natural Philosophy. As a student in Russia he worked in the Russian Diplomatic Service before becoming Commercial Secretary to Russia (1921–7) and to Stockholm (1928–9). He was UK Trade Commissioner in the Irish Free State (1929–35) and in South Africa (1937–51).

(Sir) Andrew G. Clow (1890–1957; KCSI 1941) attended the Grammar between 1896 and 1898, entering Prep. After a degree from Cambridge in 1912 he joined the ICS in 1914. He was organising Secretary to the Indian Government Labour Department in Delhi, 1920. He was the last British Governor of Assam, 1942–7. He was the first Chair of the Scottish Gas Board after nationalisation, 1949–56.

Ernest H. Lyon (1891–1985) attended the Grammar between 1902 and 1907, entering Middle II. He was Gold Medallist in the School in 1907 and then entered the Civil Service. Most of his career was spent in the Department of Agriculture for Scotland. He retired in 1953 having attained the rank of Assistant Secretary.

Herbert T. Sorley (1892–1968) attended the Grammar between 1899 and

1909, entering Lower II. He went up to Aberdeen University and Christ Church, Oxford, and joined the ICS in 1914. He was a member of the Legislative Assembly of the Governor-General, 1930–2; Chief Secretary to the Government of Bombay, 1946; and member of the Central Board of Revenue, Pakistan, until 1952. He produced a number of publications.

(Sir) William R. Tennant (1892–1969; Kt 1947) attended the Grammar between 1904 and 1910, entering Middle II. He went on to Aberdeen University. He served in both British and Indian armies from 1915 to 1919 and joined the ICS in 1919, retiring in 1949. He worked in both Audit and Financial departments, reaching the post of Deputy Auditor of India. From 1949 till 1953 he was Secretary of the Scottish Universities' Entrance Board.

Edmund B. Boyd (1894–1946) attended the Grammar between 1900 and 1912, entering Prep. He was Classical Dux in 1912 and gained a FCH in Classics at Aberdeen University in 1916. After military service he joined the Colonial Office in 1919. He was Private Secretary to Parliamentary Under-Secretaries of State, 1922–4, becoming a Principal in 1925. He was Principal Private Secretary to successive Secretaries of State, 1930–7 and was Assistant Secretary, Colonial Office, from 1937.

Alfred B. Valentine (1894–1970) attended the Grammar between 1905 and 1911, entering Middle II. He served in the Great War and after graduating MA in 1919 he entered the Home Civil Service, 1920. He was Secretary to the British Delegation at the ILO, 1921–3. He was Assistant Commissioner for Special Areas in Scotland, 1937–40. He was Principal Assistant Secretary, Ministry of Supply, 1940–1; Ministry of Home Security, 1941–5; Town and Country Planning, 1946–51. He was Under-Secretary, Ministry of Housing and Local Government, 1951–6.

(Sir) John W. Taylor (1895–1974; KBE 1954) attended the Grammar between 1906 and 1911, entering Middle II. He took an MA in 1916 from Aberdeen University before becoming a Captain in the Gordon Highlanders. He joined the Foreign Service and had consular posts in France, Czechoslovakia, Austria and USA. He became Commercial Secretary in Washington, and was Ambassador to Mexico, 1950–4. He was President of the FP Club, 1959–60.

Allan C. Anderson (1896–1986) attended the Grammar between 1907 and 1912, entering Middle I. He migrated to Canada in 1912 but served in WWI. He joined the Royal Bank of Canada. He entered Canadian government service in 1943, becoming a Latin American specialist. He worked at the Canadian embassy in Mexico and from 1959 to 1961 was Canadian Ambassador to Cuba and Haiti.

(Sir) Patrick A.B. McKerron (1896–1964; KBE 1950) attended the Grammar between 1904 and 1910, entering Lower III. He went on to Fettes before becoming a professional soldier in 1914. He joined the Malayan Civil Service in 1920, holding various posts including Political Secretary of the C-in-C of Ceylon, 1942–3, and Colonial Secretary of Singapore, 1946–50.

(Dr) James L. Mowat (1899–1984) attended the Grammar in 1915–16, entering Classical VI. He graduated in Arts at Aberdeen University in 1922 and gained a PhD in 1927. He was appointed a translator/interpreter with the ILO in Geneva in 1928. With a series of promotions he became Chief of the Maritime Division of the ILO in 1946 and then was in charge of various departments until retirement in Geneva in 1964.

(Sir) James I.C. Crombie (1902–1969; KBE 1950; KCB 1957) attended the Grammar between 1908 and 1921, entering Lower II. He was School Dux and Gold Medallist (Classical). He went on to achieve a FCH in Classics at Aberdeen and studied at Gonville and Caius, Cambridge, before joining the administrative class of the Home Civil Service in 1926. He served in the War Office, HM Treasury, Ministry of Food, and the Foreign Office, and was chair of HM Board of Customs and Excise, 1955–62.

Charles S. McLeod (1903–1989) attended the Grammar between 1908 and 1920, entering Prep. He was Dux and Gold Medallist in his final year and gained a FCH in Mathematics and Natural Philosophy in 1924 at Aberdeen University, winning in the process a number of prizes including the Fullerton, Moir, Gray and Ferguson (Mathematical) Scholarships. He studied at Cambridge, where he was awarded the Tyson Gold Medal and a distinction in the Mathematics Tripos. He joined the graduate-training scheme of the London and North Eastern Railway Co. and served with the company until it was nationalised in 1947. He then joined British Rail and became Chief Industrial Relations Officer, retiring in 1968.

Writers

Howard A. Gray (1870–1942) attended the Grammar between 1880 and 1884, entering Class II, before becoming a prize-winner at Aberdeen University. He completed his studies at Edinburgh. He was a journalist in Edinburgh, Aberdeen and Birmingham. He became leader-writer of the *Pall Mall Gazette*, 1902–23, and Assistant Editor and Leader-Writer of *The Observer*, 1920–41.

(Sir) Henry Alexander (1875–1940; Kt 1938) attended the Grammar between 1881 and 1891, entering Initiatory. He then matriculated at Aberdeen University. He was editor of *Aberdeen Free Press,* 1914–22; a member of the Town Council, 1925–35 and Lord Provost of Aberdeen, 1932–5. He was a DL for the City of Aberdeen. He was President of the FP Club, 1933–4.

(Lt Col.) Edward W. Watt (1877–1955) attended the Grammar between 1883 and 1894, entering Initiatory. After Aberdeen University he worked on local papers as a journalist, latterly as joint Manager of Aberdeen Newspapers Ltd in 1925, before becoming a member of Aberdeen Town Council, 1927–38. He was Lord Provost, 1935–8, presiding at the opening of the ARI. He was a member of Aberdeen University Court, 1928–38 and chairman of the Macaulay Institute during WWII. He was President of the FP Club, 1936–7, having been one of the first editors of the Magazine.

William M. Alexander (1880–1959) attended the Grammar between 1887 and 1896, entering Initiatory. Having taken an Arts and then Law degree from Aberdeen University he became a Law Agent in 1903. He was a journalist on local papers until 1922. From then he devoted himself to scholarship. As a polymath he published books of local, antiquarian and historical interest. He was President of the Aberdeen Philosophical Society. He contributed significantly to the School Magazine.

Theodore Watt (1884–1946) attended the Grammar between 1889 and 1901, entering Initiatory. He had been born into a newspaper family, his father being joint editor and proprietor of the *Aberdeen Free Press.* He himself was Manager of the Rosemount Press from 1914 and joint Managing Director of Aberdeen University Press from 1932 (becoming Managing Director). In 1923, he produced the *Grammar School Roll of Pupils, 1795–1919*, annotated from 1863. He was Editor of the School Magazine from 1907 to 1946, Hon. Secretary and Treasurer of the FP Club, 1919–46, and President of the FP Club in 1946. He was 'the most enthusiastic of all our Grammarians' (J.M. Bulloch, 1923).[28] His father, two brothers and four sons were all Grammarians. He served on the Business Committee and the University Court and compiled the Roll of Aberdeen Graduates, 1901–25 with Supplement, 1860–1900.

George H. Mair (1887–1926) attended the Grammar between 1899 and 1902, entering Classical V. He took his MA at Aberdeen in 1905 before his fifteenth birthday and was a scholar at Christ Church, Oxford, 1905–8, and the Sorbonne. He joined the editorial staff as Leader-Writer of *The Manchester Guardian* in 1909 and was Assistant Editor of *The News Chronicle* in 1914. He was head of the Department of Information during WWI and was Director of the Press Section of the British Peace Delegation at Paris in 1919. He was Assistant Director in the League of Nations

Secretariat, 1919–26 and Head of the League's London Office. He returned to journalism with the London *Evening Standard.*

Ernest Main (1889–1966) attended the Grammar between 1903 and 1908, entering Classical III. He gained an MA from Aberdeen University in 1912 and worked on the *Aberdeen Free Press* and *Glasgow Herald.* He was Editor of the *Times Mesopotamia* and managing director of the *Baghdad Times.* He wrote several books.

Eric R.R. Linklater (1899–1974) attended the Grammar between 1913 and 1916, entering Classical IV. He saw active service in the last years of WWI. He was a student at Aberdeen University from 1918 to 1925, first unsuccessfully at Medicine and then graduating with FCH and Medal in English. He was Assistant Editor of *The Times of India* and taught briefly. He served again in WWII. In 1945, he was elected as Rector of Aberdeen University – only the second FP to have been Rector since the Fusion of 1860. He was President of the FP Club, 1956–7. He was DL of Ross and Cromarty, 1968–73, and in 1971 was elected FRSE. He published twenty-three novels, three volumes of short stories, two children's books, two books of verse, ten plays, three autobiographies, and twenty-three books of essays and histories.[29]

Hamish F. Maclennan (1900–1964) attended the Grammar between 1908 and 1915, entering Lower III. He saw action in both World Wars. He was a writer and broadcaster and was the first Manager of the Edinburgh Festival. He was a FSA (Scot).

Arts

John R. McMillan (1868–1959) attended the Grammar between 1876 and 1879 and again between 1881 and 1884, entering Prep. II. In partnership with his father and his brother he designed buildings, winning top place in a national competition for Mackie Academy, Stonehaven. He was a founder member of the Aberdeen Society of Architects.

David West (1868–1936) attended the Grammar in 1883–4 and studied life drawing at the Aberdeen Mechanics Institute. He went on to Edinburgh and Antwerp. His exceptional ability in watercolour painting led to early exhibitions at the RSA and RA. He lived in Lossiemouth and, as a painter of the sea, sandy wastes and sky along the Morayshire coast and of old sailing boats, he was unsurpassed.

George Topham Forrest (1871–1945) attended the Grammar between 1879 and 1889, entering Prep. II, and studied further at Aberdeen University.

He was Education Architect for Northumberland, 1905–14; for Essex, 1914–19 and as superintending architect for London County Council, 1919–35 he designed many council housing estates and co-designed two bridges over the Thames River. He was elected FRSE.

Bridgeford McD. Pirie (1876–1941) attended the Grammar between 1886 and 1888, entering Lower II, and was articled to a local architect firm in Aberdeen. Later he worked in Glasgow and Malta. He was involved with a number of private and business buildings in Golden Square, Holburn Street and Hamilton Place.

Alexander G.R. Mackenzie (1879–1963) briefly attended the Grammar in 1894 before studying Architecture at Gray's School, Aberdeen, and in London and Paris. (He worked in partnership with his father, Alexander Marshall Mackenzie, 1848–1933.) A London office was at first a success with commissions for the Waldorf Astoria and Australia House, while the Aberdeen office did a great deal of conservation work, the main client being the National Trust for Scotland. He concentrated on the North-East when the London office closed post-WWI, designing the Northern Hotel in Art deco style and retrieving Provost Ross' House from ruin.

Alfred F. Milne (1883–1953) attended the Grammar between 1895 and 1900, entering Middle II. He graduated from Aberdeen University in 1904 and took an ARCM diploma in 1906. He became Music master at Madras College in St Andrews before his appointment as Head of Music at Dundee HS, 1908–17. He was organist and Director of Music at Berkhamsted School from 1920. He was Professor of Aural Training at the RAM and wrote several books.

Herbert H.E. Wiseman (1886–1966) attended the Grammar between 1896 and 1903, entering Middle I. After study at Aberdeen and the RCM in London he became the Music Master at Madras College, St Andrews, 1908–20; Director of Music with Edinburgh Educational Authority, 1920–45; and BBC Musical Director in Scotland, 1945–52.

Percival Robson Kirkby (1887–1970) attended the Grammar between 1892 and 1901, entering Initiatory. He took his MA at Aberdeen University in 1910 and studied further at the RCM, London. He was appointed as the first professor of Music at University College, Johannesburg, a post he held from 1921 until 1954. He wrote the seminal work *The Musical Instruments of the Native Races of South Africa*, 1934. His archive and collection of instruments are now housed in the South African College of Music, Cape Town.

George 'Taffy' Davidson (1893–1976) attended the Grammar between 1901 and 1911, entering Lower III, and Gray's School of Art. He exhibited at the RSA and held a Fellowship in Arts and Crafts at Aberdeen University. He was Curator of the Highland Folk Museum at Kingussie.

George A. Mitchell (1896–1964) attended the Grammar between 1902 and 1913, entering Prep. He was one of the first two students to enrol at the Aberdeen School of Architecture when it opened in 1913. He joined his father's firm after war service. He was involved in building and reconstruction of Haddo and Candacraig, hospital extensions, school buildings and the additions to King's (especially the Taylor building) and Marischal. He was three times President of the Chapter of the Aberdeen RIA.

John Maclennan (1903–1969) attended the Grammar between 1914 and 1920, entering Lower Va. He studied at the RG School of Architecture. He joined Jenkins and Marr and succeeded his father who was sole partner in the firm. He became a member of the Town Council in 1936 and President of the Aberdeen Society of Architects in 1949.

(James) Fenton Wyness (1903–1974) attended the Grammar between 1915 and 1920 and was an architect in private practice from 1929 to 1964. He was also an antiquarian expert, historian, and authority on Aberdeen and its environs. He wrote *City by the Grey North Sea*, published in 1961. He designed the School Banner and four heraldic House Standards which were presented to the School in 1947. A commemorative plaque can be found at 45 Salisbury Terrace.

Sport

(Dr) Alexander M. Kellas (1868–1921) attended the Grammar between 1881 and 1884, entering Middle III. He studied further at Aberdeen, Edinburgh and Heidelberg before teaching Chemistry to medical students at the Middlesex Hospital. He was an enthusiastic mountaineer and the Grammar's greatest mountain climber. He made six expeditions to Sikkim from 1907 to 1920, reaching numerous previously unclimbed Himalayan summits. During the Great War he researched into high-altitude and the effect of diminished atmospheric pressure on human physiology. He died mountaineering with the 1921 Mount Everest Expedition and was buried in sight of the peaks of Sikkim.[30]

Ronald C. MacDonald (1868–1942) attended the Grammar between 1882 and 1885, entering Classical I. He graduated from Aberdeen University in Medicine in 1893. He served as a Surgeon in the South African Field Force, 1901–2 and as a Captain in the RAMC in WWI. He was Scottish Chess Champion in 1901, 1904, 1905, 1906, 1927 and 1928.

(Dr) James M.P. Crombie (1873–1932) attended the Grammar between 1884 and 1889, entering Middle II (juniors). He graduated in Medicine from Aberdeen University and trained to be a Dentist. He was a Captain in the RAMC during WWI. He was a dominant figure in Badminton, winning titles at the Scottish Open in 1909–14 (incl.) and 1921 and 1923. He was also prominent in the All-England Championships in the same period. He set up a memorial fund to promote the sport in the North-East, and it began operating in 1934–5.

(Dr) George O. Gauld (1873–1950) attended the Grammar between 1886 and 1891, entering Middle II. A good all-round sportsman he captained the FP Rugby Club, 1894–6 and 1897–9. He qualified in Medicine from Aberdeen University in 1901 and after work in Yorkshire he became a general practitioner in Nottingham. He played cricket for Nottinghamshire County and fourteen matches for England between 1913 and 1919, making a highest score of ninety and taking five wickets.

Stephen H. Carnelley (1880–1976) attended the Grammar between 1889 and 1894, entering Lower I. He went on to Rugby School and Exeter College, Oxford. At the 1906 intercalary[31] Olympics in Athens he represented Britain in the Five Mile Run, though he was not placed. He became a solicitor and joined the Colonial Service. He became Resident Commissioner in Kenya.

James T. Soutter (1885–1966) attended the Grammar between 1898 and 1902, entering Classical IV. He began as an apprentice engineer and after taking a degree at Aberdeen University he went into the ministry and was a Chaplain during WWI. In 1912 at the Stockholm (Summer) Olympic Games he was a member of the British 4 x 440 yards relay team which gained the Bronze medal.

Robert G. Tait (1885–1973) attended the Grammar in 1898–9, entering Middle I. He joined the service of the North British and Mercantile Insurance Co., in Dundee. He was invalided out of WWI after fighting on the Western Front. He was one of the 'greats' of Scottish cricket and one of the finest batsmen to play for Aberdeenshire CC. He gained twelve caps including three against Australia.

Harvey G. Mackintosh (1899–1977) attended the Grammar between 1912 and 1915, entering Modern Ia. He served on the Western Front, 1918. He qualified LDS, Royal College of Surgeons, 1922. He was a Scottish Tennis internationalist and played at Wimbledon, 1926–9, losing to Jean Rene Lacoste in the third round of the Singles in 1927. He gained five caps for Tennis and three for Badminton. He was Squadron Leader and

Commanding Officer of the 107th (Aberdeen) Air Training Squadron, 1939–43.

Roderick R.F. Maclennan (1903–1986) attended the Grammar between 1909 and 1918, entering Prep., before going on to Merchant Taylor's School in London. He was capped for England against Ireland, France and Scotland at Rugby in 1925 (playing in the first Calcutta Cup match at Murrayfield). He joined ICI in 1929 and ultimately became its area manager in Northern Ireland.

Hugh M. Crombie (1903–1961) attended the Grammar between 1911 and 1920, entering Lower II. He graduated in Medicine from Aberdeen University in 1925. He was MO in charge of the Dental Department of the ARI from 1932. He gained his first Badminton cap against England in 1928 and was President of the Scottish Badminton Union, 1950–2.

TEN Recollections from the Turn of the Century

Canon Harper of Culross in 1926 looked back on his Modern Language education at the Grammar School fifty years earlier:

> The tiny room where the French and German languages were taught held twenty to thirty boys. Our master was Herr Krueger, a bi-lingual Swiss, but I think he was more German than French. He pronounced both English and French with a strong German accent. For all that, he had an adequate knowledge of the grammar, the vocabulary, and the literature of France. He compiled a French grammar for beginners, and he published an excellent French-English dictionary, which I used for many years.
>
> Herr Krueger was a little stout man with fair hair, and very Teutonic in appearance . . . He was clever and hard working, and he was much liked by his colleagues.
>
> It is to be feared that we used to 'rag' him unmercifully; that was considered the correct attitude for us boys to adopt toward foreigners. We played all sorts of tricks on him . . . One day, on resuming his overcoat at the end of his class, he found both sleeves sewn up . . . He had an over-kindly disposition . . . [and] the boys had a certain amount of contempt for the easiness and softness they experienced here, as compared with the stern discipline that they were accustomed to in the other classes.
>
> Unfortunately the members of my class had no opportunity of learning German at the Grammar. The German class was held at a time when we were otherwise engaged, so the language could not be studied by those who were taking the regular Classical curriculum.

Rev. Johnstone Murray attended the Grammar between 1879 and 1885 when he matriculated at Edinburgh University. He looked back at his schooldays when he wrote an article for the School Magazine published in October 1917:

> The two masters who impressed me most were Mr Legge and Mr Sleigh. Legge was a well-nigh perfect example of a cultured Christian gentleman. He exacted and obtained perfect order in his class . . . and took infinite pains with us . . . Mr Sleigh obtained discipline by other means . . . Corporal punishment, when he saw fit to administer it, was an experience which neither the culprit nor the spectators forgot in a hurry . . . Mr Sleigh was the only master that retained in School the use of his native Doric.
>
> I fear we regarded the French lesson as an excellent opportunity for relaxation . . . M. Klem came to the Grammar from the Gym in Old Aberdeen . . . M. Clapasson, who succeeded him, was a charming man and would have taught us excellently if we had given him a chance. But discipline was not his strong point. Mr Brebner, a member of the School Board, stepped into the breach when Clapasson resigned, and we found that we could relax no more. Mr Brebner had an enthusiasm for his subject, and kept us in order.
>
> In the Rector's class, to which we attained as seniors, we were ruled by a light hand. Mr Moir treated us as reasonable beings, and we all liked him very much. His particular care was the daily Latin 'version' . . . It certainly had the effect of turning out scholars well grounded in the Latin tongue . . . and when I left I could write Ciceronian Latin with an ease . . . English Literature was a subject which received a great deal of attention . . . It helped to give birth to the Literary [and Debating] Society [formed in 1882].
>
> It was in my time that the big Hall was fitted out properly as a Gymnasium; and Sergeant Hanna installed as Instructor. He was adored by the boys, and obeyed, and did excellent work . . . I remember that Mr A.V. Lothian did what he could to improve matters in the School field . . .

Howard A. Gray attended the Grammar between 1880 and 1884. He was ten when he joined Class II and lived at 82 Crown Street. In December 1942 he wrote an article for the School Magazine about his memories of the School:

> On the surface, indeed, nothing could seem more regular and mechanical. The School went like a clock that had been wound up.

Mr Martin, the Rector, never visibly interfered with anything but the regulation of his own classes. I was with the picturesque Legge for Latin . . . Sleigh, the preceptor in Arithmetic, was a bit of a terrorist, but I saw him thrash only two boys during the four years I was in his hands. But the English master, John Beaumont, was at this period the pick of the bunch. A year later he was transferred to the head-mastership of a Board School, on the ground, it was understood, that he did not lay proper emphasis on Bain's *Grammar* . . .

My second year at the School produced a transformation scene. Dr Moir became Rector, and the upper section of the School was divided into Classical and Modern. We Classicals scoffed at the Moderns without stint, and that department did seem to be recruited at first by a rush of dunces of every description in search of a 'soft option' . . .

The various alterations made did seem to infuse the School with more vivacity. Mr Campbell, the new English master, was a man of the world, and broadened our atmosphere from that angle. Mr Harvey, a new Classical master, was very shy, but a treasure to those who discovered his sympathies and enlisted his help in their studies . . . I must not forget to mention the popularity of Mr Lothian, the junior Mathematical master (the first pedagogue to show an interest in sport) or the stimulus that the newly founded Literary Society gave to our mental activities.

Dr Moir himself was a force in every direction. He was an inspiring teacher, he loved the School, and he had a way of shooting forth some unpremeditated observation that set the mind working in entirely new regions. Yet, sad to say, he was foredoomed by the clash between his temperament and the environment . . . His eager, candid, unsuspecting disposition laid him open to the malice of those who differed from him on any plane, and there were too many ready to lie in wait for the harvest of their grudges. This came to a head some years after I had left the School but was still in Aberdeen.

A majority of the School Board resolved to evict him from the rectorship. The stoutest opposition to this step came from many of his old pupils. The Board was a formidable body of men, but we demanded a hearing from them on his behalf. It fell to me to address it . . . I talked to these eminent citizens temperately but strongly . . . The Board eventually revoked their first decision and compromised by making Dr Moir Co-Rector. It will always be a satisfaction to feel that I may have done something to mitigate the blows of fate upon one of whose gifts the School ought to have made more use than it was allowed to do.

Charles Davidson attended the Grammar between 1882 and 1886 and from 1893 until 1920 was a member of its teaching staff:

For four years I was a pupil of the School, and for twenty-seven years I was a Master. For nineteen subsequent years I was Head of the Department of Spanish in the University.

When I was at School I lived for some time in the house of Mr Charles Sleigh in King Street, to which he had moved from Bellvue, Hardgate – now a convent. Sir Peter Chalmers Mitchell was once a boarder with Mr Sleigh. Though he had the reputation of being stern, severe and even somewhat brutal, his bark was worse than his bite. We boarders saw another side of the Mathematician. Mrs Sleigh was the essence of kindness to us . . .

For a time we were taught French by a certain Jean Simon Clapasson. His knowledge of English was poor. When he asked us to say the Lord's Prayer together we protested that we could not as we were Catholics. When he asked the Catholics among us to go outside, almost the whole class did so . . . there succeeded to Clapasson Mr William Brebner, who refused to take a salary . . . He was the incarnation of the Third Empire – moustache, imperial and all. Every week he cyclostyled for us all the French irregular verbs, with commentaries. But, alas! There were some boys who refused to rise to the bait that he had dangled in front of us. Had we done so, we should today have been accomplished French scholars . . .

'Doddie' Harvey, our Greek master, we simply loved, but he was very blushful and shy. A.V. Lothian was our ideal master then, not altogether on account of his athletic prowess and Mathematical exposition, but because every Friday after hours he gave us a demonstration of Animal Physiology, when frogs and rabbits were opened out and we saw how our own bodies were constituted.

. . . The earnest grinding for the Bursary Competition left little time for the cultivation of the graces of life. And yet when one looks back after so many years, it was not the very clever boys who were

> the successes in life. We spent too much time in encouraging the lad o' pairs so that he, neglecting all physical exercise, overstrained his nervous system and often became a physical wreck.

William George Robertson attended the Grammar between 1884 and 1890, joining Middle II (Seniors) at the age of twelve. He lived at 146 Crown Street and in June 1941 he wrote an article for the School Magazine about his recollections of 1887–90:

> Entrance into the First Classical [in 1886–7] introduced us to an entirely new set of masters, excepting Mr Maxwell Mackie. When Mr Brebner, with his fleece of patriarchal white hair, left the School in 1885, or thereabouts, the French classes came under the charge of Mr Mackie, who was a competent teacher, and very just and firm with his boys . . .
>
> After the First Classical we stopped French, and all our energies were absorbed by intensive work in Latin and Greek, in preparation for the Bursary Competition. You see that, and only that, paid in those days! Out of a grand total of 1,000 marks . . . 400 went to the Latin version, 175 to a paper on Latin Grammar, and 175 to a corresponding one in Greek. To English were assigned 100 marks, and to Geometry, Algebra and Arithmetic 50 each . . . However, thanks to Professor Bain, a concession had been made in favour of Mathematics, so that papers in that subject carrying 400 marks could be taken as an alternative to the Latin version. Mr H.F. Campbell, our English master, had been first Bursar with Mathematics in his day . . .
>
> From 1886–7 Rev. James Wilson Legge was our Classical master, Mr Charles Sleigh instructed us in Geometry and Algebra and Mr Campbell in English Literature and Grammar.
>
> Mr Legge was sharply distinguished from all his colleagues in two respects – his fanatical love of fresh air, and his refusal to maintain discipline with the aid of corporal punishment. At all seasons of the year, and very noticeably so on bitterly cold winter days, the windows of his classroom were drawn half down . . . He permitted the boys to wear coats, mufflers, gloves and caps and he was similarly clad with his silk 'topper' on . . . Stillness prevailed in the classroom, and in the event of any talking, a stern rebuke restored quiet. If an offence merited severe retribution, the unhappy

youth was given 'lines', usually five pages of Smith's *Roman History*, to copy out. This grave preceptor of our youth was universally respected and liked.

Everyone who had any dealings with gruff Charles Sleigh will recall the bald, bearded man . . . seated at his desk, with his snuffbox in one hand and his red bandana handkerchief in the other. It is not too much to say that . . . we boys positively dreaded entering his room and detested the subjects that Mr Sleigh taught. Failure to observe [an] algebraic rule . . . was impressed upon our minds by the repetition of the rule, accompanied by a cuff, first on one side of the head and then on the other. [He did not use] the tawse very often. But, when he *did* resort to the leather, he did so with a vengeance and went to reprehensible lengths . . . We must remember that he was a disciplinarian of the old school, and acted according to his lights.

Of all our teachers the only one remaining at the moment of writing is Mr H.F. Campbell. We all respected him highly . . . That he was deeply versed in the subject he taught was obvious to everyone . . . Rightly he placed a high value on the admirable qualities of Lord Macaulay's style, such as the building up of his paragraphs, the uses to which he put periodic and balanced sentences, and his preference for synecdoche and metonomy over simile and metaphor . . . Mr Campbell imparted his zeal to many of us and taught us what is implied by English scholarship . . . A great service which he rendered to many of his 'boys' was the voluntary class in Logic that he conducted in the lunch period. Many of us who were afterwards prizemen in the University lists had reason to thank Mr Campbell and the thorough training he gave us in the syllogism.

I have deliberately postponed referring to Mr A.V. Lothian, for the reason that he entered little into our lives as regards the classroom. I think that we had him only in the Third Middle for Arithmetic and Physiology, for he was really the Science master of the School, and a pioneer at that. Like Mr Campbell, he disliked correcting papers . . . He took a lively interest in our games, as was worthy of one of the founders of the Aberdeen Football Club. A good disciplinarian and a clear teacher, he was a general favourite.

When we reached the Second Classical and long trousers (1887–8) we were introduced to Mr George Harvey ('Doddy') . . . An excellent teacher, he was much liked but he retired and was succeeded by the late Dr John Clarke, who took charge of the Latin and Greek . . . the Rector taking the Third Classical in these languages . . . He [Clarke] wore a morning coat, a buff waistcoat, and striped grey trousers, a turned down pointed collar, and a scarlet tie . . . he was something more than a much-needed model to us on tasteful dress. He was a genuine Christian gentleman, deeply interested in the moral welfare of his boys. Every morning he read a few verses from the New Testament to us, and we repeated the Lord's Prayer . . .

In the Third Classical we came under the genial tuition of Dr James Moir, the Rector, florid of face, and careless of dress, sometimes forgetful of his buttons. Being very kindly, he was a universal favourite among the boys. He suddenly plunged a stunned class into four versions a week, two for homework and two in School, and assigned us five pages of Thucydides for preparation overnight! . . . He was an excellent Classical coach . . .

William McCombie Alexander (W.M.A.) entered the Initiatory department of the Grammar aged seven in 1887. He lived in Westfield Terrace and remained at the School until 1896. In February 1914 he wrote an article for the Magazine with his 'Recollections of School Life in the Early 1890s':

Suppose now that the Classes are all 'in'. Upstairs at one end of the School a bearded gentleman is about to teach Arithmetic . . . The boys take slates and he takes snuff, and proceeds to give out sums to be done. At the other end of the School Mr Morrison is likewise teaching Arithmetic, and if you listen across the years you can still hear him. 'Now say it altogether, a prime number – is a number – which can only be deevided – by itself and one!' A truly stupendous fact; and as enunciated by him, it is hammered into young heads firmly enough. It may be that in after life you have no use for prime numbers. The big world talks about prime ministers and prime bacon, but never by any chance about prime numbers. No matter, there they are, and they 'can only be deevided by themselves and one.' Mr Morrison also taught Geography out of a brown-coloured book called *Mackay's Geography,* a class-book for schools and colleges.

In an adjoining classroom English was taught. For this study, for teaching boys, that is to say, how to use their mother tongue, steam-rollers were in use. These engines, contrived by an Aberdeen professor, not unknown to fame at the time, were two in number, called respectively, Bain's *Higher English Grammar* and Bain's *Lower English Grammar.* Dr Bain expressed in his Grammar a horror of what he called 'Scotticisms', meaning thereby the rude forms of speech which were in use amongst the barbarians in whose midst he had been born, brought up, and spent his life. It was him that learned us all never to use Scotticisms; and, of course, you will never catch the writer or another body doing so.

Alongside the books mentioned, Smith's *Principia* was mere holiday reading. With Mr Legge, downstairs, one got through the *Principia* fairly comfortably. In fact, one sometimes thinks quite kindly of old man Smith: his was a capital book to learn the 'iisdem or eisdem' business out of. After Smith the Latin classes made the acquaintance of a gentleman called Barrow Allen; he was like Bain, in having a higher and lower, or first and second, treatise. One does not know if he is still in use; if not, it may be explained that he was a Latin poet. It is probably right to say that it is to him that we may trace the passionate love of Latin poetry which is so marked in all former classical pupils of the Grammar.

These were the Classicals. Not to be confused with the Moderns. Ah, yes, these Moderns. They were few in numbers, and they used to assemble a class of them, that is to say three or four – in the Chemical department, and potter about with bottles and test tubes . . .

The Moderns were a mysterious lot in those days. They are much more numerous nowadays than they were twenty years ago. They excelled in things like freehand Drawing and Gymnastics and they learned a strange language called German . . .

It is difficult nowadays to realise the relative importance of some of our juvenile activities. There was, for instance, the enormous traffic which went on in postage stamps . . .

The biggest internal change on the School has been the alteration of the Hall. The old hall had a character of its own. Who in the gallery up above has not felt a thrill when a well-aimed missile attack struck some member of a Gymnastic class down below. Sergeant Black, late 22nd Hussars used to officiate . . .; and it was accounted no small feat to climb over the gallery railing and crawl

> out on the beams and get down by the ropes . . . Sergeant Black had been in the Afghan Wars and had done the march to Kandahar or some lesser place, and he used to set us trotting round the hall at the double on a miniature march to Kandahar, he himself standing at ease in the centre, in an attitude befitting an Afghan hero. It was a fine sight, doubtless, to the boys up in the gallery, who discharged paper darts and heavier things at the gymnasticians. The old hall had its gala days when prizes were given out. It was a very dusty place, and the hollow floor resounded splendidly from our feet. The platform party in the middle seemed to object to the dust which was raised by this process, but we didn't mind a bit. And all those nice little boys with nicely-washed faces and nice clean collars, all those prize-winners and the rest, where are they now?

Herbert Tower Sorley was born in April 1892 and joined the Lower II class in 1899. He lived at 97 Hamilton Place and remained a pupil at the Grammar until 1909. Two of his brothers also attended – John Tower Sorley (born August 1899), between 1904 and 1917, and Ernest Robert Sorley (born October 1901), between 1906 and 1918. In December 1964, Herbert contributed an article for the Magazine on 'School Life at the Beginning of the Twentieth Century':

> . . . I started my Grammar career in Lower II under Miss Davidson, a gentle and kindly creature . . . In Lower III, I came under the discipline of Miss Adam, a splendid instructress whom we rather feared. She was a strict disciplinarian and kept us quiet and well behaved but she was just and knew how to handle boys. She was an LLA of St Andrews, an unusual qualification in those days before women's further education had gone very far, and it tempted us to call her Long Legged Ass, which was very unfair, as Miss Adam was neither long legged nor an ass. When we advanced to Lower IV, we came under the tuition of Miss Mackie, the sister of Max Mackie, the French master of the Upper school. She was a dear. We all loved her, a natural-born teacher with a liking for the unruly boy, who knew how to deal with us and did it all by sheer force of personality . . . After Miss Mackie we came to the first class in the Middle School and said good-bye to women teachers.
>
> The class master of Middle I was Tommy Duncan who, to our great disappointment, left very soon to take up another

appointment. He was, like Miss Mackie, a natural teacher who knew boys and did not need to threaten them with punishment. His departure left a sad blank and temporary arrangements were made to teach us so that we had 'Picker' (Davidson) and 'Spicy' (Murison), both senior masters, for Arithmetic and English, with the Rector himself taking sundry classes in History.

During the rest of my career at the Grammar, I got tuition from almost all of the other teachers except Speirs and 'Quassi' (Morrison) who were attached to the Modern side. These teachers made an imposing array – Bentley Philips, Pat Edwards, James Knox, Pat Allan, 'Puggie' Brownie, 'C.D.', Ritchie, Max Mackie, MacLeod (Towdie), 'Spicy' and 'Caesar'. Whatever education I got was the product of the combined efforts of all of these over the space of the seven years after I left the Lower School. We also had 'Popie' for Drawing, Joseph for Gymnastics and, for those who took 'Manual', Carmichael. I think my education was a worthy and solid one. Whatever I have been able to achieve since at the University and later in public service for a generation in India I lay to the credit of this noble band of educationists.

It was notable that during the whole time I was at the School there was not one single major change in the staff. The only casualties were Tommy Duncan and 'Puggie' who died while in service, to the moving grief of the whole School.

The unbroken continuity of the staff during all my time seemed to make the School a kind of settled and permanent community suffering no change and cementing a feeling of solidarity and friendship amongst all the boys. It was certainly something to have imbibed wisdom from these men whom I have mentioned and the whole experience was a joy and a privilege that has lasted me all my life. It was indeed a 'ratio confirmatioque doctrinae', as the then school motto truthfully proclaimed.

During all my years at School the building was not added to or enlarged. When I first went, Westfield Primary School was being built and has now been incorporated in the Grammar. But in those days it was a School Board Primary School with free education. The Grammar got the use of a part of the building and this was used for the Gymnasium under Mr Joseph and the Manual classes under Mr Carmichael, whom we boys helped to send to the Paris Exhibition of 1901 by collecting coupons out of the *Evening Express* or the

Evening Gazette to the number of several hundreds to let him have a free trip there and back, doubtless to help with Manual designs. The reason the School building was never enlarged in my time was, I suppose, because the number of boys during the first ten years of the century never exceeded the 600 there were when I joined, in great contrast with the 1500 the Grammar now educates. The lovely building in which our schooling took place was and is one of the architectural glories of Aberdeen.

Aberdeen was a very beautiful place in the beginning of the century, which saw the development of the West-End with the entrancing Rubislaw granite. For a small boy the daily walk from Hamilton Place where I lived (then only one-third built up beyond Fountainhall Road) was a sheer delight because the Den Burn was open all the way from Fountainhall Road to Gilcomston Dam. It was a beautiful purling stream and we boys had endless fun along its banks. But the great delight was the wooden bridge over it where there is now the road junction of Desswood Place, Whitehall Road and Osborne Place. The bridge seemed to span what was a little ford through which horses and cabs could go. Whitehall Road down to Leadside Road was a delightful country lane with Dalgarno's rose gardens on the sloping bank and some charming cottages further down. The fun of the Denburn with its prattling waters, wooden bridge, its ford and Gilcomston Dam went with the improvement of Whitehall Road.

When Mafeking was relieved [during the South African War] the School was in a ferment. The older boys paraded round the School with a flag and were allowed up on the round tower of the School and there spread out a huge Union Jack and sang and shouted 'God Save the Queen' and all the popular ditties of the day. The School got a holiday for the occasion but we small boys wondered what so much noise was about. The Rector himself did not escape the Boer atmosphere. His long streaking figure and protruding neck earned him the name of 'Long Tom' which was very appropriate, named after the big naval gun that played a part in the early British attacks on the Boers.

What were we boys like sixty years ago at School? I think we were more self-reliant than present-day boys of the same age. This may be partly due to the fact that we had to do many things for ourselves and that the masters took very little interest in us out of school hours. There was no real camaraderie between us and the masters, who as a whole were sedate creatures who played no games and certainly did not take part with us in them. There was no Games master and for training we had to rely on ourselves and do what we could by imitating 'Shire' heroes and FPs. Only towards the end of my time at School, James W. Milne, C.A., used to come and coach us in rugby. The standard of play certainly rose and latterly I formed one of a combined rugby XV of Gordon's and Grammar boys . . . The only regular society was the debater. The masters took no interest in it though we used to have lectures now and again from 'Spicy'. Max Mackie ran a tentative singing class . . . but we treated singing as more or less a joke. Dramatics were the preserve of certain interested boys only and here the great instructor, producer and impresario was 'C.D.'

What sort of boys were they who were with me during my ten years at the Grammar? Nothing is more clannish and superior than the average gang of schoolboys. We despised those who were junior to us as we were despised by our seniors. When I entered the School in 1899 I think the lot of us were a 'West-endy' kind of crowd. We were very conscious of our superiority (as we thought) over Gordon's. We despised that School because it had begun as a charity school, because it had large numbers of free scholars and many scholarships which saved parents from paying for their son's education. We were very proud of being a fee-paying school. I think the reputation we had of being 'West-endy' or 'snooty' in the modern jargon, was on the whole well deserved. We were a lot of little prigs and were proud of coming mostly from the well-to-do quarters of the lovely granite city then spreading rapidly out of the West end . . .

[How did we amuse ourselves?] . . . Photography was just beginning as a popular hobby for boys . . . we had magic lanterns and lots of slides, cut-out dioramas, model railways, steam engines . . . and we constructed and sailed model boats and learned to juggle and do conjuring tricks. We collected cigarette cards and stamps avidly and we flew kites. We played all kinds of ball games and we were in the middle of the great cycling boom . . . We skated on the ice at the Bridge of Dee, at Cults and Dyce whenever the ponds were frozen over and most of us had some sort of training for playing a musical instrument, chiefly the piano or violin . . . We were always supposed to contribute to the entertainment at a party and reciting was in fashion. All these things were individual and not made to a pattern as is the modern fashion. We did not need a multiplication of school societies to interest us. We never had much truck with the High School girls, who after all in many cases were our sisters, and what boy bothers about sisters?

At the School, before we were old enough to graduate to cricket and rugger, we played matches in the Lower School, and in the Middle School we engaged in exciting team games which did much to accustom us to taking hard knocks and preparing for rugger.

Though we junior boys did not realise it, the School was, in the first decade of the twentieth century, passing through an educational revolution. The coming of Morland Simpson had been one of the major influences in the change. The days of Melvin, which had continued in some fashion through Moir, were over. The School was changing from the rigid form of early Classical seminary to the modern secondary School. Classics were still regarded as the main backbone but there was a rapidly growing modern School for those who did not consider that a knowledge of Latin and Greek was so important in modern life or worth having at all. But the cachet was still definitely on the 'Classical' and the 'Moderns' were regarded as poor fish generally.

Simpson made it clear to us boys that it was getting to know things fully and accurately that was the aim of education and not mere ability to answer examination papers. This was one other factor in the Grammar boy's hardly disguised contempt for Gordon's. He considered Gordon's a swotting and cramming school intent on getting as many of its pupils as possible into the first ten of the Bursary Comp. Between the idea of a swot and the development of a modern type of School combined with a studied aim to make full and true education the School's ideal, Simpson steered a skilful and cautious way. We boys never loved him: he was too distant and solemn for most of us. We respected him and were keen not to anger him. We thought not of his desire for true and accurate learning. At the same time as he was instilling this principle of thoroughness he was introducing the method and ideals of the English public school with its emphasis on leadership, honesty, courtesy, truthfulness and playing for the side, instead of for oneself and the whole School. He could not go much further than general inculcation of conduct and example in a Scottish day school that had boasted of its Scottish independence for centuries. But the School as it is today with its many outside activities, its sense of continuity with the past, and its place as a moulder of character, the dignity of its masters and its insistence on good form in manners is the result of the sterling ministrations of Morland Simpson . . . He was always impressive and under him we felt a sort of awe . . . During his time decorum and order were the School ideals. All the masters wore gowns and everyone had to file in for the early morning prayer with which the School days began and which was always read by the Rector himself. There were never any disturbances in his class and he hardly ever had to threaten punishment. Boys could sense in their instinctive way that they were in the presence of something that must be obeyed.

'C.D.' (Charles Davidson) was the most imaginative and the most original of all our teachers. Not only in class but outside of it he taught us good manners and gentlemanly behaviour and he used to begin a lesson sometimes by taking the financial columns of the paper and asking us questions about it, explaining quite a lot about the place money played in the business world while doing so. He used to offer a penny every now and again to any boy who could answer a rather recondite question of general knowledge . . .

'Puggie' was another natural teacher but he was one who ruled by fear and meant to. When the fateful words were given, 'Go to locker four and bring the belt', the victim knew what to expect and the class trembled in sympathy. But he was a wonderful teacher and well-liked by everyone, despite his draconic discipline . . . 'Puggie' died suddenly one day and the whole School, realising that a great man was gone, went to his funeral . . .

Bentley Philip was another of the teachers who impressed me permanently. He was a bit of a crank but a man of extraordinary knowledge, charm and engaging openness with us boys. We laughed at a lot of his ways but we kept learning all the time. He used to insist on us all having for the Botany class what he called the 'Nine Articles' and we all had to lay them out on our desks before the beginning of the lesson . . . Bentley used to deliver fascinating lectures illustrated with lantern slides of his own taking. He was a man of many outside interests and we boys while laughing at his eccentricities liked him enormously. He introduced us to the

> mysteries of the microscope, ran the School garden, and in many ways helped to carry out happily the School's ideal.
>
> The only other teacher I shall talk of is 'Caesar' (George Middleton). He was a scholar and looked it. You felt it in everything he did. He was not interested in our getting high places in the Bursary Competition, though several of us did, thanks to him. He wanted us to be accurate and thorough and try to understand the force of ancient civilisation and its importance for an interpretation of the modern world . . . I came to admire and venerate 'Caesar' for his whole-minded pursuit of worthwhile knowledge. He was one of the two masters in my time who won doctorates at the University for scholarly research . . . [He] was a real aristocrat of teaching.

Edward James Wood was born in September 1902 and joined the Prep. Department of the Grammar in 1908. He remained until 1921, living at 31 Beechgrove Avenue. In June 1968 he wrote an article for the Magazine on 'Life at the School, 1908–21':

> . . . The School I remember was not quite so grand as it is now, though it seemed grand to me in those days. There was no Byron statue – Byron arrived during my time at School, and a number of people were just a tiny bit shocked at the idea of having a statue in his honour, even though he *was* the most distinguished son of the School – there was . . . no swimming bath or dining hall, and the assembly Hall that I knew occupied the space now taken up by the magnificent Library and the rooms underneath it. There was no Rubislaw field. Our games and sports took place in the ground, bounded by Leadside Road on the north, lying between the Osborne Place gate and the wall that separated the School property from that of Westfield School.
>
> School games in those distant days were looked after by Mr James Davidson who for many years was a well-beloved Mathematics master. Twice a year, in autumn and summer, Mr Davidson visited every class . . . so that in his presence the members of each class could choose their rugger and cricket captains and vice-captains. The Infant School [of Junior Infants, Senior Infants and Lower I] confined their games to their own gravel playground.
>
> A few days before the autumn term of 1908–09 began, my mother took me to the School to register me as a new boy. We were

taken in to the presence of Morland Simpson . . . the man who pulled the School up out of medievalism and put it on a modern footing . . . I cannot think of the School without thinking of him at the same time . . . We were received by Miss Anderson, a most kind lady, whose skill and patience in teaching were beyond praise. She was in charge of Junior Infants . . . Miss Adam . . . taught Lower I. The intermediate class was looked after in the morning by Miss Adam along with Lower I, and in the afternoon by Miss Anderson . . . Fortunately before I had passed beyond the Infant School, Miss Sutherland was added to the teaching strength . . .

One of my most vivid memories of those early days is the presentation made to Mr Samuel Pope on the occasion of his retirement. He had been Art master for an incredible number of years and when he departed, the whole School . . . was assembled in the Hall to bid him farewell. His dignified presence, his grey hair and kind face made a deep impression on me.

The Lower School consisted of four years, Lower II, III, IV and Va (Latin) and Vb (French). The ladies who taught these, Miss Maydon, Miss Elizabeth Davidson, Miss Jessie Mackie, Miss Ledingham and Miss Reid respectively were all fine teachers. Miss Mackie exercised a kind of supervision over the Lower School and she was noted for the strict discipline she kept. But be it said at once that she always retained the respect and even affection of her young charges. I had been introduced to the *scudder* as early as Lower I. Miss Adam, small of stature as she was, could ply it with a stout arm, and we all had a healthy fear of her . . . But it was Miss Mackie of Lower IV who was *the* disciplinarian. She was reported to have four scudders to suit the various degrees of crime we committed.

After the Lower School came the Middle School, Classical and Modern I, II, and III, while the Upper School was made up of Classical and Modern IV, V, and VI. The Middle and Upper schools were taught by masters. Beside Mr James Davidson and Mr J.C. Knox . . . I had encountered only one master before reaching the middle School, 'Caesar'. He became my greatest friend among the masters, and that is saying a lot . . . All our senior masters were looked upon with the greatest respect and affection. There was Charles McLeod (Teodie) who taught Mathematics, and along with him should be mentioned Peter Edward (Pat) who also taught Maths . . . there was William Murison (Spicey) whose subject was English and Maxwell Mackie (Max) whose French was fluent.

When I first entered the Middle School, war had brought havoc to the world and even the tenor of our young lives had been disrupted. There were no School games. Our splendid Gymnastic instructor, Mr Summers, had gone to the war. And what physical exercise we had took place in the school grounds under the charge of an aged ex-sergeant. And I fear we gave him a bad time of it. Kitchener's army trained daily in our grounds. The Gymnasium, which was part of the Westfield School buildings, was taken over along with the Westfield School as a hospital for wounded soldiers and the war was not many weeks old before we saw figures clad in light blue hospital garments hobbling about in front of the Gym. We used to bring cigarettes from home for them. In wartime we went to School at 8am. There was a break of fifteen minutes about eleven o'clock and lessons then went on till 1.30pm. From that time onwards we were free for the rest of the day. The pupils of the Central School occupied our buildings from 2pm till sometime in the evening as their own buildings had, like our Gym, become a military hospital.

Several of the younger masters went off to the army, and those who were left did a heroic job coping with the extra work that faced them. None can have done more valiantly than George Hay (Doddy) who had the gigantic task of teaching Greek to both sections, at one and the same time, of Classical II – forty-six young ruffians . . . packed into one room. His achievement was little short of marvellous, though it must have strained his good nature nearly to breaking point . . . He was a splendid teacher, and I mentally take my hat off to him every time I think of him. It was Roderick McCrae to whose unfortunate lot it fell to try to drive Mathematics into my head . . . [He], like all our masters, was superb...and I owe it to the grounding that he patiently gave me that in the end, with a mighty effort, I somehow achieved Higher Mathematics . . .

I must mention also Mackenzie Forbes (Tiny) who, besides slowly but very thoroughly teaching us Latin, founded the School Orchestra . . . The unique Charles Davidson (C.D.) was one of the most entertaining characters I've ever known. He was supposed to teach us English but his method was, let us say, unorthodox. He told us wonderful stories of faraway things and places. He later became the first master to teach Spanish at the School and the first head of department of Spanish at Aberdeen University.

I always felt that I couldn't have found a better school . . . [The teachers] gave us boys a feeling that they cared for us as human beings, and that we meant something to them . . .

ELEVEN A Time of Rectors

This chapter follows the School through the inter-war period from the uncertainties of the early 1920s into the calmer waters of Andrew's rectorship. The other major themes are staffing arrangements and the usual remarkable biographies of successful Former Pupils.

JOHN MACKAY THOMSON: RECTOR, 1920–1921

The year 1920 proved to be an important one in the School's history. The wartime restrictions came to an end and the normal school hours were resumed. The School came under new management as the decision was made to abolish the School Boards and to replace them with new bodies – Education Authorities – elected to cover wider geographical areas of responsibility, though in Aberdeen's case it meant that a new body replaced the old Board which had controlled the Town's state education since 1873. Continuity was established by the election of former Board members to the new body, notably George Duncan, who was its chairman. A Director of Education was appointed, James Dawson MA, and the procedures to be followed were listed in great number in the Members' Directory. Among the many details was one which stated that in the case of corporal punishment the use of the cane was forbidden and punishment had to be inflicted only on the hand. The cane had been introduced into the School by Morland Simpson.

One of the first tasks of the new Authority was to find a replacement to fill the vacant Rectorship. From a short-list of four, which included the Acting Rector, Charles McLeod, the choice fell on John Mackay Thomson, aged 33. He had been educated at Glenalmond, taken an MA at Edinburgh (1908) and gained a FCH in Mods at Oriel College, Oxford in 1911. Like Simpson, Thomson had had experience as a master at Fettes College in

Edinburgh, in his case since 1915. He came with a glowing reference – 'the most conscientious of men, and, to anyone who wanted to learn, a born teacher'.[1] To his intense disappointment he had been declared unfit for war service. He was also a son of an FP of the Grammar School, the Rev. Peter Thomson, who had attended the School in 1862–3.

There were several issues resulting from the First World War which had to be resolved. The contribution made to the war effort by former pupils was enormous and plans were laid to make suitable recognition. It was decided that a Roll of Honour commemorating the 243 Former Pupils who had given their lives during the hostilities would be placed in the School Hall. This memorial was designed by Dr William Kelly and carried out by local tradesmen. In addition, a major undertaking was to provide a suitable Pavilion at Rubislaw Field as another memorial to those lost in the war. This building with the inscription 'Caesorum Comitum Memores' (In memory of friends who fell in battle) was completed in 1923, and while extensions have been added from time to time the original building remains the outstanding central piece of the Rubislaw Pavilion.

Two other enterprises came to fruition in the early 1920s. The long-awaited erection of the Byron Statue in 1923 and the publication of the Roll of Former Pupils edited by Theodore Watt. The statue of Byron had been the brain-child of Morland Simpson but it took thirty years before the scheme was completed by its official unveiling on 14th September 1923 before a gathering of members of the Gordon family and other local dignitaries.

For a historian of the School it is hard to give adequate praise and recognition to the work of Theodore Watt for both the School and the FP Club. Not only did he fill the role of Editor of the FP magazine until 1942 but he was also Secretary and Treasurer of the Club and represented parents on the committees of the Education Authority. However, probably his greatest contribution was the *Roll of Former Pupils 1795–1919*. It took nearly fifteen years to produce with the help of Louis Wilson (who attended the School in 1872–5), the son of the famous Aberdeen photographer, George Washington Wilson. When it seemed ready for publication in 1913, the outbreak of the war delayed it and this led to the addition of war service details to those of civilian occupations. The impressive volume finally made its appearance to great acclaim in 1923.

Meantime, Mackay Thomson was making an impressive start as Rector. He carried on the drive to provide a widely based course, academic and athletic, for the boys. To involve the senior boys in the running of the School he created Prefects. Introducing the compulsory wearing of caps to and from School received as enthusiastic a response as had Simpson's abortive attempt to encourage the wearing of the kilt. Accommodation for changing at Rubislaw was provided by the purchase of an army hut which survived as a First World War relic up to the present time.

But, after only a year in the post Thomson resigned in April having been offered and accepted a call to join the School Inspectorate, a career in which he eventually reached its highest rank as Secretary of the SED between 1940 and 1952. He was also to be knighted for his services to Scottish education.

DOUGLAS G. MILLER: RECTOR, 1921–1924

So, unexpectedly, the Authority had once again to advertise for a new Rector. Fifteen candidates came forward and from them a short-list of three was selected, all Oxford graduates, two from the London area but the final choice fell on Douglas G. Miller, the Rector of Kelvinside Academy. He had gained fourteen rugby caps for Scotland between 1905 and 1911. However, the list of those who were capped for Scotland includes no Miller! The reason for this was that his original name had been Schultze and to avoid the anti-German prejudice of the pre-war years he had adopted his mother's maiden name.

Miller had the advantage of experience as a primary pupil of a day school, Glasgow Academy, before going on to Fettes for his secondary education between 1893 and 1900. There he showed himself an athlete and scholar. He played rugby, cricket and hockey for his school, was prominent in the Literary Society, held office as school Prefect as well as being Head Boy of his House and won four Governors' Prizes and a Fettesian Exhibition. He attended Merton College, Oxford where he studied Literature and Philosophy and won his rugby blue in 1903. His teacher-training took place at Manchester University and there followed spells of teaching at the Royal Naval College, Christ College Brecon, and Uppingham, where he was assistant master and house tutor. He became Rector of Kelvinside Academy and was in post there from 1913 till 1921, increasing the school roll from 142 to 306. He also introduced Russian and a definite Science scheme, which allowed Kelvinside to develop its curriculum.

Miller had the same views on the need for a broad education as his two predecessors and in what proved to be a short term of office he had a tremendous impact on pupils, staff and parents. He had great charisma and personal popularity, far removed from the traditional remote figure that headmasters tended to be at that time. One of the few people who until recently could still recall personal contact with Douglas Miller was the late Dr J.R.S. Innes ('Donny') who spoke with great delight about walking to school with the Rector while only a young boy, a pleasure which other boys shared from time to time. Miller took an interest in all aspects of school life, attending society meetings, coaching the 1st XV backs while the forwards were coached by Sheriff Dallas (also a Scottish internationalist).

They were stirring times over which Miller was to preside. At long last, the Byron Statue was unveiled and the Roll of Honour was officially dedicated. The memorial Pavilion was brought into use at Rubislaw and the roll increased from 807 to 937 boys. The centenary of Byron's death was celebrated with due ceremony in 1924.

In the organisation of the School one important innovation was the introduction of a system of 'Houses'. Every pupil and member of staff was allocated to one or other of the four sub-groups, called Houses, named after an important personality connected to the School: Byron, Melvin, Dun and Keith. As the School grew in numbers, Miller realised that something more intimate than commitment to the School would help to strengthen a boy's sense of loyalty. The House System took root and for many years vied with the Scouts for the affections of the pupils and great rivalry was established between the Houses.[2]

All of this was achieved by a man who was noted by all for his friendliness and his modesty. But this success was not going unnoticed in the educational world and when a vacancy in Manchester Grammar School occurred for a new High Master the thoughts of its Governors turned to the Grammar and Miller. Manchester GS was recognised and accepted as probably the most prestigious school of its type in Britain. What followed reminds one of a modern football transfer. Aberdeen EA raised the Rector's salary to £1,250 per annum to match the offer of £1,250 (rising to £1,500) offered by Manchester, in order to keep him at the Grammar. By now it was obvious that Manchester was determined to get its man and it made a new offer of £2,000. Miller held to his position that he was not a candidate for the post but now the salary on offer was higher than that of a university principal. Manchester just refused to take no for an answer and Miller was persuaded to go to Manchester for an interview, after which he took the job on offer, to the universal regret of the School and the Authority.

Miller left behind a flourishing School. The considerable rise in the income from fees made the School free from requiring a subsidy from the school rates. Academically, the School still performed well in the Bursary Competition and athletically the rugby fixture list now included not only its old rival, Gordon's College, but also Heriot's, Edinburgh Academy and Glasgow Academy. Many tributes were paid to Miller on his departure but one that was quoted by Professor George Pittendrigh was the shrewdly philosophical remark of a pupil: 'Well sir, it is good that we have had him for a short time.'

DAVID ANDREW: RECTOR, 1924–1942

So as Miller departed south to continue a distinguished career the Authority faced, for the third time in four years, the task of finding a new Rector. Again it was a hard act to follow and after due consideration David Andrew, who came from Bothwell, was interviewed and appointed. Like his three predecessors in office he was an Oxbridge graduate in Classics. He himself was not a former pupil but both his father and brother, who were both school inspectors, were! Andrew had gone to Hamilton to teach Classics after graduating with FCH in the subject at Aberdeen University in 1897. After a brief time there he was appointed Rector of Hamilton Academy at the very young age of twenty-nine. His record had been so successful that he was appointed unanimously to the Grammar.

After the two very short rectorships, no doubt the Authority was hoping for a long period of settled progress. When Andrew was introduced to the School he stated that his aim would be to continue the policy of a balanced education. 'Scholarship on the one hand and athletics on the other must go together in any properly thought-out scheme of educational training.' He was to remain in office from 1924 until 1942 and on leaving then he modestly hoped that he had maintained the traditions of the School. In choosing Andrew, the Authority had gone for a 'safe pair of hands' and this was what they got. A quiet, unassuming man with apparently few interests outside the School's welfare, reading the Classics and playing golf, he safely led the School through the period of the inter-war years and then the early stages of the Second World War. Eight years after retirement he died starting a round of golf at Royal Aberdeen. Colonel Dawson, the Director of Education, wrote a brief review of his tenure in the School Magazine in which he suggested that the rather reserved manner he presented to the public had led to his contribution to the School's progress being under-estimated.

In a short book which surveyed the twenty-five years of George V's reign as far as they affected Aberdeen from 1910 to 1935, Andrew contributed the section devoted to the GS. As achievements in his time, he pointed to the provision of a new Gymnasium which was built in 1927 and the absorption of the Westfield School building by 1930 – which provided accommodation for the Lower School and increased workshop space – and a Dining Room in the old Chalmers School building. One of the most important developments was the acquisition in Queen's Road of two houses which provided the accommodation for the Boarding House in 1928. This was another scheme which was carried out by the FP Club which recognised the advantage of having premises which could provide for the sons of the many former pupils who pursued their careers abroad. Previously several masters including the Rector had opened their homes to receive pupils as a useful supplement to their income. In a way, this practice was continued by using members of the School staff as senior and junior house masters. The Boarding House remained in operation until 1956 when the need for education for expatriates had dwindled and there was uncertainty about how the changing school policy in post-war Aberdeen could affect it. The boys from abroad like the Serbians during the First World War introduced a modestly exotic element to the School mix. The coming of the oil industry in the seventies was to revive this element, while the Boarding House itself was taken over by the Scottish Youth Hostel Association, which has retained the accommodation up to the present time.

As one would expect from the modest targets he had set himself, in 1935, Andrew noted only minor adjustments to the curriculum, pointing to the introduction of Spanish and the provision of Music for all the senior boys. The School continued to produce successful candidates in the University Bursary Competition and its reputation among leading Scottish rugby schools was maintained.

Having threaded its way through the difficult years of the period between the wars, the School again faced new challenges produced by the outbreak of war in 1939. In many ways the challenges were similar to what had been faced back in 1914. The Central School was again required for military accommodation and this led to the sharing of the school's premises and a drastic alteration of the school's organisation. For an account of what happened one can turn to the Magazine contributions which Andrew offered it from 1926 until his retirement in 1942 under the heading 'Messages to Former Pupils'. In these he provided a humorous but well-informed survey of the happenings in the School year. The seed for this had been sown by the decision of the FP Club in 1925 that long speeches would no longer be permitted at the Annual Club Dinner.

The information and observations provided by those long, worthy speeches was replaced by persuading Andrew to write an account 'To FPs abroad', reviewing the activities of the year. This was so well received that this became an annual feature in the Magazine and provides a first-hand account of what was going on in the School. During the War this was a very effective way of maintaining the link between servicemen and their old School. There he recorded various gifts to the School, the most notable being the gift of the clock to fill the space in the eastern tower of the School, the Shanghai clock donated by the FPs who were resident in China in 1927. This was, of course, not only a boon for the School but also for the whole community of Aberdeen. The practice of clock gifts was maintained in 1939 by the provision of a clock by the FP residents of Malaysia, which was placed in the Hall and later transferred to the new Library in the 1960s where it became a victim of the fire of 1986. In more recent times still, a clock was presented by FPs in Canada to instal in the Memorial Pavilion at Rubislaw.

Sharing with the Central School was arranged by running a six-day week with the schools having three alternate days per week. Games went on very much as usual apart from the trenches dug across Rubislaw field to prevent any enemy landings. The main hall was taken over for air raid precaution facilities, various air raid trenches were dug and the school buildings had their windows protected against blast and black-out curtains were installed. In July and August, boys took part in forestry camps and harvesting. Space around the School was turned into a market garden providing vegetables and fruit for the Boarding House, Feeding Centres and individuals. The Scouts carried out a variety of services and the danger of fires brought a call for volunteers, which was enthusiastically taken up by senior pupils, attracted by the 3s per night reward which was offered.

The arrangement of having three alternate days for school at the outbreak of war was replaced by what was deemed a more satisfactory one, of having the pupils attend for four-and-a-half hours per day morning or afternoon on alternate months. These arrangements were to last till 1944 when the Central School returned to Belmont Street. By then D.M. Andrew had retired, having reached the age of sixty-five. Thereafter, he only once in his eight years of retirement attended an official School function, the extending of the School Roll of Honour to cover the years 1939–46 which included many of his 'boys'. Unfortunately the collection of personal diaries Andrew left behind has been missing for some time.

STAFFING: 1920–1942

In 1929, William Murison retired from his many years in charge of the English department and was succeeded by his assistant, George Farquharson. Murison's friend and colleague Dr George Middleton, last of that famous four, retired shortly after and was followed by an assistant, Andrew Milne, who was a Former Pupil and Dux of the School.

William McL. Dewar taught briefly in the Classics department before leaving to become a very prominent figure in Scottish education as the Headmaster of first Greenock Academy and then of George Heriot's in Edinburgh. George Hay, who had joined the staff before WWI, remained in Classics until 1949.

Figures like Henry Paterson and John Lynch joined the staff in the 1920s but also continued for many years, gaining well-deserved promotions first as principal teachers and later as Deputy Rectors. Bentley Philip, after a difficult start, came to be recognised as an enterprising teacher of Botany and Geography. Dr McAndrew helped to develop the teaching of Spanish which had been pioneered by the redoubtable Charles Davidson, whose namesake James Davidson was a stalwart Secretary for the sporting activities of the time. Between the Wars few members of staff played a greater part in school life in general and in athletic and games activities in particular than Duncan McGregor, who created and developed the role of Games Master envisaged by Morland Simpson.

But as the old giants of the past gradually disappeared, their places were filled by a new generation of teachers. Some like Sandy Bruce and Archie Baxter were to spend most of their long careers with others such as Ian Park and James Collie at the School. However, for many others, after relatively brief successful contributions to various departments, opportunities for promotion, either locally or further afield, presented themselves. W.W. Dickie and T.H. MacRea were amongst those who moved to win promotion. The School seems to have been a kind of apprenticeship, whereby – after a spell with the younger classes in the Middle School – folk like William Hendry and James Walker, both old soldiers, rose to principal teacherships in Geography and History respectively. The latter succeeded Dr Alex Miller, who had been recruited from Bathgate but whose distinguished career was cut short by an early death.

James Eddison filled a dual role in the School community, not only serving in the English department but also being the first Housemaster of the Boarding House in Queen's Road. While the School continued to lay great stress on the usual academic subjects there was a considerable contribution on the cultural side from Music, under the guidance of Gavin Falconer, while Leslie Miller and his successor Charles Hemingway did much to develop an appreciation of Art. The latter was accomplished not only through formal teaching but also by encouraging individual talent through the Art Club after school hours. Commercial Subjects under David Macara and George Laing and Technical Subjects under James Winkley and George Strachan, were the forerunners of the later growth of the practical elements of the curriculum.

PUPILS ATTENDING THE GRAMMAR SCHOOL, 1920–1942

Merchants and Manufacturers

Joseph R. Carry (1912–1994) attended the Grammar between 1918 and 1930, entering Junior Infants, and studied at the London School of Optics. He joined the family business of Jamieson & Son, jewellers and watchmakers, which in 1933 was renamed Jamieson & Carry, and he became the sole owner in 1939. He served on the Western Front in 1939–40 and was a POW until 1945. He represented Rosemount Ward on the Council for three years. He was chairman of the FP Executive, 1955–57 and President of the FP Club, 1967–8.

(Sir) Maitland Mackie (1912–1996; Kt 1982) attended the Grammar between 1926 and 1928, before graduating in Agriculture from Aberdeen University. He was a farming pioneer and a Governor of the North of Scotland College of Agriculture, 1968–92; Chairman of the Aberdeen District Milk Marketing Board, 1965–82; and first Chairman of the North East of Scotland Development Agency, 1969–75. He chaired the Education Committee of Aberdeen County Council and unsuccessfully contested parliamentary seats for the Liberal Party. He was Lord Lieutenant of Aberdeenshire, 1975–87. His autobiography *A Lucky Chap* was published in 1993.

Douglas D.S. Craib [= Simpson] (1914–2001) attended the Grammar between 1925 and 1929, and Dundee HS. He was a farmer, 1937–83, and served in the Second World War. He was chair of the Royal Highland and Agriculture Society of Scotland, 1967–9, its Honorary Secretary and Treasurer, 1970–4, and its Hon. Vice-President, 1978–9 and 1987–8. He was a member of the Potato Marketing Board of GB, 1968–83. He was DL of Moray, 1974–90.

J. Gordon Dawson (1916–2007) attended the Grammar between 1921 and 1934, when he was Classical Dux. He graduated from Aberdeen University with FCH in Electrical and Mechanical Engineering. He joined Rolls-Royce and later became Chief Engineer at the Shell Aero Engine Laboratory at Thornton. He moved in 1955 to Perkins in Peterborough where he modernised their product range. He was chair and Managing Director of Zenith Carburettor Company. He was made a Fellow of the Institute of Mechanical Engineers and in 1979 he became its President.

Basil D.D. Emslie (1917–2005) attended the Grammar between 1929 and 1935, joining Scottish Oils on leaving school. He served in the TA and RA. He worked tirelessly for the FP Glasgow Centre and this was recognised by his election to the office of Honorary Vice-President of the Club in 1999.

Robert A.E. Mennie (1919–1994) attended the Grammar between 1924 and 1936. Despite the interruption of WWII he graduated from Aberdeen University with a FCH in Classics in 1942. He served in the RA but was discharged through ill-health. He had a very successful career with British Petroleum in the oil industry and from 1977 played a key role in BP's involvement in North Sea Oil. He was President of the FP Club in 1976–7.

Andrew M. McLaren (1921–1998) attended the Grammar between 1926 and 1939. He completed an Engineering apprenticeship with a local firm and remained in its employment until 1956. He worked as a consultant to the Locomotive Co. at Springburn, Glasgow, and became a successful manufacturing manager in Dundee. He was President of the FP Club, 1995–6.

Harold M.R. Watt (1921–2003) attended the Grammar between 1926 and 1938, graduating from Aberdeen University with FCH in Classics in 1941. He served in the RAF in WWII. He became joint Managing Director of Aberdeen University Press in 1948 (sole from 1958). He was Vice-Convener of the Business Committee of the University, 1971–82, and a member of the University Court, 1970–84. He was a son of Theodore Watt.

(Dr) Alexander J.R. Murray (1922–2008) attended the Grammar between 1928 and 1939 and graduated in Chemistry from Aberdeen University in 1943. He was part of Slim's 'forgotten' 14th Army in Burma. He spent a thirty-two-year career with ICI, as a research chemist and then a General Manager, spending some time as manager of its Rotterdam plant.

Douglas N. Georgeson (1924–2001) attended the Grammar between 1929 and 1939, and was in the RAF during WWII. He joined the family vehicle repair business (until 1985). An FP rugby stalwart, he captained the

1st XV for five seasons in the 1950s and was Rugby section President for three years. He was President of the FP Club, 1985–6.

Eric Craig (1927–2008) attended the Grammar between 1934 and 1946. He joined the family firm of Craig Stores, involved in the catching side of the fishing industry. He was a notable FP rugby player. He was President of the FP Club, 1989–90.

Churchmen

(Right Rev.) Ian F. Begg (1910–1989) attended the Grammar between 1926 and 1928. He graduated in Arts from Aberdeen University in 1931 and became an Episcopal priest in 1934. He served St Ninian's in Seaton until 1973. He was appointed a Canon of St Andrew's Cathedral, Aberdeen, in 1965, Dean of the united diocese of Aberdeen and Orkney in 1969 and a Bishop in 1972. Following retirement he took over the charge of St Machar's Episcopal Church at Bucksburn. He helped found Aberdeen Samaritans.

Horace Walker (1910–1994) attended the Grammar between 1922 and 1928. He went on to Aberdeen University, where he qualified in Classics and then, in 1935, Divinity. His first charge was in Hawick between 1939 and 1944, before returning to Aberdeen. He became Secretary-Depute of the Church of Scotland's Home Board in 1948 and was its Secretary from 1957 until 1977, being involved in creating fifty new parishes and 150 building projects.[3]

(Very Rev. Dr) J. Fraser McLuskey (1915–2005) attended the Grammar between 1920 and 1931, graduating from Edinburgh University in Arts and Divinity. He became Chaplain to Glasgow University in 1939. He was a member of the SAS in WWII winning an MC and an account of his experiences was contained in *Parachute Padre*. After ministries in Broughty Ferry and Bearsden he moved to St Columba's in London's Knightsbridge (1960–86). He was Moderator of the General Assembly in 1983. His autobiography, *The Cloud and the Fire*, was published in 1994. He was President of the FP Club in 1974–5.

Military

(Maj. Gen.) Robert A. Stephen (1907–1983) attended the Grammar between 1919 and 1925 and qualified in Medicine from Aberdeen University in 1930. He joined the RAMC in 1934 and during WWII served in France, Egypt, Libya, Greece, Crete, Belgium, Holland and Germany. He was Director of

Army Surgery, 1959–67, being created a Major General in 1961. He was consultant in Surgery, Royal Hospital, Chelsea.

(Dr) Robert S. Slessor (1913–1985) attended the Grammar between 1927 and 1929 and went on to qualify in Medicine at Aberdeen University in 1935. He was a surgeon Lieutenant Commander in the RN in WWII. In 1948 he was appointed senior Medical Officer in the Falkland Islands, remaining till 1970. He participated in two Polar expeditions to Antarctica.

(Maj. Gen.) R.A. (Robin) Smart (1914–1986) attended the Grammar between 1919 and 1931, graduating in Medicine from Aberdeen University in 1936. He joined the RAMC and during WWII served in Palestine, North Africa, France and Germany. He then specialised in hypothermia, frostbite and snow blindness. He led an expedition to Antarctica in 1956 and was awarded the British Polar Medal. From 1960 on he held top medical positions in the Rhine Army, the Ministry of Defence, Far East land forces and Strategic Command HQ.

(Air Marshal Sir) Leslie D. Mavor (1916–1991; KCB 1940) attended Grammar between 1923 and 1933, going on to RAF College at Cranwell. He was commissioned in 1937 and spent the first years of the War defending the North-West frontier of India. He had a series of staff jobs until, in 1959, heading the bombing school at Lindholme. He returned to Whitehall in 1968 as C-in-C of Training Command. In 1980 he became Britain's Co-ordinator of the voluntary Civil Defence effort for four years. He was President of the FP Club, 1972–3.

Thomas J.T. Nicol (1917–1998) attended the Grammar between 1930 and 1935, graduating from Aberdeen University in Arts in 1939 while he trained as an Army Chaplain. He served as such with the Black Watch in North Africa in 1942. After the War he decided to return to the army and he remained there until 1972, when he was called to the ministry of Crathie Church (until 1979).

(Brig.) (Roderick) 'Fergie' M. Semple (1922–2003) attended the Grammar between 1927 and 1938, graduating from Aberdeen University in Engineering in 1941. He was commissioned into the RE in 1942. During WWII he helped create glider landing zones in preparation for the D-Day landings. He was Chief of Staff of a Parachute Brigade and CO of the 131 Parachute Engineer Brigade. He was Director of the SAS from 1969 to 1972. In retirement he was Director-General of Administration in the Omani department of Defence and a member of the Sultan's National Defence Guard.

(Dr) Ian M. Brooker (1928–2009) attended the Grammar between 1934 and 1945 and graduated in Medicine from Aberdeen University in 1950. He joined the RAF and was promoted to Squadron Leader. An experienced climber from his school and student days he was part of a small expedition to South Georgia which mapped previously uncharted areas of the Antarctic. Mount Brooker was named after him by the RGS. He was in general practice in Shetland from 1958 until the mid-1980s.

(Air Vice-Marshal) William K. MacTaggart (b. 1929) attended the Grammar between 1933 and 1945, graduating in Engineering from Aberdeen University in 1948. He joined the RAF in 1949, attending its staff college and the joint services staff college. He was President of the Ordnance Board before he retired and went into commerce in 1980.

Medical

(Prof.) William M. Davidson (1909–1991) attended the Grammar between 1914 and 1928, entering Junior Infants. He graduated in Medicine from Aberdeen University in 1934 and specialised in pathology. His war ended with capture in May 1940 and he spent time in his camp treating prisoners of all nationalities. He returned to Aberdeen becoming senior lecturer and then was appointed Head of Clinical Pathology at King's College Hospital. A Professorship in Haematology followed at London University and he was elected FRSE in 1964. His research, on congenital diseases and immunology, was ground-breaking.

(Prof.) Alan D. Morgan (1910–1992) attended the Grammar between 1919 and 1928, entering Lower I. He graduated in Medicine from Aberdeen University in 1935, having previously gained an Arts degree there. He specialised in pathology and was appointed to Aberdeen University before WWII took him to the Middle East and the rank of Major. In 1946 he was invited to Westminster Medical School, where he quickly became Head of the Histopathology Department. In 1962 he was its first Professor of Histopathology, the science of disease in the tissues of the body. He gained a wide reputation for his research into pathology of the testes and pathology of arterial disease. He wrote a number of academic papers and was a founding fellow of the Royal College of Pathologists in 1964.

(Dr) Alexander J. Slessor (1912–1954) attended the Grammar between 1918 and 1930, entering the Senior Infants, and went on to Aberdeen University, graduating with honours in Medicine in 1935. He became a Lt Col. in the RAMC during WWII. From 1948 he held the post of assistant surgeon at the Western General Hospital in Edinburgh. 'Of the undergraduates that it has been my privilege to teach, A.J. Slessor, taken all-in-all, was the best' (Sir James Learmonth in *The Lancet*).

(Dr) Logie S. Bain (1914–1988) attended the Grammar between 1919 and 1931, entering Junior Infants. He qualified in Medicine at Aberdeen University in 1937. He spent much of WWII in the Middle East but returned home in 1945 and took charge of Rheumatology at Stracathro. In 1953 he took over the new Department of Physical Medicine and Rheumatology at the ARI. He was also Director of the School of Physiotherapy at Woolmanhill, 1962–79. He was President of the Aberdeen Medico Chirurgical Society in 1980 and chair of the Aberdeen branch of the British Rheumatism and Arthritis Society. He was notable in rugby and golf.

(Prof.) Eric K. Cruickshank (1915–2007) attended the Grammar between 1920 and 1932, graduating as a prize-winner in Medicine at Aberdeen University in 1937. He was a Fellow of Harvard before service with the RAMC in WWII. He was a prisoner in Malaya for much of the war. After lecturing at Aberdeen he became the first Professor of Medicine in the new University of the West Indies in Kingston, Jamaica, in 1950, and helped shape the practice of medicine in the Caribbean. He was Dean of Postgraduate Medicine at Glasgow University from 1972 to 1980 and a Professor in Grenada. He also was a WHO consultant on nutrition and medical education.

(Prof.) Bernard H. Smith (1917–1985) attended the Grammar between 1932 and 1935 and graduated with FCH in Medicine at Aberdeen University in 1941. He joined the RAMC during WWII and served in India and Burma. Between 1951 and 1953 he worked at Montreal Neurological Institute and lectured at McGill. He was chief neurologist in a hospital in Buffalo before becoming Professor of Neurology at the State University of New York from 1955 until 1979. He wrote a number of books on neurological subjects.

(Dr) J.R.S. (Donny) Innes (1917–2012) attended the Grammar between 1923 and 1935, graduating from Aberdeen University in Medicine in 1940. During WWII he was commissioned in the RAMC and saw action in 1944–5. He went into general practice in Aberdeen in 1946, retiring in 1987. He held the position of MOH at Craiginches Prison from 1949 to 1987. He led the almost all-conquering FP rugby side of 1947–8 and won eight caps for Scotland (five as captain) at the sport. Captaining Scotland to a 6–3 win over England on 20 March, 1948, meant that his name was inscribed on the Calcutta Cup. He was President of the SRU in 1973–4 and President of the FP Club, 1991–2. He was the first nominee for a place in Aberdeen Sports Council Hall of Fame.

(Prof.) James K. Russell (1919–2006) attended the Grammar between 1932 and 1937 and qualified in Medicine from Aberdeen University in 1942. He became Professor of Obstetrics and Gynaecology at Durham then Newcastle Universities, 1958–82. He was Dean of Post-graduate Medicine at Newcastle from 1968 to 1977. He was a consultant in human reproduction for WHO. His main research interest was pregnancy in young teenage girls.

George E. Mavor (1919–1973) attended the Grammar between 1928 and 1936. He graduated MA at Aberdeen University in 1939 and MB ChB with honours in 1944, winning a number of prizes. He became FRCSE and was internationally known for his specialisation in vascular surgery.

(Dr) Alexander L. Speirs (1921–2008) attended the Grammar between 1926 and 1938 and graduated from Aberdeen University in Medicine in 1943. He joined the RN as a surgeon-lieutenant. After WWII he trained as a paediatrician and took charge of the children's wards and neonatal units at both Stirling and Falkirk Royal Infirmaries. He gained an international reputation for his research into babies born with severe limb abnormalities which led to the withdrawal of distaval (thalidomide) from use in Britain. His work and persistence, described as 'single-handed clinical detective work of the highest order', ensured an even greater tragedy was avoided.

(Prof.) Robert B. Duthie (1925–2005) attended the Grammar in 1934 before going on to King Edward GS, Chelmsford and reading medicine at Edinburgh University. Following service as a Captain in the RAMC in Malaya he worked in Edinburgh, London and New York. In 1966 he became the Nuffield Professor of Orthopaedic Surgery at Oxford University, a post he held for over twenty years. He built a leading reputation for musculoskeletal medicine, developing new ways of dealing with injury management.

(Prof. Sir) Alexander C. Turnbull (1925–1990; Kt 1988) was educated at RGC and the Grammar, where he studied between 1939 and 1942 and was the modern Dux in his final year. He graduated in medicine from Aberdeen University in 1947. After working in Dundee and Aberdeen he was appointed chair of Obstetrics and Gynaecology in Cardiff in 1966. Seven years later he became Nuffield Professor of these same disciplines at Oxford University, working in the new John Radcliffe Maternity Hospital, and a fellow of Oriel. He was a prolific author of original scientific papers and books. He influenced a whole generation of doctors and scientists in his outstanding life-long contribution to his profession.[4]

Ian M. Duguid (b. 1926) attended the Grammar between 1938 and 1943. Having graduated in Medicine at Aberdeen in 1948 he specialised in ophthalmology, spending his entire career at Moorfields Eye Hospital in London. He obtained an MD at Aberdeen, was awarded FRCS of London and the French Ordre du Merit. He was President of the FP Club in its Centenary Year, 1993–4, and gifted the Duguid Decanter to the then newly formed Canadian Centre of the Club.

(Dr) Alexander H. Innes (1927–2008) attended the Grammar between 1933 and 1945, graduating in Medicine from Aberdeen University in 1952. He set up a work therapy unit at Cornhill Hospital and provided sheltered employment for patients with severe mental illness. He came to be recognised as a pioneer of Forensic Psychiatry and was deputy superintendent physician at Cornhill before becoming Medical Administrator. He won two international Hockey caps.

(Prof.) William I. Cranston (1928–2001) attended the HSOG and the Grammar between 1936 and 1938, before graduating in Medicine from Aberdeen University in 1949. After working in Aberdeen, London and Oxford he was Professor of Medicine at the United Medical and Dental Schools of Guy's and St Thomas' Hospital between 1964 and 1993.

Lindsay Symon (b. 1929) attended the Grammar between 1934 and 1946. At Aberdeen University he was the most distinguished graduate in Medicine in 1951. He had a role in developing cerebro-vascular research and was Professor of Neurological Surgery at London and senior surgeon in the National Hospitals Group from 1981 until retiring in 1995. He researched extensively and wrote and lectured widely. Honours include CBE and several fellowships.

Legal

(The Hon. Lord) (Douglas H.) Johnston (1907–1985) attended the Grammar between 1913 and 1926, entering the Junior Infants. He went on to study Law at both St John's, Oxford, and Edinburgh University. He was called to the Bar of the Inner Temple in 1931 and in the following year he was admitted to the Faculty of Advocates. He became an Advocate-Depute in 1945 and took silk two years later. In 1947 he became Solicitor-General in Attlee's government and shortly after Labour MP for Paisley. He was elevated to the Scottish College of Justice in 1961. Following an active war career as a Lieutenant Colonel in the RA, he investigated war crimes. He chaired the Royal Fine Arts Commission. He was President of the FP Club, 1961–2.

Allan C. Frazer (1911–1995) attended the Grammar between 1925 and

1930 and graduated from Aberdeen University with FCH in English Language and Literature in 1934 and Law in 1937. He served his apprenticeship as a solicitor in Aberdeen but spent the rest of his professional career in Edinburgh. He served in WWII and was commissioned in the RAOC. He became a WS in 1948 and was Rector's Assessor on the Court of Edinburgh University. He was President of the FP Club, 1970–1, having been Secretary of its Edinburgh Centre for thirty years, 1937 to 1967.

(His Hon) Alastair G. Sharp (1911–2001) attended the Grammar between 1918 and 1924, entering Lower I, and Fettes. He won an Exhibition to Clare, Cambridge, graduating in 1933. He became a Barrister of the Inner Temple in 1935. His legal career was interrupted by war service. He took Silk in 1961 and became a judge of county courts before becoming a circuit judge, 1962–8.

Norman R. Wylie (1913–1983) attended the Grammar between 1927 and 1930, going on to graduate from Aberdeen University in Arts and Law in 1935 and 1939 respectively. He was held POW in Poland, 1940–5. He was admitted to the Faculty of Advocates in 1958 in Edinburgh. After working as a judge in Hong Kong he became a Legal Assistant in the Scottish Office until 1974.

David M.C. Donald (1914–1985) attended the Grammar between 1926 and 1932. At University he was President of the Students' Conservative Association. He graduated with a Law degree in 1935 and joined Shepherd and Wedderburn in Edinburgh. In 1960 he moved to London merchant bankers, Robert Fleming & Co., as Managing Director.

J. Scott MacLachlan (1914–1971) attended the Grammar between 1922 and 1932 being Senior Prefect in his final year. He qualified at Aberdeen University in Arts (1935) and Law (1937). He became an Advocate in Aberdeen. For several years he was a Progressive Councillor. In 1946 he succeeded Theodore Watt as Secretary and Treasurer of the FP Club and retained these posts until 1965.

Alexander Milne (1915–1975) attended the Grammar between 1929 and 1933, graduating MA LLB from Aberdeen University. He became a solicitor in 1940. He was Chief Executive of Kincardine and Deeside District Council from 1974 until his early death.

James F. Watt (1916–2009) attended the Grammar between 1921 and 1925, completing his education at Daniel Stewart's and Edinburgh University, where he graduated in Law. After work as a legal assistant for Aberdeen Corporation he became Town Clerk in 1972 and was Chief Executive of Aberdeen District Council from 1974 to 1977.

James S.G. Munro (1917–1983) attended the Grammar between 1922 and 1928 and graduated in Law from Aberdeen University. He was President of the Society of Advocates, secretary of a branch of the Red Cross and a wartime Major in the Gordon Highlanders. He was leader of the Progressive group on the Aberdeen Town Council for a number of years. He was a notable FP rugby player. He was President of the FP Club, 1971–2.

Neil I.W. Meldrum (1919–1991) attended the Grammar between 1925 and 1937. He suffered a severe leg wound whilst a serving officer with the Gordon Highlanders at El Alamein in 1942. He completed his education after the war and having qualified MA LLB he set up business on his own. He was a notable district rugby referee. He gave over forty years' service to the FP Rugby Club and was President of the FP Club, 1981–2.

Douglas Reith (b. 1919) attended the Grammar between 1924 and 1935. He qualified from Aberdeen University with MA LLB, served in WWII and was a POW from 1940 to 1945. He became a member of the Faculty of Advocates in Scotland, 1946. He was Advocate-Depute, Crown Office, Scotland between 1953 and 1957, and became a QC in Scotland in 1957. He was President, Pensions Appeal Tribunal from 1958 until 1964. He was chairman of the NHS Tribunal, Scotland, 1963–5. He was a Social Security Commissioner, 1960–92.

(Sheriff) William O. Pattullo (1921–1975) attended the Grammar between 1934 and 1941. He took degrees in Arts and Law at Aberdeen University. He practised at the Scottish Bar (1951–9) and was senior lecturer in Mercantile Law at Aberdeen University (1959–62). He was a Sheriff in Glasgow, 1962–75.

William L. Connon (1922–2000) attended the Grammar between 1930 and 1940 and his higher education was interrupted by war service in WWII in the RAF. He graduated in Law from Aberdeen University in 1949 and remained with the one legal firm throughout his career (Mackenzie & Wilson). From 1946 to 1953 he played in the front row in the FP rugby team which shared the Unofficial Championship with Kelso in 1947–8, and won three Sevens Tournaments in 1951. He was president of the FP Club, 1979–80. He succeeded Doug Smith as SRU President, 1987–8.

Lawrence Milne (1925–2011) attended Inverness Royal Academy and between 1939 and 1943 the Grammar, where he was Senior Prefect. During WWII he served with the RN before completing a Law degree at Aberdeen University. He joined his father-in-law's firm and following amalgamation he retired from Milne, Mackinnon and Peterkins. He played rugby for the FPs.

William A.B. Forbes (1926–1981) attended the Grammar between 1932 and 1942. He gained a FCH at St Andrews and studied further at Cambridge.

He was called to the English Bar in 1953, taking Silk in 1972. He sat on the Law Commission on Criminal Procedures for England and Wales.

Ronald L. MacKinnon (1926–1994) attended the Grammar between 1932 and 1945. He joined the RN shortly before the end of WWII and saw service minesweeping in the Adriatic. He graduated in Law in 1951 and spent his professional life with firms in Aberdeen. He unsuccessfully contested local elections for the Liberal party, was a founder member of Aberdeen Solicitors' Property Centre and Secretary of Stockethill Community Council.

(Sheriff) Roy A. Wilson (1928–1985) attended the Grammar between 1937 and 1942, achieving a degree from Oxford and a Law degree from Edinburgh in 1953. He was a solicitor in Edinburgh before he became a Sheriff in Elgin in 1975.

Brian K. Crookshanks (b. 1929) attended Grammar between 1934 and 1946. He gained an MA (1949) followed by LLB (with distinction) and worked in private legal practice until 1975 when he joined the Procurator Fiscal Service (until 1994). He was Editor of Notes for FP Magazine, 1959–65; Club Secretary and Treasurer, 1965–76; Club Centre Secretary and Treasurer, 1969–74; President of the FP Club, 1983–4; Chairman of the Club Centre, 1990–5; Magazine Notes Editor 1959–65 and again from 1993; and General Editor from 1997.

Academic

John H. Speirs (1906–1979) attended the Grammar between 1911 and 1924, entering Junior Infants. He went on to study at Aberdeen and Cambridge Universities and lecture at Edinburgh, Riga and Egypt Universities. He wrote a number of publications on Scottish and English literature.

(Prof.) Alfred A. Harper (1907–1996) attended the Grammar between 1918 and 1925, entering Lower VB. He was influenced in becoming a physiologist by Professor J.J.R. Macleod of Aberdeen University. After working at Leeds University, St Thomas' Hospital, London and Manchester University, he was appointed chair of Physiology in Newcastle at the medical school of Durham University in 1949, retiring in 1972. He was elected FRSE in 1959.

Hugh A. Murray (1907–1973) attended the Grammar between 1919 and 1925 and won the Classical School Gold Medal. He took a FCH in Classics at Aberdeen University in 1929 and went on to study at St John's, Cambridge. He taught Classics at the GS then lectured at Aberdeen and Durham Universities before becoming Professor of Classics at Wellington University, NZ, in 1946.

Charles Strachan (1907–1993) attended the Grammar between 1919 and 1925 and was First Bursar in Mathematics and Natural Philosophy in 1925. He took FCH at Aberdeen University and an accelerated tripos at Corpus Christi, Cambridge achieving the distinction of becoming Junior Wrangler. (He later took his PhD.) He lectured in Natural Philosophy and Applied Mechanics at Aberdeen and Liverpool, before becoming senior lecturer, then Reader, at Aberdeen, 1946–77. He was elected to the RSE in 1942.

Adam J.G. Barnett (1908–1957) entered the Junior Infants of the Grammar in 1915 and went on to study at Edinburgh University. He lectured in Chemistry in Nigeria, 1932–45, being elected to the RSE in 1937. He taught at Aberdeen University from 1949 to 1957.

George E.C. Barton (1909–2005) attended the Grammar between 1923 and 1926, graduating in Arts from Aberdeen University in 1929. He trained as a teacher and took up a position in Brechin. From 1933 until 1974 he was Head of the Junior School of RGC. He was Housemaster of the Sillerton Boarding House from its opening in 1937 until his retirement in 1974. He was FP Club President in 1973–4 filling the role with distinction.

Norman F.M. Henry (1909–1983) attended the Grammar between 1915 and 1927. He graduated from Aberdeen University with FCH in Geography in 1931 and FCH in Geology in 1934. He gained a research scholarship to St John's, Cambridge, where he became a lecturer. His important work was on quantitative reflected light microscopy.

Arthur J. Adams (1910–1982) attended the Grammar between 1919 and 1930. He graduated from Edinburgh University in Vet Medicine in 1935. He worked his whole career in private and public practice in Yorkshire. He was President of the FP Club, 1978–9.

(Prof.) Joseph A.C. Knox (1911–1984) attended the Grammar between 1916 and 1923, entering Junior Infants, and also the HSOG and Glasgow University, where he graduated in Medicine in 1935. He lectured in Physiology at Glasgow, 1940–4 and held a similar post at King's, London until 1948 when he was appointed a senior lecturer there. In 1954 he became Professor of Physiology at Queen Elizabeth, London, a position he held until 1974.

David D. Murison (1913–1997) attended the Grammar between 1922 and 1929, entering Middle I, and became Classical Dux of the School. He graduated from Aberdeen University with FCH in Classics in 1933. He then progressed by scholarship to Cambridge, graduating in 1936 with a First in the Classical tripos. He also studied comparative philology and Old English, Celtic and Norse. In 1946 he became first Deputy Editor of the *Scottish*

National Dictionary (SND) and then the editor of eight four-part volumes. In doing so he helped give respectability to the modern Scots language.[5]

August H.L. Slater (1917–1996) attended the Grammar between 1922 and 1935 and was Classical Dux. He took a FCH in Classics at Aberdeen University and after war service studied further at Merton College, Oxford. He became a senior civil servant and President of the London Centre of the FP Club.

(Prof.) Alexander J.B. Youngson (1918–2004) attended the Grammar between 1923 and 1936. Having been a pilot in the Fleet Air Arm (1940–5) he graduated from Aberdeen University in 1947. Following lectureships at St Andrews and Cambridge he became, in 1963, Professor of Political Economy at Edinburgh University (till 1974). He was Vice-Principal of the University 1971–4; Professor of Economics at Hong Kong (1980–2); and chair of the Royal Fine Arts Commission for Scotland (1983–90). He published extensively on a wide variety of subjects.

William Dallas (Dally) Allardice (1919–2003) attended the Grammar between 1934 and 1939, entering Middle II. He was an all-round athlete. In season 1938–9 he captained one of the most successful pre-war school rugby XVs. Aged nineteen at the outbreak of WWII, instead of starting at Loughborough PE College, he opted for commando training. He took up a PE teaching post at the GS in 1947, leaving in 1959 for Dundee HS, where he became Assistant Rector and retired in 1984. He gained eight rugby caps as scrum-half for Scotland. His wartime exploits were revealed in his autobiography, *Friendship in a Time of War*.

Ian S. Flett (1920–2001) attended the Grammar between 1925 and 1937 and graduated in Classics from Aberdeen University in 1940. He served in the RAF during WWII. He taught in Aberdeen, was an educational psychologist in Sunderland, and an educational officer in Preston, Southport and Hull before becoming Director of Education for Fife from 1966 to 1984. He expanded provision for nursery and special education, reorganised secondary schools on comprehensive lines and enriched and developed the curriculum.

(Prof.) Alexander E. Anton (1922–2011) attended the Grammar in 1932–3 and between 1935 and 1940. He graduated from Aberdeen University with an MA LLB with distinction and became a solicitor in 1949. He lectured at Aberdeen before becoming Professor of Jurisprudence at Glasgow University, 1959–73. He was a member of the Scottish Law Commission, 1966–82, and Chair of the Scottish Rights of Way Society, 1988–92.

(Prof.) E. Kerr Borthwick (1925–2008) attended the Grammar between 1933 and 1942, being Classical Dux in his final year. At School and at

Aberdeen University he was a multi-prize-winner and achieved a FCH in Classics in 1946. He won a Classical scholarship to Cambridge, where he graduated in 1948 with FCH in both parts of the tripos and a distinction in Literature. He taught at Leeds and Edinburgh Universities before gaining a personal chair at the latter in 1980. He headed the department of Greek until retiring in 1989. He was President of the Classical Association of Scotland in 1987–92. He was a prolific writer and accomplished musician.

(Dr) Harry G. Macpherson (1925–2001) attended the Grammar between 1938 and 1944, then serving in the RE at the end of WWII. He graduated in Geology from Aberdeen University in 1952 and did further study at Toronto. He did prospecting work in Canada, was Curator of Geology in Edinburgh's Royal Museum and in 1984 the mineral Macphersonite (discovered in Leadhills in Lanarkshire) was named after him.

Donald E.R. Watt (1926–2004) attended the Grammar between 1931 and 1943. He joined the RAF and still managed to achieve a FCH in History at Aberdeen University in 1950 and a scholarship to Oriel, Oxford. In 1953 he became a lecturer in Medieval History at St Andrews. He was appointed to a personal chair in Scottish Church History in 1977 and elected FRSE in 1988. He produced two major, remarkable works: his *Biographical Dictionary of Scottish Graduates to 1410* and his *Scotichronicon*, both of which involved years of painstaking research. He was a son of Theodore Watt.

Ian A. Watt (1926–2010) attended the Grammar between 1931 and 1943. His university education was interrupted by war service. In 1950 he gained a FCH in History at Aberdeen University and proceeded to Merton, Oxford and a degree in PPE. He became Dean of Academic Studies at the Police Staff College at Bramshill until retirement in 1986.

(Prof.) Ronald W. Hepburn (1927–2008) attended the Grammar between 1936 and 1944, and was Classical Dux in his final year. He served for a short time in WWII before graduating with FCH in Moral Philosophy and English from Aberdeen University in 1951. He became Professor of Philosophy at Nottingham (1960) and then Edinburgh (1964). He changed to Moral Philosophy in 1975, the chair of which he retained until retirement in 1996. He published extensively.

Financial

A.D. Stewart Anderson (1906–1962) attended the Grammar between 1918 and 1924, entering Modern IA. He was Classical Dux and First Bursar in 1924. He graduated in Arts in 1927 and became a CA in 1931. He was a wing-commander in the RAF in WWII. He was a director of Hecht, Levis and Kahn group of rubber merchants.

William J.A. Nelson (1907–1993) attended the Grammar between 1914 and 1924, entering Lower I. He was apprenticed as a CA and qualified in 1930 with distinction in his final examination. Between 1930 and 1939 he worked for leading London accountants. He served as a captain with the RA in the Middle East in WWII and was wounded in 1944. He was appointed Treasurer and Assistant Secretary to Aberdeen University and held these posts from 1948 until retirement in 1975. He published books on fortifications in the Indian Ocean in his retirement.

John A. Cruickshank (b. 1920) attended the Grammar between 1925 and 1929 going on to complete his schooling at Stewart's. He became an apprentice in the Commercial Bank. He enlisted in the RA in 1939 transferring to the RAF in 1941. For his brave actions in July 1944 in sinking a U-boat and saving his crew he was awarded the Victoria Cross. He returned to Grindlays Bank after the War, retiring in 1977.

Robert W. Adam (1922–1993) attended the Grammar between 1928 and 1933, going on to Fettes. He was commissioned in 1943 in the Royal Scots, but he transferred to the Indian army rising to the rank of Major. After the War he qualified as a CA in 1950 and joined British Petroleum. His commercial instincts and financial acumen led him to Director and General Manager of the Finance and Planning Department of BP Chemicals in 1967. Within two years he was President of BP North America. By 1975 he was one of BP's five managing directors, specialising in finance and the western hemisphere. He became Deputy Chairman in 1981 and retired aged sixty in 1983. He was still much in demand with many directorships.

James A.N. Watt (b. 1922) attended the Grammar between 1927 and 1939, taking up a CA apprenticeship in Glasgow. During WWII he served in the RAF in India and the Far East and returned to qualify as a CA in 1948. He spent thirty years in industry mainly as secretary and Chief Accountant. He was President of the FP Club, 1982–3.

Administrative

Cecil A.G. Savidge (1905–1975) attended the Grammar between 1913 and 1924, entering Lower II. He took his MA at Aberdeen University and entered the ICS in 1928 serving in various posts including Under-Secretary of External Affairs to the Governor of India. After the sub-continent's partition he was appointed the Chief Commissioner to the first Governor-

General of Pakistan. He was President of the FP Club, 1964–5.

Norman D. Begg (1906–1956) attended the Grammar between 1915 and 1924, entering at Lower IIB. He graduated in Medicine in 1929. After WWII he joined UNRRA Mission to Poland as an epidemiologist. From 1949 he was in charge of the special office for Europe for the WHO in Geneva. In 1951 he was made UN Regional Director of the WHO for Europe, holding this position at his death.

George E. Crombie (1908–1972) attended the Grammar between 1916 and 1921, entering Lower II. He went on to Fettes and Aberdeen University where he gained a FCH in Classics in 1930. He joined the Colonial Civil Service and was with the India Office from 1930. In 1947 he was appointed UK Deputy High Commissioner in Rangoon then Counsellor at the British Embassy there. Various diplomatic posts followed – Madras, Ottawa, Kuala Lumpur, Dublin and Bathurst in Gambia. He was President of the FP Club, 1969–70.

(Lord) John-Mackie (1910–1993) attended the Grammar between 1924 and 1926 and studied at the North of Scotland College of Agriculture before taking over the 700-acre family farm at The Bent, Laurencekirk. He went on to farm 750 acres in Lincolnshire, and a further 500 acres at Waltham Abbey, Essex. In 1951 and 1955 he failed in attempts to get into Parliament but was elected in 1959 as Labour MP for Enfield East. He was joint Parliamentary Secretary to the Minister of Agriculture from 1964 to 1970. He retired from Parliament in 1974 but became a life peer in 1981 and was Labour's spokesman on agriculture in the Lords until 1989.

William A.B. Hamilton (1910–1982) attended the Grammar between 1921 and 1927. He was Classical Dux of the School and took first place in the Aberdeen Bursary Comp. in 1926 and 1927. He graduated with a FCH in Classics in 1931. He was first in the open entrance examination for the Civil Service and was appointed to the Board of Education. He became Assistant Secretary in the Ministry of Food during WWII and Under-Secretary to Education, 1946–9. He was director of Personnel and Under-Secretary at the UN in New York, 1959–62 and Under Secretary at FCO, London, 1962–8.

(Dr) Louis Findlay (1912–1956) attended the Grammar between 1924 and 1930, graduating from Aberdeen University in Medicine in 1936. He worked in New York and London before going with the Red Cross to Abyssinia, 1941–3. He was Director of Health for the UNRRA Middle East at Sinai and then Cairo. He was chief MOH, then chief of operations, for the international refugee body in the American zone of Germany, 1946–51 and then worked in Korea, 1951–3. He was Chief of the Health Division of UNRRA for Palestinian Arab Refugees at the time of his early death, which was a great loss to the international community.

Robert G. Sangster (1912–2001) attended the Grammar between 1919 and 1930, graduating from Aberdeen University in Forestry in 1933 and going on to further study at Oxford and Edinburgh. He joined the Colonial Service and spent his career as a conservator of forests in Uganda and Tanganyika, retiring in 1965.

(Dr) Charles G. Cruickshank (1914–1989) attended the Grammar between 1925 and 1932. He gained a degree in History from Aberdeen and studied at Hertford, Oxford before joining the Civil Service in 1940. Work at the Board of Trade led to his appointment as Trade Commissioner to Ceylon, then Canada and New Zealand. He retired from the post of Assistant Secretary. He became well known as a serious writer on the subject of war.

Richard M. Fraser (Lord Fraser of Kilmorack) (1915–1996) attended the Grammar between 1925 and 1929 and later claimed that this was more important to his development than his army service. He completed his schooling at Fettes and graduated in History from King's, Cambridge. He volunteered in 1939 and emerged in 1945 as a Lt Col. He joined the Conservative Research Office and his gifts for organisation and diplomacy resulted in him becoming Deputy Chair of the Party from 1964 to 1975. He was also Secretary to the Shadow Cabinet, 1964–70 and 1974–5.

Arthur R.H. Kellas (1915–2007) attended the Grammar between 1926 and 1932 and, after winning several prizes, graduated with FCH in Classics at Aberdeen University in 1936. He was awarded a scholarship to Balliol, Oxford and gained a FCH there in 1938. He studied further in Paris before winning a place in the Foreign Office. Instead he joined the SAS and worked with the French resistance and Greek partisans. He then served as Third Secretary in Teheran, and then Helsinki, Cairo, Baghdad, Tel Aviv and Nepal. He was Ambassador to Aden and finally High Commissioner to Tanzania.

(Sir) Richard L. Sharp (1915–2002; KCVO 1982) attended the Grammar between 1920 and 1927, going on to Fettes. From there he proceeded to Aberdeen University, where he was a prize-winner and achieved a FCH in Classics in 1937, and Cambridge where he repeated this success in 1939. During WWII he was posted missing in Malaya in 1942 and spent three years as a POW. On return he joined the Civil Service and from 1948 to 1950 was Private Secretary to Sir Stafford Cripps at the Treasury. He served in Washington and between 1966 and 1968 was Under-Secretary at the Prices and Incomes Board. From 1977 until retirement in 1982 he took charge of the honours system as Ceremonial Officer in the civil service department.

Gordon M. Hector (1918–2001) attended the Grammar in 1924–5 and went on to Edinburgh Academy and Lincoln, Oxford, graduating in History. After war service he joined the Colonial Office. He was an administrative officer in Kenya, Secretary to the Governor of the Seychelles, and Deputy Commissioner of Basutoland. On returning home he was Clerk to Aberdeen University Court from 1967 to 1976 and then its Deputy Secretary. In 1980 he became Secretary to the Assembly Council of the General Assembly, 1980–5.

William W. Gauld (1919–2002) attended the Grammar between 1928 and 1932, graduating from Aberdeen University in 1943 with FCH in Classics. He served for six years in the Pioneer Corps, reaching the rank of Major. He joined the civil service in 1947, becoming an Under-Secretary at the Department of Agriculture and Fisheries for Scotland from 1972.

Baron (George Y. Mackie) Mackie of Benshie (b. 1919) attended the Grammar between 1933 and 1935, becoming a farmer. He served in Bomber Command in 1944. He was Liberal MP for Caithness and Sutherland, 1964–6; chair of Scottish Liberal Party, 1965–70; and later Liberal Democrat spokesman in House of Lords on Devolution, Agriculture, Scotland and Industry. He was chair of Caithness Glass, 1966–84. He was a member of the Council of Europe and Western European Union, 1986–96.

Alan C.R. Watt (1919–1989) attended the Grammar between 1925 and 1937. His degree course was interrupted by war service in India. He returned and graduated from Aberdeen University with a FCH in History and became a lawyer. On the death of his father he took over as sole editor of the FP Magazine for eight years (producing two a year). He held the post of Town Clerk of Ballater for almost twenty years. In 1971 he was appointed Chair of Industrial Tribunals and was the most senior Tribunal Chair in Scotland on his retirement in 1987. He was President of the FP Club in 1975–6. He was a son of Theodore Watt.[6]

Leslie T. Carnegie (1920–1998) attended the Grammar between 1925 and 1938, graduating in Law from Aberdeen University. He qualified as a solicitor and served in WWII in North Africa and the Middle East. He took up an apprenticeship with the Town Clerk of Aberdeen and then worked for East Lothian CC. He became county clerk for Dumfries in 1954 and was Chief Executive of Dumfries and Galloway Regional Council from 1975 until retirement in 1985.

Robert S. Couper (1921–1993) attended the Grammar between 1932 and 1939, being Classical Dux in 1939. He achieved a FCH in Classics at

Aberdeen University and was commissioned in the army shortly after, seeing action in South-East Asia. He joined the GS staff as a teacher of Classics and English in 1947 and became principal teacher of classics at Kirkcaldy HS in 1951. He was Rector of Forres Academy from 1968 to 1981.

(Dr) John L. Kilgour (1924–2008) attended the Grammar between 1936 and 1941, graduating in Medicine from Aberdeen University in 1947. Joining the RAMC he served in Korea and Cyprus leaving the army in 1966. He served in the civil service as British delegate to the World Health Assembly from 1971 to 1976, as member of the WHO Commission on International Control of Communicable Diseases and when seconded to WHO in Geneva played a major part in the smallpox eradication campaign.

(Sir) Iain J.M. Sutherland (1925–1986) was educated at the Grammar between 1933 and 1941 and went on to Aberdeen and Balliol, Oxford. He served in WWII and entered the Foreign Service in 1950. He was Third Secretary, Moscow, 1951; First Secretary, Belgrade, 1958–61; Minister, Moscow between 1974 and 1976; Ambassador to Greece, 1978–82; and Ambassador to the USSR, 1982–5.

John W.R. Gray (1926–1999) attended the Grammar between 1931 and 1945, graduating from Aberdeen University in Arts in 1949 and Law in 1952. He joined the Faculty of Advocates in 1954. He was appointed by the Colonial Office as resident magistrate in Uganda. He was a lecturer in Scots Law at Dundee University, 1964–86.

(Prof.) Roy D. Weir (b. 1927) attended the Grammar between 1932 and 1944, graduating in Medicine from Aberdeen University and becoming a lecturer in Public Health there in 1955. In time he became the Head of the Department of Community Medicine. He was Vice-Principal of the University, Vice-Chair of Grampian Health Board and in 1987 he became Chief Scientist of Scotland at the Home and Health Department.

Patrick K. Booker (1928–2002) attended the Grammar between 1933 and 1945, graduating from Aberdeen University in History in 1949 and continuing his studies at Oriel, Oxford. He joined the Overseas Civil Service spending thirteen years in the Middle East, centred on Aden. He became Assistant Secretary to Aberdeen University in 1969.

Writers

George Sutherland Fraser (1915–1980) attended the Grammar from 1924 until 1933 when he went up to St Andrews University as a bursary student. He qualified in English and History and was employed as a reporter on *The*

Press and Journal. After war service he lived in London as a poet and writer. His first major critical work was published in 1953. He took a post in the English department of Leicester University in 1958 and his output of writing increased. His vocation then became that of a teacher although he believed that poetry was his main gift. He was poetry editor of the *Times Literary Supplement*.[7]

Eric B. Mackay (1922–2006) was educated at the Grammar between 1930 and 1940 and Aberdeen University, although his studies were interrupted by service in WWII. He became a journalist and in 1957 was appointed London Editor of *The Scotsman*. By 1961 he was Deputy Editor of the paper and in 1972 he became the eleventh Editor in its history. *The Scotsman* led the debate for devolution and its circulation increased. He recruited a distinguished team of journalists and despite a drop in morale after the failure of the referendum bill he held circulation at over 90,000 until his retirement in 1985.[8]

Kenneth J. Peters (1923–2000) attended the Grammar between 1929 and 1941. After serving in WWII he became Editor of the *Evening Express* in 1953 and Editor of the *Press and Journal*, 1954–60. He was Managing Director of Aberdeen Journals Ltd, from 1964 to 1983. He was a pillar of FP cricket.

Arts

Andrew J.M. Cruickshank (1907–1988) attended the Grammar between 1919 and 1925. He joined provincial repertory and in 1930 made his West End debut, His career mixed classical and lighter drama. He served in WWII rising to the rank of Major. He resumed his career and was successful in both commercial and art theatre. He performed Ibsen with distinction. He was also popular in the BBC television series of *Dr Finlay's Casebook* (1962–71). Its 150 episodes made him well-known and loved. He wrote a number of books on philosophical and religious themes. He was Chair of the Edinburgh Festival Fringe for ten years.[9]

Philip A.T. Bate (1909–1999) attended the Grammar between 1917 and 1927 where he learned the clarinet. He won a Carnegie award to attend University and studied science at Aberdeen. Work with the BBC in Aberdeen led to work with the Corporation in London, mostly with its music department. He produced some of the first live broadcasts of Edinburgh Festival performances and pioneered live interviews. Throughout his life he collected musical instruments and was the first Chair of the Galpin Society for the history and study of musical instruments. He gave over his collection to Oxford University.[10]

John A. Gray (1918–2006) attended the Grammar between 1926 and 1935 before going on to RADA to study stage management. From 1940 he worked in radio for the BBC, producing many feature and documentary programmes. He co-founded the Edinburgh TV Festival and was chair of Scottish Ballet. He was awarded a prestigious Radio Academy Fellowship in 1998.

Sport

Richard F. Combe (1912–1952) attended the Grammar between 1923 and 1930. He graduated in 1936 in Law at Aberdeen University and was the most distinguished graduate of his year. He was a solicitor by profession. He was runner-up in the Scottish Chess Championships of 1938 and won the British Chess Championships in Nottingham in 1946.

(Dr) Doug W.C. Smith (1924–1998) attended the Grammar between 1930 and 1941, and was coached rugby by 'the finest of games-masters' – Duncan McGregor ('The Gamey'). He graduated from Aberdeen University in Medicine in 1947 and went into general practice in Essex. He gained eight caps for Scotland between 1949 and 1953, and also played against Australia in 1950. He managed the successful Lions tour of New Zealand and Australia in 1971 and was President of the SRU in 1986–7.

TWELVE Robertson and Skinner, 1942–1972

This chapter covers the leadership of Rectors Robertson and Skinner, both of whom had to face the challenges of the reorganisation of Scottish education in the post-war period. The other sections concentrate on staffing and the continuing success of Former Pupils in their careers in later life.

JAMES J. ROBERTSON: RECTOR 1942–1959

The announcement of Andrew's retirement triggered the search for his replacement and the Education Committee (which had taken over from the EA in 1929) identified one outstanding candidate, James J. Robertson MA, BD, who had recently been appointed Rector of the Royal High School in Edinburgh. After some negotiations the Committee felt it had pulled off something of an educational coup when it persuaded Robertson to move north to Aberdeen, although it must be said that his decision had also something to do with how frustrated and depressed he felt with his dealings with Edinburgh's Education Committee.

Robertson had been a pupil at Kilmarnock Academy, Hutchesons' GS in Glasgow and had spent a sixth year at the High School of Glasgow before being placed first in Glasgow's Bursary Competition in 1913. His career was then interrupted by military service for three years in France but he graduated MA with Honours in Classics in 1919. After training as a teacher he rapidly passed from Hillhead High School in Glasgow to the Hermitage School in Helensburgh to Bell-Baxter in Cupar and to his first appointment as Headmaster of Fort William Secondary School in 1926. Five years later he moved to Falkirk High School where he presided with great success and distinction for nine years before being appointed to the rectorship of the Royal High School in 1940. He was clearly a man of great intellectual gifts as well as great eloquence and the Committee's pride in its capture was to be entirely justified over the next seventeen years.

As soon as he took up office at the Grammar he started keeping a log-book. Much of the space is taken up by recording staff absences and noting school trips to various events. The most interesting aspect of the recorded absences are those of the Rector himself, because it becomes clear there of how important a national figure he became, particularly in education. It is recorded in the later part of 1942 that, having taken office in March of that year, he was attending a Council meeting of the Headmasters' Association and, more importantly, the first meeting of the Scottish Advisory Council on Education (SACE). By the end of the year he had been at a meeting of the EIS and another meeting of the Advisory Council. These commitments became a frequent feature of the Rector's routine and in a way became almost a parallel career with his duties at the GS. Later, he was invited to join the Advisory Council for Education in the Colonies and when, in time, a new Advisory Council on Education was set up he was again invited to take part.

Looking back on his career after he retired in 1959, one can only express astonishment that one man could successfully fill so many different roles in so many different fields. The fact that he was invited to participate in such a wide range of commitments is testimony to the very high regard in which he was held by so many different bodies. And yet as honours and distinctions showered down upon him he obviously regarded his role at the Grammar to be of primary importance to him. When Glasgow University offered him a Professorship of Education he declined the offer, staying as Rector of the School until his retirement.

Robertson was active in professional circles becoming Secretary and later President of the Scottish Secondary Headmasters' Association. The post-war educational scene in Scotland involved work on producing new directives from the Advisory Council and the greatly admired Report on Secondary Education of 1947 was largely his product. It summed up what it (or he) saw as the purpose of schooling: 'the good school is to be assessed not by any tale of examination successes, however impressive, but by the extent to which it has filled the years of youth with security, graciousness and ordered freedom'. He advised on School Broadcasting policy for Scotland and the UK and was Vice-Chairman for the Scottish Council for the Training of Teachers in 1959. At the meeting of the British Association in 1959 he was President of the Educational Section.

Outside Scotland he was an influential figure in the development of Education in the Colonies, particularly in Africa and also was a delegate to the General Council of UNESCO held in Montevideo in 1954. He also found time to accept the invitation of the Secretary of State to act as an assessor in the important John Waters Tribunal of 1959.

It is interesting to follow how the list of honours accumulated over the years of his rectorship. He started modestly in 1942 as an MA, BD, FRSE and acquired an OBE in 1948, became FEIS in 1949 and Hon. LLD of Aberdeen University in 1956. Finally the supreme recognition of his contributions to society came in the form of a knighthood in 1956.

Such a career would have placed a considerable strain on any individual but Sir James remained a pleasant, modest, cheerful man who was greatly admired and respected by the pupils and staff as well as the wider community. He had become a JP in 1951.

Despite his many commitments and frequent absences from the School he still managed to keep a close eye on the School's activities. Nonetheless, it was recognised that some sharing of the responsibility for running the day-to-day School routine had to be made. And so a Deputy Rector was appointed in 1946. The first holder of the office was Henry Paterson, the Head of the French and German department and he was succeeded in 1951 by John Lynch, the Head of Science. Another interesting development had been the appointment of separate heads of department for both History (Dr Alexander T. Miller) and Geography (Mr William M. Hendry) in 1943. Miller had been School Captain at Heriot's as a pupil and had graduated with FCH from Edinburgh University before completing his teaching qualification at Oxford. Hendry had already proved his versatility, originality and initiative in thirty years at the School teaching English and History. It was Robertson's view that being a Head of Department in a senior secondary school was the most desirable position in Scottish education. Certainly separate departments gave a lead to the rest of the country and History and Geography received new prominence in the curriculum.

It is important to remember that when he assumed control in 1942, the Grammar School shared with the Central School the dubious distinction of being the only schools in the country on part-time education. Nevertheless, extra-curricular organisations like the ATC and ACF flourished alongside the Scouts. Besides the long-established Literary and Debating Society there was an active Dramatic Society producing quite ambitious efforts. Games continued, rugby matches against other schools took place, swimming competitions were organised, while summer terms were devoted to cricket and athletics. Hockey was introduced in order to offer a wider choice as an alternative to rugby. Tennis was also popular.

Every effort was made by the Rector to encourage a broader curriculum, emphasising the development not only of Spanish as an alternative to French but also a wider choice of Technical and Commercial courses. All this activity continued with the background of the Second World War raging throughout the world, but signs of a return to more normal times started with the Central School returning to its own premises in April 1944.

As the War moved toward closure in 1945 the feeling of uncertainty about the future mingled with the joy and relief at the end of hostilities. It was generally accepted that there would be major changes in education at a national level in the post-war period, plans in whose direction Robertson was deeply involved but the question was how would they affect Aberdeen and particularly the School? Fortunately, Robertson had continued Andrew's practice of contributing his thoughts on the current scene in his 'Messages to Former Pupils' in the Magazine. These are an invaluable insight into his views on developments.

Locally one of the major decisions taken was the ending of fees in Aberdeen Authority's senior secondary schools. At a meeting on 21 October 1946 the Town Council decided by a majority of 19 to 15 that fee-paying at the GS and High School for Girls would be abolished 'at the earliest possible date'. This seemingly simple policy decision in fact created major headaches about the future of the schools. How were pupils to be enrolled when 'free places' became available for all? Some kind of selection would have to be introduced, but on what basis should this be made? How were the interests of the current pupils to be safeguarded when they moved from Primary to Secondary when a selection procedure used in the Central School was to be introduced? Was the selection to be on a residential qualification or were family connections to be considered for admission? For many years there had been a considerable number of pupils from outside the City who had attended the School, and a decision had to be made about their position. And what about the boys who stayed in the Boarding House? Was the Primary section of the School to be abolished?

After considering the many pitfalls which lay before the School the Rector offered the opinion, no doubt bolstered by a great deal of hope, that at the end of the day nothing too drastic would happen, and so it turned out. Country boys could continue at School if their area authority came to a financial arrangement with the town. The Boarding House boys were to be accepted if their parents paid a fee, although it was pointed out that no parents could be required to pay fees under the new legislation.

In his article in the Magazine of July 1947 the Rector made clear that he had reservations and questions about the Authority's policy and its impact on the School. In some quarters feelings and fears about the future of the School ran high, but the Rector's review of the various issues and his recognition of the Authority's effort to ensure continuity for the pupils and the sympathetic approach to special interests was carried out so diplomatically that he avoided the animosity which Morland Simpson had aroused over the Westfield School issue. He also pointed out that the new situation might even lead to where 'the general level of diligence and attainment in the School may well rise and that would be no trifling gain, provided always that it was not bought at the price of that tolerant, generous spirit which in the past has welcomed diversity of type and talent and seen its pupils as boys to be schooled and not simply examinees to be tutored'. He went on to remind the North-East 'with its admirably strenuous but somewhat narrow conception of schooling . . . that education is life and preparation for life in its entirety and not simply equipping of the young for remunerative employment'.

The transition to the era of free education was carried out smoothly and the admission of a pupil to the School at all stages depended on the new criteria of availability of places, the capacity to benefit from the education provided and the desire of the parents to enrol him.

One of the saddest occasions in Robertson's period of office was the unveiling of the Roll of Honour for those who had died in the Second World War. The Grammar FPs had made heavy sacrifices and a total of 194 lives were lost. On Friday 19 May 1950 a large gathering including the then Lord Provost, Duncan Fraser, parents and relatives of those who had given their lives, various local notables and others assembled to witness the ceremony. The actual unveiling was carried out by Lord Alness, one of the school's most eminent former pupils, who in his address remarked that little did he think in 1923 when he had unveiled a memorial to the dead of the Great War, that he would be called upon to carry out a similar role twenty-seven years later. What had been decided was that the Memorial would take the form of an extension of the Kelly-inspired memorial of 1923, which was placed on the north wall of the Hall. In addition, Alan Watt, the son of Dr Theodore Watt, as editor of the Magazine, had produced a Memorial Book including pictures and career details of those whose names appeared on the School Hall wall. Copies of this handsome work were presented to the families represented and were received with great gratitude.

An issue which was still to be resolved was that of the Primary department and the criticism that it was easier to enter the Grammar secondary from its own primary than from other primary schools. The Education Committee of the Town Council was made up of 12 Labour, 5 Progressive and 10 external members with knowledge of education when on 22 November 1957 a decision was taken on the future of the Primary Departments of both the GS and High School for Girls. The vote was tied at 12–12: with 10 Labour and 2 external against 1 Labour, 5 Progressives and 6 external. The decision to close the Primary was taken on the casting vote of the chair, Colin MacIver, who had attended the GS in 1902–3 and taught there from 1927 to 1939.

Recognising how much the Lower School contributed to the well-being of the School it is not surprising that this decision to close the Primary Departments of the High School for Girls and the Grammar raised a storm of protest from the FP Clubs of both schools and a variety of other interested bodies. Since the 1940s the separation of the early stages from the secondary and a succession of Lower School masters established what virtually had become a separate Grammar School Primary school.

The first notable Master of the Lower School had been Alfred (Freddy) J.M. Edwards, himself a former pupil (1908–21), who could recall the opening of Rubislaw Field in 1916. He had gained an MA from Aberdeen University in 1924 and a BComm in 1927. He was a fine athlete, a talented swimmer, and a county cricketer; he left in 1949 but was to remain a highly respected member of the FP community and a fund of sporting information about the Aberdeen area. He was succeeded by Duncan Annand who was in charge of both the Boarding House and the Lower School before he went abroad for several years, returning as Head of Ashley Road School, one of the Grammar's main feeder schools. Having worked as Annand's associate, Jimmy Morrison succeeded him as Head of the Lower School in 1954 and remained in that post until 1965. He was a most cheerful and efficient Head, taking great interest in the welfare and development of his charges who responded to his efforts on their behalf with great respect and affection. Along with the ladies on his staff he was fortunate to have the assistance of several young male teachers – Fergus Davidson, Harry Lawson, Sandy Farquhar and Hamish Paterson – all of whom went on to secure various promotions as the doors began to close on the Lower School. Though hardly young in years, Monty McRobert made up in a zest for life which was communicated to the boys under his charge.

The course offered to the boys fitted them well academically in most cases to play a prominent part when they joined the ranks of the Upper School. Well taught, encouraged to pursue many interests and hobbies and to embrace an active life in games and outdoor activities the Lower School boys were thoroughly imbued with the ethos of the School and proved a great influence when they were absorbed into the ranks of those who joined the School at the beginning of the Secondary course from the primary schools of the Town, the District and the Boarding House.

The matter of closure had gone to the Secretary of State who suggested that the proposal should be left in abeyance until it was clear that a change would offer reasonable assurance of its permanence. The Education Committee accepted this and the Primary Department was temporarily reprieved.

In the school log-book for 24 August 1959, there is the simple record 'Sir James J. Robertson retires today' with the Latin addition 'Vivat atque floreat Schola Grammatica Aberdoniensis' (May the Aberdeen Grammar School survive and prosper). So ended the great contribution that Sir James had made to the School and Scottish education in general and he left having been presented with gifts from FPs and parents and his portrait, painted by J.B. Souter. Unfortunately this was another victim of the fire of 1986.

Robertson should be added to our list of great Rectors mainly for his remarkable and inspirational vision spelled out in his 1947 Report for Secondary Education. He convinced educationists in the years after the Second World War that they were heirs to an actively democratic system of national education serving a society characterised by pride, democratic patriotism and freedom from class consciousness. It was Scotland's loss that his proposals for a national system of omnibus schools reconciling social and intellectual diversity through a general curriculum and liberal pedagogy were not implemented, mainly because of the Scottish Education Department's wish to retain control of the Leaving Certificate and, through the Certificate, control of the schools.

JOHN VASS SKINNER: RECTOR 1959–1972

The vacancy caused by Sir James' retiral was filled by yet another Classical scholar from Glasgow, John Vass Skinner, who assumed office at the beginning of session 1959–60. After early education in Clydebank High School he entered Glasgow University as Sir Walter Scott bursar in 1927. He had a glittering academic career, winning prizes in Roman History, Greek and Arabic before graduating with FCH in 1931. He proceeded to Jordanhill for teacher-training. After teaching Classics in several schools he became a lecturer at Jordanhill for two years after his war service, 1940 to 1945. Although he never spoke publicly about his wartime experience in the Intelligence Corps his very wide knowledge of various European languages – German, French, Italian, Spanish, Russian, Swedish, Danish, Norwegian and Arabic – had been put to great use in a career which had involved both secrecy and adventure. In 1949 he became Rector of Alloa Academy and stayed there, in a school which included both primary and secondary pupils, until he was offered the Grammar post.

At a dinner given by the FP Club to welcome him to Aberdeen, the Club President, George Barton, expressed the curiosity and apprehension which was felt about who would be asked to follow Sir James. However, considering his scholarship and experience the feeling was that someone well-suited for the task had emerged – and so it was to prove. Skinner acknowledged that there might be difficult times ahead but was reassured by the certainty of support from the FPs. In a quotation from the Alloa Academy Magazine the point was made: 'Our loss may be Aberdeen's gain but this does not console us . . . His greatest success would be to make Aberdeen Grammar School as pleasant a place to work in as Alloa Academy has been for the past decade'. He did!

Skinner took over the School at a time when the desire for change in education was still strong. As the roll grew and wider prospects of advancement elsewhere appeared, the days of staff spending whole careers in one school were numbered. The School log-book relates long lists of staff changes, arrivals and departures, retirements and temporary placements affecting every department. One interesting innovation was the appointment of a specialist teacher of Religious Education. Hitherto religious provision was probably most actively carried out in the morning assembly with curricular contribution being carried out none too enthusiastically by ordinary members of staff. It is interesting to note that the prospectus first noted Eric Duncan's appointment under the heading 'Religious Instruction' but this was quickly replaced with the less controversial 'Religious Education'.

In 1962 the Education Committtee returned to the issue of the Primary School and agreed by 15–7 to terminate the Department at the end of session 1970–1. (11 Labour and 4 external were opposed by 4 Progressives and 3 external members.) Despite meetings and resolutions, on 1 November 1963, the Secretary of State agreed to the proposal as the loss of the Primary did not prejudice the fulfilment by the Education Committee of its statutory duty to provide adequate and efficient primary and secondary education for the area.

He also rejected the suggestion of a Public Inquiry as all views were known. So eventually the long-drawn out elimination of the Lower School began in 1965 and by simply having no intake in early stage provision the process was complete by 1971 and it was noted in the 1971–2 Prospectus laconically that 'By the start of the session 1971–2 the last classes from the Lower School will have passed into the Senior School and the Lower School will have ceased to exist.' The staff had retired or dispersed to other posts with Jimmy Morrison going off as Head Teacher to Walker Road School and his short-term successor, Jimmy Niddrie, going to Westerton School.

A notable change in the cover of the Prospectus for 1970–1 was the new name of the School, Rubislaw Academy (Aberdeen Grammar School). This change resulted from the decision of the Education Committee to introduce comprehensive education throughout the city. The existing junior secondary schools were raised in status to academies and much speculation arose as to what would happen to the existing senior secondary schools. They had to accept renaming on a territorial basis and before the final choice was made Dr Norman Walker, from the Committee, met with the Rector, his Deputy and the Principal History master to consider what preferred name should be suggested to the Authority. After poring over various maps it was felt that the district along with the name of the playing fields justified the suggestion of 'Rubislaw'. This was accepted and along with that was linked the traditional name which produced the clumsy but useful reminder of the School's roots. A promise was made at a Prize-Giving that a final decision on the name would be made when the last boy who had entered the GS left. This did not occur until 1977 when by then Skinner had retired and a reorganisation of local government (in 1975) had led to a different political and educational situation.

In addition to these challenges Skinner was also faced with the decision made by the Committee to undertake a major building programme. The proposals involved two significant changes: the extension of the School buildings and radical alterations to the interior of the School. In the magazine for June 1961 there was a useful map which showed how extensive the new buildings were. A new Hall was built on the north side of the site and this linked up with the new Dining Hall and kitchen to the east and the new Technical Department to the west. The biggest development was the creation of a three-storey block for Mathematics and Science, which was built in a very simple style more functional than the original Scottish Baronial pile with its extensions.

In some ways the greatest difficulty rose from all the internal modifications which had to be introduced into the older buildings. New corridors provided better access, old Science laboratories were converted into classrooms and a new Staffroom, while the old staffroom became a Language Lab. As the Primary was run down its classrooms were immediately taken over by Secondary classes, mostly Language rooms though Geography came to share what was called the Language Block until recently. The old Chalmers School, which had served as a school dining room and later the old technical classrooms, was eventually transformed into the Total French School in 1974 when the oil industry brought many foreign nationalities to Aberdeen.

The old school Hall, which Simpson had transformed into what he referred to as the school Valhalla, which was devoted to the purpose of reminding the pupils of the School's long history, underwent a major adaptation to modern requirements. The Library was repositioned in the Hall following Charles Hemingway's ('The Bush') suggestion that the floor should be raised to take advantage of the hitherto remote high windows at the front of the original building with a further two side galleries to allow the use of most of the wall space. The area underneath was used for two tiered areas for lectures and visual aids projection.

All this took time to build and for many months the School shared its site with workmen, but the dislocation had a positive result. In 1963 the long-awaited Swimming Pool was officially opened on 23 October by Lt Col. H.J. Butchart, a distinguished FP who was Secretary of Aberdeen University. That evening there took place in the old school Hall a dinner for FPs and guests, chaired by Dr Douglas Simpson, the son of Morland Simpson, and addressed by Sir James Robertson with his customary eloquence. He offered a survey of the School's history since 1863 reminding the company that this was the centenary of the move from Schoolhill to its present location. It was a reassuring view, based on his sure belief that the uncertainties of the time, e.g. the closure of the primary department, would be met and coped with.

In the Magazine for December 1966, Rector Skinner gave a 'state of the School' message in which he offered a 'good news, bad news' view of affairs. The 'good news' was the final completion of the building programme and the internal renovations which had lasted for five or six years and had been formally opened by Princess Alexandra on the first Royal Visit in its history on Wednesday 2 December 1964 (although the Duke of York had represented Gordonstoun School on the rugby field at Rubislaw during his schooldays!). Due notice was taken of the School's continued successes, academic and on the games field, but Skinner, like his predecessor Sir James, expressed reservations not about the policy of comprehensive education, but about how it was to be implemented locally.

The future of the Grammar and the High was not only to be comprehensive but also co-educational! With his experience of both single sex and co-educational schools Skinner had no strong views in general but recognised that the policy of comprehensive education raised a variety of issues. There was a serious debate about whether the system adopted should be 'one tier' or 'two tier'.[1] After consideration the 'one tier' was chosen and ten academies were to be set up. Each Academy would draw its pupils from the area round it and Skinner pointed out that this raised difficulties with the argument that the policy would break down social barriers and that it might in fact reinforce them unless very careful thought was given to zoning.

At first the zoning was to be done on a geographical basis and this involved lines being drawn down the middle of Union Grove with one side going to the Grammar and the other to Harlaw (High School). It was later decided to base the catchment areas on schools. Originally only parts of Mile-end and Ashley were to be assigned to the Grammar along with Skene Street, Skene Square and Causewayend. However, it proved simpler to base the intake on complete school populations of Mile-end, Ashley, Skene Street and Skene Square.

One outstanding problem in assigning pupils in the west end of the town was St Joseph's School at Queen's Cross which provided education for Roman Catholic pupils. Actually the question of Catholic education at the secondary level was a serious problem. The Convent School at Queen's Cross was about to close its secondary department and provision had to be made for all the Catholic secondary pupils. The establishment of a separate Catholic secondary was reckoned to be impractical because there were not enough Catholic pupils in Aberdeen to create a viable academy. This was the result of the historical migrations of the mid-nineteenth century when there had not been the industrial opportunities to attract large numbers of Catholic families to the North-East of Scotland. The issue was settled to the satisfaction of the Catholic Church authorities by an arrangement whereby Catholic provision was to be provided in three secondary schools with a suitably qualified and approved member of staff teaching RE to Catholic pupils separately from the rest of their form class. The Grammar was one of the designated schools and the school policy was simply to distribute RC pupils throughout the classes of their year; the occasional students from the College of Education with a central Scotland background were astonished by the completely non-sectarian ethos in the School.

For a short time the introduction of co-education had to be delayed while the School had to make its accommodation suitable for both sexes. This resulted in all the boys who would have gone to Harlaw having to be drafted into the Grammar for two years where they completed their secondary education. The first girls to become Grammar School pupils entered the school in 1973 and were quickly absorbed into the school community where they made substantial contributions to its academic, cultural and games traditions.

In its comprehensive situation staff now had wider opportunities for personal advancement through promotion to senior posts in the other city academies and beyond and the old practice of spending long periods of one's career in the Grammar became less common, but at the same time a wider range of promoted posts on the administrative side of school life was an inducement to stay. One of the most important sides of education to be developed in the 1970s was that of pastoral care and this led to the introduction of 'guidance' teachers or year staff who enjoyed equal status with the departmental principals of subjects on the academic side.

In another direction, literally, Rosemount School was not converted into an Academy but was added to the Grammar as a very considerable annexe where accommodation for Home Economics, Mathematics, Commercial, Technical, Art, RE and PE became immediately available for the growing roll of pupils. While this accommodation seemed just a stone's throw from the main School area it did involve a considerable movement of pupils between the two sites and the residents of Grosvenor Place had to endure the passage of hundreds of pupils up and down several times a day for many years with surprisingly little friction.

By the time much of this activity was underway, John Vass Skinner had decided to retire as 'the last Rector of the Grammar School' though that remark proved to be a little premature as events turned out. All the academies in Aberdeen were to have a Headmaster or Head Teacher and when Skinner retired he was to be followed by the former not a Rector.

It is difficult to do justice to how much John Skinner did for the School during his twelve years in charge. For a teacher joining the staff from a different authority it did seem like entering a haven of calm and relaxation. The Rector had managed to develop a School which very much reflected his own character. While the whole educational scene in local authority's control was going through what seemed to be drastic changes, many of which affected the Grammar deeply, there was very much an attitude of "don't panic!" which was conveyed by the Rector's quiet, humorous outlook on life.

Like his predecessor, Skinner was a notable scholar whose talents were widely recognised. As an experienced timetabler he ensured that the School ran smoothly. Any requests for help in developing departmental initiatives in curriculum or staffing could depend upon a sympathetic ear and practical support and in this it must be recorded that the Director of Education, J.R. Clark, and the Authority gave generous support. Skinner believed that teachers as professional people should be treated professionally and this led to cordial relations with his staff. His quiet, friendly personality made his contacts with pupils very easy to manage and he won their respect and affection. His shrewdness in judgment of character meant that he was from time to time called away to sit on the Boards selecting recruits for army, navy and air-force at various establishments.

The school log-book for the period records the practice of Skinner to call together the parents of groups of pupils to explain procedures which affected them. This meant that in a sense the School opened its doors more widely than had previously been the custom and this enlisted the understanding and support of a very important part of the school community, the parents. In addition, the close relationship with the FP Club was maintained and this was welcome support in difficult times.

Certainly one of the most unusual situations in modern times that the Aberdeen community had to face in June 1964 was the outbreak of typhoid. Its origin was in the west end of the city but the whole city had to face a serious epidemic with large gatherings discouraged and isolation imposed by the outside world. Schools were closed to the pupils and efforts were made to provide work for home. But with the term drawing to a close and examinations over, it could have come at a worse time. Nevertheless, one member of staff and two pupils from the Lower school and two pupils from the Senior school fell victims. Fortunately all recovered completely. Gradually the restrictions were relaxed but senior pupils only came to school half-time after 16 June and the Lower School only returned for the forenoons on the 25 June. Apart from the Prize-Givings held in early July all other school activities were cancelled from the beginning of June until 3 July. When the School reopened after the summer vacation on 24 August normal schooling was resumed.

In 1972, when he retired, Skinner could look back on a successful period of office having guided the School through the restless years in Scottish education at both a national and local level. He left a School whose academic standards had been upheld; which offered a wide range of extra-curricular activities and which maintained its high reputation on the Games field. When he was presented with his portrait on Friday 22 June 1973 warm tributes were paid to him by the President of the FP Club, George Barton.

The FP Club had continued its loyal support of the School but it found itself facing the problem of deciding where its future lay. Were those pupils who had entered Rubislaw Academy to be accepted as Club members? Some members expressed the opinion that, since the change of name, the Grammar School was now dead and the Club should be allowed to decline and die also. The prospect of the School becoming co-educational also filled some with a sense of horror raising the question of whether female former pupils might be admitted. It was also necessary for the Club to come to an arrangement with the Education Committee about the future administration of Rubislaw field when the Club, like many similar bodies throughout Scotland, became "open" and accepted membership of those who had no direct connection with the School. In the long run no problems arose about membership and the Club in its imposing Club Centre on Queen's Road continued its happy relationship with the School.

STAFFING

With the coming of the War in 1939 once again the Central School was commandeered and the Grammar School and the Central had to resume the situation of 1914–18, sharing the accommodation in Skene Street West. As air-raid shelters were hastily prepared and the ARP regulations were imposed in the School and at Rubislaw, the School settled down to six years of disturbed existence. Eventually nine members of staff were listed in the Prospectus as being absent on military service. This, understandably, led to the employment of temporary staff, male and female, to fill the gaps. Even so it sometimes proved very difficult to follow a regular timetable and reports were made of classes having four or five different teachers during one session.

Regular staff members left at home took a very active part in School extra-curricular commitments. Freddy Edwards, the master in charge of the Lower School, assumed the role of Games master in the absence of Duncan McGregor on war service and occupied the position for most of the war. Although the School was not really a 'military' school by tradition, it was not long before a squadron of the Air Training Corps and a company of the Army Cadet Force were established. The task of providing officers for these organisations was taken up by the staff and John Lynch first commanded the ATC and Bill Stewart took command of the army unit. Both bodies recruited healthy numbers of boys – 120 for the ACF and 140 for the ATC at their peak. Ronald McAndrew later took over the ATC while the army cadets were led by James Eddison, Ian Park and Bob Wilson. Two of the early visitors to inspect the units were W.W. Wakefield, the famous English rugby internationalist and C.M. Usher, the Scottish rugby cap. The involvement in these activities during the Second World War must have imposed a considerable strain on everyone and the Rector noted with regret the death of Bill Stewart who had, in addition to the classroom and cadets, been an important rugby coach in the Upper School. He had also been assistant Housemaster at the Boarding House, a post filled comfortably by a succession of junior staff from the School.

When one considers what sort of an education was offered at the Grammar during the War what strikes one is how normal the scope was despite the abnormal conditions. The main clubs still functioned, Games carried on and inter-school matches were quickly resumed though travel restrictions and conditions caused problems. Hockey emerged as an additional choice beside rugby, and cricket followed its summer season. The alternating pattern of school attendance meant that Games practice had to take place sometimes in the morning and sometimes in the afternoon until the Central School returned to its home at Belmont Street in April 1944.

In his magazine articles J.J. Robertson had warned his readers that the post-war education scene would be subject to many changes and the destiny of the Grammar was uncertain. One of the more immediate problems was the need to welcome back the various members of staff from the forces. The structure of the school staff also witnessed important changes with the introduction of the new deputy rector post. One notable resignation was that of Duncan McGregor who decided after the War to resign as Games master. A man of similar mould was chosen to succeed him, J.C. Hunter, who was soon joined on the PE staff by his brother, E. Hunter, Dallas Allardyce and Fordyce Paterson, all of whom turned out regularly for the FP rugby club.

The period after the War witnessed a large turnover of staff. In 1945 Ron McLeod joined the Classics department and began a long career in the School, closely linked with the Cadets, and eventually becoming head of a department which recruited over the years a large proportion of Gordonians. Soon after in 1947 a new Principal Teacher of Geography was appointed to replace William Hendry. Bob McNay arrived from Lanarkshire, an enthusiastic Motherwell fan who took up the sport of hockey and was responsible in his forthright way for producing a continuous flow of very successful teams and players. In Geography he joined Mary Matheson, for years the only female member of the secondary staff. James Walker, promoted to Principal History master, was joined by Clem Bell in 1947. The following year Ian Stephen arrived in the Mathematics Department: he was another example of one who was to spend his whole very active and diverse career at the School.[2] The same year saw the appointment of Nan Boyd as Librarian. She made a notable contribution to School life over many years. Another lady who came at this time was Betty Gibb who was to preside over the School office and also acted as Rector's secretary. The increasingly important subject of Commercial was led by Jack Lawson.

No doubt the reputation that the School enjoyed made it a convenient base from which to seek promotion and a steady stream of masters sought pastures new. The English department proved to be an especially successful recruiting ground, as Forbes, Russell, Brown and Tom McRea all moved on. While Principal Teachers departed for other posts, in a department of such central importance in the School it must be remembered that many very able people had been appointed as their assistants. While some filled the posts that new internal prospects offered like James Tinto and Marion Smith, others opted to follow careers usually in promoted posts elsewhere, like Bruce Finlayson, Ronald Caie and Bob McIntyre. At least two, Alex Nisbet and Quentin Cramb, joined the Inspectorate and Kenneth Henderson and David Northcroft pursued careers at the College of Education.

Albert Johnstone left the Maths Department and shortly after in 1950 was replaced by John Flett, who became a most successful and awe-inspiring teacher of Mathematics under Alec Gray and later Archie Baxter. In later years he took on the additional responsibility of Guidance teacher until his retirement in 1980.

With Henry Paterson's retirement in 1951 John Lynch was promoted but, like his predecessor, he retained his departmental responsibility until eventually the Science and Mathematics posts were separated in 1960. As staff came and went, the Log-book for the 1940s and 1950s records the many absences of staff for illness and other reasons and also notes the high number of temporary staff who were employed in the running of the School. The many times the Rector was away from School suggests that the Deputy Rectorship was no honorary post.

In 1953 a new member of the Modern Languages department took up his post. James Michie served for only a short period before seeking wider fields for his energies and was to return as the Director of Education for Grampian Region. On a more modest level, Norman King joined the staff and after general service settled as a Special Assistant in the History department. Beside his classroom work he played a large part in the dramatic activities of the School, supervising and producing notable stage productions, both modern and Shakespearean. A Liberal in politics he stood as a candidate in General Elections before setting out to try his fortunes in Canada.

The Inspectorate claimed the services of the Head of Modern Languages William Cunningham, in 1954, and he was replaced by Harry Davidson, a most pleasant and acceptable colleague in the classroom and staff room. Soon after another of the long-established departmental heads (Alec Gray) handed over to Archie Baxter and the Department continued to produce able Mathematicians who performed well in the Bursary Competition, which was still recognised as an important indicator of a school's educational status. General results in the Leaving Certificate were also impressive. Andrew Milne in Classics retired in 1955 and was succeeded by Robin Brown. One of the successes of the expanding curriculum had been the introduction of Spanish and much of this was due to Dr Ronald McAndrew, who had followed Charles Davidson. He joined the list of long-serving masters when he retired in 1956 after thirty-five years' service. Spanish was taken over by Douglas McClean.

Young blood was brought in either to replace or expand various areas. Jim Will, Dycie Paterson, Donald Hawksworth (who went on to teach Music at the GS from 1956 until 1973) and Ian Galloway all came into this category. Some were promoted like Bill Williams, who became Head of the Biology department.

J.C. Hunter left to become adviser in PE for the City and was followed by Andrew Stevenson who brought to the job the unusual qualification of a degree in Law. He was later to teach in the Training Centre, become a town councillor and close his career by becoming a Church of Scotland minister in Fife. In the same year – 1957 – Alex Tait took over the English Department and he stayed until the end of his career, when yet another Gordonian appeared to assume charge, Bill Hall, a colourful character who entered into the life of the School in many capacities.

When an assistant teacher joined the staff, if he was professionally ambitious, he faced the dilemma of whether to wait in the hope of moving into the top post in his department or to move elsewhere. After all, the structure of every department was simple: a principal teacher and 'the rest'. Beneath the Rector only a Deputy held office and until 1962 he retained his departmental responsibilities, so the internal prospects of promotion were very limited. In some cases, notably PE, opportunities for promotion outside one's subject area hardly existed at all, and to gain promotion one was forced to move.

In the 1960s this rather grim picture was brightened up by the introduction nationally of a more varied departmental structure and a widening of promotion prospects beyond the departmental level. Departments were able to reward loyal staff with Special Assistantships and these were later extended to allow for Principal Assistantships in larger departments. Later still in the 1970s after Robin Brown and Bob McNay[3] had held the post of Deputy Rector and had left to become Head Teachers at Grangemouth and Dumfries respectively, their successor, Archie Baxter, was joined in 1973 by a Second Deputy. This duplication was the result of the Education Committee policy to have two deputy heads, male and female, in Academies after the introduction of comprehensive education but in the case of the all-male Rubislaw Academy this led to the appointment of a second male Deputy. This allowed the School to give control to the latter of the Rosemount Annexe, until Archie Baxter retired in 1976 and the School reverted to a single Deputy.

Just as important for the internal promotion prospects was the introduction of Assistant Head Teachers with special areas of responsibility, one of whom, Jean Downie, took charge of the girls who first entered the School in 1973.

PUPILS ATTENDING THE SCHOOL BETWEEN 1942 AND 1972

Scotland has witnessed, in recent years, the transformation from a society of manual work to one of administrators and professionals. In 1921 some 74% of people were in manual work, while today the figure is down to 33%. However, although there has been a great deal of absolute mobility, rates of relative mobility have not changed very much. This suggests that if you come from a higher social class then you are liable to remain there. The following profiles bear this out and also show the diversity of careers available. It seems that even when middle-class children do not achieve the highest educational qualifications they have other forms of cultural capital or networks available to them to maintain their social position.

Merchants and Manufacturers (Businessmen)

John W. Cradock (1929–2010) attended the Grammar between 1940 and 1946 and became Chief Executive of Richard Irvin & Sons (founded by his great-grandfather in 1871). He was chair of the Harbour Board, 1985–94. By the time of his retirement in 1994 he held executive positions in eleven companies. He was president of the FP Club, 1977–8.

(Sir) Denys H. Henderson (b. 1932) attended the Grammar between 1938 and 1950 and graduated in Arts and Law at Aberdeen University in 1953 and 1955 respectively. He joined ICI as a solicitor in 1957. He chaired the University of Aberdeen Quincentenary Appeal Committee, 1993–6. He was chair of ICI, 1987–95 (the youngest chair in its history), chair of Zeneca Group, 1993–5, chair of Rank Group, 1995–2001, and was the First Crown Estate Commissioner, 1995–2002.

Roy H. Thomson (1932–2009) attended the Grammar between 1941 and 1950, graduating in Psychology from Aberdeen University in 1955. For a considerable time he ran the garage business founded by his grandfather. He was elected to Aberdeen City Council as a Liberal in 1974 (later becoming the Council leader). He spent fourteen years on the Council. He was chair and President of the Liberal Democrats in Scotland. He was a founding member of the Aberdeen Mountain Rescue Association and chair of Mental Health Aberdeen. He was much involved with the development of the Aberdeen International Youth Festival. He was appointed a DL of the City of Aberdeen in 2005.

Ronald R. Comber (b. 1934) attended the Grammar between 1947 and 1952. His career was in the building trade and latterly in the Licensed trade. He gained a Final Trial in rugby for Scotland. He organised (with Douglas Georgeson) a Golden Oldies' rugby team in the 1960s, which developed into Aberdeen Strollers and for some years it was the only Scottish team participating in the World and European Rugby Festivals.

Andrew S. Noble (1934–2000) attended the Grammar between 1939 and 1952, becoming Senior Prefect and Dux, as well as captain of rugby and cricket. He went to St Andrews on a scholarship and gained FCH in Mathematics and Applied Mathematics in 1956 and was also President of the Students' Union. He went on to St John's, Cambridge for further study. He worked for ICI from 1959 to 1973 and was Managing Director of Debenhams, 1979–86. He was President of the FP Club, 1986–7.

Charles P. Skene (b. 1935) attended the Grammar between 1940 and 1947 before going on to Loretto. A successful businessman he has been a governor of RGIT, chairman of Aberdeen Chamber of Commerce, industrial consultant to the Scottish Education/Industry Committee and a visiting professor of entrepreneurial studies at RGU.

(Dr) David V.S. Williamson (b. 1936) attended the Grammar between

1948 and 1954, being joint Dux in 1954 and First Bursar in the Aberdeen Bursary Competition. After further study at Leeds University he joined Du Pont International in Geneva in 1963. He retired in 1993 from his position as President of Du Pont Europe.

D. Euan Baird (b. 1937) attended the Grammar between 1942 and 1954, graduating from Aberdeen University and Trinity College, Cambridge, where he gained a PhD in Geophysics in 1960. He then joined the global technology services company of Schlumberger Ltd, serving as Chief Executive and Chairman from 1986 until 2003 (the first non-Frenchman to hold those posts). He has been a Trustee of the Carnegie Institute of Washing-ton DC since 1997.

Maitland Mackie (b. 1937) attended the Grammar between 1946 and 1954 and is a farmer, chair of Mackie's Dairy and director, Farmdata. He is a member of the Court of Aberdeen University and an honorary professor at RGU. He is a former chairman of the Scottish Agricultural College, vice-president of the NFU of Scotland, and former director of the Rowett Research Institute and Lloyds TSB Scotland.[4] He became Rector of Aberdeen University in 2011.

(Prof.) David J. Murray-Smith (b. 1941) attended the Grammar between 1947 and 1959 and then Aberdeen and Glasgow Universities. He worked in Ferranti Ltd before lecturing, from 1965, in Electrical Engineering at Glasgow. He held various posts before holding the personal chair of Electronics and Electrical Engineering at Glasgow between 1985 and 2005. He was Dean of the Engineering Faculty, 1997–2001. He is past chairman of the UK Simulation Council.

(Edward) Michael Walker (b. 1941) attended the Grammar between 1956 and 1959. He became President of the Edinburgh and District Master Builders Association, 1987 – 1996, and the Scottish House Builders' Association. He was Dean of Guild for Edinburgh, 1992–6. Most recently he was chair of Walker Group (Scotland) Ltd, Westerwood Ltd, and Lothian and Edinburgh Ltd.

George K. Yule (b. 1951) attended the Grammar between 1963 and 1967 and trained as a mechanical engineer before a brief spell as a professional footballer with Bury FC. He was employed in the offshore gas and oil industry, latterly for twenty years with Shell UK. With colleagues he then launched Clean Ocean Ltd seeking to provide environmental solutions to the problems of ocean pollution worldwide.

Iain G. Gray (b. 1957) attended the Grammar between 1969 and 1975, graduating in Engineering Science from Aberdeen University in 1979. He did further study at Southampton University. He joined British Aerospace in 1979. He became Managing Director and General Manager of Airbus UK in 2004 and three years later he was appointed chief executive of the Technology Strategy Board. He is a fellow of the Royal Aeronautical Society.

Churchmen

Gordon S. Cowie (1933–2006) attended the Grammar between 1937 and 1949 and 1950–1, when he was Gold Medallist. He graduated from Aberdeen University in Politics, History and Law. He lectured in Law at St Andrews and was admitted to the Faculty of Advocates in 1962. He was appointed the first Professor of Public Law at Glasgow University but took early retirement in 1983 and qualified for the ministry. In 1986 he was ordained into the Moray charges of Birnie and Pluscarden.

(Prof.) I. Howard Marshall (b. 1934) attended the Grammar between 1946 and 1951, being Dux of the school. He went on to Aberdeen University, Cambridge and Göttingen Universities graduating MA, BD and PhD. He tutored at Bristol then was a Methodist minister in Darlington. He was lecturer, senior lecturer, reader, before being, between 1979 and 1999, Professor of New Testament Exegesis, all at Aberdeen University. He has written numerous publications.

(Very Rev. Dr) David W. Lacy (b. 1952) attended the Grammar between 1963 and 1965, the HSOG, and the Universities of Strathclyde, Glasgow and Trinity College. After parish posts in Edinburgh and Glasgow he was appointed minister of Henderson Parish Church, Kilmarnock, in 1989. He was Moderator of the General Assembly of the Church of Scotland, 2005–6.

(Rev.) Colin G.F. Brockie (b. 1942) was educated at Musselburgh GS and the Grammar between 1955 and 1960 before going on to Aberdeen University. He was parish minister of St Martin's, in Edinburgh, 1968–78 and Grange in Kilmarnock, 1978–2007. He was appointed Clerk to the Presbytery of Irvine and Kilmarnock in 1992.

Military

(Col.) Albert (Jack) Paterson (1930–2012) attended the Grammar between 1935 and 1947. After taking an MA at Aberdeen University he served a law apprenticeship with Paull and Williamsons. In 1956 he joined the Directorate of the Army Legal Service and served in Britain, Europe, the Middle and Far East, advising on which cases should proceed to courts martial. Following a thirty year distinguished military career he retired to manage an estate in Moray.

(Air Vice-Marshal) William M. Rae (b. 1940) attended the Grammar between 1946 and 1953 before joining the RAF in 1958. Ultimately, in 1996, he became Director, United Services Trustees.

(Wing Commander) Graeme W. Fraser (b. 1944) attended the Grammar between 1956 and 1962 and took a degree in Geography from Aberdeen University. He joined the RAF as an Education Officer and on retirement made a second career in banking. A talented rugby player he played for the FPs and London Scottish.

(Commander) Hugh S. Clark (1946–2010) attended the Grammar between 1951 and 1965 and gained a Scholarship to Britannia Royal Naval College, Dartmouth. He trained as a flying instructor and his naval air squadron supported the RM in the Falklands conflict. He won the DSC for his gallant and distinguished service. Following instructor posts he became Naval and Air Attache at the British Embassy in Muscat, Oman.

Medical

(Dr) Edward R.H. Tennant (1928–2006) attended the Grammar between 1945 and 1946, graduating in Medicine from Aberdeen University in 1951. He spent time in India when in the RAMC. He was MOH in Inverness and senior medical officer to Esso Standard in Libya. He joined the Diplomatic Service, becoming Medical Officer to the High Commission in Delhi and later the British Embassy in Poland.

(Dr) Alexander (Sandy) Lawrence (1929–1993) attended Grammar from 1940 to 1946 and was Senior Prefect, captain of rugby and cricket and winner of the All Round Trophy. A Medical graduate of Aberdeen University, he spent over thirty years as a general practitioner in Buckie. While a student he played cricket for Aberdeenshire for three seasons in the Scottish Counties Championship.

(Dr) Alexander Addison (b. 1930) attended the Grammar in 1947–8 and went on to qualify in Medicine at Aberdeen University. He was senior partner in a medical firm, 1978–95; chairman, Lanarkshire LMC, 1989–95; member of the Scottish Committee of the BMA since 1984, and Fellow of the BMA since 1993; and medical officer and anti-drugs officer, RCCC, 1996–2000.

(Prof.) Derek Ogston (b. 1932) attended the Grammar between 1937 and 1939, and 1946–7, and Aberdeen and Edinburgh Universities. After lecturing in Aberdeen from 1962 in medicine he was appointed Professor of Physiology (1977–83), Dean of the Faculty of Medicine (1984–7), and Vice-Principal (1987–97). He was vice-chair of Grampian Health Board (1993–7) and a member of the University Court (1998–2002). He has written extensively and established prizes at Aberdeen University for the History of Art and for Music.

(Dr) Michael James Williams (b. 1931) attended Grammar from 1936 to 1945 and graduated in Medicine from Aberdeen University. He lectured in therapeutics before becoming a consultant physician in 1968. From 1983 he was consultant in charge of the Diabetic Clinic in Aberdeen. He published a widely acclaimed biography of Professor J.J.R. Macleod, the Nobel-winning co-discoverer of Insulin. He was co-author of a book on the treatment of epidemic diseases in Aberdeen and the history of the City Hospital, one of the first in Scotland to be devoted to sufferers from contagious diseases.

(Prof.) David T. Baird (b. 1935) attended Grammar between 1940 and 1952 then was educated at Aberdeen, Trinity College, Cambridge and Edinburgh Universities. He completed his clinical training in endocrinology and obstetrics and, between 1977 and 1985, was Professor of Obstetrics and Gynaecology at Edinburgh. From 1985 to 2000 he was Medical Research Council Professor of Reproductive Endocrinology also at Edinburgh. He has produced a number of publications and served on national and international committees.

(Dr) Martin M. Lees (b. 1935) was schooled at the Grammar between 1947 and 1952 and qualified in Medicine at Aberdeen University. He became consultant Obstetrician and Gynaecologist at the Royal Infirmary in Edinburgh and senior lecturer and director of studies at Edinburgh University. He was chairman of the senior fellows of the RCPE.

(Dr) Donald G. Jamieson (1936–2010) attended the Grammar between 1944 and 1952. He graduated from Aberdeen University with honours in Medicine in 1958. He became a consultant Neurologist in Birmingham and gained a reputation as a first-class clinician.

(Prof.) John G.R. Howie (b. 1937) attended the Grammar between 1944 and 1951 when he moved to Glasgow High School. He qualified MB ChB and MD from Glasgow University in 1961 and 1966 respectively. After GP work he was a lecturer/senior lecturer in General Practice at Aberdeen University, 1970–80. From 1980 to 2000 he was Professor of General Practice at Edinburgh University.

(Prof.) Michael G. Walker (b. 1939) attended the Grammar between

1946 and 1957 and was a leading member of FP Rugby for a number of seasons. He spent his career as a general/vascular surgeon in Manchester Royal Infirmary.

(Dr) David B. Galloway (b. 1940) attended the Grammar between 1944 and 1958 and became a lecturer at Aberdeen University in 1972. He was with Beechams and Roche before working in the Napp Research Centre Cambridge as Director of Clinical Pharmacology. Returning to Aberdeen as a senior lecturer he has been Director of the Medicines Assessment Research Unit at the Aberdeen Royal Infirmary, Chairman of the medical research charity Tenovus (Scotland) Grampian and President of the Aberdeen Medico-Chirurgical Society (2010).

(Dr) George G. Shirriffs (b. 1940) attended Grammar between 1947 and 1957 and went on to study Medicine at Aberdeen University. He was in general practice in Aberdeen but became involved in medical teaching in the 1970s and was an Associate Regional Adviser for several years. He obtained a Master's degree in Education in 1989 after which he sat on many national education committees as a representative of the Royal College of General Practitioners. He was awarded the President's Medal of the College in 2001.

(Dr) G. Gordon Milne (b. 1943) attended the Grammar between 1950 and 1961, being rugby captain at School. He graduated in Medicine from Aberdeen University in 1968 and was a GP in Elgin, 1973–99. He was President of the FP Club, 2005–6.

(Dr) Douglas G. Fowlie (b. 1946) attended Grammar between 1950 and 1964, being senior prefect, captain of rugby, cricket and athletics and winner of the All Round Trophy. Awarded a flying scholarship by the RAF, he studied Medicine at Aberdeen University and on graduation joined the RAF, specialising in psychiatry and becoming a consultant in neuropsychiatry. He retired from service in 1983 and became a consultant psychiatrist with the NHS with a special interest in community psychiatry. He was chairman of the FP Club Executive in 1994–96 and President of the Club in 2002–3.

(Prof.) (Alexander) Allan Templeton (b. 1946) attended the Grammar between 1953 and 1963, and Aberdeen University, where he qualified in Medicine in 1969. He was lecturer and senior lecturer at Edinburgh before being appointed Professor and Head of the Department of Obstetrics and Gynaecology of Aberdeen University, a post he held from 1985 until 2007. He was the President of the RCOG, 2004–7. He published a number of works.

(Dr) Murdoch J. Shirreffs (b. 1947) was educated at the Grammar between 1951 and 1964 and Aberdeen University. Since 1974 he has been a

GP in Aberdeen. He specialised in medical hypnotherapy and homoeopathy and took charge of the NHS Grampian Homoeopathy Service. Between 1977 and 1999 he was a GP Trainer. He is a member of the Scottish Veterans' (over 60s) Hockey Team.

(Dr) David S. Carroll (b. 1951) attended the Grammar between 1956 and 1969 and became a GP in Banchory. He went freelance on a range of medical activities – writing, teaching and hospital work. His main interest is in cancer with a clinical commitment to Roxburghe House and a long association with Cancer Relief Macmillan.

(Dr) John L. Duncan (b. 1953) attended the Grammar between 1958 and 1971 and then began a distinguished career in Medicine. He spent a number of years in Sheffield before becoming consultant General Surgeon at Raigmore Hospital, Inverness.

Legal

T. Gordon Coutts (b. 1933) attended the Grammar between 1938 and 1949 and 1950–1. He followed his MA LLB at Aberdeen University by becoming an Advocate in 1959. He worked on various Tribunals and was appointed a QC in 1973 and a Barrister at Lincoln's Inn in 1994. He was a temporary Judge of the Court of Session, 1991–2004 and a Special Commissioner, Income Tax, 1996–2004.[5] He was President of the FP Club, 1980–1.

Alexander E. McIlwain (1933–2008) attended the Grammar between 1945 and 1951, graduating in Arts and Law from Aberdeen University in 1954 and 1956 respectively. He was Hamilton burgh and district prosecutor and became an honorary Sheriff for Strathclyde, Dumfries and Galloway. He was President of the Law Society in 1983, the third FP to hold this office in five years. He was President of the FP Club, 2003–4.

(Rt Hon.) Lord Marnoch (Michael S.R. Bruce) (b. 1938) attended the Grammar between 1943 and 1949, going on to Loretto and Aberdeen University, graduating with MA LLB. He was called to the Scottish Bar in 1963 and took Silk in 1975, serving as Advocate-Depute in the High Court in 1983–6. He was a senator of the College of Justice in Scotland, 1990–2005.

Ian Michael S. Park (b. 1938) attended the Grammar between 1942 and 1955 and then Aberdeen University. He was a partner in Paull & Williamsons, advocates in Aberdeen, from 1961 to 1991. He was President of the Law Society of Scotland, 1980–1 and a temporary Sheriff, 1976–84. He was a member of the Criminal Injuries Compensation Board, 1983–2000, and the Criminal Injuries Compensation Appeals Panel, 1996–2002.

Rae C. Barton (1939–2001) attended Grammar between 1942 and 1955 and went to Aberdeen University where he graduated in Arts in 1958 and in Law (with commendation) in 1960. He was in practice as a solicitor in Aberdeen and later in Aboyne before merging his business with another firm and becoming a consultant in 1992. He was then for a few years secretary of the Aberdeen & Northern Marts Group at Inverurie. He was General Editor of the FP Club Magazine for five years from 1963.

(Prof.) Philip N. Love (b. 1939) attended the Grammar between 1952 and 1958 and Aberdeen University, becoming a solicitor and advocate in Aberdeen in 1963. He was Professor of Conveyancing and Professional Practice of Law at Aberdeen, 1974–92. He was President of the Law Society of Scotland, 1981–2; vice-principal of Aberdeen University, 1986-90 and president of the FP Club, 1987-8. He was honorary sheriff of Grampian, Highland and the Islands from 1978, and vice-chancellor of Liverpool University, 1992–2002.

Melville F. Watson (1939–2002) attended the Grammar between 1943 and 1956, graduating in Arts in 1959 and Law in 1961 from Aberdeen University. He became a partner in a legal firm in 1964. He was chair of Social Security Appeal Tribunals in Aberdeen and a founder member of the Aberdeen Solicitors' Property Centre. He was a Trustee of VSA for twenty years and its chair from 1981 to 1983. He was President of the Society of Advocates in 1995–6 and President of the FP Club, 1994–5.

David L. Allan (b. 1940) attended the Grammar between 1944 and 1958. He joined Aberdeen City Police and rose to the rank of Inspector. He moved to Glasgow in 1972 and retired in 1991 as Assistant Chief Constable of Strathclyde. He graduated in Law from London and in Philosophy from Glasgow. After retirement he worked with the Overseas Development Agency as an adviser on policing to various overseas countries. He was President of the FP Club in 2006–07.

John F. Hendry (b. 1947) attended the Grammar between 1951 and 1965. He qualified as a solicitor and has been a partner in Campbell Connon & Co. since 1974. He served on the FP Club Executive from 1969 and became Secretary of the Club in 1976. He is a member of the Society of Advocates in Aberdeen.

(Prof.) Colin R. Munro (b. 1949) was educated at the Grammar between 1954 and 1967, and Aberdeen University where he gained a FCH in Law. He lectured in Law at Birmingham and Durham Universities and held the post of senior lecturer, then Reader, at Essex University (1980–5). He was Professor of Law at Manchester University, 1985–90 and Professor of Constitutional

Law at Edinburgh University, 1990–2009 (and Dean of the Faculty of Law, 1992–4).

(Hon.) Lord Kinclaven (Alexander F. Wylie) (b. 1951) attended the Grammar between 1960 and 1962 and graduated from Edinburgh University in Law. He was called to the Scottish Bar in 1978 and took Silk in 1991. He was an Advocate-Depute, 1989–92, part-time Sheriff, 2000–5, and from 2005 a Senator of the College of Justice in Scotland.

John Watt (b. 1953) attended the Grammar between 1958 and 1971. He began his fiscal career at Jedburgh in 1976, moving to Aberdeen in the 1980s and later serving in the Crown Office and in Glasgow. He was Procurator Fiscal of Kilmarnock from 1999 to 2002 and of Grampian in 2003.

Gary J.G. Allan (b. 1958) was educated at the Grammar between 1963 and 1976 and Aberdeen University. Having completed his legal apprenticeship in Glasgow and Edinburgh he worked as an assistant solicitor before becoming a partner in a legal firm in Glasgow. He was admitted to the Faculty of Advocates, 1994, and became a QC in 2007. He was senior Advocate-Depute (Crown Counsel) between 2007 and 2011. He was President of the FP Club, 2007–8.

James H. Rust (b. 1958) was educated at the Grammar between 1963 and 1971, Loretto and Aberdeen University. Following his legal apprenticeship in Aberdeen he became partner in a legal firm in 1985. He is Clerk and Collector, Society of Writers to Her Majesty's Signet.

Duncan L. Murray (b. 1959) attended the Grammar between 1964 and 1971 and Aberdeen University qualifying as a solicitor in 1982 following his legal apprenticeship. He has been a partner in legal firms since 1985. He was President of the Law Society of Scotland, 2004–5 and was appointed a part-time sheriff in 2006.

Academic

Ian R. Fraser (b. 1930) attended the Grammar between 1942 and 1948, graduating in Geography from Aberdeen University in 1953. He taught in Stirling and Elgin before becoming Rector of Waid Academy, Anstruther, 1966–71. He was Rector of Inverness Royal Academy, 1971–93. He was president of HAS, 1977–8 and vice-chair of the Scottish Consultative Council on the Curriculum, 1987–91.

William D. Brooker (1931–2011) attended the Grammar between 1938 and 1950 and Aberdeen University where he studied Geography from 1950 to 1953. After working as an engineer he converted his degree to honours in

1958 and began teaching at Aberlour High School and Keith Grammar. He became tutor organiser in extra-mural studies for Aberdeen University, retiring as Head of Department in 1991. He was President of the Scottish Mountaineering Club, 1972–4 and editor of its journal, 1976–86.

Alan S. Hall (1931–1986) attended the Grammar between 1937 and 1940 and from 1943 to 1950. He was Dux in his final year and gained a FCH in Classics at Aberdeen University in 1954. His brilliant academic career continued and he won an Exhibition to Balliol, Oxford. He became an authority on the archaeology and epigraphy of Anatolia.

David Edge (1932–2003) attended the Grammar between 1937 and 1944, going on to the Leys School, Cambridge and Caius College, Cambridge in 1949 to read Physics. He gained a PhD in 1959 on radio astronomy. After working as a BBC radio producer he became Edinburgh University's first Director of its Science Studies Unit in 1966. It was aimed at broadening the horizons of its Science graduates. He created the journal *Social Studies of Science.*

Peter A. Murphy (b. 1932) was educated at the Grammar between 1945 and 1951, and Aberdeen University, before returning to become a member of the English teaching staff of the GS. Promotion followed – Summerhill Academy; Logie Secondary School, Dundee; and from 1976 to 1993 he held the post of Rector, Whitfield HS, Dundee. In 1999 he became a Labour member of Angus Council. He wrote a biography of R.F. MacKenzie of Summerhill (*A Prophet without Honour*, published 1999).

(Prof.) Alastair M. North (b. 1932) attended the Grammar between 1937 and 1950. He spent sixteen years at Strathclyde University as chair of the Department of Pure and Applied Chemistry, Dean of the School of Chemical and Materials Sciences and University Vice-Principal and Deputy Principal. From 1983 to 1996 he was President of the Asian Institute of Technology in Bangkok, a multi-national foundation providing post-graduate study and research for the countries of South-East Asia.

(Dr) John L. Brebner (1934–2001) attended the Grammar between 1938 and 1951, graduating with FCH in Natural Philosophy at Aberdeen University before working in Ottawa and Geneva. From 1974 to 2000 he was Professor of Solid State Physics at Montreal, a French-speaking university.

(Prof.) Anthony Wren (b. 1936) attended the Grammar between 1941 and 1944, graduating from Edinburgh University in Mathematics and Natural Philosophy. He joined Leeds University and became a Professor there in 1994. He pioneered the world's first computerised train timetable and went on to revolutionise the scheduling of transport operations across the world. His software has been placed among the top hundred world-changing discoveries, innovations and research projects to come out of British universities in the last fifty years.

Norman J. Horne (b. 1937) attended Grammar between 1950 and 1956. He graduated FCH in Classics and trained as a teacher. After five years at Hamilton Academy he became principal teacher of Classics at the Nicolson Institute, Stornoway, then at Inverness Royal Academy. He was Assistant Rector of Inverness High School for five years, Rector of Milne's High School, Fochabers for eight years and Headmaster of Harlaw Academy, Aberdeen from 1985 until retiring in 1993. He is an accomplished jazz musician.

(Prof.) Jon A. McCleverty (b. 1937) attended the Grammar between 1944 and 1955 and followed his BSc at Aberdeen with degrees at Imperial, London and London. He was a research fellow at Cambridge, Massachusetts, lecturer and reader at Sheffield University and Professor of Inorganic Chemistry at Birmingham University. He was Professor of Inorganic Chemistry at Bristol, 1990–2003 and Senior University Research Fellow, 2003–7.

W. Stewart Wilson (b. 1937) attended the Grammar between 1942 and 1955 and qualified with a BSc from Aberdeen University. He returned to the GS to teach Mathematics before, in 1966, becoming principal teacher of his subject at Banchory Academy. Following internal promotion he was Rector between 1978 and 1995. He was consultant to Grampian Regional Council on staff appraisal.

(Prof.) Bruce P. Lenman (b. 1938) attended the Grammar between 1946 and 1956 and studied further at Aberdeen and St John's, Cambridge. He lectured at Dundee and St Andrews Universities, becoming senior lecturer at the latter in 1978. He was appointed Professor of Modern History at St Andrews (emeritus since 2003) and since 2004 has been an Honorary Professor at Dundee. He has written extensively.

Iain R. Bishop (1938–2007) attended the Grammar between 1950 and 1955, graduating from Aberdeen University in Zoology and Botany in 1959 and then studying further at Southampton. He lectured at Guy's in London and Leicester University and led the RGS Mato Grosso Expedition to central Brazil. He became Deputy Keeper of Zoology at the Natural History Museum.

(Prof.) Alan K.G. Paterson (b. 1938) attended the Grammar leaving in 1956 to study Spanish at Aberdeen and Cambridge, where he gained a PhD in 1965. He lectured at the University of London, 1964–84, and was appointed to the chair of Spanish at St Andrews in 1985. He was Dean of the Faculty of Arts, 1991–5. He has written extensively.

(Prof.) Harry J.C. Hill (1940–2005) attended the Grammar between 1948 and 1959, and the University of Alberta, before teaching English in Minnesota and, for over thirty years, in Montreal. He was equally accomplished as actor and teacher and was a gifted musician. His textbook *A Voice for the Theatre* was a guide to actors and for students of literature.

(Prof.) Francis Lyall (b. 1940) attended the Grammar between 1944 and 1957, graduating from Aberdeen University in Arts in 1960 and in Law in 1962 with commendation. He studied further at the Institute of Air and Space Law at McGill University and taught at Auckland University. He became Professor of Public Law at Aberdeen in 1974, retiring in 2005, and was Dean from 1976 to 1979. He became a Board member of the European Centre for Space Law and a Director of the International Institute of Space Law.

(Prof.) Neil K. Buxton (b. 1940) attended the Grammar between 1948 and 1958, graduating in Political Economy from Aberdeen University and studying further at Heriot-Watt. After lecturing at Aberdeen and Hull he became a Professor at Heriot-Watt, 1979–83. He was depute-director of Glasgow College of Technology, 1983–7, Director of Hatfield Polytechnic, and Vice-Chancellor of Hertfordshire University. He held the posts of manager and selector of the Scottish hockey team and gained nine caps for Scotland.

(Dr) Joseph Leiper (b. 1941) was educated at the Grammar between 1953 and 1959 and Aberdeen University before becoming a teacher. He held posts in English at RGC and Bankhead Academy and senior management posts at Ellon Academy before his appointment as Rector at Oldmachar Academy, 1984–2004. He was Convenor of Aberdeen University Business Committee, 2000–2006, and was a member of the University Court, 2000–8. He was appointed a DL for Aberdeen in 2005.

(Prof.) Charles Mulvey (b. 1941) attended the Grammar between 1945 and 1959, graduating from Aberdeen University in Economics in 1963. He became Professor of Industrial Relations at the University of Western Australia in 1981, and Professor of Labour Economics in 1996. He was Dean of the Faculty of Economics and Commerce, 2001–5.

Clement A. Stewart (b. 1941) attended the Grammar between 1952 and 1959. He trained as a Mathematics teacher and became Head of Lochgilphead HS, Argyll in 1977, and was the first Head of Portlethen Academy, 1987–97.

Ronald I. Lewis-Smith (b. 1942) attended the Grammar between 1946 and 1960, graduating in Botany from Aberdeen University in 1964. That same year he joined the British Antarctic Survey (BAS) as a cryptogamic ecologist, and in 1975 he was made Head of the BAS Plant Biology Section. He was awarded the British Polar medal in 1977 and a clasp in 2002 in recognition of his contribution to Antarctic science.

Hugh W. Reid (b. 1942) was schooled at George Watson's, Glasgow Academy and the Grammar between 1955 and 1960 before graduating from Edinburgh University. He was veterinary research officer (1968–74) and principal vet research officer (1974–90) before becoming Head of the Virology Division at Moredun Research Institute, a post he held till 2002. Since then he has been Transmissible Spongiform Encephallopathy Research Co-ordinator there. He has written numerous papers and book chapters.

Hugh Barron (1943–2012; OBE 2005) attended the Grammar between 1953 and 1960, graduating with FCH in Physics from Aberdeen University in 1964. He stayed on at university, completing a PhD in 1971 and became a lecturer in Physics and then Engineering. In the 1980s he pioneered techniques with Grampian Police and became Scotland's foremost road traffic accident investigator.

(Dr) Andrew D.H. Wyllie (b. 1944) attended the Grammar between 1947 and 1960, graduating from Aberdeen University in Science and then Medicine in 1964 and 1967 respectively. He took a PhD under Sir Alastair Currie, head of Pathology. In 1972 he discovered the significance of natural cell death, called by him and his colleagues, apoptosis. After lecturing at Aberdeen and Edinburgh he became Head of the Department of Pathology at Cambridge University and Fellow of St John's. He was awarded FRSE in 1991 and FRS in 1995.

(Dr) Richard Grieve (b. 1943) attended the Grammar between 1948 and 1961, graduating from Aberdeen University in Geology and doing further study in Toronto. He was involved in a research programme of Geophysics in Ottawa. An asteroid, discovered in 1988, was named after him to mark his work with the Geological Survey of Canada.

(Prof.) William L. Miller (b. 1943) was educated at the Grammar in 1959–60 and Royal HS, Edinburgh, going on to Edinburgh and Newcastle Universities. He was lecturer, senior lecturer and Professor at Strathclyde University before, in 1985, being appointed Professor of Politics at Glasgow University. A frequent contributor to press and TV he has produced numerous publications.

(Prof.) Graham G. Ross (b. 1944) attended the Grammar between 1951 and 1962, going on to graduate in Natural Philosophy at Aberdeen University and gaining further qualifications at Durham and Pembroke. He has been a Fellow of Wadham, Oxford since 1983 and Professor of Theoretical Physics at Oxford since 1992. He was elected FRS in 1991.

(Prof.) Graham D. Caie (b. 1945) was educated at the Grammar between 1949 and 1963 before going on to Aberdeen and McMaster Universities. He worked at McMaster and Copenhagen Universities. He became Clerk of the Senate and Vice-Principal of Glasgow University, and has been professor of English Language there since 1990. He was Senate Assessor of Glasgow University's Court from 1998–2003.

(Prof.) Michael Lynch (b. 1946) attended the Grammar between 1954 and 1964 and Aberdeen University where he gained a FCH in English and History in 1969. After posts at Bangor and Edinburgh he was appointed Professor of Scottish History and Palaeography at the latter, a post he held from 1992 until 2005, when he became a Research Professor. He chaired the Ancient Monuments Board of Scotland, 1996–2003, and was President of the Historical Association of Scotland, 1992–2002. He has a number of publications to his name.

(Prof.) Roderick A. McDonald (b. 1946) attended the Grammar between 1951 and 1964 and Aberdeen University, before gaining his PhD from Kansas University in 1981. He became Professor of History at Rider University and from 2004 to 2009 was editor of the *Journal of the Early Republic* – the premier publication on the history of US between 1776 and 1861. He lives in Philadelphia.

Douglas Marr (b. 1947) attended the Grammar between 1959 and 1965, and Aberdeen University before embarking on a teaching career. He held History posts at Hilton Academy and the GS (1971–6) and senior management posts at Kemnay Academy and the Gordon Schools, Huntly, before taking up headships at Hilton Academy (1987–8), St Machar Academy (1988–95) and Banchory Academy (1995–2002). He was a member of the Business Committee and Court of Aberdeen University and since 2004 has been an HMI (part-time).

John H. Garvie (b. 1948) was educated at the Grammar between 1960 and 1966 and Aberdeen University before becoming a teacher. He held Science (Physics) posts at the Nicolson Institute and Balfron HS and senior management posts at Gairloch HS (1985–94). He became Rector at Dornoch Academy in 1994.

(Prof.) Eric Grove (b. 1948) attended the Grammar between 1960 and 1966, graduating in History from Aberdeen University in 1970. He went on to King's, London and lectured at Dartmouth College. He became a defence consultant and a reader in Politics at Hull University. In 2005 he became Professor of Naval History and Director of the Centre for International Security and War Studies at Salford University. He is a prolific writer.

James Brian Kenworthy (1949–2011) attended the Grammar between 1954 and 1967 and studied Archaeology at Cardiff University. He lectured at St Andrews, moving in 1987 to Nottingham and finally to Aberdeen. He was the author of several academic papers and made a valuable contribution to the appreciation of Scottish archaeology. He was elected FSAScot.

James Fiddes (b. 1951) attended the Grammar between 1963 and 1969 and graduated in Arts at Aberdeen before studying librarianship. He held posts in Wigan and Falkirk before appointment as librarian for the Faculty of Design in Aberdeen. In 2000 he merged the libraries of the School of Architecture and Gray's School of Art into a new facility at Robert Gordon University's Faculty of Management.

Albert V. Swinborn (b. 1953) was educated at the Grammar between 1964 and 1970 and Aberdeen University before becoming a teacher of English at Lossiemouth HS, Inverurie Academy and Hilton Academy. He held a senior management posts at Westhill Academy and in 1997 became the Headteacher of Portlethen Academy.

(Prof.) Craig Clunas (b. 1954) attended the Grammar between 1959 and 1972, graduating with FCH in Chinese Studies from King's, Cambridge, in 1977. He worked as a curator in the Victoria and Albert Museum. He was Professor of Art History at Sussex University, 1997–2003, and then at the School of Oriental and African Studies, London, 2003–7. Since 2007 he has been Professor of Art History and Fellow of Trinity, Oxford. He was elected a Fellow of the British Academy in 2004.

(Prof.) Peter G. Bruce (b. 1956) attended the Grammar between 1968 and 1974, and Aberdeen University. He was a research fellow at Oxford, 1982–5; lecturer at Heriot-Watt University, 1985–91; reader at St Andrews, 1991–5; and Wardlaw Professor of Chemistry at the latter since 2007. He was elected FRS for his pioneering work on the chemistry of materials.

Financial

Colin C. Allan (1928–1990) attended the Grammar between 1936 and 1945. He qualified as a CA and served as a company accountant with various firms, and was latterly group accountant with J.W. Holdings, the demerged part of the Wood Group. He was Treasurer of the FP Club from 1976 till his death.

John P. Grant (1930–2004) attended the Grammar between 1937 and 1945, completing his schooling at Fettes before proceeding to Aberdeen University, where he graduated in Law in 1953. He qualified as a CA in 1955. He joined his family firm which merged with Ernst & Young. In 1989 he joined the University's Audit committee, which he went on to chair. He was co-opted onto the University Court in 1990. He was an outstanding golfer, having won all the major amateur competitions.

Charles Ritchie (1933–2008) attended the Grammar between 1945 and 1951. He was for many years with the Royal Exchange Assurance before taking early retirement. He was manager of the Scottish rugby touring party to Australia in 1992 and was elected as President of the SRU, 1997–8 (the fifth FP to hold this office). He was President of the FP Club, 1999–2000.

Ronald Scott Brown (b. 1937) attended the Grammar between 1946 and 1955 and took the degrees of MA and LLB at Aberdeen University in 1958 and 1960 respectively. He specialised in Investment Management. In 1983 he was one of the founding directors of Aberdeen Fund Managers – later changing its name to Abtrust. He has been involved in many local and national institutions and was a member of the University Court for over a decade.

George A. Robb (b. 1942) attended the Grammar between 1946 and 1960, thereafter qualifying in Law and becoming a solicitor in Aberdeen. He was co-founder of Aberdeen Asset Management in 1983 with Ronnie Scott Brown and Martin Gilbert. He moved to Surrey a number of years ago.

Ian P. Souter (b. 1943) attended the Grammar between 1947 and 1961. He gained an MA from Aberdeen University then CA before becoming a partner in Whinney Murray in London. He returned to establish their Aberdeen office in the late 1970s. He became an insolvency specialist with Ernst and Young. He was a Governor of RGIT for twelve years, the last four as chairman.

Harvey E. Morrison (b. 1947) attended the Grammar between 1951 and 1965. He qualified as a CA and has been a partner in Williamson & Dunn since 1976. He became Treasurer of the FP Club Centre in 1975 and apart from a break of two years in the 1980s remained in office until retiring in 2012.

Iain D. Saville (b. 1948) attended the Grammar between 1952 and 1966. He studied Mathematical Physics at St Andrews and joined the Bank of England in London, 1973–6, working as an analyst and programmer. He was seconded to the LSE to study economics and he worked as an economist, 1978–83. He was the founder and CEO of CREST, one of the world's largest and most sophisticated securities settlement systems and joined Computershare, as the executive director responsible for the group's European operations and chair of its Treasury Review Committee. He was awarded a CBE in 1999.

Marshall Byres (b. 1951) attended the Grammar between 1960 and 1969 and took degrees at Aberdeen and RGU. He was an inspector of taxes before he became involved in the financial services sector as Managing Partner of Ernst & Young in the Far East. In 2005 in Hong Kong he was awarded an honorary doctorate from the University of Aberdeen.

Graeme W. King (b. 1954) attended the Grammar between 1966 and 1972. He qualified as a chartered insurer and chartered loss adjuster spending over twenty-five years in the Far East. He was heavily involved in the aftermath of the 2004 Indonesian tsunami.

Stephen J. Davidson (b. 1955) attended the Grammar between 1967 and 1973 and studied Maths and Statistics at Aberdeen University. After posts with NM Rothschild Merchant Bank and America's Chemical Bank in New York, arranging finance for movies, he became treasurer at Lorimar Pictures, the producers of 'Dallas'. Back in the UK, after a spell with Bankers Trust he was appointed chief executive of the cable giant TeleWest Communications. He is now on the boards of several companies, mostly in the communication field.

Alan W. Marr (b. 1957) attended the Grammar between 1969 and 1975. He qualified as a CA and is a partner in Bain Henry Reid in Aberdeen. He became Treasurer of the FP Club in 1998 and served until retiring in 2012.

Administrative (Politicians)

(Sir) Alan Donald (b. 1931) attended the Grammar between 1942 and 1944, going on to Fettes and Trinity Hall, Cambridge. He joined the Foreign Service in 1954 and saw service at Peking, Paris, Athens and Hong Kong before becoming Ambassador to Zaire, Burundi and Rwanda, 1977–80; the Congo, 1978–80; Indonesia, 1984–8; and China, 1988–91. He was President of the China Association, 2003–8.

J. Edward Fraser (b. 1931) attended the Grammar between 1936 and 1949 and went on to Aberdeen and Christ's, Cambridge. He joined the home Civil Service and in 1962 became a Principal and in 1970 an Assistant Secretary for the SHHD. He was Under-Secretary at the SHHD from 1981 to 1991. He was Secretary of Commissions for Scotland, 1992–4 and Assistant Local Government Boundary Commissioner for Scotland since 1997.

(Prof.) Urlan A. Wannop (b. 1931) attended the Grammar between 1936 and 1949, going on to Edinburgh and Liverpool Universities. He was Senior Deputy Director of Planning, Strathclyde Regional Council, 1975–81 and Professor of Urban and Regional Planning, Strathclyde University, 1981–96.

John F. McClellan (b. 1932) attended the Grammar between 1944 and 1950 and went on to Aberdeen University before joining the home Civil Service in 1956. He became a Principal in 1960 and an Assistant Secretary in the Scottish Office in 1969, before becoming Under-Secretary of the Scottish Office, 1977–85. He was Director, Scottish International Education Trust, 1986–2001.

Robert Middleton (1932–2002) attended the Grammar between 1944 and 1948 and became an engineer with Post Office Telephones. A life-long Labour party supporter he was elected to local Councils from 1961 until 1999. He played a prominent role in the introduction of comprehensive education in Aberdeen as Convener of the Education Committee in the late 1960s. He was Convener of Grampian Regional Council, 1990–4.

David B. Haggart (1934–2002) attended the Grammar between 1945 and 1952, graduating in Psychology from Aberdeen University in 1956. He was appointed the first Head of the Careers and Appointments Service at the University in 1963. He had a life-long interest in music and was active locally in the Church and the Ferryhill community.

D. Ivor M. Sutherland (b. 1938) attended the Grammar between 1951 and 1955 and went on to Aberdeen and Zurich universities before returning to the GS as a Modern Languages teacher, 1962–6. After lecturing in education-related areas in Ireland and Scotland he held posts in the Education Directorate, becoming Depute Director of Education in Highland Region, 1975–85. He was Registrar of the General Teaching Council for Scotland between 1985 and 2001.

(Dr) Edward Alistair Smith (1939–2012) attended the GS between 1943 and 1957. He graduated with an MA and PhD before returning to Aberdeen University as a Geography lecturer in 1963. An active Conservative he was President of the Scottish Conservative and Unionists for two years. He was a member of Grampian Health Board, 1981–9. He was head of the inaugural fund-raising development for Aberdeen University, 1982–90, and then Director of its International Office.

M. Quentin Cramb (b. 1940) attended the Grammar between 1944 and 1958, graduating from Aberdeen University. He taught in Huntly, was for a time Special Assistant in English at the GS and then Principal Teacher of English in Madras College, St Andrews. He joined HMI and became the specialist in English and Drama and district inspector for Strathclyde.

(Prof. Sir) C. Duncan Rice (b. 1942) attended the Grammar between 1949 and 1960, graduating with FCH in History at Aberdeen University in 1964 before further study at Edinburgh. He lectured at Aberdeen and Yale before becoming a Professor in New York. He was Dean and then Vice-Chancellor at New York University and then from 1996 to 2010 Principal and Vice-Chancellor at Aberdeen University.

(James) Hamish Hamill (b. 1943) attended the Grammar between 1951 and 1961. He became a senior career civil servant. He was Head of the Scottish Home and Health Department and first head of the Scottish Executive Justice Department, 1992–2002.

Stuart J. Mitchell (1943–2001) attended the Grammar between 1948 and 1961, being Dux of the school and a bursar to Aberdeen University. He graduated with FCH in Chemistry in 1965 and took his PhD in 1968. He spent his working life in government service, initially at the Atomic Weapons Research Establishment at Aldermaston and then with the Ministry of Defence in London, this last including a secondment to the British Embassy in Washington between 1979 and 1984.

Alistair R. Cruickshank (b. 1944) attended the Grammar between 1956 and 1962 before joining the MAFF as assistant principal in 1966. He became a Principal (1970), Assistant Secretary (1978) and Under-Secretary (1986). Since 2001 he has been secretary, and chair from 2007, of EcoLocal – formerly the Centre for Environmental Initiatives.

Alan G. Campbell (b. 1946) attended the Grammar between 1959 and 1965 and graduated in Law from Aberdeen University in 1968. He became a solicitor in 1970 and held a number of local government appointments. He was Chief Executive of Grampian Regional Council, 1991–5, and Chief Executive of Aberdeenshire Council, 1995–2008. He gained a CBE for services to Scottish local government in 2002 and an honorary LLD from Aberdeen University in 2005.

Robin F. Cook (1946–2005) attended the Grammar between 1950 and 1960 and the RHS in Edinburgh. He was an academic high achiever. He read English at Edinburgh University, where his debating skills were further honed and where he was politically active. He advanced in the Labour Party and his leadership and work helped reorganise the local party and won power for it in Edinburgh from 1980 to 2007. He became an MP in February 1974 and joined the centre-left Tribune group. He made U-turns on devolution and the EEC but was the kingmaker for Neil Kinnock in 1983 and John Smith in 1992. Blair and Brown kept him out of domestic affairs. He was Foreign Secretary from 1997 to 2001 but in Blair's second Government was demoted to Leader of the House of Commons. In March 2003 he resigned over Blair's Iraq policy and his speech won a rare 'unparliamentary' standing ovation. He is remembered as a parliamentarian and probably the most accomplished orator of his generation.[6]

William G. U'ren (b. 1946) was educated at the Grammar between 1958 and 1964 before going on to Aberdeen and Strathclyde Universities. He held various planning officer posts before becoming Director of Planning and Technical Services for Clydesdale District Council, 1982–96. Between 1997 and 2007 he was Director, Royal Town Planning Institute in Scotland.

(Dr) Alexander Hardie (b. 1947) attended the Grammar between 1954 and 1963, Bristol GS, Edinburgh University and Corpus Christi, Oxford. He was a member of the Diplomatic Service between 1973 and 2001. He was First Secretary, Budapest, 1977–8, then Bucharest, 1979–81 and Lusaka, 1986–90. He was a Counsellor in Pretoria, 1993–7. He was a Fellow and Bursar of Oriel, Oxford, 2001–4.

Donald A. Lamont (b. 1947) attended the Grammar between 1952 and 1965. After graduating from Aberdeen University he worked for British Leyland, 1970–3, before joining the Foreign Office. He worked in Vienna, Moscow, London and Berlin. He was Ambassador to Uruguay, 1992–4; Head of the Republic of Ireland department, 1994–7; Governor of the Falklands, 1999–2003, and then Ambassador to Venezuela. He was President of the FP Club, 2010–11.

Michael Forbes Smith (b. 1948) attended the Grammar between 1959 and 1966 and took a BSc in Geography at Southampton University, 1968–71. He was an officer in the Gordon Highlanders, 1971–8 before joining the Diplomatic Service until 2004. His career culminated in his appointment as the first British resident ambassador in Tajikistan, set up following 9/11. He has been Director General of the Chartered Institute of Arbitrators since 2006.

Writers

(Dr) F.L. Pierre Fouin (b. 1929) attended the Grammar between 1944 and 1947, graduating in Medicine at Aberdeen University in 1953. He was a GP in Cults and Culter until 1990. He is author of *Glentanar Exile: A History of Glentanar Estate* and *Kick those Sleeping Dogs.*

M. David Bonavia (1940–1988) attended the Grammar between 1946 and 1953, going on to Clifton College in Bristol and graduating in Modern Languages from Corpus Christi, Cambridge. He worked for Reuters and

Far Eastern Review, before in 1967 starting work for *The Times*. His coverage of the Cultural Revolution led to his work as foreign correspondent in Vietnam. He moved to Moscow where he was expelled in 1972. He then was posted to China. He produced several important books.

(Prof.) Roderick Watson (b. 1943) attended the Grammar between 1955 and 1961, graduating from Aberdeen University and Peterhouse, Cambridge. He is a poet, literary critic and writer, producing a number of publications. He became Professor of English Studies and Director of the Centre for Scottish Studies at Stirling University.

Harry W. Reid (b. 1947) was educated at the Grammar between 1952 and 1961, Fettes and Oxford University, graduating in Modern History. He became educational correspondent for *The Scotsman* in 1973 and worked on the *Sunday Standard* before moving to the *Glasgow Herald* in 1983 and being appointed the Editor of *The Herald*, a post he held from 1997 to 2000. He has produced a number of publications.

David K. Yule (1947–2007) attended the Grammar between 1951 and 1965, graduating in English from Aberdeen University. He served the University from 1971 being Clerk of the Medical Faculty then Clerk to the University Court. For fourteen years he was editor of the School Magazine and was responsible for the conception, compilation and production of *1256 and All That*.

Alan Cowie (b. 1948) was educated at the Grammar between 1954 and 1966, and in London and Glasgow before becoming, for a short period, a teacher in Glasgow. In 1972 he was appointed a reporter/presenter with Radio Scotland. He joined Grampian TV as a news presenter and was its Head of Current Affairs, 1998–2000. He is now a freelance television producer, journalist and broadcaster.[7]

Roddy Phillips (b. 1957) was educated at the Grammar between 1969 and 1975 and Gray's School of Art. He was an illustrator and portrait artist before working as a graphic designer for Shell UK (1976–9). In 1980 he became graphic designer for Aberdeen Journals. He has produced a weekly column for the *Press & Journal* since 1996. Since 2006 he has been Creative Director of *The Agency*.

Paul Gough (b. 1958) was educated at the Grammar between 1969 and 1973 before graduating in Fine Art from Wolverhampton Polytechnic, 1976–9, and gaining an MA and PhD at the RCA. From 1988 to 1998 he presented, wrote and researched arts programmes for TV and radio. Since becoming Professor of Fine Art at the University of the West of England, he has been Pro-Vice-Chancellor for Research and Development, and since

2010 Pro-Vice-Chancellor and Executive Dean in the Faculty of Creative Arts.

Arts

Iain Cuthbertson (1930–2009) attended the Grammar between 1946 and 1948 (following time at Glasgow Academy). He graduated in French and Spanish from Aberdeen University in 1952. He became a freelance actor, writer and lecturer. He was general manager of the Glasgow Citizens' Theatre and director of productions, then assistant director at the Royal Court Theatre, London and director of Perth Theatre. From the late 1960s he concentrated on TV appearances culminating in the title role in *Sutherland's Law*. He took parts in many films. From 1975 to 1978 he was Rector of Aberdeen University and was awarded an honorary doctorate of laws.

James Reith (1932–2011) attended the Grammar between 1947 and 1950, studying further at the RSAMD and Jordanhill Training College. He taught at Torry and Ruthrieston before in 1970 becoming PT of Music at Cults Academy, retiring early in 1990. He conducted the Aberdeen Orpheus Choir from 1963 and was Musical Director of the Aberdeen Scout Gang Show. He was appointed honorary vice-president of Aberdeen Opera Company in 1995. He was a great champion of Scottish music, composing and arranging and was also a gifted accompanist.

John McLeod (b. 1934) attended the Grammar between 1946 and 1950. He went on to study composition at the RAM, winning several prizes, and was elected a FRAM in 1989. He was Head of Composition for Film and Television at the London College of Music (Thames Valley University), 1991–7. He has become a 'major force in contemporary Scottish music' (*The Scotsman*). His Clarinet Concerto was premiered in Edinburgh in 2007.

Stephen A.C. Robertson (1934–2011) attended the Grammar between 1939 and 1951, graduating in Law from Aberdeen University. He was President of the Union, 1955–56. In 1983 he retired from his practice as a solicitor to concentrate on a career on the professional stage with his partners, Buff Hardie and George Donald. He was given the Freedom of the City of Aberdeen in April 2007 along with the other members of *Scotland the What* 'for services to the fine arts, the Doric language and north-east of Scotland culture'. He was President of the FP Club, 2001–2 and Rector of Aberdeen University, 2008–11.

Alan Hamilton (b. 1938) attended the Grammar between 1943 and 1956, qualified as an architect and was a partner in George Bennett Mitchell & Son in Aberdeen. A long-time member of the FP Club Centre Committee he served as its chairman for four years in the 1980s. He then served a lengthy term as vice-chairman of the Club executive.

Douglas R. Kynoch (b. 1938) attended the Grammar between 1948 and 1956 before graduating in Arts at Aberdeen University. He trained as a teacher and became involved in broadcasting in 1961 with Grampian TV in Aberdeen and BBC TV in Glasgow. He became a freelance broadcaster with BBC Radio Scotland. His interest in the Doric language has led to several books and he has published many poems.

David Bruce (b. 1939) was educated at Dundee HS and the Grammar between 1947 and 1956 before Edinburgh University. His involvement with films led to his appointment as Director of the Edinburgh International Film Festival in 1965–6. He was Deputy Director of the Scottish Film Council between 1977 and 1986 and its Director from 1986 till 1994. He was chairman of the Glasgow Film Theatre, 2002–8. He has written a number of publications.

Patrick E.B. Chalmers (b. 1939) attended the Grammar between 1943 and 1949, going on to Fettes, North of Scotland Agricultural College and Durham University. He joined the BBC as radio talks producer in 1963 and became Head of Television, Scotland, 1979–82, and Controller, BBC Scotland, 1983–92. He was a member of Aberdeenshire Council, 1995–9.

Patrick F.C. Milne (1940–2007) attended the Grammar between 1944 and 1959 and after graduating from Aberdeen University in 1962 he went to the RCM to study bassoon and piano. He played with the Royal Philharmonic Orchestra and from 1966 to 1976 with the London Symphony Orchestra. He then played as principal bassoon with the Bournemouth Sinfonietta.

Brian Dargie (b. 1941) attended the Grammar between 1953 and 1959. He studied Music at Aberdeen University and was awarded a scholarship to continue his studies at the RAM. He played with leading London orchestras, including the Royal Philharmonic, before returning to Aberdeen where he established himself as a leading violinist and violin teacher. He is leader of the Aberdeen Sinfonietta.

J. Martin Dalby (b. 1942) attended the Grammar between 1946 and 1960 followed by study at the Royal College of Music. He was music producer for Radio 3, 1965–71; Head of Music, BBC Scotland, 1972–91, and Executive Music Producer, BBC Scotland, 1991–3. He is now composer, freelance music/recording producer, music lecturer and has been chair and director of national guilds of composers, songwriters and performers.

Nigel Murray (1943–2007) attended the Grammar between 1953 and 1962 and went on to study at the RCM in London and also in Lucerne and Italy with the foremost violinists. He played with many of Britain's most prestigious orchestras until an arm injury ended his professional career. He taught at music schools and at the RSAMD and was one of Scotland's most gifted and admired musicians.

(Prof.) Neil Mackie (b. 1946) attended the Grammar between 1963 and 1966, and then went on to the RSAMD and the RCM. He also studied singing in Munich and with Peter Pears. From 1983 he was Professor of Singing at RCM and became Head of Vocal Studies there in 1993. He moved to the RAM in 2008.

Malcolm F. Rennie (b. 1947) attended the Grammar between 1952 and 1965 before further study at the Central School of Speech and Drama in London. He has had a successful career on stage and in television and has performed in around twenty London West End shows. He is involved in a large volume of commercial and corporate work. He married Tumara Ustinov (daughter of Peter Ustinov).

Ray Davis (b. 1948) attended the Grammar between 1963 and 1966, RGU and Heriot-Watt University. He worked as an architect in Edinburgh and Glasgow before setting up his own organisation in 1981–2. He lectured at the Mackintosh School and Strathclyde University.

Alisdair G. Gracie (1948–1998) attended the Grammar between 1953 and 1966. He was a reporter on Aberdeen newspapers before joining Grampian TV in 1971. He was Head of News and Current Affairs at Grampian, 1986–97, and Controller of Grampian TV, 1997–8. He was Editor of the FP Magazine, 1968–74.

John (Iain) A. Dickson (b. 1951) was educated at the Grammar between 1956 and 1969 and the Scott Sutherland School of Architecture. From 1973 he worked in architectural practices and was senior partner with George Watt & Stewart. He was President, Royal Incorporation of Architects in Scotland, 1999–2001.

Arthur J. Watson (b. 1951) attended the Grammar between 1956 and 1969 and Gray's School of Art. In 1974 he founded Peacock Printer-makers, an artists' print workshop gallery and publisher. Since 1996 he has been senior lecturer at Duncan of Jordanstone College of Art and since 2007 Secretary of the Royal Scottish Academy.

(Prof.) Lennox R. Dunbar (b. 1952) was educated at the Grammar between 1964 and 1969 and Gray's School of Art. Since 1987 he has been

Head of Printmaking, Gray's School of Art. He has lectured in painting and printmaking extensively at home and abroad.

(Prof.) Ian Howard (b. 1952) attended the Grammar between 1957 and 1970 and Edinburgh College of Art. He lectured in Painting at Gray's School of Art from 1976. He was appointed Dean of Faculty, Duncan of Jordanstone College of Art in 1999. He has been Principal, Edinburgh College of Art, since 2001.[8]

Sport

T. Ian Morison (1929–2012) attended the Grammar between 1934 and 1947 and graduated in Science at Aberdeen in 1951. After teaching in Stirling and Jordanhill, he was assistant rector of Brechin High School and then adviser in secondary education in Tayside. He captained both FP Cricket and Hockey and was twice President of the Scottish Hockey Association. He was chairman of the Great Britain Men's Hockey Board and was Chief of Mission of the GB Men's team which won gold at the Seoul Olympics in 1988. He was FP Club President in 1990–1.

(Dr) Bruce Thomson (b. 1930) was born in Assam, India, of Scottish parents. He was educated at the Grammar between 1940 and 1943, Glenalmond, Keble College, Oxford and the Royal London Hospital. He won blues for rugby and boxing at University and played rugby for Scotland in 1953 against Wales, Ireland and France. He practised Medicine as a GP in Horsham, Sussex, and retired to Crieff. He plays, and composes for, the bagpipes.

Eric D. Watt (b. 1932) attended the Grammar between 1937 and 1950 and he played for Scotland at hockey against Wales in his final year at School. This unique event was marked with a half-holiday. His hockey career was to last sixteen years and he accumulated fifty-two national caps and two Great Britain caps. He graduated in Engineering from Aberdeen University and entered his father's wholesale fish business. In 1974 he obtained a BEd degree and began Primary Teaching. He was President of the FP Club, 1984–5.

Ernest J.S. Michie (b. 1933) attended the Grammar and played rugby for Aberdeen University and other sides including the FPs. He played for Scotland and went on the 1955 British Lions tour to South Africa.

Dennis Hay (b. 1940) attended the Grammar between 1952 and 1959. He taught PE at various Edinburgh schools and was Director of Hockey at Edinburgh University. He has been awarded sixty-two Scottish and seventeen British Hockey caps. His younger brother, Kenneth Hay, who attended the GS between 1960 and 1966, gained thirty-one hockey caps.

Meldrum B. Edwards (b. 1942) attended the Grammar between 1947 and 1960. He was a civil engineer with the City Council. An athlete, he has made an outstanding contribution to athletics at local, national and international levels and narrowly missed out on a place in the 1968 British Olympic running squad.

Fred K.S. Lawson (b. 1943) attended the Grammar between 1947 and 1962. He was a business manager for different companies. He has been involved with FP Hockey since leaving school and has been 1st XI captain and club captain. He won fifty-four caps for Scotland at hockey and he is still involved in coaching junior and school hockey.

John A. (Jocky) Scott (b. 1948) attended the Grammar between 1960 and 1963, leaving School to join Chelsea FC. He was transferred to Dundee in 1964, and subsequent transfers took him to Aberdeen and Dundee again. He has had three managerial spells with Dundee FC. He played football for Scotland (two caps in 1971).

David McDonald (b. 1949) attended the Grammar between 1961 and 1967 and worked in the licensed trade in Shetland and Aberdeen before serving in Aberdeen Leisure department. A former President of the FP Rugby Section, he has had a long involvement with Golden Oldies Rugby and was President of the European Golden Oldies from 2001. Being a below-knee amputee, he has taken a huge part in organising disability groups, in particular Disability (Sport) Scotland.

Nigel Watt (b. 1950) attended the Grammar between 1963 and 1969. He graduated in Law from Aberdeen University and became a partner with an Edinburgh firm and a WS. In 2004 he changed careers and became Secretary of Gullane Golf Club. He served on the Rules Committee of the R & A Club in St Andrews, and in 2008 became a professional golf referee. He was Secretary of the Edinburgh FP Centre from 1976 until 2005. He was elected FP Club President for 2012–13. He is the first third-generation President, following grandfather Theodore (1946–7) and father Alan (1975–6).

Dallas Moir (b. 1957) attended the Grammar between 1969 and 1975. He was a Maltese-born cricketer who played first-class cricket for Scotland in 1980 and 1986, and for Derbyshire, 1981–5. His twin brother, Jeremy, played first-class cricket for Scotland in the NatWest Trophy and Benson & Hedges Cup between 1989 and 1992.

THIRTEEN Recollections from more Modern Times

David Morland Craig, grandson of Morland Simpson, attended the School between 1937 and 1950. These were his recollections when he visited his old School in the early 1990s:

> I went back into the School grounds, past the prefabs in which the girls and boys were taught for a time after the fire of 1986. Everything was familiar: the crow-stepped granite gables, the green metal fence between the grass and Esslemont Avenue, and the bronze statue of Byron by Pittendrigh MacGillivray . . . When I looked through the window of the classroom furthest to the southwest, the unchanging character of the place became almost comical. The declension of *miles*, Latin for 'soldier', was written in chalk on the blackboard – as it had been when I spent hundreds of laborious, often frightening, hours in that same room, doing Latin (and more often Greek) under the high-minded bullying of Happy Harry – Mr Andrew Milne, Head of Classics . . .
>
> Happy Harry was the very type of the martinet teacher, whose mission was to exorcise by well-focussed rage the demon of Inaccuracy from the child mind. Or it was a sin, damnation for which could be averted only by unremitting toil and taking-pains. When your answer was wrong, by so much as a vowel, his pink face flushed scarlet and his blue eyes blazed and bulged. His very corrections were blood-red, written with a steel nib, on a bad day so copiously that a page of your own blue-black Quink was overwhelmed by his deadly scarlet.
>
> Milne worshipped verbal accuracy. He was so good with language that he had helped Hugh MacDiarmid with points of Lallans when they both lived in Montrose, in the 1920s, and the great poet was writing some of his finest work.

The best of our teachers were scholars manqués, intellectual sergeant majors devoted to drilling and shaming us sinners into doing our very best. The worst ones were exhausted foot-soldiers in the front line of the war between old and young.

Pizzie Henry (Geography) had probably once cared about the configuration of the Earth and the products of its countries. He was also rumoured to have been an amateur boxing champion, and to have held a boy by the ankles over a thirty-foot stairwell. He did throw chalk at us, hard and accurately, and occasionally schoolbags, if the noisy inattention got too much.

Doddy Hay taught Classics and Suivie Souter taught French. Both of them had tobacco-stained moustaches, shabby suits, and shoulders drooping under the weight of disappointment and failure. Both came from a generation who tended to get jobs because their peers had been wiped out in the trenches. Suivie's nick-name came from his habit of saying 'Suivez – you follow?' after a sentence of explanation, spoken in a low-pitched Scottish (rather than French) accent.

Some like Berty Johnson (Mathematics with bursts of Geography) went in blatantly for comic turns, to relieve the sheer sameness of straight teaching. Berty excelled at speed chalk work. He covered the tall roll-over blackboard with quadratic equations or occluded weather fronts, scribble-scribble-scribble in a cloud of chalk dust, then plunged his hands into his pockets and made bird-like jabs of his large aquiline nose at one section of the class after another, grinning hugely at his own prowess and egging us on to admire him. By then I'd given up on Maths. When he pretended to teach us the Geography of low-pressure systems and anticyclones, because he'd been in the Meteorological Division of the RAF, he communicated so little that to this day my keen interest in the weather has a blind spot in the area of occluded fronts.

Creeper McLeod (Latin) was a more complicated case. 'Creeper' was short for Creeping Jesus and he may have been dubbed that because he tended to walk close to walls, in a furtive way, like a private eye tailing a target, and also because he gave sideways looks and meaning grins so that whatever he said was suspected of being filthy, although he never made particularly dirty jokes. And he played the trumpet in the Palais de Danse in Diamond Street, the Las Vegas or red light quarter of Aberdeen (or so we excitedly supposed). Perhaps he was rather good at his subject, because he did shepherd us through ornate tracks of Vergil's *Aeneid.*

There was this tendency to teach us more or less useless knowledge. It also put us in danger of the snobbery that goes with schooling people in material they can never actually *apply* or put to use in any area of living interest, like Modern Languages or Cooking. James J. Robertson, the Rector, known as The Beak, was clearly gratified when some of us bookish lads opted for Greek instead of French. Some years later he himself chaired an Education Department Committee in Edinburgh which recommended that less Classics should be taught and more Modern Languages. The favouring of the traditional or archaic over the up-to-date infected many parts of the syllabus. One of the teachers I most respected, James 'Paasie' Walker (History), must have taught us the German Reformation at least three times and 'the Tudors' more like forty-three times. His grave and learned style made everything seem equally important. His classes were lectures, delivered from notes propped up on a late nineteenth century attaché case. His tests were written on the board in pale chalk copperplate and the questions were extremely long. He limped heavily from a Great War wound and according to my mother 'shrapnel was still coming out of his leg'. As he spoke, he pulled hairs out of his steel-grey moustache with the thumb and little finger of his left hand and it occurs to me now that this may have been to distract him from the agony of his leg. What a shame that the syllabus stopped short of the Great War. For that matter it stopped short of the Industrial Revolution, just as Scottish history concentrated on Robert the Bruce and Mary, Queen of Scots and never so much as mentioned Clydeside or the Highland Clearances.

Our teachers tended to be old because the younger men were away at the War, at least until 1945 or so. This meant that some of them had to double up and teach outside their specialisms. Bouncer Bruce was a chemist who sometimes taught us Geography, and was called Bouncer because he was more or less spherical, or heading that way. But why if he taught us Science, and Geography, did he once instruct us in the making up of sentences using common phrases?

Although English Lit. was to be my life's work I had rather written off School English as a waste of time. Jimmy Ed (Eddison)

> actually liked the footling essays of Charles Lamb and the creaking antiquarianism of Scott's *Ivanhoe*, or did he pretend to for professional reasons? Had he really no liking for anything written after, say, 1850? When a modern-minded teacher at last arrived, it was like pure oxygen. A.B. 'Sandy' Russell saved our sixth-year English from stupefaction in our very first lesson with him, by reading out passages from some of the best poetry published in that very decade, T. S. Eliot's *Four Quartets*. Sandy was what would now be called cool, and quite aware of his own heterodoxy.
>
> By that time the refreshment of new and newish waves of teachers was making us feel that the stale dust of ages was being blown away at last. In our final year of Greek, Scottie Cooper, who looked young enough to be our elder brother, so enthused us that we used to voluntarily translate thirty lines of Sophocles for homework instead of the allotted twenty. If someone made a howler, there was no shaming rage from Scottie, not even pained reproach, just a nimble suggestion of something better and more correct, and lo and behold! His method worked! The years of being bullied for our own good had been unnecessary after all.

From a slightly later period R. Halsey G. Bradford, who attended the School between 1951 and 1965, told of his memories of that time:

> From Nursery we moved into the Kindergarten proper, where a new intake doubled our numbers, and we were divided into the As and Bs, the As being, on average, six months older. We learned to read and write, under the tutelage of Miss Brown and Mrs Grant, which prepared us well for the years and careers ahead, but I sometimes wonder if I would have been more successful had my mother heeded the then Rector, Sir James J. Robertson. We were going back to Ireland for Christmas and permission was sought for me to be absent for an extra couple of days. Somehow the request was escalated to the Rector, and my mother was summoned to explain this heresy. She was much chided and told of her irresponsibility and reminded that rules were rules. Be it on her own head if she put Ireland before her son's education, and he wasn't all that well-behaved anyway and this would just encourage him to disobey. Both of us felt awful but my father said to hell and we went anyway and my education and character suffered and society is still paying the price.

We played football and 'foot-cricket' in the playground, and more football after School in Thistle Lane. We collected bubblegum cards and team photos of football teams, we bought gobstoppers and sherbet sookers from Beggies [in Esslemont Avenue] and we lied about the victories of our conkers. We made slides in the playground and used them briefly before the jannies salted them. In the days after the Timmer Market pea-shooters were much in evidence, and marbles too had their season and their vocabulary.

In the classroom the Bs learned much from Miss Swan, Miss Gracie, Miss Stewart and Miss Valentine, while the As had Miss Andrews, Mrs Angus, Miss Hunter and Mr Farquhar. We all had Mr Sawdust for speech therapy and all learned to recite 'Algy met a bear'. We all studied the Geography of Europe. When one of our class proudly announced that he never washed and never cleaned his shoes – Moozie, James D. Morrison, the Lower School Headmaster, brought in brushes and polish and made the hapless boy clean his shoes in front of the class.

Some of us joined Cubs, often the Grammar packs (1st, 9th and 17th). We learned rugby on Friday afternoons at 'the field'. What came along with rugby were showers, and our first experience of group nudity.

So on to 1959 and to the Middle School, there to be joined by all kinds of new faces from other schools. They had all done well in the Control, whereas we didn't even have to pass. As and Bs finally became irrelevant and we became 1S or 1G or whatever, following the initial of your class-master. Some were already in long trousers and every week someone new graduated to them. Those still in shorts would have loved to have changed, but most probably had, like me, mothers who felt that they were 'growing up too quickly'. O those months and years of embarrassment.

Science teachers seemed to come and go with regularity, but the boredom of the curriculum overrode the staff changes. For one particularly awful term we did calorimetry under Dr Milligan. We had to write down each experiment in pencil then transcribe it at home in ink to black hard-covered notebooks. We were seldom even allowed to conduct the experiments ourselves – punishment for being too noisy.

Teachers were always, I suppose, in that quandary of whether to teach us to pass exams or to educate us. Of course there was some overlap, but there was a different emphasis. Bob McNay was a student of Higher papers, and his department was dedicated to getting as many of us as possible to pass that exam. But it was fun; I sometimes won a prize and I ended up taking Geography at university, where, for me, education was secondary to passing. I too, pored over old papers and figured out the odds and studied as little as possible and was glad for Bob McNay's advice.

Not judged good enough for sporting teams, I turned to the Hill Walking Club, with whom I had several years of much enjoyment if several days of sheer misery. The triumvirate of Donald Hawksworth (Music), Jimmy Will (Art) and Ian 'Twinks' Stephen (Maths) aided and abetted by others, led us up and down and through the Grampians, the Cairngorms, and the mountains of the west coast.

The scouts were also big in my life and I progressed through the 1st Troop to become the patrol leader of the Swifts . . .

Punishment ranged from extra homework to detention to the belt to Joseph the gumshoe (Andy Stevenson) [Head Games master] to a visit to Vass. Detention for being late was accompanied with a warning from Jessie Lynch, Deputy Rector, 'If you're late again within a fortnight the Rector shall wish to see you'. In 5th and 6th years, you had some mates who were prefects, and being late was more often overlooked.

I have somehow meandered my way to Sixth Year, having missed out the Mitsukoo, Madam's, the Rendez [respectively, a Japanese themed restaurant at Holburn Junction, a dancing class at the Cowdray Hall and a cafe on Forest Avenue, but all facilities for the mingling of the pupils of the then single sex schools in the City] and the typhoid (Summer 1964). By this time some had left School for some reason or another, some were completing the requirements to advance to their next desired step, and some were just marking time, 'readying themselves for university', or, in truth, enjoying the absolute freedom of having little to do. I took Dynamics, which was one third of a Higher. I painted maps of the Great lakes, the Damodar valley and Australia. I watched Test matches in the projection room. I took meteorological readings on top of the new Science/mathematics block. I planned summer jobs in the canneries of Peterborough and I played cricket for the FPs.

There was a new Hall by now and morning assembly moved

there. The denizens of the front row, 6th Year non-Prefects, were a motley crew who could have been expected to renounce this pomp and ceremony. But they loved singing and somehow enjoyed their spot in the limelight of sorts.

It had been fourteen years for some of us, shorter for most. Some enjoyed it, some didn't, but at worst it was the best of a necessary evil. We launched forth into the next episode in our lives and were generally glad that School was behind us.

Some have become accountants or tradesmen or entrepreneurs or managers or teachers or spies or salesmen or whatever. Some too became doctors or lawyers or diplomats. It is of no matter. What remains important, at least to me, is that I still feel a strong bond to those I knew at School, and trust it will remain strong in the years to come.

FOURTEEN Gill and Johnston, 1972–2004

This chapter gives a resumé of the major developments which took place in more recent years at the Grammar School. The other sections relate to staffing changes and the influx of French pupils and, more significantly, girls whose arrival in the last thirty years has further changed the ethos of the School.

ROBERT DOUGLAS GILL: RECTOR 1972–1987

The vacancy created by Skinner's retirement was filled by the appointment as Headmaster of Rubislaw Academy of Robert Douglas Gill. He was the first non-Classical graduate to take control of the School. Moreover, he was a native of Aberdeen and had been educated at the Central School before going on to Aberdeen University where his studies were interrupted by military service from 1942 to 1946. He completed his University training in 1949 when he graduated with an Honours degree in Modern Languages. After teacher-training he had a brief spell at Larbert before joining the staff of Gordon's College, where he spent eleven years as a Special Assistant in Modern Languages. While there he was also commanding officer of the Combined Cadet Force (CCF). His career then took him to Peterhead Academy and Perth Academy as principal teacher, and in 1969 he became Headmaster of Beath High School in Fife. With this experience behind him he was well qualified to take up his new post and face the challenges which awaited him.

As could be expected with his interest in languages, Gill loved travel and greatly enjoyed leading trips of staff and pupils abroad. Like his predecessors, he adopted a cautious approach to change and his policy was one of evolution rather than revolution. Not only did each year add a larger contingent of girls to the School roll but a working relationship with the Annexe at Rosemount had to be established under the control of one of the two deputy heads. Both of these situations were quietly and effectively dealt with. A new structure of guidance teachers was gradually introduced to meet the changing social composition of the School and the two original guidance teachers, Ian Stephen and John Flett, were joined by two more males and four ladies.

A change which was to have important effects for the School took place when local government was restructured in 1975 by the introduction of regionalisation. Aberdeen Town Council as a statutory body ceased to oversee local education and control passed into the hands of the Grampian Regional Council, a much wider and larger body covering most of North-East Scotland. Apart from the wider geographical provision one of the most significant results of the change was political. The Labour majority which had dominated Aberdeen's government now found itself facing a non-Labour majority.

One of the first reactions of the Aberdeen Town Council was to show its appreciation of its employees' efforts by spending some of its funds in providing them with lavish free hospitality in the Beach Ballroom. For School pupils the opportunity of enjoying a trip on the cruise ship the *Uganda* was made available. The Rubislaw pupils eagerly seized this chance and a hundred boys and two girls joined hundreds of pupils from the other Academies and set sail for the Baltic Sea under the command of the Deputy Rector, Arthur McCombie, and six other members of staff. The two girls, one of whom was Chinese, were linked with the group from Torry Academy. Starting and ending in Dundee the trip lasted a fortnight from the beginning of June 1974 and took the party as far as Leningrad and Moscow with a variety of trips ashore as well. It was a memorable experience for all who took part.

As had been promised, a final decision about the School's name was to be made when the last pupils who had entered the Grammar School as far back as 1965 completed their secondary education. In 1977 the decision had to be made by the Grampian Regional Council and it passed the matter over to the School Council for its view. This School body represented staff and pupils. The views of Gill were bound to play a decisive part in any discussion and at a meeting with the Headmaster, McCombie made the point that the first question that would be asked would be 'What do the pupils think?' McCombie stressed the need for hard evidence on the opinions of the pupils going as far as to suggest holding an Australian-type election where everyone had to vote. Gill agreed and as a further refinement it was decided that no warning of the vote would take place to avoid any lobbying.

On the day decided on for the election every class in the school was presented with a batch of voting papers: pink for the girls, blue for the boys, marked with three choices: 1 = Aberdeen Grammar School; 2 = Rubislaw Academy; 3 = No preference. The result was: 1 = 70%; 2 = 20%; 3 = 10%. The idea and execution were so successful that the Staff was also balloted and the result of their voting was: 1 = 60%; 2 = 40%.

Armed with this information, Gill met the School Council and as predicted the first question was about the pupils' views. Gill was able to give the overall result and could have given the details for every teaching group in the School. The outcome was questioned by one of the Staff members on the grounds that it was not known why they had voted in this way. A pupil member who later became a prominent broadcaster with the BBC (William B. Whiteford, GS 1972–8) gently pointed out that in an election by ballot you never knew why people voted as they did. Incidentally, the member of staff who had called for a staff ballot then voted against the finding of his referendum. The School Council voted for the proposal to restore the original name and the title of Rector and this was accepted by the Grampian Regional Council.

The one constant in a school is change. Buildings, staff and pupils are never the same for long. Aims and objectives in teaching are often subject to review and modification, even the means of enforcing discipline have had to be replaced by different systems. The resources for teaching have been greatly increased. When Gill came to the School, departments with film strip projectors and banda spirit printing facilities felt that they were at the forefront of educational technology. Radio and television began to offer visions of new approaches to the presentation of subjects. The introduction of Rank Xerox printing was at first received with a fair amount of doubt in some quarters about its value but before long staff came to recognise its possibilities and as these machines became progressively more sophisticated so they increased their potential assistance. To any retired member of staff returning now to the scene of his or her former endeavours probably the greatest impression must be the huge battery of technological resources which is available in a modern school.

And yet, looking back to the 1970s one can remember a 'phone call from a former pupil, Paul Cook, saying that he was going to upgrade his computer and was there any chance that the school would like to take the model he was replacing. The offer was duly accepted and Gill gratefully received the school's first computer. It was not long before an intense interest developed in Information Technology and instruction in IT became an established part of the curriculum. Not only the office but the Library and many classrooms became a different kind of resource centre. In a different direction, the teaching of Drama in a curricular setting was established as part of the English department by the later part of the decade. It was later decided to set up a department for Drama and Media Studies.

As the 1970s drew to a close and a Head Girl, Ruth Hutchison, became the first occupant of that position in 1978–9, the School could claim to be a fully comprehensive co-educational district school. Gill must have looked forward to a more settled and peaceful decade to follow but the 1980s proved to be just as challenging as previous times.

With the majority of pupils now coming from the catchment area stretching from Anderson Drive in the west to George Street in the east and from Ashgrove Road in the north to Great Western Road in the south there were still occasions when appeals had to be settled when parents applied for admission on special grounds. At one point a senior education official expressed the view, privately, that it would be interesting to see what would happen if the zoning restrictions were removed. He had not long to wait to find out because in August 1982 the 'Parents' Charter' was introduced nationally and this gave parents the right to choose which school they wished their children to attend.

One report on the outcome of the Charter emerged on the pages of the *Daily Record* where its education correspondent reported on Thursday 11 April 1982, 'Parents are queuing up to get their children into Scotland's most popular comprehensive school.' He pointed to an intake into the GS of 165 pupils 'from outside its normal catchment area'. He then speculated on the reasons for this influx. Gill, when approached, simply replied, 'Parents do not have to give reasons for their selection.' In the years which followed the School roll continued to grow until it reached 1,719, which created great pressure on its facilities and staff.

In order to provide staff for the new comprehensive system, a major recruiting campaign had brought many into the teaching profession who had experience in other occupations. Teachers had became increasingly unhappy over their working conditions and all the teaching professional bodies soon found themselves in dispute with their employers. In the long drawn-out dispute – with its strikes and work-to-rule – it says much for Gill's diplomatic skills that what could have caused bitter divisions in staff relations was avoided and in the course of time normal service was mostly, if not entirely, resumed and the strikes and work-to-rule gradually came to an end.

Challenges of a different sort arose with the move to introduce a new national type of examination, the Standard Grade, which meant that all departments had to undertake a review of the presentation of their subject. It had become obligatory for all schools to produce a Prospectus. The Grammar School had had prospectuses for over a century but now a much more detailed survey of the history, organisation, examination results, disciplinary procedures, relations with parents, curriculum guidance provision and accommodation, was required.

Despite all the disruption, in 1986 Gill could still report that the results in the national examinations continued to be very satisfactory but that year brought major problems for the School when serious fires occurred twice in the first half of that year. The first fire started in the Science/Mathematics Block in laboratory 2 on the ground floor early in the morning of 13 February. Fortunately, the serious structural damage was restricted to the west end of that area although smoke spread beyond there. Four laboratories were out of commission for some time and this caused serious inconvenience and disruption for the Science Departments.

As the 1985–6 session gradually wound down and the summer holiday promised a welcome break from a hectic period, at the morning interval of Wednesday 2 July, there suddenly appeared a cloud of smoke above the east end of the main building. The fire alarms sounded and the buildings were evacuated, although most pupils were outside enjoying a break from classes. This was the start of the catastrophic fire which was to destroy the whole of the original building and the nineteenth-century extensions to the north.

The cause of the fire was quickly established as the result of work being carried out on the windows on the upper floor of the original building. The fire had been caused by the use of a blow lamp which ignited the frame of the window and then spread rapidly westwards to the rest of the central area. Apparently it had been the practice in the nineteenth century to pack the window frame surrounds with paper before sealing them with cement and after a hundred years this would have been very easily combustible.

The much earlier fears expressed about the limited supplies of water available, in case of fire, were realised. The Denburn was a mere trickle in July and for some reason the water in the swimming pond was not used probably because of chemical additives. The primary concern of the Fire Brigade was to ensure that there were no casualties and they refused to allow any effort to retrieve the many School treasures and personal belongings. The main losses were in the area of the Library where most of the books in Special Collections and its general Library stock were destroyed. The corridor which had contained the collection of stuffed birds and the oriental relics gifted by Cromar Watt was completely destroyed except for a small statue of Buddha which was thought to be metal but oddly enough survived although made of wood.

The progress of the fire was helped by so much wood which was a century old. The Art Department had long complained about lack of ventilation in its rooms until it was revealed not long before the fire that a long forgotten ventilation system actually existed and this helped to provide vents throughout the building to spread the fire. By late afternoon the fire was extinguished and the extent of the damage could be assessed. The wings which had been added in 1914 were untouched but access to the east wing had been made impossible. The Rector's room in the west wing and the Office were not affected and what archives there were, were held in these two areas.

Everyone who witnessed the fire probably has his or her own recollections of the event or some aspect of it. For example, when surveying the smouldering ruins Deputy McCombie said he wondered if the eighteenth-century long-case clock which had come from Schoolhill and which had been placed in the new main staffroom (the old Chemistry laboratory) had been destroyed. Retreating to the edge of the lawn in front of the school he was able to see the top of the clock had survived whereupon to his great surprise the clock duly struck five o'clock. Later firemen entered the building and retrieved the clock intact! The next day when the firemen were sifting through the debris which covered the area of the sanctum off the main library, the semi-jocular enquiry was made 'Have you found a gold watch?' They laughed but shortly after produced the gold watch which had belonged to Dr Melvin. It too had amazingly survived, though much damaged.

The period after the fire saw the immediate closure of the School for the summer holidays and an immediate consideration of the long-term and short-term planning for the School's future. The most important decision was made when the Convener of the Region assured everyone that the School would be rebuilt. The decision was not universally welcomed and a minority speculated on alternative uses of the site, though as a listed building its restoration in the long run was assured as a structure. Plans for rebuilding the School were approved by the Education Committee on 14 June 1988. They entailed a single-site school of 1,000 pupils with most of the new part open-plan. The rebuilding was to take place between 1988 and 1991 at a cost of £3 million.[1] The new structure was formally opened by the Regional Convener Robert Middleton on 4 March 1992.

Of course, what was of most immediate concern for the Rector was ensuring that accommodation would be available for the pupils when the School reassembled after the summer holidays. One idea which was floated was to bus pupils to Northfield Academy where empty accommodation might be used. It was met with the argument that apart from the complications of timetabling such a move, the so-called 'host' school might resent the intrusion and become the 'hostility' school. It was finally agreed to find the remedy closer at hand and spare space at Gilcomston (Skene Street) School could be used as it was within easy walking distance. However, the greatest innovation was the providing of extra temporary classrooms sited on the front lawn of the School. Hitherto, one had always been grateful that the decision in the years before 1863 to ensure plenty of space round the school meant that extensions could always be developed to the north and west and the view of the main building was unobstructed. But not so any longer and the result was what Gill gleefully called 'the Village'. The temporary classrooms in many ways offered the teachers who were drafted into them better facilities than they had endured previously in the now fire-damaged areas.

Against all the odds the School was ready after a frantic holiday period to open for business at the beginning of the new session and the staff and pupils settled into the new set-up quite smoothly. It was suggested that the reopening might be marked with the ringing of the school bell which had welcomed pupils in the past for many years but had been silent for some time. The suggestion was not acted upon.

In January 1987 Gill retired from the Rectorship after fourteen years in post and could look back with satisfaction over the period which had seen the transformation of the School from a selective boys' school into a co-educational comprehensive. In a time when there was constant pressure from some quarters for radical change his policy of caution, sticking firmly to his ideas of how the School should proceed, was justified by the popular demand for admissions when the Parents' Charter was introduced. To the outside world Gill presented a rather serious, solemn even stern appearance but the private person was quite different. Few could remember how in his student days as an accomplished pianist he had been a key figure in a local dance band. But many got the chance to witness his great sense of fun on trips abroad and at social gatherings at his home after a variety of School occasions. He was always greatly interested in the fortunes of Aberdeen Football Club and the sporting activities of School and FP teams. He was a very keen bowler and was a popular member of the Woodend Bowling Club. He was very fortunate to have the support of his wife, Isobel, who

The old Library was created in 1900. In the 1960s it was converted into English classrooms.

The Physics lab of Alex Speirs is now replaced by a corridor and guidance rooms.

The Chemistry lab became the main staffroom from 1964 until the fire in 1986.

The post-1914 School with its new East and West wings (the photograph being taken before 1927).

LEFT. Lord Alness was a famous former pupil who became Secretary of State for Scotland and who unveiled the War Memorials in 1923 and 1950.

BELOW. The modernised School Hall containing the War Memorials and Malayan Clock before the construction of the new Hall post-1960.

Theodore Watt was noted for his dedicated service to the School and the FP Club in many capacities.

Sir James J.R. McLeod was the famous former pupil who shared the Nobel Prize in Medicine in 1923 for his contribution to the discovery of insulin.

ABOVE. The School cap of Donny Innes for rugby, when caps and sports blazers were a feature of School life.

LEFT. Lt R.G. Combe gained a Victoria Cross posthumously for his bravery in WWI.

RIGHT. Flt Lt John A. Cruickshank gained a Victoria Cross for his outstanding courage in WWII.

BELOW. 'Petit France' was the Total French School established in 1974 in the former Chalmers School.

LEFT. The fire of June 1986 destroyed the School building.

BELOW. Another photograph of the 1986 fire. The School was rebuilt by 1992.

ABOVE LEFT. William Johnston, Rector, 1987–2004, oversaw the rebuilding of the main block and the modernisation of a one-site School.

ABOVE RIGHT. Graham Legge became the Rector of the Grammar School in August 2004.

RIGHT. Tracey Menzies (née Robb) was elected the first Lady President of the FPs for 2011–12.

shared his sense of fun in attending so many School social events. He died suddenly in January 1997 and details of his career were recorded in the same School Magazine in September 1997 as the notification of the death of the previous Rector, John Vass Skinner.

STAFFING

In the early 1970s pastoral care became a serious concern for Scottish schools and the development of Guidance staff or Year Teachers offered yet another opportunity for staff to widen their opportunities for internal promotion. However, these changes were not an exclusive monopoly and, as the posts increased in number, so competition came from outside the School and several new members of staff were welcomed to the GS. This was particularly the case for lady members of staff who were appointed to ensure each year group had a female and male member of staff to look after them as the School population became fully co-educational by 1979.

For a time the Guidance staff had a mathematical appearance as the originals – Ian Stephen and John Flett – were joined by Pat Scott and an incomer, Bill Barber. When Stephen moved up to Assistant Head, Tom Henderson, who had been a member of the old Rosemount staff, Ian Spence, Russell Gray and later Steve Parry became members of the Guidance team as year teachers. On the ladies side, Mary Dutch, Janette Black, Enid Blaikie, Sandra Ramsay and Doris Kinghorn, all made notable contributions to the development of this new structure. By 1980 the ranks of the year teachers were supplemented by the inclusion of two assistant principals on general non-subject duties – Eva Cowie and Hugh Diack.

While these changes were taking place, teaching in the classroom, laboratory, workshop and Gymnasium still went on. A completely new department for Home Economics was set up under Mrs Clark to cater for the influx of girls, although some boys also trickled into the facilities situated at Rosemount Annexe where, after a brief spell under the Deputy Rector, supervision was taken over by an assistant head, Stanley Allan, who virtually created an 'imperium in imperio'.[2] He had the challenging task of controlling a large number of diverse departments and semi-departments in a scattered collection of buildings with a shifting complement of pupils who trekked between the main area and the Annexe in their hundreds each period changeover. He was able to do this very successfully while still maintaining the integrity of the School.

The School roll grew and the teaching staff swelled to cope with it. By 1980 its teaching staff numbered about a hundred. The English department numbered twelve; the Mathematics department had eleven; and Science, which had been separated into Chemistry, Physics and Biology, totalled sixteen. The PE department had risen to ten but some of the ladies there were part-time. But the great increase in numbers was not shared by Classics, where Ron McLeod was left as the sole teacher of what had once been the most prestigious department in the School.

Many changes in personnel took place in the 1970s. When Archie Baxter retired in 1976, he was the last member of staff to have been appointed before the Second World War. His only rival for this distinction had been his old friend and colleague, Sandy Bruce, who had succeeded John Lynch as head of Chemistry after many years teaching in that department.

As the opportunities for promotion in the school increased so they did elsewhere. So principal teachers such as Drew Low and John Wiseman in Physics and Alistair Marr in RE only stayed briefly; others such as Mike Wilson in Mathematics, Brian Anderson in Physics, Bill May[3] in Chemistry, Ian Milne in Modern Languages and Alan Smith in RE all settled in for the longer haul into the 1980s and beyond. They were joined by Guinevere Thomaneck, in charge of German, and David Swanson[4] in PE. Archie Fraser had taken over the Technical department and Douglas Milne succeeded Laurence Murray in History. Another notable character came to replace Bob McNay, when Jim Gelly found his way to the Geography department.

Looking forward to the 1980s Gill suggested, or at least hoped, that the decade would bring a less fraught period for the School. Even then there were problems of a declining school population, shortage of funding and staff reductions and transfers to contend with, but all Authority schools at that time faced these difficulties. However, what the GS had to deal with in the period was the consequences of the Parents' Charter. Far from a declining roll, this move to give parents an unrestricted choice of school brought as many as two hundred and sixty pupils who would previously have been ineligible to come. The result was a roll of 1,720 and the arrival of staff from other schools whose rolls were declining.[5] The situation led to criticism of the School in some quarters.

In the late 1970s the national report of the Dunning Committee into assessment led to the decision that a drastic overhaul of external school examinations was required. The relatively straightforward Ordinary Grade was replaced by the more complex Standard Grade. All of this put increasing pressure on the School staff who shared with teachers generally the feeling that they were being overworked and underpaid. Throughout Scotland a more militant attitude surfaced as morale sank and the teaching unions pressed the authorities with demands for improved conditions. The problem was how to put pressure on the authorities without involving teachers generally in heavy financial sacrifices. The tactic adopted by the unions was to target particular schools rather than call for national strikes. The schools so selected had to be "prestigious" so that the public and the policy makers would have to take notice of the campaign. The GS fell into this category. Hitherto, representatives of the teaching unions had acted as distributors of union information and collectors of annual subscriptions but now they had to adopt the role of shop stewards as they performed the duties that their unions required of them. Strikes took place and 'work-to-rule' took place. Outside the classrooms more or less all the extra-curricular activities came to a stop, with clubs and societies and games restricted.

Fortunately, the potential for internal union rivalry and personal animosity was largely avoided and the long period of unrest came to an end leaving a legacy which hindered the resumption of some of the extra-curricular actively at weekends. For many staff the 'work-to-rule' had freed them from weekend commitments and freedom once tasted was not easy to give up. Keen walkers on the staff such as Ian Stephen, Jim Will and Pat Scott still enjoyed the hillwalking trips and others such as Neill Montgomery maintained the practice encouraged by Morland Simpson to take an active part in coaching games and travelling with teams. By the mid-1980s the staff reached 120 members, but at least half of them were ladies, often with domestic ties, so Joyce Webster, Sandra Ramsay, Ellie Shepherd shared with Dave Swanson and Brendan Adey the problem of recruiting help from other departments' teaching staff.

As the School emerged from the difficult mid-1980s it suffered major blows with the fires of 1986. With Gill's retirement shortly after, it was his successor, who was faced with a devastated building when he arrived on 30 March 1987.

WILLIAM JOHNSTON: RECTOR 1987–2004

Since 1863 the School had undergone major redevelopments in 1914 and 1964, so if any good came out of the fires it was the opportunity to undertake a major internal reconstruction of the interior within the shell of the original building. Apart from the two major redevelopments there had also been a series of changes at the end of the nineteenth century, with the result that while the School presented an imposing appearance to the outside world, internally it had become something of a warren.

Trying to explain where everything had been to the new Rector proved a difficult task for Deputy McCombie and Head Janitor, Ron Foulger. It was probably fortunate then that the Rector and the architects had a blank sheet to start the planning of the replacing of the old building. It took some time but eventually there emerged from behind the fence a modern layout, admirable and functional but to Former Pupils pre-1986 'not our School'. No flagstones in the corridor, no lists of names of team members and no photographs of teams of yesteryear along the corridor walls, though some of these were saved to puzzle later generations.

Despite all the disruption of the 'troubles' the staff adjusted to the changed conditions, temporary and permanent. The decision had been taken to cut the School roll by limiting the intake for the first year so that the roll gradually reduced. The other main aim was to bring the whole School together on one site and so Rosemount Annexe was vacated and no longer did the legions march up and down Grosvenor Place.

The plans for the reconstructed building were printed in the magazine for 1989 along with an account of the plans approved by the Education Committee on 14 June 1988. When the rebuilding was complete there was an official ceremony on 4 March 1992 to mark the occasion. A lunch was followed by a gathering in the School Hall presided over by a Former Pupil, the regional convener Councillor Robert Middleton JP. The event was commemorated by the presentation of a bronze plaque and a board of photographs. From the board a statue of Lord Byron looks steadfastly in the wrong direction, but if this is seen as a mark of his disdain the tour of the new sections was met with a sense of wonder and admiration for the great ingenuity that the architects had shown by fitting so much into such a relatively small area. Again the Magazine produced plans of the finished articles and the 107 guests were able to go home with a brochure containing a brief history of the School supplied by the retired Deputy Rector, Arthur McCombie.

Gill was succeeded by William Johnston, an Ayrshire man, the first Rector to be a graduate of Science and au fait with the modern technology which IT had begun to offer to education. His earliest experience in teaching had been in Glasgow and this had been followed by a number of appointments and promotions up and down the A9 from Perth to Inverness culminating in his Deputy Rectorship of Culloden Academy in Inverness.

His move to Aberdeen Grammar faced him with unusual challenges, a scattered site and a fire-damaged central building with all the difficulties these created. He was immediately involved in the architectural planning for the restoration of the fire-damaged area as well as the day-to-day running of a large co-educational secondary school. The official reopening of the building in 1992 was proof of the fact that he had proved himself a very capable successor to his many distinguished predecessors.

His office was always meticulously well-organised, a model which was both admired and envied by his colleagues. He was able and ready to lead the school into the 21st century of modern educational practice. His previous experience in Guidance work fitted in well with his kind and considerate concern for the welfare of pupils and staff. He took a very keen and active interest in every aspect of school life, academic, cultural and sporting. He was found most Saturdays on the touchline at Rubislaw Field and it was one of his greatest aims to obtain the provision of modern Physical Education facilities in the shape of a Games Hall and improved accommodation at Rubislaw. These the school now enjoys.

So it was something of a surprise when he decided to take early retirement in 2004 aged only 57 though having sadly lost his wife, Katie, in 2003 and with a grown-up family of three daughters perhaps, though much regretted, his decision was understandable.

Retirement saw him continuing to take an active interest in helping with coaching at Rubislaw but also providing him with the opportunity to pursue an academic course in Gaelic Studies leading to a first-class honours MA as well as continuing to take an active interest in educational developments in the Aberdeen area. He also had more time for his great interest in hillwalking.

For many it was almost unbelievable to hear of his tragic death in 2011 in the hills he loved so much. The sense of loss over a wide section of the community was illustrated by the huge congregation from many walks of life which gathered at Skene Parish Church for his funeral.

Graham Legge became Rector of the GS in August 2004. He was educated at Buckie High School and Aberdeen University. After holding Geography posts in several schools in the North-East he moved into school management. He had been Rector of Kemnay Academy, 1998–2004.

PUPILS: THE FRENCH INVASION

In the 1970s as Aberdeen became deeply involved in the oil industry, a variety of oil companies set up headquarters here. Foreign companies brought in many employees and their families who had to be accommodated and educated. One of these companies was Total which came to an arrangement with Aberdeen Town Council that the Council would provide accommodation for the French schoolchildren in Skene Square Primary School and Aberdeen GS.

The Grammar itself enrolled a mixture of different nationalities – American, Argentinian and Venezuelan among others connected with the oil industry – while others joined the American School set up independently at Cults. Wherever the French went they provided schools which operated on their national pattern, a system which allowed pupils to transfer easily wherever their family circumstances took them in the world. The old Chalmers School, available because of the various alterations to school accommodation, became the 'French School', where all instruction was given in French. The headmaster and most, but not all, of the staff were French.

The pupils quite happily accepted the requirement to wear the GS uniform and made use of the various PE facilities of the school. One of the trials which they faced was to accept the Scottish cuisine which was provided in the School Dining Hall. Wherever possible they were welcomed to share School facilities. Many of their homes were scattered round the town and surrounding district so the company provided buses to collect them in the morning and then to take them home after school. This meant that their ability to take part in after-school activities was very restricted though some played in the rugby teams and the football teams at Skene Square.

Most of the senior teachers stayed for only a few years so a succession of very interesting friendly French people followed M Hervier, the first headmaster. M Gallion, M Chevreau and M Albert were followed by M Lebresne who stayed for several years. M Albert had enjoyed his spell in Aberdeen so much that he and his wife returned for a second spell. Two Aberdeen ladies, Mrs Robertson and Mrs Morrison, taught in the French School, and along with Bill Kemp, who helped in PE, undoubtedly proved of great assistance in explaining any of the mysteries of Scottish and Aberdonian customs and practices which might have puzzled their French colleagues.

The Total Oil Company was extremely generous in inviting Grammar staff to enjoy their hospitality after the presentations which the French produced to mark their end of session in the School Hall. They quickly established the practice of inviting two senior GS pupils and a member of staff to visit Paris each year to experience the delights of that city accompanied by members of the company's staff. For everyone who enjoyed this trip it was a wonderful experience.

Perhaps one way of illustrating the extent of the interest and support which the Company provided for the GS was when it said it wished to mark its gratitude for the welcome that its school had received from the GS staff and pupils by giving a gift. Rector Gill and his Deputy were faced with the difficult task of suggesting something suitable and acceptable. After much thought it was agreed that a computer would be a reasonable request. But the company rejected the suggestion and instead offered a minibus! This it duly provided.

As the Company dug its roots deeper into Aberdeen the number of French families was reduced and the move to establish a school on one site for all ages was accomplished by building an extension block near Whitehall Place in the area of the old playground of Westfield school and Chalmers School. All in all it had been a splendid example of the *entente cordiale.*

PUPILS: GIRLS

When the decision was taken that the Grammar School would progress to becoming a co-educational School, in the first intake during transition over a hundred girls joined the First Year and moved on through the School in the following five years. Accepting a year at a time proved a great success as the girls were able to be integrated gradually into the traditions and values of the Grammar. Although there was an appreciation, in all parts of the School community, that Grammar girls would not gain equal status with boys immediately, there was also an acceptance that this was the goal and that within a reasonable timescale it would be achieved.

In a number of respects the Grammar had already changed significantly from its selective past to a more comprehensive institution and the introduction of girls was but another phase in the development of the modern GS. Indeed, it was argued in some educational quarters that girls 'civilise' a school and strengthen its academic record. Be that as it may, issues such as discipline policy needed to be applied fairly to all pupils. Thus when the new Rector, R.D. Gill, determined that girls would not be subject to corporal punishment, it became increasingly difficult to continue to use the tawse to punish boys while giving a different punishment to girls for the same offence. National developments, banning physical punishments in schools, solved this problem for the School and detention for forty-five minutes after 4 p.m. became the uniform punishment for pupils.

A survey of the existing buildings led to an early realisation of the need to build a new toilet block for the girls on part of the interior quadrangle. This was completed before the first girls arrived. It was a worthy addition to the premises and had washbasins and mirrors, essentials for young ladies. However, the toilets soon became a smokers' haven and refuge, as they did in other such establishments. The newly appointed lady Assistant Rector, Mrs Jean Downie, and the lady janitor, were kept busy dealing with such matters, until they were helped in their task by the appointment of Girl Prefects in Fifth and Sixth Years.

The wearing of uniform was not an issue, although wearing it tidily was another matter. The girls were expected to wear ties, as the boys did, and skirts were also standard dress, and the School was in a strong position to enforce high standards given the support of parents and staff. Tight control was also exacted by the use of School dress suppliers, Esslemont and Macintosh.

By 1973 all pupils entering first year (S1) were new to the School and the girls and boys, organised in mixed classes, were escorted from class to class by senior boy pupils round what was after all a fairly complicated and scattered School environment. For most subjects the girls just took their place with the rest of the class but one problem arose with the requirement that 'practical' classes had to be restricted to a maximum of twenty pupils. While a very few girls expressed a wish to concentrate on Technical rather than Home Economics, on occasion the numbers of girls and boys in a Technical/HE group forced the Rector to the pragmatic solution of making the pupils take both subjects so that creating the appropriate number for a 'practical' class was simple. In Home Economics this was possible as the department was fortunate to share the services of several guidance staff: Janette Black, Enid Blaikie and Eleanor More being all experienced teachers.

Presiding over the task of incorporating the girls into the Physical Education activities was Roy Falconer, a Gordonian who had taught in St Albans in England before returning to Aberdeen. His strong leadership in this area was a major contribution to the School's successful transition into co-education before he returned to his old school, Gordon's College, as the Head of its PE department.

One of the main characters in developing the PE side of education for Girls was Carrie Welsh, who for twenty-seven years in feminine garb personified the type of teacher that Morland Simpson sought in vain when he arrived in Aberdeen. Carrie was just as much at home in the History classroom as she was in the games field and she made a massive contribution to the development of girls' hockey both locally and nationally. Her husband, Gary, was also on the PE staff before moving to the International School at Cults.

The girls of the Grammar took advantage of the opportunities offered to them. Academically, they competed well with the boys and prize lists began to include increasing numbers of girls. Girls, too, soon raised their career expectations and worked hard, in general, to prove themselves capable of taking on, and succeeding at, even the most competitive of courses in Higher Education including Medicine and Law.

Out of the classroom the girls also played their full part in the life of the School. The Hill-Walking Club became popular and they were supported by female staff members who accompanied them. Similar arrangements enabled girls to join the Duke of Edinburgh Award Scheme in Fourth Year and above and by that time the number of female staff appointed had increased making logistical problems less of an issue. The track record of the girls in the Scheme is good and a number have succeeded in attaining the challenging Gold Award and have usually travelled to Edinburgh to receive it. Girls also took to Debating, one of the School's strengths over the years, and Skiing and the CCF were also areas where the girls played their full part.

As the girls progressed through the School in the 1970s they were fortunate to be arriving as a new era was being introduced into Scottish Schools. 'Guidance' or 'Pupil Support', as it is now called, originated with a publication from the SED in 1968. Although Scottish schools had always been concerned with the welfare of their pupils, the move to comprehensive education in the 1960s was the first time that the education system as a whole had had to face up to the challenge of S1–S6 all-through secondary schooling. Schools now had a wider ability range and socio-economic mix than ever before. So the GS too had on its agenda the problem of accommodating pupil needs. True, the School had a House system but the SED now expected the development of personal, vocational and curricular Guidance. Each pupil would now be entitled to receive advice or help from a teacher with a special and continuing responsibility to do so. Guidance would be for all pupils, not only for those with problems. Such an ethos resulted in the growing recognition that all teachers had a role in the area of guidance and the girls benefited from this. A strong team was on hand to support them.

The teaching profession itself was changing markedly and a growing number of teachers were female providing the role models needed for the increasing number of girls in the School. Mary Matheson, Nan Boyd, Jeanette Shaw and Eva Cowie were joined by Jean Downie and Jeanette Massie. Their numbers warranted the provision of a small staffroom in the English department. The promotion of Mrs Clark to the post of Principal Teacher of Home Economics was another sign of the progress of women in the School.

The first Head Girl was Ruth Bradshaw (née Hutchison) (GS 1974–9), the first of a family including also a sister and two brothers who all attended the School. It is unlikely that Ruth, a schoolgirl hockey internationalist, will ever have a successor to equal her record of holding the office for two years in Class V and Class VI.

Head Girls for some time created a kind of medical sorority as Lesley Galloway (née Fraser) (GS 1974–80), Fiona McKay (née McCombie) (GS 1975–81), Lesley Watson (née Carson) (GS 1981–5) and Sui-yen Allison (née Ah See) (GS 1978–84) all joined that profession. Two of them also married the Head Boy of their vintage. The legal profession attracted several girls, Louise Sutherland (GS 1973–9), Yvonne McAllister (GS 1984–90), Lindsay Dron (GS 1975–80), Margaret Macrae-Gibson (GS 1977–82) and Tracey Menzies (née Robb) (GS 1981–6). Others followed different career paths. Margery Taylor (née Coutts) (1975–81) qualified in Physical Education and took up teaching as well as having an outstanding career in women's hockey, both indoor and outdoor, winning over a hundred caps for Scotland; Shona Marshall (née Milne) (GS 1979–82) won a silver medal in Shooting at the Commonwealth Games in Delhi in 2010; Gillian Jack (née Taylor) (GS 1975–81) trained as an opera singer at the RSAMD; Jennifer Laing (née Lamond) (GS 1977–83) was elected as a Labour Councillor to Aberdeen City Council. Ruth Dukes (GS 1989–95) took up a teaching post at LSE, while Alison Smith (née Smart) (GS 1982–6) and Emma Mair (née Hendry) (GS 1985–91) went into business. Gillian A. Thomas (née Crookshanks) (GS 1975–80) became the President of the FP Canadian Centre in 2004–5 and the Secretary from 2011.

Another Head Girl, Fiona Bennett (GS 1982–88), pursued a career in Theology and Social Work which took her to Europe and America and various religious posts until she took up her present position as a minister of Augustine United Church on George IV Bridge, Edinburgh. Karen

McCombie (GS 1975–81) went south to London where she followed a career as a writer of popular fiction for the younger ages. Another who followed a career in the south was Jenny Turner (GS 1975–80) who worked as a journalist with *The Guardian*.

Possibly lady-like modesty seems to have made girls reluctant to subscribe in numbers to the 'Notes on Former Pupils' in the Magazine and for many the ties of married life interrupted the advancement in their careers. One exception was Lorraine (Lori) Manders (née McKenna) who attended the GS between 1979 and 1985. For twelve years she was Director of Development and External Affairs, as well as Director of Marketing, at Aberdeen University. In 2011 she was appointed Director of Development and Alumni Relations at University College London.

One Head Girl epitomises the talent exhibited by many of the girls who have attended the GS. By the time Tracey Robb (later Menzies) joined the School from Mile End in 1981 the Grammar could claim to be a co-educational School. It was certainly not a boys' school with girls added, if it ever was. She knew she was privileged in attending; after all, her parents in their recent move to Aberdeen had been advised that the Grammar was the School their daughter should attend. She took all the opportunities on offer and had a very successful schooling. She was Head Girl in her final year.

Tracey completed a Law degree from Aberdeen University, worked with Ledingham Chalmers from 1992 until 2006 and now is a partner in the Aberdeen office of Pinsent Mason, dealing mainly with real estate. She became a Governor of 'the other place' – RGC – in 2006. Her grounding for a successful career clearly says much for her and her former school. So does her extra-curricular success. She was capped 153 times for Scotland at hockey (as goalkeeper) and eight times for Britain. She captained the Scottish team in the 1988 Hockey World Cup and the 2002 Commonwealth Games. In 2011 she gained an OBE and in 2011–12 she was elected the first female President of the FP Club, inaugurated by Morland Simpson in 1893. Needless to say, she won't be the last.

PUPILS: A SELECTION OF MALE FPS EDUCATED AT THE SCHOOL AFTER 1972

David Pitt-Watson (b. 1956) left the GS in 1974 to attend Queen's, Oxford, reading PPE. He has gained a global reputation in responsible investment and advises on industrial and financial policy.

(Prof.) Peter Davidson (b. 1957) attended the Grammar between 1970 and 1975 and was First Science bursar in the Bursary Competition. He took a FCH in Engineering Science at Aberdeen and a PhD at Cambridge. He worked for Westinghouse in Pittsburgh before taking up a lectureship at Imperial College. Since 2006 he has been Professor of Fluid Mechanics at Cambridge and has published extensively.

(Prof.) Philip C. Hannaford (b. 1958) was educated at the Grammar between 1973 and 1976 and Aberdeen University, before completing his GP training in Sheffield, 1982–5. He was NHS Grampian Professor of Primary Care and from 2002 was Director, Institute of Applied Health Sciences, Aberdeen University. Since 2011 he has been a Vice-Principal.

Arthur D. Stewart (b.1958) attended the GS between 1963 and 1976 and then took a degree in Geology at Edinburgh University. He studied further at Calgary University and lectured at Aberdeen University in Sports Science. In 2005 he became a senior lecturer at RGU in the department of Obesity and Epidemiology and recently advised Olympic athletes on protecting their health from the dangers of extreme weight-loss.

Robert B.M. Howie (b. 1960) attended the Grammar between 1972 and 1978 before studying Law at Aberdeen University. He became an advocate in 1986 and took Silk in 2000.

(Prof.) Murray Pittock (b. 1962) was educated at the Grammar between 1973 and 1978, Glasgow and Balliol, Oxford (where he was a Snell Exhibitioner). He was a lecturer then Reader at Edinburgh University, 1989–96. He was Professor of Literature at Strathclyde University, 1996–2003, then Professor of Scottish and Romantic Literature at Manchester University, 2003–7. He is now Bradley Professor of English Literature, Head of College and Vice-Principal (Arts) at the University of Glasgow. He has written a number of publications.

Michael D. Clark (b. 1962) attended the Grammar (Rubislaw Academy) in 1974–5, the Royal Ballet School and Ballet Rambert. In 1984 he launched his own company, Michael Clark and Company, which was an immediate success. He has become an internationally renowned dancer and choreographer and was awarded an honorary degree of Doctor of Art by Robert Gordon University in 2011.

(Andrew) John Stevenson (b. 1963) attended the Grammar between 1975 and 1981, graduating from Dundee University in History and Politics. He studied Law at Chester before qualifying as a solicitor. He became a councillor in 1999 and a Conservative MP (for Carlisle) at the general election in 2010.

Timothy McKay (b. 1962) attended the Grammar between 1976 and 1981, entering Class II and was Head Boy in 1981. He trained in PE and taught in Aberdeen primary and secondary schools before becoming Principal Teacher of Guidance at St Machar Academy. He took an MEd degree from Aberdeen University and was appointed Assistant Head at Banchory Academy, Deputy Head at Kemnay and Rector of Alford and Ellon Academies. In 2012 he was seconded as Temporary Rector of Peterhead Academy.

Brothers Michael J. Smith (b. 1966) (GS 1978–84), and Roderick C. Smith (b. 1968) (GS 1980–6) have been involved with Aberdeenshire and Scottish cricket since the mid-1980s. Mike was awarded his first full cap in 1987 against Ireland, was dropped in 1990 but returned in 1994. He was involved in the ICC Trophy in 1997 and in the World Cup in 1999. Roddy represented Scotland at every level, U16, U17 and U19 and was capped against Denmark in 1994. He was Scottish Batsman of the Year in 1998. After 10 years with Sport Scotland he became Chief Executive Officer of Cricket Scotland in 2004.

Douglas M. Watson (b. 1967) attended the Grammar from 1979 to 1985 when he was Head Boy and winner of the All Round Trophy. He graduated in Law at Aberdeen University and is in practice as a solicitor in the city. He served on the FP Club Executive and Club Centre committees for several years and has been chairman of each. His wife was Head Girl in 1985, Fiona Carson.

Russell Anderson (b. 1978) attended the Grammar between 1982 and 1987 and played centre-back for Aberdeen FC, 1997–2007. He was transferred to Sunderland and Derby. He played eleven times for Scotland.

Barry J. McGlashan (b. 1974) attended the Grammar between 1986 and 1992 and graduated with FCH at Gray's School of Art in 1996. He returned to teach at Gray's until 2005 when he became a full-time artist. He has exhibited widely and won a number of artistic awards.

Jonathan W. Rowson (b. 1977) attended the Grammar between 1989 and 1995. He gained FCH in PPE at Keble, Oxford and became Scotland's third chess Grandmaster in 1999 on winning the Scottish Chess Championships. In 2004 he became the first Scot to win the British Chess Championships for over fifty years.

Neil Stirton (b. 1981) attended the Grammar between 1992 and 1998, and took a first-class degree in Computing which led to work as a business analyst. He took up 50-metres rifle shooting and gained a Silver medal at the 2006 Commonwealth Games and was travelling reserve at the Beijing

Olympics in 2008. He won Gold with team-mate Jon Hammond in the 2010 Commonwealth Games.

Kyle J. Coetzer (b. 1984) attended the Grammar between 1996 and 2002 and represented Scotland at all levels of cricket, captaining U15, U17 and U19. He gained his first cap against Pakistan in 2003. He played for Durham and Northants. He is one of three cricketing brothers who attended the Grammar.

David Law (b. 1991) attended the GS between 2002 and 2008. He took up golf at the age of six and rose through the junior ranks. In 2008 he won the North-East Boys' Championship and two Scottish Junior Boys' Tour events. In 2009 he won both the Scottish Boys' and Scottish Men's Amateur Championship, the first time this has been done by a player in the same year. After a year of injury he won, in 2011, the Scottish Men's Amateur title again as well as the Northern Open before turning professional in October. In April 2012 he won his first professional title at the Dar Es Salaam Open.

PARENTAL INVOLVEMENT

In the School prospectus it was held that 'the Rector is responsible for the internal management of the School' but towards the last quarter of the twentieth century opinion began to favour allowing other voices to have some say in the running of the School. To represent their interests a School Council was formed that included parents, local councillors, staff and senior pupil representatives. Its first chairman was a parent who was also an FP, Brian Crookshanks. Strangely, neither in the Prospectus nor the School Magazine was there any record of its activities. Its moment of glory came when the Regional Education Committee referred to it the question of the school name and the title of Rector in early 1977. The outcome is referred to elsewhere and the details were recorded in the Magazine of that year.

Thereafter, the School Council resumed its rather shadowy existence. In 1982 a formal body, a Parent–Teachers' Association was set up and it proved to be a supportive body in many School activities. In 1989 a School Board was formed 'to establish much closer links between schools and parents and to give parents a greater say in the running of the school'. This body had clearly defined duties and responsibilities. It had to have reports from the Rector and the Education Authority on school business, to take part in the appointment of senior staff, to scrutinise School expenditure, to settle dates for occasional holidays and to supervise the use of School accommodation outwith normal School hours. The membership was made up of elected parent members, co-opted members and staff members.

However, the search for an effective and acceptable way of representing the views of parents continues, as the Scottish Executive abolished the School Boards and replaced them in 2007 with Parent Councils. A PTA continues to fulfil its functions of raising funds and supporting all School activities.

The Former Pupils Club, whose members include many parents, continues to act vigorously in the School's interests and support it by providing prizes for academic achievements and financial support for extra-mural activities and sport.

FIFTEEN The Grammar School: An Overview

From the days of John Knox in the sixteenth century onwards Scotland proudly boasted of a national system of education. The provision of a school in every parish was an admirable and worthy aim although critics sometimes suggested it was not as comprehensive as it sounded. The emphasis on the instruction in the three Rs and little else for long was the staple diet of the parish schools. In the burgh schools, including Aberdeen Grammar School, the assumption was that the basics had been already learned or could be acquired in the many private or occasional public schools to be found in a town. The fare which a Grammar pupil could look forward to was several years of Classical education, mainly grammatical, based on Latin and a little Greek. While following this apparently very narrow curriculum the diligent pupil could and did acquire incidentally a fair amount of knowledge of Ancient Geography and History and a sound knowledge of English grammar.

By the time pupils entered the new Grammar buildings in 1863 they could choose from a wider range of subjects: Modern Languages, English, Arithmetic and Mathematics, Writing, Drawing and Drill had been added to the Classics. These were available but not compulsory and a boy or his parents selected what they wanted and could pay for. There was little encouragement for pupils to stay beyond the end of the formal school day until well into the later years of the century. By then the School Prospectuses were able to offer an even wider choice as Science, Phonography (Shorthand), Elocution[1] and Vocal Music had been added. The reorganisation of the School in 1881 prescribed courses for Classical or Modern pupils to follow and the haphazard individual choices largely ended.

In those early days, while much attention was applied to the mind and a great deal to the soul, no attention was paid to the body at all. Physical Education was strictly extra-mural and informal. Not everyone thought that the introduction and development of Games was something to be applauded because it was claimed that the lack of school opponents meant that the boys had to face adult teams whose attitudes and behaviour were felt to have a bad influence on the Grammar pupils.

The result of this uncertainty about the value of organised games was that the staff only very occasionally interested themselves in an activity which they themselves had very seldom experienced. The struggles to establish an interest in football, both of the soccer and rugby forms, is well illustrated by an article in the Magazine in December 1941 entitled 'Pioneering in Football', written by The Very Rev. Dean MacRae, a former pupil from 1883 to 1887. Looking back to his youth, this pillar of the Scottish Episcopal Church recounted the difficulties he recalled. No games master, only A.V. Lothian, a soccer player of note, took any direct part in helping the boys in the weekly task of trying to raise fifteen players, often having only thirteen willing to take the field. No one was too sure about the rules and the result was disputed decisions where the losing side just walked off the pitch. The school pitch was the area behind the School near Whitehall Place, which was either a sea of mud or frozen hard. A player played in shoes and any old clothes with little effort to have a team strip. Results were of little concern as there were no leagues or cups. As much interest was given to soccer as to rugby. There was no organised practice for teams but the boys used to practise drop-kicking in front of the School. Despite all the drawbacks the games took root and the writer claimed that this perseverance made an important contribution to the School and through it to the University and other city teams.

In spite of the lack of interest in active participation in Games, the School Magazine from earliest issues faithfully reported the results of games and also accounts of how the matches had been played and where they had been played. Matches took place at the University and Mannofield as well as at the School and various other venues in town and country. The covers of the Magazine in 1890 indicate that cricket was played on the area in front of the School after the valley of the Denburn was filled in. The poor condition of the ground left by the rugby games made cricket behind the School difficult and probably helps to account for the low scores usually recorded in the Magazine.

Another important development in the 1880s was the setting up of a Literary and Dramatic Society which survives to the present day. This was an opportunity to take part in debates, to listen to talks given by staff and guest speakers and to meet staff and other adults in a less formal atmosphere. Alongside this, the first steps were taken to produce a School Magazine, a modest affair which grew into the remarkable production which also has flourished up to the present day.

These ventures into the areas of Games and Literature received an enormous boost with the arrival of Morland Simpson whose experience in education had made him an enthusiastic disciple of the doctrine of 'mens sana in corpore sano' (a healthy mind in a healthy body). While he continued to maintain the study of Classics and other academic subjects as important, he pointed out that the object of a good education should be to produce a rounded boy with wide interests and attainments. It was a view which was at first received with a degree of scepticism by parents and public but came to be accepted as a legitimate objective. Not only the pupils but the staff were also encouraged to take part in extra-curricular interests if not as an active participant at least as coaches, referees and umpires.

Simpson pointed out that when he came to Aberdeen he found that the type of teacher commonly found in England, a man with a sound academic background and a wide experience of involvement in Games just did not exist in Scotland except in the public schools. At the Grammar the boys were offered an alternative to rugby in the form of hockey which the Rector himself played with the pupils. In the years to come hockey rivalled rugby as the game of choice. When reviewing other sports to introduce, Simpson condemned tennis because it spoiled good cricketers in his opinion and rejected rowing as well because he felt it led to physical problems in later life. He did, however, encourage swimming and it was one of his great disappointments that the scheme to include a Swimming Pool in the Westfield project was abandoned – and the School had to wait another seventy years before it eventually was built.

While Dean MacRae lamented that there had been no Games master, he noted that there was some attention given to Gymnastics and every summer there was an athletic sports. Two events – the opening of Rubislaw Field in 1916 and the arrival of Duncan McGregor as Games master – marked the beginning of the establishment of a Games tradition which saw the School compete with many of the major rugby, hockey and cricket school sides in Scotland. This helped the FP sides too. The diet offered to the boys was very narrow in the inter-war years: rugby or hockey in the winter and cricket and athletics (with some tennis) in the summer. Yet this concentration was a factor in the resulting success, despite the Spartan facilities at Rubislaw and the School.

Fortunately Simpson's two immediate successors were also progressive in their outlook and encouraged the development of Games. In the inter-war period there was a great expansion of inter-school competition in the major School games. Athletics flourished and the Sports Day at the end of session stretching over two days was as much a social occasion for a gathering of parents, friends and former pupils as it was a test of individual prowess and inter-house rivalry. At such events the School was on display to the public.

Music was another interest and activity which took root in the School and the early prospectuses note the existence of an Orchestral Society. Under such as Gavin Falconer and later Donald Hawksworth a very successful musical interest was fostered. With the individual tuition of Peddie Willox and Bill Spittle, groups of musicians were developed which drew the admiration and respect not only of parents and local public audiences but even of the BBC. This tradition led to close ties with Regensberg in Bavaria and many years of alternate visits of orchestral and chorus groups. In later years the School took advantage of links established by an American exchange teacher to arrange an exchange visit to schools in Pennsylvania. This trip was possible only when the low-cost Laker Airways offered cheaper flights to the USA. One wonders how other passengers reacted to Anne Brown, the Principal Teacher of Music, boarding the flight with her harp!

The Magazines of the 1920s mention the practice of exhibiting the work of members of the Arts Club which had been started after the First World War. There was a demonstration of the talents which existed among the boys of the time. The outcome was sketches of many local scenes and buildings which are now of historical as well as artistic merit. More recently Charles Hemingway, James Will and Frank Boag led the Department not only into painting and drawing activities but also photography and pottery. The Art Department attracted individuals who could also share their own interests with pupils. Many of them spent only a short time at the School before finding opportunities elsewhere. One must not forget the contribution made by Miss Horn, who looked after the department during the Second World War, having been given a temporary transfer on loan from the Central School. In their various ways, Hamish Cruickshank, Helen Smith, Norman Constable and Belle McCoig all added to the interesting array of opportunities for the successful work that the SCE demanded for its certification.

In a Classical school the struggle for recognition and acceptance of Technical Subjects was hard and not helped by the nomadic existence it had to accept over the years. From the Language Block to the Chalmers School only in the 1960s did the Department move into purpose-built accommodation. The technical facilities in Rosemount Annexe proved a useful and welcome addition to their resources. There were still only three members of staff listed in 1960–1, one of whom, Bill Watt, defected to Mathematics soon after. By 1978 the number of its staff had risen to seven. The Technical staff also benefited from the opening up of promotion opportunities which had not previously existed for the like of Messrs Winkley and Barron. There they were, time-served craftsmen with industrial experience and great personal ability but with little chance for promotion outwith their own department. So Jim Gilbert, John Cruickshank and Sandy Duncan laboured on until Jim Murray, an ex-POW, arrived as Head of Department and was later promoted to Assistant Headteacher. He earned great kudos for his Department by encouraging some of his pupils to enter a national competition with a scheme which involved using the Denburn as a source of power. It aroused great interest in various quarters and years later they were consulted about the Project.

For long Science was also regarded as a minor concern tacked on to the Mathematics Department, although in John Lynch at least it had a Principal Teacher whose teaching skills were widely recognised. That arrangement persisted until 1961 when Science was split into specialist subjects with Lynch retaining Chemistry, Dr Milligan coming in briefly to hold the Physics post before going to the College of Education, and Bill Williams being promoted to become Head of Biology. Sandy Bruce took over from Lynch in 1962. By this time, young teachers like Gordon Forbes, John Lockie, Jim Wilson and Bill May were filling the posts previously held by Peter Cook (the father of the late Robin Cook MP) and Ian Park. The demand for qualified Science teachers was great and the opportunities for promotion considerable. John Wiseman, a former pupil, had replaced Milligan but he too did not stay long before moving to Dundee. Alex Garrow, after a spell in the Physics Department and a departure for promotion, actually returned as an Assistant Head for several fruitful years before again moving for further promotion elsewhere. In recent times the Physics Department has been run by Brian Anderson and Alistair Milton.

But in this constantly changing scenario not everyone moved on. Bill Williams was to stay many years amid the flora and fauna of Skene Street West and Bill May rose to head the Chemistry Department. Apart from running a successful academic department, he encouraged his pupils to enter successfully all kinds of competitions and challenges which brought distinction to themselves and their School. Colleagues did not escape his love of practical jokes and any activity could count on his enthusiastic support. Organising trips to Hampden and School dances were among his contributions to School life. Celebrated by the tune 'Bill May of Boddam' composed by Jim Hunter (who became a prominent figure in BBC Scotland), when the time for retirement arrived he assumed the peripatetic role of supply teacher to spread his ideas, energy and experiences among a variety of schools in Aberdeen and district.

The School and Science department suffered a great loss with the sudden death of Brian Gordon, who had played a prominent part in many School activities.

Russell Gray is another with a long connection to the School. He first started as a pupil in the Nursery department in 1951 and apart from his studies at Aberdeen University he had unbroken attachment until his retirement in 2007. In that time he filled many roles, assistant in Geography and Modern Studies, Guidance teacher and finally Assistant Head and Deputy Rector. But that tells only part of the story because he was for many years in charge of the CCF rising to the rank of Major. In these later stages few School activities did not enjoy his willing participation. Even after retirement he acts as the knowledgeable tour guide for any Reunion groups, and has also assumed the important role of senior invigilator for the national examinations.

It is difficult to imagine a time when a subject like Science had to struggle for recognition and acceptance in the School curriculum, as more than an adjunct to Mathematics. Modern Languages also had to face a long battle to challenge the monopoly of Classics. Part of its problem was that, after 1863, the early teachers of Languages, usually of foreign origin,[2] had to accept unsympathetic timetabling and the reluctance of parents and pupils to recognise their value. One of the colleagues of Mackie, who headed the Department of French and German in the early twentieth century, was in constant conflict with the Rector and often with parents and pupils as well over his harsh discipline. It took the Rector years to persuade the School Board to put pressure on this awkward member of staff to leave and follow an unlikely career in the Episcopal Church. By perseverance the position of the two main languages became established but teachers like Souter could be called upon to take classes in different subjects as required and this versatility was still a feature of staffing expectations till after the Second World War. Specialisation in Spanish came in with Dr McAndrew after the First World War when he replaced Charles Davidson. Briefly the two languages were run separately with Cunningham in charge of French and Henry Paterson having the dual responsibility of Deputy Rector and sole teacher of German. The two departments were reunited under Cunningham after

Paterson retired. Henry Davidson came as Principal and after his retirement German was split off again to allow for Guinevere Thomaneck to take over a separate department. The French Department was able to enlist the services of an Assistant Head, Alistair Aitken, who joined the staff from St Machar's Academy.

Widening the choice of Languages further Ian Galloway, from Classics, turned his many talents to spreading the cause of Russian before accepting the responsibility of providing also a very much reduced demand for Classics as Ron McLeod retired. Galloway's sudden death left the Rector with a problem to replace him. Ian Milne, a former pupil, succeeded Harry Davidson in French and also branched out in teaching some Italian. Ron Scott continued 'the Spanish connection'. For a time Bill Hardwick, who also assisted in the Religious Education Department, offered a very limited number of pupils the chance to learn Japanese.

Social Subjects, including History and Geography, were perceived as subjects which any self-respecting teacher could deal with, particularly those in the English Department. William Hendry was the first to secure status as Principal Teacher of Geography and Dr Alex Miller was appointed Principal of History. The retirement of the former and the death of the latter meant the arrival of Bob McNay to Geography while James Walker was promoted to the post in History. Mary Matheson, for a brief time, was not only the sole lady on the secondary staff in 1946 but also the sole teacher listed in the prospectus for Geography until McNay. The department grew with the recruitment of David Anderson, Andrew Tait and Graeme Traill. When McNay left to become Deputy Rector (and later Rector) at Dumfries Academy his place was taken by Jim Gelly. One feature of the department's premises was that it had the only room, in Aberdeen at least, which had a tiered floor, much favoured in older times. Primary school pupils sometimes appeared with a request to see what a Victorian classroom looked like.

James Walker had been a pupil at the School before fighting and being wounded in the Great War. After a short spell in Fraserburgh Academy he joined the English and History Department in the early 1920s, becoming Head of History from 1946 until 1961. Norman King moved from general subjects to assist in History. When Walker retired he was succeeded by Arthur McCombie, who stayed as Principal Teacher of History until 1973 when he became Deputy Rector with Archie Baxter and then sole Deputy until 1990 when he retired. He was replaced in the History post by Laurence Murray, one of his assistants.

After Murray's retirement through ill-health he was succeeded by

Douglas Milne, who later became Head at Inverurie Academy. The department was situated in the two rooms which lay behind the Hall and now provide the main staffroom. The opportunity offered by the vacating of the old Science labs established the main History room in Room 4 opposite the east entrance door. The fire in 1986 forced the department to wander about to Rosemount and Gilcomston School before settling into the Language Block, where Kathleen Hay became head of the department.

While the History Department had a nomadic existence the Geography Department had no such upheaval to face. However, the tiered floor in the main block is now gone, no doubt in the interests of health and safety, but during the renovations a workman approached Gelly, well known for his careful harbouring of his department's resources, and asked him what lay behind a door in the department. Gelly admitted he did not know because in his many years of tenure he had never opened it. While hardly rivalling the opening of Tutankhamun's tomb, when it was forced open it revealed a collection of relics from the old School Museum much cherished by Morland Simpson. While Shirley Milton came to be Gelly's assistant at headquarters, the Geographical colony in the Language Block grew with the presence of Lilian Arthur, Sheila Tough and Jim Rodwell.

The old Westfield School became the Lower School until that was phased out in the 1970s. It then acquired the title of the Language Block but this is misleading because other occupants of its premises included two Geography teachers, Gordon Cruickshank and Bill Porter; three History teachers, Eileen Strachan, Doug Marr and Ron Grant; and Gordon Hutcheon who joined this group as Head of Modern Studies, a discipline which had at first been treated as a supplementary course for pupils doing Higher History and Higher Geography involving no extra instruction. However, as the SCE examination requirements became more complex and specialised, instruction had to be undertaken, hence the creation of a new department.

It is difficult to attempt to follow the trails of departments as they shifted from one location to another in quite a complex collection of buildings. Religious Education moved from the main building when Eric Duncan was in charge up to Rosemount where Alistair Marr and later Alan Smith operated for a time. One complication was the agreed requirement to provide Roman Catholic instruction in the School and who could have been more appropriate to carry this out at one point than Sister Margaret Pope who transferred to the Catholic Girls' School at Kilgraston before returning to live in Aberdeen after retirement from teaching. The assistance of committed members of staff like Sheila Watt and Ian Forbes meant that both Alan Smith and Alistair Marr were spared the task of recruiting from the general staff to supply the department's needs.

Business Studies was fortunate to inherit the ready-made facilities which Rosemount offered and this meant that the different requirements of a growing number of girls could be met. Richard Greig and Leslie Hutton followed in the footsteps of Jack Lawson and Jack Waters in organising a commercial-based choice. Equally fortunate was the Home Economics Department which had to be started when the School became co-educational. Most 'new' subjects could trace their roots back to an older department in the School but Home Economics had no such heritage. The first lady to take charge was Mrs Clark and the foundations which she laid have been built on by Mrs Reid and Mrs Belford. Now the department enjoys premises, much more modern, in the main block north wing.

Another 'new' subject was Computing Studies which through John Guthrie had links with Mathematics. It too had a varied locational history, for a time sharing exile in Gilcomston with History after the fire of 1986. Now the department has also been able, after the reconstructions post-1986, to settle in the main block. Another offshoot department was that of Drama and Media Studies. Pat Wood was originally attached to the English Department but acquired premises in another building at Rosemount where she was eventually accorded independent status and set about establishing the department, ever on the look-out for possibilities of extending the accommodation her department might claim. Like other departments Drama returned to the main block after the reconstruction and was established along with Janet Adam's help appropriately in the area where the stage in the old Hall would have been.

Another small peripatetic group was added to the staff when a Remedial Teaching group was created to support pupils with learning difficulties. This very valuable work was carried out effectively by Sheila Niven, Ethel Hill, Edna Jamieson and Moira Leiper and the department grew in numbers as the service developed and it was renamed the Learning Support Department.

The arrival of co-education in the 1970s and a post-war widening of choice for the boys opened up many outlets for PE activities. The girls entered wholeheartedly into the School's traditions of games involvement and soon were producing teams in hockey, athletics, netball and basketball which brought success in local and national competitions and matched standards being achieved by the boys. The School produced internationalists in most of these activities and in the case of netball both Anne Watt and later Marie Milne were internationalists, while Marie enjoyed the further distinction of captaining her country. The opening of the School swimming pond in the 1960s and more recently the extending of the facilities at Rubislaw and the splendid Games Hall in the back area of the playground have now made available an even wider choice of games activities including badminton.

It would be a mistake to imagine that the School offers only class-work and games to its pupils. As the School began to widen the scope of education a variety of clubs began to take root. Staff and pupils came to share interests of many sorts. It is difficult to do justice to the variety of interests that were catered for over the years. By 1980 the School Prospectus listed some forty clubs and societies and pointed also to the involvement in the Duke of Edinburgh's Award Scheme and the Combined Cadet Force (CCF) which had started in 1941.

The CCF provided a disciplined opportunity to experience the rigours of parade ground drills, to enjoy the summer camps at air stations and military camps and to be instructed in the use of firearms, as well as learning a plethora of other useful skills. Even after the Second World War ended there was a ready supply of officers with war or national service experience to carry on the contingent's work. Eventually the girls too took the chance of serving in the ranks of the army section. The air cadet section was taken over by Raymond Nugent who did a power of work for this School activity amongst a number of others. But this type of experience declined in popularity in Education Authority schools and, bucking the trend for some time, the Grammar was one of the last to close down its cadet force. Its demise was hastened by the difficulty of obtaining officers with commitment and experience. The loss of the Pipe Band was particularly felt.

Unfortunately, the number of extra-curricular activities was also reduced, as a number were casualties of the teachers' strike in the mid-1980s. Nonetheless, the modern School has arranged numerous trips to many locations at home and abroad. For the pupils of the Lower School visits to places of local interest were a common experience. The Edinburgh Festival provided annual visits from staff and pupils. Foreign travel to the Continent became more and more possible so there are records of visits to France in Dr Cormack's time in the 1920s and more recently trips to Switzerland, the Mediterranean and the Baltic have given Grammar pupils experience of different cultures. The Art Department organised trips to Italy. A contact in Germany with Markdorf led to a fruitful relationship established by

Guinevere Thomaneck and Gordon Cruickshank.

No history of a school would be complete without acknowledging and appreciating the contribution that non-teaching staff make and have made to the well-being of the School community. One of the key figures in Scottish education was the Janitor, usually a man of many talents which allowed him to deal with emergencies and everyday routines. The first Janitor to be referred to by Former Pupils was 'snuffy old John Gray' described by (Sir) George Reid in the mid-1850s as having a 'fresh complexion and a white beard, and being small of stature and somewhat infirm'. Perhaps this was a factor in why he was 'occasionally subjected to a good deal of hustling and annoyance'.

The most notable successor in this role was Sergeant Charles Duncan, a veteran of the Indian Mutiny, who retired from the army to take over the position of Janitor from 1877 to 1895. Not very long after, William Kennedy joined the staff in 1901 and remained as a general factotum for twenty-nine years to the great satisfaction of everyone in the School as well as the FPs.

In 1969 Harry Hopkins took the post. He always took a keen interest in School activities and was known to don military uniform to take part in the summer camps of the School ACF. As Head Janitor he was responsible for a group of assistants and one unexpected recruit for his squad was Margaret Reid, the first and only female janitor in the School. By the early 1980s a new arrangement for wider teams of janitors saw Ron Foulger acting as the Senior Janitor in one such group having previously been an assistant in the School.

When Rosemount School was incorporated into the Grammar in the early seventies, many of its staff were transferred to the GS. One such was its janitor, Bob Davidson, who remained at Rosemount, living and working there for many years more or less independent of other janitors.

In another direction, as administration in the Grammar School became more onerous, Rectors had limited clerical assistance but this changed when the redoubtable Miss Beattie Brown became the Rector's Clerk in 1924. By the outbreak of war in 1939 she was the Rector's Secretary and retained that post until 1946. How much she contributed to the running of the School in that period would be hard to over-estimate but having resigned she returned to teach in the Kindergarten Department to everyone's delight. Her replacement was Betty Gibb, who, having already served for most of the War in the Wrens, was well-qualified to deal with an ever more complicated School office for the next twenty years mostly as Administrative Assistant with four assistants.

After her retirement she was succeeded by Jenny Archibald who had to deal with office work which became increasingly technological in nature, and yet she also had to deal with the day-to-day routines of staff and pupils at a human and personal level. By January 1991 Mrs Ross had taken over and held the post until retirement.

The Library, once the finest in a Scottish school, became a resource centre and the role filled by Miss Boyd and Pat Fraser is now filled by Miss Allard who has held the post for a number of years.

The task of ministering to the sick and ailing has been taken over by a succession of School Nurses, Mrs Brown, Mrs Heffren and until recently by Mrs Moya Cromar. An army of technical assistants has been created for a large number of departments.

One group of people who played a very important part in School life and yet were never listed in the School Prospectuses was the succession of individuals who were the groundsmen at Rubislaw Field. As soon as the Memorial Pavilion was completed in 1924 it became possible to have a groundsman living on site in the accommodation above the Pavilion.

The first notable character was Frank Findlay, a prominent sportsman in his younger days. His two sons, Tom and Frank, were Scottish international cricketers and excellent rugby players – unfortunately both were Gordonians! He was followed in the 1940s by Eric Tyson, a former professional cricketer whose great enthusiasm and experience saw the square at Rubislaw recognised as one of the best in the North-East. His coaching saw the Grammar cricket teams reach very high standards and for many years he was a significant figure in the FP cricket teams which benefited from his bowling skills as well as his experience.

Quite a different individual was David Matthew, a quiet, humorous character who maintained the high standards people had come to expect on the cricket, rugby and hockey pitches at Rubislaw. His successor, Bill Allan was followed by Hughie Millar, both of whom continued the tradition of providing support for the Games staff and pupils of the School as well as helping with hospitality and catering for the visiting teams.

The accommodation at Rubislaw was extended and altered many times, most recently witnessing a large-scale redevelopment which modernised the premises and greatly extended them. The good humour and tolerance of these men was greatly appreciated by the staff and pupils over the years.

All in all, the general impression is of a School which has prospered through the ages and in its modern guise is offering a variety of choice in both academic and extra-curricular fields which must surely astonish the pupils of the past. Even 'expert' opinion in the form of the most recent HMI Report, based on the inspection of the School in October 2008, highlighted the strengths of the menu available to its pupils.

Such views of the Grammar School were not always so complimentary and while great pride was usually taken in the achievements and successes of the School there was also hostility in some quarters towards an institution perceived as a bastion of privilege. But by 1900 developments in secondary education in Aberdeen had resulted in the closure of The Gymnasium and the Grammar School of Old Aberdeen and the growth of Gordon's College and the Central School. This led to keen rivalry particularly between the Grammar and Gordon's academically and in games throughout the twentieth century. A by-product was the softening of the animosity towards the Grammar's supposed social elitism, though the desire to see it turned into 'Esslemont Avenue Comprehensive' never completely disappeared.

The abolition of fee-paying in the Grammar in the late 1940s and the introduction of comprehensive education in the early 1970s fundamentally changed the nature of its social mix. But Gordon's also changed socially after 1975 following its decision to go down the different route of independence and the higher fees that this involved. The social pendulum swung and the two schools assumed the social role which their rival probably had held in the eyes of the Town. Gordon's College lays stress on increasing the number of bursaries available to widen its social base and avoid charges of elitism, but Aberdeen Grammar probably has a more comfortable position now that it is no longer the school 'a town loved to hate'.[3]

The main challenge in the future for the present Board of Studies – Rector Graham Legge and his four Deputies, Helen Innes, Janet Adams, Alan Martin and Noelle Straiton – is to emulate the School's distinguished past and to continue to produce a cohort of outstanding individuals who rank amongst the most notable of Aberdeen's citizens. Given the history, traditions and ethos of the Grammar School there is no reason to suppose that they cannot succeed in doing so.

'Vivat et Floriat Grammatica Schola Aberdonensis.'

'May the Grammar School of Aberdeen live and flourish.'[4]

NOTES

CHAPTER ONE

1 Correspondence of March–May 1924 can be consulted in the Special Archives of Aberdeen University.
2 Joseph Robertson: 'On Scholastic Offices in the Scottish Church in the Twelfth and Thirteen Centuries' in *Spalding Club Miscellany* (Aberdeen 1852) vol. V pp. 56–77.
3 Richard Oram: *David I: the King Who Made Scotland* (Stroud 2004) pp. 49–50.
4 D.E.R. Watt: *Fasti Ecclesiae Scoticanae Medii Aevi ad Annum 1638* (Scottish Record Society 1969) p. 6.
5 Ian B. Cowan (ed. by James Kirk) *The Medieval Church* in Scotland (Edinburgh 1995) pp. 77 and 102. Leslie J. Macfarlane: 'St Machar's Cathedral Through the Ages' in John S. Smith (ed.): *Old Aberdeen: Bishops, Burghers and Buildings* (Aberdeen 1991) pp. 14–37.
6 *Registrum Episcopatus Aberdonensis* ii, p. 45
7 Ibid. p. 49.
8 *Registrum Vetus de Aberbrothoc*, No. 254 p. 193. William Kennedy: *Annals of Aberdeen* (London 1818).
9 John Vaus attended the Old Aberdeen Grammar School under his kinsman, Alexander Vaus, before studying in the arts faculty of the University under Hector Boece between 1500 and 1504.
10 Leslie J. Macfarlane: 'St Machar's Cathedral through the Ages'.
11 Janet P. Foggie: *Renaissance Religion in Urban Scotland. The Dominican Order, 1450–1560* (Leiden 2003) p. 103.
12 *Extracts from Burgh Records* vol. 1 pp. 4 and 5.
13 *Extracts* 1 p. 36.
14 *Extracts* 1 p. 80.
15 *Extracts* 1 pp. 97 and 107.
16 *Extracts* 1 p. 120.
17 University teacher who took his students through from first to fourth year.
18 He went on to become Principal of King's between 1542 and 1553.
19 *Extracts* 1 pp. 151, 202 and 276.
20 *Extracts* 1 pp. 277, 278 and 306.
21 *Extracts* 1 pp. 324 and 326.
22 *Extracts* 1 p. 186.

23 Leslie J. Macfarlane: *William Elphinstone and the Kingdom of Scotland 1431–1514* (Aberdeen 1985) p. 247.
24 F.C. Eeles: *King's College Chapel, Aberdeen* (Aberdeen 1956) p. 210.
25 John M. Fletcher: "The Foundation of the University of Aberdeen in its European Context" in Paul Dukes (ed.): *The Universities of Aberdeen and Europe. The First Three Centuries* (Aberdeen 1995) pp. 9–56.
26 *Rudimenta puerorum in artem grammaticam* (Paris).
27 *c.*1484–*c.*1539, a grammarian from a well-established Aberdeen family. *ODNB*: Leslie J. Macfarlane.
28 H.F. Morland Simpson: *Bon Record* (Aberdeen 1906).
29 Publius Terentius Afer (*c.*190–159BC), Roman comic dramatist, whose surviving six comedies were based on the New Greek Comedy.
30 Publius Vergilius Maro (70BC–19BC) has come to be regarded as one of Classical Rome's greatest poets.
31 Marcus Tullius Cicero (106–43BC) is widely viewed as one of Rome's greatest orators, lawyers and statesmen. His prose writing is held to be as the paragon of Classical Latin.
32 Marcus Fabius Quintilianus (*c.*35–100AD) was a Roman rhetorician from Hispania who has been described as the 'earliest spokesman for a child-centred education'.
33 James Grant: *History of the Burgh Schools of Scotland* (London, 1876)
34 = under-masters.
35 Jenny Wormald: *Court, Kirk and Community: Scotland 1470–1625* (Edinburgh 1981) p. 87.
36 *Extracts* vol. 1 p. 366; vol. 2 p. 24.
37 Ibid. vol. 2 p. 24.
38 Ibid. vol. 2 p. 39.
39 Ibid. vol. 2 p. 45.
40 Ibid. vol. 2 p. 66.
41 Ibid. vol. 2 pp. 58, 90 and 154.
42 Ibid. vol. 1 p. 120; vol. 2 pp. 66 and 176.
43 Andrew of Wyntoun (*c.*1350–c.1422): *The Orygynale Cronykil of Scotland* Book V, chapter 10 line 3376; Grant: *History* p. 48; Helen M. Jewell: *Education in Early Modern England* (Basingstoke 1998) p. 101.
44 These can all be found in the Special Libraries of Aberdeen University.
45 Norman F. Shead: 'Glasgow: An Ecclesiastical Burgh' in Michael Lynch, Michael Spearman and Geoffrey Stell (eds): *The Scottish Medieval Town* (Edinburgh 1988) p. 127.
46 1518/9–1592: *ODNB*: Mark Dilworth.
47 *c.*1467–1550 historian, philosopher and theologian. *ODNB*: Alexander Broadie.
48 John Durkan: 'Education in the Century of the Reformation' in David McRoberts: *Essays on the Scottish Reformation 1513–1625* (Glasgow 1962) p. 165.
49 William Keith Leask (ed.) *Musa Latina Aberdonensis* vol. 3 Spalding Club (Aberdeen 1910). Leask was a Grammar pupil.
50 James K. Cameron: 'Some Aberdeen Students on the Continent in the late sixteenth and early seventeenth centuries' in Paul Dukes (1995) pp. 57–78.

51 *Ane breve descriptioun of the pest quhair in the causis, signis and sum speciall preseruatioun and cure thairof ar contenit. ODNB*: Thompson Cooper rev. Sarah Bakewell.
52 *ODNB*: Athol Murray.
53 *ODNB*: Charles Platts rev. George Molland.
54 Alexander Broadie: 'The Rise (and Fall) of the Scottish Enlightenment' in T.M. Devine and Jenny Wormald (eds): *The Oxford Handbook of Modern Scottish History* (Oxford 2012) pp. 372–3.
55 *ODNB*: G.T. Bettany rev. Anita McConnell.
56 *ODNB*: James K. Cameron.
57 *ODNB*: J. Derrick McClure.
58 *ODNB*: Shona MacLean Vance.
59 £1 sterling equalled eighteen merks equalled twelve pounds Scots.
60 *ODNB*: John Durkan.
61 *ODNB*: Marja Smolenaars.
62 *ODNB*: Alexander Du Toit.
63 Supporting evidence for this is thin.
64 *ODNB*: Nicola Royan.
65 *ODNB*: Shona MacLean Vance.
66 *ODNB*: W.G. Blaikie rev. R.P. Wells.
67 *ODNB*: James Cooper rev. David George Mullan.
68 *ODNB*: R.P. Wells.
69 *ODNB*: Duncan Thomson.
70 *ODNB*: David Allan.

CHAPTER TWO

1 *Extracts* vol. 2 p. 223.
2 *ODNB*: T.P.J. Edlin.
3 Ian J. Simpson: *Education in Aberdeenshire before 1872* (London 1947) p. 63.
4 *Extracts* vol. 2 pp. 262–4.
5 *Extracts* vol. 2 p. 313.
6 *Extracts* vol. 2 pp. 251, 298, 308 and 310–18.
7 It was confirmed in 1696 as the textbook to be used in Edinburgh's High School by its Town Council. It was only ousted by Ruddiman's *Rudiments* in 1714.
8 *ODNB*: A.S. Wayne Pearce.
9 *Extracts* vol. 2 pp. 389 and 392.
10 *Extracts* vol. 2 p. 353.
11 In 1633 he became minister of Old Meldrum.
12 Probably Dr Patrick Dun.
13 Dr J.M. Bulloch.
14 Morland Simpson *Bon Record* p. 128.
15 Ibid. p. 132.
16 W. Douglas Simpson: *School Magazine*, November 1934.
17 William Kennedy: *Annals*. He was a former employee of the Council and wrote a restrained account of these events.

18 William Kennedy: *Annals* vol. 2 p. 129.
19 Colin A. McLaren: *Aberdeen Students 1600–1800* (Aberdeen 2005) p. 35.
20 Fenton Wyness: *City by the Grey North Sea* (Aberdeen 1965) p. 150.
21 *ODNB*: John Coffey.
22 *ODNB*: John Callow.
23 *ODNB*: Davis Coakley.
24 *ODNB*: Anita Guerrini.
25 *ODNB*: Gerald M.D. Howat.
26 *ODNB*: Terry Friedman.
27 *ODNB*: Mark Dilworth.

CHAPTER THREE

1 *ODNB*: William Donaldson.
2 *ODNB*: Roger J. Robinson.
3 *ODNB*: Edward M. Furgol.
4 *ODNB*: Paul Dukes.
5 *ODNB*: Lionel Alexander Ritchie.
6 *ODNB*: William Donaldson.
7 *ODNB*: Joan Lane.
8 *ODNB*: H.M. Scott.
9 *ODNB*: A.N.L. Grosjean.
10 *ODNB*: Alan Ruston.
11 *ODNB*: John Westby-Gibson rev. Patrick Bullard.
12 *ODNB*: Jeffrey M. Suderman.
13 *ODNB*: Paul Lawrence.
14 *ODNB*: Alan Ruston.
15 *ODNB*: William Donaldson.
16 *ODNB*: G.T. Bettany rev. Caroline Overy.
17 Youngest son of James Gregory (1674–1733) and half-brother of James Gregory (1707–1755). *ODNB*: Paul Lawrence.
18 *ODNB*: P. Wood.
19 *ODNB*: G.S. Boulger rev. Marcus B. Simpson Jnr.
20 *ODNB*: H. Lesley Diack.
21 *ODNB*: Roger J. Robinson.
22 *ODNB*: Roger J. Robinson.
23 *ODNB*: John Booker.
24 *ODNB*: Alexander Du Toit.
25 *ODNB*: John S. Reid.
26 *ODNB*: T.F. Henderson rev. H.V. Bowen.
27 H. Lewis Ulman: *The Minutes of the Aberdeen Philosophical Society, 1758–1773* (Aberdeen 1990).
28 Nicholas Hans: *New Trends in Education in the Eighteenth Century* (London 1951) pp. 25–30.

CHAPTER FOUR

1 In 1826 a sub-committee recommended the introduction of Greek for eight of the eighteen hours a week; but this was thought by the Town Council too great an inroad on the time devoted to Latin, and only three hours were allotted, for grammar and easy sentences.
2 As of 1860.
3 = a fancy but insubstantial cooked dish, especially one of foreign origin.
4 I. Carter: *Farm Life in Northeast Scotland, 1840–1914. The Poor Man's Country* (Edinburgh 1979) p. 112.
5 R.D. Anderson: *Education and Opportunity in Victorian Scotland: Schools and Universities* (Oxford 1983) pp. 3–10 and 22–23.

CHAPTER FIVE

1 Given the relatively small numbers in the senior classes it has been estimated that Cromar's 'allowance' would be about £23 10s per annum. Perhaps this explains his actions. Morland Simpson: *Bon Record* p. 178.
2 The largest number of extranei throughout the School was 197 in 1860.
3 The others were George Buchanan, tutor of James VI; Thomas Ruddiman, who produced what was to become the standard Latin textbook in 1714; and Arthur Johnston, an eminent Latin poet.
4 *ODNB*: A.F. Pollard rev. Richard Smail.
5 Who had joined the staff in 1853.
6 Alexander Beverly had attended the GS between 1835 and 1840, and been Dux in his final year.
7 However, it should be mentioned that Evans came from a family with connections to the Irish peerage and in 1849 he strengthened that connection further by marrying his first cousin, Emily-Mary Evans. She died in 1873 but there were no issue from the marriage.
8 William Carnie: *Reporting Reminiscences* (Aberdeen 1902) vol. 1 p. 1.
9 Under Melvin the Fifth Class number reached 111 in October 1850; under Geddes the number in October 1855 (when Evans inherited the School) was 97.
10 Some of the evidence also suggested that Kelman had aggravated matters by making injudicious remarks to the boys.
11 Laurence H. Officer: Purchasing of British Pounds from 1245 until the Present (Measuringworth.com). He also sold 300 acres in the barony of East Carbery, County Cork, in November 1859 in the Irish Landed Estates Court.
12 Westland's father was one of the twenty witnesses who gave evidence to the Enquiry and stated that 'there was nothing like order in his son's class' and Evans had 'no moral influence with the boys'. *Enquiry anent Aberdeen Grammar School*, 22 August 1859.
13 With some difficulty for he had disciplinary problems at first.
14 The buildings cost £16,605 in total.
15 George MacDonald: *Alec Forbes of Howglen* (1865).
16 John S. Smith: 'The Growth of the City' in W. Hamish Fraser and Clive H. Lee (eds): *Aberdeen 1800–2000: A New History* (East Linton 2000) p. 23.

17 *ODNB*: J.C. Hadden rev. S.R.J. Baudry.
18 The GS Dux was the student who won the First Prize in the Fifth Class at the Annual Examinations.
19 Fraser and Lee: *Aberdeen 1800–2000* p. 179.
20 Ibid., p. 86.
21 Ibid., p. 271.
22 Ina Mary Harrower: *John Forbes White* (Edinburgh 1918) p. 24.
23 *ODNB*: Freda Harcourt.
24 *ODNB*: R.J. Irving.
25 *ODNB*: W.G. Blaikie rev. Rosemary Mitchell.
26 *ODNB*: John R. McIntosh.
27 The degree of MA in Scotland was generally written AM until the 19th century.
28 *ODNB*: Michael Gauvreau.
29 Biblical Exegesis is the critical explanation or interpretation of Biblical text.
30 *ODNB*: Lionel Alexander Ritchie. New College opened its doors in 1846 as the College of the Free Church but is now part of the University of Edinburgh.
31 *ODNB*: Lionel Alexander Ritchie.
32 *ODNB*: J.C. Hadden rev. Douglas Brown.
33 *ODNB*: Rosemary Mitchell.
34 *ODNB*: Rosemary Mitchell.
35 *ODNB*: W.G. Blaikie rev. Rosemary Mitchell.
36 *ODNB*: Lionel Alexander Ritchie.
37 *ODNB*: Rosemary Mitchell.
38 *ODNB*: Lionel Alexander Ritchie.
39 *ODNB*: George Stronach rev. Lionel Alexander Ritchie.
40 *ODNB*: H.C.G. Matthew.
41 *ODNB*: T.B. Johnstone rev. Lionel Alexander Ritchie.
42 *ODNB*: T.F. Henderson rev. Lionel Alexander Ritchie.
43 *ODNB*: Lionel Alexander Ritchie.
44 *ODNB*: J.W. Rogerson.
45 *ODNB*: Christopher Saunders.
46 *ODNB*: John Huxtable.
47 *ODNB*: G.C. Boase rev. Kaye Bagshaw.
48 *ODNB*: H.M. Chichester rev. J.S.G. Blair.
49 Wikipedia.
50 *ODNB*: Roy Bridges.
51 *ODNB*: Roger T. Stearn.
52 *ODNB*: Elizabeth Baigent.
53 *ODNB*: Irvine Loudon.
54 *ODNB*: Paul Lawrence.
55 *ODNB*: Carolyn Pennington.
56 *ODNB*: R.A.L. Agnew.
57 *ODNB*: Bill Luckin.
58 *ODNB*: A.H. Millar rev. Brenda M. White.
59 *ODNB*: Ornella Moscucci.
60 Open to all four Scottish Universities the Ferguson Scholarship (Philosophical) was regarded as the 'blue ribbon' of Scottish scholarship.

61 *ODNB*: C.S. Sherrington rev. Michael Bevan.
62 *ODNB*: Alexander G. Ogston.
63 Fraser and Lee: *Aberdeen 1800–2000* p. 32.
64 Alexander Keith: *Eminent Aberdonians* (Aberdeen 1984) pp 1–4.
65 *ODNB*: Michael Fry.
66 Fraser and Lee: *Aberdeen 1800–2000* p. 185.
67 The Dux was the boy placed first in the Fifth Class, while the Silver Medal was awarded to the top boy of those who had attended the GS for five years.
68 *ODNB*: Theobold Mathew rev. Patrick Polden.
69 *ODNB*: Michael Lobban.
70 *ODNB*: David Gavine.
71 *ODNB*: Lionel Alexander Ritchie.
72 *ODNB*: Roger J. Robinson.
73 *ODNB*: Thomas Seccombe rev. Peter Osborne.
74 *ODNB*: R.S. Simpson.
75 *ODNB*: Thomas Seccombe rev. Richard Smail.
76 *ODNB*: Robert Ralph.
77 *ODNB*: Cecil Bendall rev. Parvin Loloi.
78 *ODNB*: D.T. Moore.
79 According to John Bulloch (ed.): *Scottish Notes and Queries* (Aberdeen 1897).
80 *ODNB*: E. Kerr Borthwick.
81 *ODNB*: William Bayne, rev. H.C.G. Matthew.
82 *ODNB*: Tristam Clarke.
83 *ODNB*: B.D. Jackson rev. D.E. Allen.
84 *ODNB*: N.J. Girardot.
85 His father, a hand-loom weaver, could not afford the fee for the GS (half-guinea a quarter with books extra) at the end of Bain's schooling in 1831. *Autobiography of Alexander Bain* (London 1904) p. 14.
86 *ODNB*: William Bayne rev. S.R.J. Baudry.
87 *ODNB*: E.I. Carlyle rev. Thomas Prasch.
88 *ODNB*: E.M. Craik.
89 Robert Machray: *Life of Robert Machray, Archbishop of Rupert's Land* (Toronto 1909) chs. 1 and 2.
90 *ODNB*: Horace Lamb rev. Isobel Falconer.
91 *ODNB*: J.H. Morgan rev. Eric Metcalfe.
92 *ODNB*: Christopher J. Schmitz.
93 *ODNB*: A.F. Pollard rev. David Huddleston.
94 *ODNB*: F.H. Brown rev. B.R.Tomlinson.
95 George Croom Robertson attended the GS (1853–7) and pursued an academic career in Aberdeen and London (see separate entry). His other brothers included John Grant Robertson (GS 1850–5), who followed Charles into the Bengal civil service, and Alexander Webster Robertson (GS 1856–62) who was the librarian of Marischal before becoming Aberdeen's Public Librarian.
96 *ODNB*: Gillian Bickley.
97 *ODNB*: David Prain rev. Andrew Grout.
98 Gregory Claeys: *Imperial Skeptics: British Critics of Empire, 1850–1920* (Cambridge 2010) pp. 67–71.

99 *ODNB*: E.A. Smith.
100 *ODNB*: R.M. Healey.
101 Loula Solomou-Dalgarno: 'Byron and the Grammar School', *School Magazine* vol. 91 (June 1988) pp. 21–5.
102 *ODNB*: Jerome McGann.
103 *ODNB*: G.G. Smith rev. Sondra Miley Cooney.
104 *ODNB*: Ronald Bayne rev. H.C.G. Matthew.
105 *ODNB*: G.S. Woods rev. Guy Arnold.
106 *ODNB*: T.W. Bayne rev. H.C.G. Matthew.
107 Fraser and Lee: *Aberdeen 1800–2000* p. 36.
108 *ODNB*: Ian Gow.
109 *ODNB*: Derick S. Thomson.
110 *ODNB*: J.C. Hadden rev. Douglas Brown.
111 *ODNB*: William Hunt rev. Nilanjana Banerji.
112 *ODNB*: Tim Barringer.
113 Profiles with no endnotes attributed are from *WWW*.

CHAPTER SIX

1 John Bower, teacher of English.
2 James Ross (1760–1824), teacher of Writing and Arithmetic. He became a minister of the East Kirk of St Nicholas in 1795.
3 John Paterson attended the GS in 1795–6, entering Class V. He was First Bursar at Marischal of twenty-six competitors and graduated in 1800.
4 William Duncan, teacher of Writing and Arithmetic.
5 The library of Dr Melvin was believed to contain 365 editions of Horace, or one for every day in the year.
6 Ogilvie resigned from the staff in 1844 and became head of the Educational Institution in Calcutta for twenty-five years.
7 There was one important difference between the College arrangements for the Bursary Competition: Marischal allowed the use of dictionaries in the Exams, while King's did not.
8 King's and Marischal fused into one university in 1860.
9 Alexander Russel was editor from 1846 to 1876.
10 Conley attended the GS from 1858 to 1860, entering Class III.
11 Barrack went on to become head of Dollar Institution (later Academy) from 1868 to 1878 and then the first Rector of Kelvinside Academy dying suddenly in 1881.

CHAPTER SEVEN

1 Macdonald was only on the staff from 1861 till 1863.
2 Brebner and Beverly were both active in the YMCA Movement, which began its activities in Aberdeen in 1858.
3 All profiles unattributed in this chapter come from *WWW*.
4 *ODNB*: A.H. Millar rev. Michael Twaddle.
5 *ODNB*: Michael D. McMullen.
6 The coming together of the Free Church and the United Presbyterians in 1925 to

form the United Free Church signalled the diminution of the intra-Presbyterian conflict of the nineteenth century.

7 *ODNB*: C.V. Owen rev. A.J.L. Blond.

8 *ODNB*: Joan Mottram.

9 *ODNB*: Claire E.J. Herrick.

10 *ODNB*: Ronald M. Birse.

11 Reid's Base Line is used for an unambiguous definition of the orientation of the human skull in conventional radiography, computer tomography (CT) and magnetic resonance imaging (MRI) studies.

12 Theodore Watt: *The Roll of Former Pupils of AGS* (1923) p. 112.

13 *ODNB*: Eric J. Sharpe.

14 *ODNB*: F.P. Sprent rev. Lynn Milne.

15 *ODNB*: Ray Desmond.

16 *ODNB*: Ian Levitt.

17 *ODNB*: J.C. Edwards.

18 *ODNB*: F.H. Brown rev. Francis Robertson.

19 *ODNB*: H.C.G. Matthew.

CHAPTER EIGHT

1 Livy (59BC–AD17) – Roman historian who described the foundation of Rome.

2 Tully = Cicero (106–43BC) – Roman statesman, lawyer, scholar and writer.

3 Virgil (70–19BC) – Roman poet.

4 Virgil's Latin epic poem in twelve books.

5 Entrance to the underworld. A lake near Naples, filling the centre of an extinct volcano.

6 The monstrous watchdog guarding the entrance to Hades (the underworld).

7 The old man who ferried souls of the dead across the rivers Styx and Acheron to Hades.

8 (Greek) One of the three Fates.

9 (435–354BC) – Greek historian, writer and military leader.

10 (570–478BC) – Greek lyric poet.

11 In Greek mythology the 'waterer'.

CHAPTER NINE

1 Much of the biographical profile which follows is based on the correspondence between Arthur McCombie and Simpson's grand-daughter, Ann Simpson, in November 2011, with additional material being supplied by her cousin, Morland Craig.

2 Fettes had been opened in Edinburgh in 1870 as an English public school in Scotland.

3 References here are from H.R. Pyatt (ed.): *Fifty Years of Fettes: Memories of Old Fettesians, 1870–1920*. (Edinburgh 1931).

4 This was based on the presumed assumption that the School had been founded about 1256 – this was later held a date pertaining to the Grammar School of Old Aberdeen.

5 Dr John Clarke had been Classical master at the GS between 1888 and 1898. He had previously been Headmaster of the Chanonry School from 1879 to 1897 when it closed.

6 Menzies had been educated at Fettes and Edinburgh University. He left the GS in 1896 to become Rector of Wallace Hall Academy, Dumfriesshire. He gained four rugby caps for Scotland in 1893–4.

7 Maxwell H. Mackie qualified at Edinburgh University. After working in the Prep. department under Green, in 1885, he became French master in succession to William Bremner. He retired in 1924 reaching the age limit of sixty-five.

8 After Cambridge, Murison in 1893 became Head of English at the Grammar until his retirement in 1929.

9 George Middleton was Head of the Classical department from 1900.

10 George Dawson (1883–1916) attended the GS between 1896 and 1901. He joined the staff in 1911.

11 A number of Former Pupils were appointed to the staff in this period. George Harvey (GS 1868–9) taught Classics between 1881 and 1887; George Stewart (GS 1889–92) taught Science and Mathematics in 1897-8; and Charles Simpson (GS 1897–1909) taught English between 1916 and 1918.

12 *Reminiscences: Academic, Ecclesiastic and Scholastic* (Aberdeen 1904) pp. 76–7.

13 Graham Walker: 'The Religious Factor' in T.M. Devine and Jenny Wormald (eds): *The Oxford Handbook of Modern Scottish History* (Oxford 2012) p. 585.

14 *ODNB*: Alan Main.

15 *ODNB*: George E. Godber.

16 *ODNB*: David E. Evans.

17 *ODNB*: David Pyke.

18 *ODNB*: D.M. Abbott.

19 *ODNB*: H.G. Champion rev. David E. Evans.

20 *ODNB*: W.J. Bishop rev. Caroline Overy.

21 *ODNB*: W.S. Urquhart rev. Mark J. Schofield.

22 *ODNB*: Susan Howson.

23 *ODNB*: David Ferguson.

24 *ODNB*: A.T. Hall.

25 *ODNB*: Yolanda Foote.

26 *ODNB*: John Orbell.

27 *ODNB*: Gordon F. Millar.

28 His brothers also attended the GS: Edward William Watt (b. 1877) attended from 1883 to 1894, entering Initiatory, going on to be a newspaper man and joint Manager of the P&J in 1922; and George Robertson Watt (b. 1879) attended between 1885 and 1895 and in 1897, also entering Initiatory. He graduated from Cambridge but soon after his appointment as a Professor in 1908 he died early.

29 *ODNB*: Andrew Rutherford rev. Isobel Murray.

30 *ODNB*: Doug Scott.

31 An additional Games placed in the calendar between the 1904 and 1908 Olympics.

CHAPTER ELEVEN

1 *Fifty Years of Fettes: Memories of Old Fettesians, 1870–1920* p. 220.

2 Only in recent years has the House system been changed to three Houses.
3 *ODNB*: R.D. Kernohan.
4 *ODNB*: Gordon Stirrat.
5 *ODNB*: Mairi Robinson.
6 See separate entries for Donald and Alan Watt. A fourth brother, George, graduated in Medicine but was killed while on Navy service in 1941.
7 *ODNB*: R.P. Draper.
8 *OODNB*: Magnus Linklater.
9 *ODNB*: David Hutchison.
10 *ODNB*: Helene la Rue.

CHAPTER TWELVE

1 'One tier' made all district schools the same, all-through secondaries. 'Two tier' was based on the concept of retaining the three Senior secondaries (which included the Grammar) as post-16 selective colleges.
2 He retired in 1985 after thirty-seven years' service to the School.
3 He had been PT Geography at the GS from 1947 until his promotion to Deputy Rector in 1967. He went on to Dumfries in 1970.
4 *WWS*.
5 *WWS*.
6 *ODNB*: Christopher Hardie.
7 *WWS*.
8 *WWS*.

CHAPTER FOURTEEN

1 Drawings of the plans for rebuilding were set out in the School Magazine vol. 92 (June 1989).
2 = an independent state.
3 Bill May retired after forty years' service, thirty of them as Head of Chemistry, in 2003.
4 He taught on the PE staff from 1979 until retirement in 2003.
5 The *Daily Record* claimed the Grammar was the 'most popular School in Scotland'.

CHAPTER FIFTEEN

1 The School Board organised Elocution which was taught by Alfred Macleod between 1874 and 1919. It had early success and a Shakespearian Society was started.
2 Monsieur Leon Klem was a Pole remembered for his quiet, slow guttural speech. He was succeeded by M Jules Simon Clapasson, who had a degree from Paris University, was vivacious and immaculately dressed in frock-coat and black tie.
3 Arthur McCombie.
4 The farewell remark of Sir James J. Robertson.

MEMORABILIA AND SELECT BIBLIOGRAPHY

MEMORABILIA: FOUND AND LOST

In a School with as long a history as the Grammar it is not surprising that much interesting material was accumulated. One of the earliest examples of this was the collection of *Aldines* – fifteenth- and sixteenth-century printed Classics, which fell victim to a burglary in the twenty-first century. Of a more permanent nature was the seventeenth-century School bell donated by Robert Fergusone in 1625, which survived the fire of 1986.

Relics of the building in Schoolhill include the portico which faced the building in 1758 and was placed in various sites in the Skene Street building and is now in the corridor beside the Gymnasium and also the eighteenth-century grandfather clock which obligingly struck the hour when the School was visited by members of the Byron Society. The Archery medals from the seventeenth century must also have come from Schoolhill.

While there are many books and documents in the Rector's room all awaiting the attention of an archivist the janitors from time to time unearth interesting pieces of memorabilia. Though most of the library books perished in the fire those stored in the Rector's room survived.

There have been many internal changes in the School and one of the unfortunate effects was the dispersal of much of the School museum to provide a projection room which later involved a corridor with collections of birds' eggs, oriental birds and eastern artefacts, donated by Cromar Watt – practically all of which were victims of the fire.

A collection of Victorian campaign medals covering the Crimean War, the Indian Mutiny and various African campaigns disappeared and is probably the proud possession of some collector now. Similarly a copy of the original etching of the School went missing but was very generously replaced by the University of Aberdeen. One interesting relic which was also lost was a Boxer Flag dating back to the Boxer Rising in China in 1900.

In the store rooms there is a large portrait of a gentleman whose identity has never been certainly established though suspicion falls on George Williamson who was not a pupil of the school but who donated bursaries to the School in the nineteenth century.

In November 1928, the School received a gift of the silver snuff box which had been presented in 1853 to the Rector, Dr James Melvin along with a sum of £300. The snuff box was placed in the school museum but went missing after the dispersal of the museum in the 1950s. However, it was purchased by the FPs when it was offered for sale in the 1980s. It now is on display at the FP Centre in Queen's Road.

The School recently acquired the copies of the original paintings by J.B. Souter which were gifted to Sir James J. Robertson and John V. Skinner when their portraits were presented to them on their retirements. These generous gifts from their respective families replace the originals which were destroyed in the 1986 fire.

A few years ago the School was contacted by a descendant of William Barrack, the Rector 1860–9, and a promise was made to present the School with his portrait. His initials are on the front of the building, to mark his being the first Rector in the Skene Street Building.

The School was very fortunate over the years to receive other generous gifts from, or on behalf of, Former Pupils. The organ donated by the Waters family to grace the School hall was a notable example. However, from time to time groups of Former Pupils have joined to present significant gifts. In November 1927, the empty space in the original clock-tower was filled by a clock donated by a number of FPs from Shanghai. This was followed by the decision of fifty-two FPs, who worked in Malaya, to present a clock for the School hall in 1939. This clock was relocated to the new Library set up in the upper area of the original School hall in the 1960s where, unfortunately, it was a victim of the 1986 fire.

In a similar vein the opening of the extension and refurbishment of the Pavilion at Rubislaw in 2009 had inspired the FPs in Canada to present a new clock to replace the original in the upper front area of the original building.

SELECT BIBLIOGRAPHY

Primary sources

Old Aberdeen Records

13 ED/GR6S/A58 Records of Aberdeen Grammar School (AGS) 1864–1994.
14/ED/GR6S/A58/1 AGS Log Books 1881–91.
15/ED/GR6S/A58/1/1 AGS Log Book 1881–1906.
19/ED/GR6S/A58/2 AGS Admission Registers and Class Lists 1864–1994.
ED/GR6S/A58/10 AGS Library Records 1820.
ED/GR6S/A58/11/1 AGS List of Lantern Slides in School, 1901.
ED/GR6S/A58/14 AGS Ink Blocs of Masters (n.d.).
ED/GR6S/A58/29/1 AGS Class Lists, 1826–66.
ED/GR6S/A58/65 Former Pupil Photographs.
ED/GR6S/A58/70 Scrapbook.

The Town House

Aberdeen has a wealth of sources and the starting point is the Council Registers. References to the Grammar School can be followed in *Extracts from the Burgh Records* vols 1 and 2.

Committee of the Council of the City of Aberdeen on the Town's Public Schools: Interim Report (Aberdeen 1834).

Report on the Grammar School and other educational institutions under the patronage of the Town Council of Aberdeen (Aberdeen 1854).

Government Commissions are a useful source of information especially the Reports of 1834 and 1839; the Reports of the 1866–8 period and the 1881 Report.

The fortunes of the Grammar School can be followed in local newspapers – the *Aberdeen Journal* from 1748 onwards, the *Aberdeen Chronicle* between 1806 and 1832, the *Aberdeen Herald* between 1832 and 1876, and the *Aberdeen Free Press* from 1869 forward.

Minutes of the Aberdeen School Board (1873–1919).

The Grammar School

The School lost much in the fire of 1986 but still has some memorabilia (mentioned elsewhere) and more modern records in the Rector's Study. Many of the book's illustrations came from the School.

The AGS Magazine is an invaluable source of material especially about Former Pupils. The School has a complete set from 1893 onwards.

AGS Prospectus is also a fund of information about the School. It has been produced annually since 1861.

The Roll of Former Pupils of AGS produced by Theodore Watt (1923) is a unique record and the starting point for any and all research into boys who attended the School from 1795 until 1919.

Class Lists from 1945 onwards.

Other sources

Registrum Episcopatus Aberdonensis vol. ii.

Registrum Vetus de Aberbrothoc no. 254.

Secondary works (listed alphabetically)

R.D. Anderson: *Education and Opportunity in Victorian Scotland, Schools and Universities* (Oxford 1983).

R.D. Anderson: *Education and the Scottish People 1750–1918* (Oxford 1995).

T.R. Bone: *School Inspection in Scotland 1840–1966* (London 1968).

Alexander Broadie: 'The Rise (and Fall) of the Scottish Enlightenment' in T.M. Devine and Jenny Wormald (eds): *The Oxford Handbook of Modern Scottish History* (Oxford 2012).

James K. Cameron: 'Some Aberdeen students on the Continent in the late sixteenth and early seventeenth centuries' in Paul Dukes: *The Universities of Aberdeen and Europe: The First Three Centuries* (Aberdeen 1995).

Jon Cannon: *Cathedrals: The Great English Cathedrals and the World That Made Them 600–1540* (London 2007).

William Carnie: *Reporting Reminiscences* 3 vols (Aberdeen 1902, 1903 and 1906).

I. Carter: *Farm Life in Northeast Scotland: The Poor Man's Country* (Edinburgh 1972).

Jennifer J. Carter and Colin A. McLaren: *Crown and Gown 1495–1995* (Aberdeen 1994).

Ian B. Cowan (ed. by J. Kirk): *The Medieval Church in Scotland* (Edinburgh 1995).
E. Patricia Dennison, David Ditchburn and Michael Lynch: *Before 1800: A New History* (Aberdeen 2002).
John Durkan: 'Education in the Century of the Reformation' in David McRoberts: *Essays on the Scottish Reformation 1513–1625* (Glasgow 1962).
John Edgar: *History of Early Scottish Education* (Edinburgh 1893).
F.C. Eeles: *King's College Chapel, Aberdeen* (Aberdeen 1956).
John M. Fletcher: 'The Foundation of the University of Aberdeen in its European Context' in Paul Dukes (ed.): *The Universities of Aberdeen and Europe: The First Three Centuries* (Aberdeen 1995)
Janet P. Foggie: *Renaissance Religion in Urban Scotland: The Dominican Order, 1450–1560* (Leiden 2003).
W. Hamish Fraser and Clive H. Lee: *Aberdeen 1800–2000: A New History* (East Linton 2000).
Alexander Gammie: *Churches of Aberdeen* (Aberdeen 1909).
James Grant: *History of the Burgh Schools of Scotland* (London 1876).
Nicholas Hans: *New Trends in Education in the Eighteenth Century* (London 1951).
Helen M. Jewell: *Education in Early Modern England* (Basingstoke 1998).
Alexander Keith: *A Thousand Years of Aberdeen* (Aberdeen 1972).
Alexander Keith: *Eminent Aberdonians* (Aberdeen 1984).
William Kennedy: *Annals of Aberdeen* 2 vols (London 1818).
William K. Leask (ed.): Musa Latina Aberdonensis *vol. 3 Spalding Club* (Aberdeen 1910).
Brian R.W. Lockhart: *Robert Gordon's Legacy* (Edinburgh 2007).
Roderick A. McDonald: 'Mystery and Scandal at Aberdeen Grammar School in Byron's Student Days' in *Aberdeen University Review* vol. 57, No. 1 (Spring 1997).
Leslie J. Macfarlane: 'St Machar's Cathedral through the Ages' in John S. Smith (ed.): *Old Aberdeen: Bishops, Burghers and Buildings* (Aberdeen 1991).
Leslie J. Macfarlane: *William Elphinstone and the Kingdom of Scotland 1431–1514* (Aberdeen 1985).
A. Allan MacLaren: *Religion and Social Class: The Disruption Years in Aberdeen* (London 1974).
Colin A. McLaren: *Aberdeen Students 1600–1800* (Aberdeen 2005).
Alexander Morgan: *Rise and Progress of Scottish Education* (Edinburgh 1927).
Richard Oram: *David I: The King Who Made Scotland* (Stroud 2004).
James Rettie: *Aberdeen One Hundred and Fifty Years Ago* (Wakefield 1972) (originally published in Aberdeen in 1868 as *Aberdeen Fifty Years Ago*).
Joseph Robertson: 'On Scholastic Offices in the Scottish Church in the Twelfth and Thirteen Centuries' in *Spalding Club Miscellany* vol. V (Aberdeen 1852).
James Scotland: *The History of Scottish Education. From Beginning to 1872* vol. 1 (London 1969).
Norman F. Shead: 'Glasgow: An Ecclesiastical Burgh' in Michael Lynch, Michael Spearman and Geoffrey Stell (eds): *The Scottish Medieval Town* (Edinburgh 1988).
Alexander Shewan: *The Record of the Gym (Chanonry House School) Old Aberdeen* (Aberdeen 1923).
Dr H.F. Morland Simpson: *Bon Record: Records and Reminiscences of Aberdeen Grammar School from the Earliest Times by Many Writers* (Aberdeen 1906).

Ian J. Simpson: *Education in Aberdeenshire before 1872* (London 1947).
David Stevenson: *King's College, Aberdeen 1560–1641: From Protestant Reformation to Covenanting Revolution* (Aberdeen 1990).
John Strong: *A History of Secondary Education: An Account of Scottish Secondary Education from Early Times to 1908* (Cambridge 1910).
Katherine E. Trail: *Story of Old Aberdeen* (Aberdeen 1929).
H. Lewis Ulman: *The Minutes of the Aberdeen Philosophical Society 1758–1773* (Aberdeen 1990).
Shona M. Vance: 'Mortifications (Bursaries and Endowments) for Education in Aberdeen 1593–1660 and their Implementation in the 17th Century', *University of Aberdeen PhD thesis*, 2000.
Rev. Dr W. Walker: *Reminiscences: Academic, Ecclesiastic and Scholastic* (Aberdeen 1904).
D.E.R. Watt: *Fasti Ecclesiae Scoticanae Medii Aevi ad Annum 1638* (Scottish Record Society 1969).
Theodore Watt: *Aberdeen Grammar School Roll of Pupils 1795–1919* (Aberdeen 1923).
Paul B. Wood: *The Aberdeen Enlightenment: The Arts Curriculum in the Eighteenth Century* (Aberdeen 1993).
Jenny Wormald: *Court, Kirk and Community: Scotland 1470–1625* (Edinburgh 1981).
Fenton Wyness: *City by the Grey North Sea* (Aberdeen 1965).

INDEX I: FORMER PUPILS

Note: All AGS Former Pupils mentioned or listed in the book are included in this index, with their dates of attendance at the school, where known. Where these dates are not known or uncertain, birth and death dates are provided. For FPs with the same name who attended at similar times, their eventual profession is shown to more clearly identify them. FPs who later taught at the School have their teaching career summarised.

INDEX 2: MEMBERS OF STAFF

Note: All members of the GS staff mentioned in the text are included here, with their dates of service and subjects taught or positions held (where these are known). Some of the dates are inevitably approximate, especially for the early years. Rectors of the School are highlighted in **bold type**.

INDEX 3: GENERAL